# Currencies of the Anglo-Norman Isles

A. L. T. McCammon

Spink & Son Ltd.

London

1984

Published by Spink & Son Ltd., London

© 1984 A. L. T McCammon

All rights reserved. No part of this publication
may be reproduced, stored in a retrieval system,
or transmitted in any form or by any means
(electronic, mechanical, photocopying, recording
or otherwise) without the prior permission of the
copyright owner.

ISBN 0 907605 13 3

Photography by
Simmen & Della Pietra, Zürich
Typeset and printed by
Druckerei Schulthess AG, Zürich

# Contents

Preface and Acknowledgements ... 1

**Part I**
The Beginnings ... 5
Armorica ... 9
The Finds ... 21
The Coriosolites ... 45
Interpretation of the Design ... 50
The Celtic Connection ... 59

**Part II**
The Romans ... 69
The Merovingians ... 75
The Carolingians ... 81
Normandy ... 83
The *Tournois* Period ... 88
The Jersey Mint ... 113
The Century of Transition ... 124

**Part III**
1800–1830 Token Coinage ... 135
Philippe d'Auvergne's 5 *Franc* Piece ... 141
The Sir Isaac Brock Half Pennies ... 143
Channel Islands Paper Money ... 145
Guernsey and Jersey Coinages ... 155
The German Occupation ... 163
Commemoratives & Decimals ... 168
Medals, Checks and Other Curiosities ... 173
The Present ... 184
The Future ... 185

**Part IV – Catalogue**
Private Channel Island Tokens ... 191
Guernsey Banknotes ... 199
Jersey Banknotes ... 215
Guernsey Coins ... 305
Bibliography ... 349
General Index ... 359

*Front cover:* With perhaps two exceptions, coins illustrated will be known to Channel Island collectors. The significance of the *gros tournois* of Louis IX, symbolic of the close connections to the currency of France, is explained on page 90. Lower right is a facsimile in aluminium of the *reverse* of the first Channel Island pattern, which is described on page 101. The positions of all coins on the map have been carefully chosen.

*Back cover:* A design of the late Edmund Blampied, which graces the *reverse* of an emergency banknote issue (see JN246), is a reminder of the peace and serenity still to be found in the Channel Islands.

*Frontispiece:* Bronze medallion (diameter 14.5 cm) of an Armorican Chieftain by the late Major N.V.L. Rybot, after Rybot I 18 (see illustration k on page 16).

# Preface and Acknowledgements

Channel Island history both unites and contrasts the stories of France and Britain while – somehow – maintaining its own strong identity. Each of the Islands has in fact such a strong, distinct character that it has been quite a challenge to paint each scene of this numismatic history on one Channel Island canvas.

Set against this tough insular streak, the well-known loyalty, over many centuries, of the Channel Islanders to the British Crown has a puzzling aspect to it. A casual student of Channel Islands history is often struck by the curious French-sounding names on the Islands, and may even be made conscious – perhaps by a flash of sunlight on a distant church window – of the proximity of the Islands to the French mainland. However, there it usually ends, and, beguiled by the current welter of literature on the German Occupation, and the sturdy concrete relics of that era – 40 years ago – our student departs little the wiser.

If he were only to pause for a moment and jangle his remaining Jersey or Guernsey coins at the 'duty-free' counter at the airport or on board the *Earl Granville,* it might dawn on him that the customs privileges he is enjoying are over 800 years old, and that the coins in his hand are only the very latest development in a numismatic association with France, and later England, which has lasted for well over 1000 years.

The aim of this book is to introduce the currencies of the Channel Islands to students and collectors of three distinct series: the Gaulish – particularly the Armorican – series, current in the Channel Island region over 2000 years ago; the French series which was the staple currency of the Islands for a millenium; and the 'modern' series, current for the last 200 years. These three subjects are bound together by the history of the Islands, of France and of Britain; and throughout the later narrative it will also be seen that British currency plays its part.

Coins illustrated are from the author's collection, and the cataloguing of later tokens and coins and their varieties is also based on the author's collection; although it is extensive, the catalogue does not pretend to be complete and a listing method has been chosen which allows for the discovery of further varieties. The classification of the early banknotes is largely based on lists of note-issuing entities published in contemporary trade directories ('almanachs'), and examples extant in private collections, mainly the William Barrett collection, the Jersey Museum collection and the author's own.

The subject of feudal or seigneurial *'rentes'* (payments in kind: corn, vegetables, eggs etc), though fascinating in itself, is felt to be outside the scope of this work.

All shortcomings of this study are the responsibility of the author, a dedicated amateur historian, whose peregrinations as an overseas banker over the last twenty years may have kept him away from certain source material. He is also responsible for any inaccuracy in the measurements specified, which have been undertaken with a 'Weso' measuring microscope, a 'Royal' micrometer gauge, and Harris 'Micro-minor' precision scales.

His thanks are due to Dr. J. Renouf, past Curator and Mr. G. P. Drew, present Acting Curator of the Museum of the Société Jersiaise, who have over the years provided information whenever it has been requested, to Mr. P. Finn for his support, to Mr. I. Monins for some timely words of encouragement, to Mr. R. M. L. Marsh and Mme K. Gruel for their constructive comments on parts of the manuscript, to Mr. H. Wolfensberger of Buchdruckerei Schulthess for his patience and guidance during printing, and to many other friends who have helped in this project.

He is indebted to the following individuals and institutions for providing illustrations of items referred to in the text and catalogue section:

Mr. William L. S. Barrett: GN1, GN4 (Specimen), GN5, GN15, GN16, GN17, GN19, GN21 (Trials), GN23, GN26, GN28, GN29, JN12, JN23, JN48, JN96, JN104 (*l.*), JN131, JN132, JN146, JN178.

The Bodleian Library: Sir Edward Hyde's letter (see Bibliography).

The Trustees of the British Museum: T7.

Mr. G. Charman: G57 ii.

Mr. I. Monins: AN1.

The Jersey Museum (Société Jersiaise): JN2, JN5, JN7, JN11, JN13, JN61, JN66, JN83, JN87, JN88, JN100, JN103, JN104 (*r.*), JN116, JN118, JN133, JN138, JN148, JN162, JN168, JN184, JN186, JN189, JN190, JN192, JN216, JN217, JN229, JN232, JN233, JN240, JN241.

The Bibliography contains as complete a list as possible of other relevant works and publications. The author has drawn on material from some of them, notably studies by Allen, Colbert de Beaulieu and Rybot for the Gaulish period, and Marshall-Fraser and Pridmore for the modern series.

While a completely new classification system for the 19th and 20th century Channel Island issues has been utilized, a few sub-classifications of die varieties already published have been adopted (e.g. G3) in deference to the earlier publications and for the convenience of collectors; full details of the original sources are to be found in the Bibliography.

This book contains, necessarily, a comprehensive – if concise – summary of French numismatic history; spurred on by the fact that so little has been published in English about French currencies, the author has drawn heavily on the works of Blanchet, Dieudonné, Ciani, le Blanc and Prou.

Opinions expressed, particularly in the chapter on 'The Future' are the author's alone.

This book is dedicated to the late Ernest Huelin, a Channel Islander and a great man in his time, whose idea it was, and to the late Ernesto Meissner, another great man, albeit in another hemisphere. Much of the credit for the book's completion must rest with the author's family for their forbearance in the spending of '... our midday sweat, our midnight oil'.

Zurich, August 1984                                                A. L. T. M.

# Part I

The Beginnings
Armorica
The Finds
The Coriosolites
Interpretation of the Design
The Celtic Connection

Philologists who chase
A panting syllable through time and space,
Start it at home, and hunt it in the dark,
To Gaul, to Greece, and into Noah's ark.

William Cowper
*Report of an Adjudged Case.* l. 619

# The Beginnings

In the study of history and prehistory, few objects have been as engaging as coins. Not only may coins be studied in the light of their artistic qualities and significance in a bygone culture, but they are also relatively common – having been the property of the average man through the centuries. And, unlike most of the other properties of the average man – a point of particular importance to the archaeologist or historian – they are durable.

The existence of coinage, in general terms, mirrors the spread of commerce and the continuity of civilization, as the absence or interim absence of such evidence suggests anarchy or perhaps the presence of a non-trading society, priestly or agricultural; the existence of slavery, in some instances, is also shown to have diminished the importance of coinage.

Perhaps as early as 300,000 B.P. (i.e. 300,000 years before the present, as measured by the radiocarbon dating method), Acheulian man had occupied the caves at la Cotte in Jersey where animal remains (such as bones of mammoth and woolly rhinoceros) suggest that a land-bridge to the Island, from what we now call the Cotentin Peninsular, still existed to facilitate their coming. There is also evidence, at the same site, of a Mousterian flint industry, dating to the earlier half of the last Glaciation or the preceding interglacial (130,000–40,000 B.P.).

*Fig. 1: Stylized stone circle from a 19th century Jersey currency note.*
*Illustration from a 'renewed' £1 note of the Town Vingtaine of St. Helier (JN233).*
*This dolmen was removed from Mont de la Ville (now Fort Regent, Jersey) in 1785 and presented to the then Governor, General Conway; he had it taken to his country seat at Wargrave, Berkshire, where it now stands. Horace Walpole called it 'little Master Stonehenge'.*

The cavemen's Stone-age successors, who flourished from 7000 B.C., may have dragged their huge stone monuments across that same land-bridge from the Armorican hinterland. However, these first inhabitants of the Channel Islands area left no clues to enable us to determine if there was any commerce or measure of wealth in those distant times. Studies of the most primitive chopper-core and hand-axe industries, and the exchange of these implements, are progressing steadily, but a definitive study of the excavations at La Cotte is still awaited.

Recent excavations on L'Ancresse Common, Guernsey, have turned up pottery similar to that found in the very ancient sites in Brittany, dated to 4500 years B.C. The pottery was found in stone structures which are believed to pre-date the Pyramids by at least 1000 years.

The Palaeolithic remains found in Jersey at la Cotte and la Cotte à la Chèvre only confirm the presence of a very primitive hunting society which does not appear to have had the simplest notions of trade, though it is interesting to speculate that barter, on a 'silent' basis, might have been practised. Such barter might have been conducted between two families or tribes each of whom, in turn, would leave weapons, food, tools or ornaments at a recognized spot, then withdraw and allow the other to make an inspection and remove favoured articles; this 'silent' system of barter is still practised by primitive tribes in Brazil. Among the remains of the later, Neolithic, era, such as the beads found in the Hougue Bie tomb and the coloured pebbles found in the Monts Grantez passage-grave, there are no items which can be construed as primitive forms of currency.

From Ireland to India, during the last 5000 years, wealth has frequently been measured in cows, and it is not strictly true to say that the custom has died out today. Cows were also used as a medium of exchange before a currency medium was invented for convenience. They survived as such down to the fifth century B.C. in India when purchases were made by means of the *gopuchha* – literally a cow's tail; this still survives in the Hindu rituals of *go-dān,* where a cow is given to a priest by physically putting the tail in his hands. Down to the late Iron age in Ireland, the value of the currency bar was reckoned as 1 female slave *(cumal)*

*Fig. 2: Obverse of a silver medal for the Birmingham Jersey Show of 1894.*
*This medal was awarded to Fowler and De la Perrelle 'for best Guernsey cow or heifer'.*

or 6 heifers or 3 milch cows. The farmer from the Channel Islands can still be said to measure his wealth in the famous and distinctive strain of cattle which is so sought after as breeding stock.

At some time between 2000 B.C. and 1500 B.C., perhaps earlier, the Bronze age overtook the Channel Island area. Our knowledge of this period has recently been increased by excavations at St. Ouen's Bay, Jersey, which have uncovered not only pottery which links the site with others in the Côtes-du-Nord, across the Gulf of St. Malo, but also an area where pottery firing took place.

In the later Bronze age, perhaps around 700 B.C., at about the same time as the Lydians were beginning to strike the first known 'coins' of electrum from the washings of the river Pactolus in Asia Minor, the Ibero-Celtic peoples of the Armorican coast of Gaul were already trading with Britain in copper and tin and working their own lead mines. Bronze 'socketed' axeheads from this period have been found in Brittany and Normandy in large numbers, and also scattered along the South Coast of Britain. These axes provide us with the first evidence of a currency system in the area.

Many of the axeheads found are too small to have been of any practical use, and of these, some were struck in an alloy of such a high lead content as to be completely useless as anything more than 'token' axeheads. The lead content reached a 'high' of over 98% in samples from a hoard found at Nivillac, Morbihan, in Brittany. This suggests a currency function comparable in concept to that of the ancient Chinese 'knife' or 'spade' money or the wealth-by-weight systems employed by other ancient civilizations (cf the Greek *'talent'* and the Jewish *'shekel'*). An analogy has been drawn between these token axeheads, which have been dated by the radiocarbon method to 560 B.C. ±130, and the ancient Roman *'aes rude'* ingots which preceded the first Roman coins – *'aes grave'*.

*Fig. 3: Small socketed axe from Brittany c. 1000 B.C. (1:1).*
*Found in the South of England.*

Among Channel Island Bronze age finds, mention should here be made of a hoard of weapons and indistinguishable lumps of metal such as might have been the property of a travelling smith, discovered in St. Lawrence Valley, Jersey in 1871. Several examples of this Armorican socketed axehead were found in the hoard – the tenuous beginnings of Channel Island numismatic history.

# Armorica

At about the time that our Bronze age smith was providing us with a basis for the above introduction, the first Celts were beginning to migrate into the eastern and central parts of what came to be known as Gaul. Amber and salt began to be traded and bronze appears to have reached the area simultaneously from the east (via the Danube) and from the west (via the earliest coastal trade routes). There is evidence that, as early as 1000 B.C., tin was being carried to the region from Britain. This was the dawn of European commerce.

Towards the end of the Halstatt era (c. 500 B.C.) the Celtic influx from the east was at its most intense and the deposits of iron in today's Burgundy and Lorraine were being heavily exploited for the manufacture of tools and weapons. Only then did the first descendants of those immigrants begin to reach Armorica, that part of the Atlantic coast which had hitherto been left to more primitive peoples, perhaps with ethnic connections to the Iberians in the south.

Mention should be made of the golden *torques* (twisted metal ornaments) and rings which have been dug up in many places in the British Isles, Ireland and Northern Europe. One magnificent specimen of a *torque* was found during a dig in St. Helier in 1888. These Bronze age objects are often thought to have been used as a primitive form of currency. They may have been, though the evidence seems to indicate that they were used rather as personal ornaments. The famous Gundestrup cauldron, for example, dated to c. 100 B.C., has a panel on which the deer-antlered Kernunnos (a Celtic 'Lord of the Beasts') is shown holding a *torque* in one hand and wearing another tight-fitting *torque* round his neck. There are many other instances of Gaulish statuettes showing the *torque* in this position, a decorative and convenient place, perhaps, for a warrior to carry his wealth.

Fig. 4: Gold Torque, dated to 1500 B.C., found in St. Helier in 1888 (enlargement from J284). Jersey Museum; the torque has since been reshaped to what is believed to be its original form.

It is clear that, when Julius Caesar chronicled his marches and counter-marches through Gaul, there already existed in that country a society which – if not as organized as that of Republican Rome – was ordered enough to challenge Roman might on many occasions. Gaulish society in pre-Roman times left comparatively few relics behind. Perhaps they did not have the same notions of posterity as for example, the Ancient Egyptians and the Ancient Greeks had. Life for those Celts who flourished in the hundred or so years before the Roman invasions, was probably of an intensely mobile nomadic nature. Very few artifacts of this period have been discovered which are of any great size. Their dwelling places appear to have been essentially temporary (perhaps seasonal); there is evidence that some of them lived in 'dug-outs'. Migrations and sub-migrations were so frequent that archaeologists have only very tentatively been able to map the areas in which the various clans or tribes lived. One field which – perhaps more than any other – has contributed towards a knowledge of this period in history, is that of the study of the coins of these tribes.

How and when coins came to Gaul is an old chestnut among students of the subject. There are many theories; some hold that coins were first introduced into the Greek colonies in the neighbourhood of Marseilles and filtered northwards; others that settlers from as far east as the Danube gradually brought the coins westwards in a process of trade and migration; others, still, that marauders seized stocks of coins from Italian treasuries and carried them off, until the purchasing power of the coins was appreciated and they were eventually copied and re-copied; Brennus, the Senonian Chieftain, was persuaded to desist from his siege of the Capitol in Rome by the payment of a large sum in gold after the battle of Allia in 390 B.C. An older school of thought has it that coins were carried round the earliest Atlantic trade routes along the coast of Brittany, Normandy and the Netherlands to permeate through Gaul from the north-west.

Whatever the origins, the fact is that hoards of Gaulish coins of clearly definable types have come to light throughout modern France, and to a lesser extent in neighbouring territories. De la Tour's *'Atlas de monnaies gauloises'* has been the standard reference work on this subject for many years, and the sources or differentiations of the coins illustrated in this book are still used as a base by numismatists, although experts are at last making some further headway in the study of this family of coins. The difficulty is that, although the find of a hoard or a single coin may be clearly established and recorded, it is in many – if not most – cases still unknown which tribe was inhabiting the area at the time the coin or hoard in question was 'in circulation'. Opposite is a tentative map showing the approximate areas of occupation of most recorded Gaulish tribes.

Examples of coins ascribed to many of the tribes shown on the map have been found in the Channel Islands, usually in hoards. By far the most numerous have been coins attributed to the Coriosolites; in fact, so many of these particular coins have been found in the Channel Islands (principally Jersey) that the type has become known – by some – as the 'Channel Island' type, and the term has been extended misleadingly to cover many other coins of the Armorican *système* or series, i.e. the coins of those tribes who once occupied north-western Gaul. For the purposes of this study I am going to dispense with the 'Channel Island type' epithet – however unpatriotic this may sound – as it will avoid confusion, and give due weight to recent advances made in the study of the Armorican series as a whole. I cannot, however, rule out the possibility that those coins, which are now generally attributed to the Coriosolites, may one day be re-attributed to the Channel Islands and may become known as a 'Channel Island' type in their own

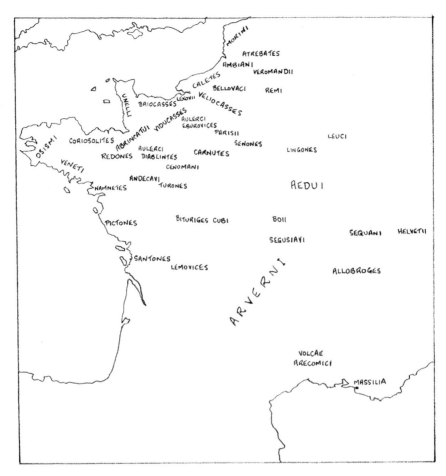

*Fig. 5: Tentative map of the principal peoples of Gaul c. 100–50 B.C.
Map is based on de la Tour, Forrer, Colbert de Beaulieu, Lecoq-Kerneven and others.*

right. In any event, as this type is so little known but has a special importance for the Channel Islands, I will devote a few extra pages to it below.

Purists may argue that the Armorican series – or even Gaulish coins as a whole – should not be included in a book on Channel Island currency, as there is little indication that these coins circulated – or were destined for circulation – in this area, but that they should be seen rather as the buried hoards of refugees or marauders from the east. One authority at least was of the opinion that the coins, with particular reference to those of the Armorican series, could not have been destined for circulation anywhere, but should be regarded as a foundry consignment. There is, however, considerable evidence that the coins *did* circulate as currency over a large area, and a small number of coins have been found singly in Jersey; the possibility that they did circulate in the Islands is therefore not excluded. In any event I feel that a synthesis of Gaulish coin finds in the Channel Islands, the publications of which have often been in learned journals, not always easily accessible (see Bibliography), will certainly be of interest to the Channel Islands numismatist.

For convenience and clarity I have divided the Gaulish and Celtic coins found in the Channel Islands into three groups, as follows:

A) The Armorican series – subdivided into
   (i) the Coriosolite type and
   (ii) other Armorican types
B) All other Gaulish types
C) Celtic types from Britain

The Roman coins found in some Gaulish hoards will be listed in a later section.

## A) The Armorican Series

Coins of the Armorican series are generally regarded as homogeneous. This series consists roughly of the coins struck by those tribes once frequenting the areas north and west of a curved line drawn between the mouth of the Seine and the Gironde (see map). With very few exceptions, the coins of the series are 'mute' (without inscription), and this absence of any epigraphic clues adds greatly to the difficulties of classification.

Whereas hoards of coins have often been found in the Armorican region (including the Channel Islands) containing many types from central and southern Gaul – and even some Roman Republican coins –, Armorican coins have seldom been found in any other continental area; they have, however, quite often been found in Southern Britain. This suggests a pattern of trade which Caesar confirmed when he mentioned the number of vessels – particularly of the Veneti – which traded between Armorica and Britain. Although the metallic sequence of Armorican coins roughly follows that of Gaul as a whole, i.e. gold – base gold – silver – billon – base copper, coins of billon (gold or silver with a preponderating admixture of a baser metal) are to be found in much larger quantities in Armorica than in any other region of Gaul. This factor, which suggests that the series was, in a metallic sense, more developed than other types, together with the distinctive mute designs, lends support to the theory that the Armorican series may be older than the other Gaulish types and may therefore have originated from the ancient Atlantic trade routes. There is, however, as yet, no solid evidence to support this theory.

Many facets of the design together with a strange – at times crude – symmetry, are common to most coins of the Armorican series. This has led experts to look for a pattern of development in the coin types of the region. Perhaps the most well-argued and attractive theory is that most coins of the *système* are derived from a series which has been recently attributed to the Veneti who, after the fall of the Empire of the Arverni (122 B.C.) when each region in Gaul began to coin its own money, succeeded in monopolizing the Armorican system for a time.

*Fig. 6: Prototype gold stater of the Veneti.*
DLT 6830 7.80 g (Bank Leu auction 25, 23.4.1980; photo courtesy of the Numismatic Department of Bank Leu AG, Zurich).

The prototype in gold and of impressive workmanship (itself originally derived, as were most early Gaulish types, from the gold *stater* of Philip II [382–359 B.C.] of Macedon), figures on the obverse a head with ornately curled hair, surmounted either by a boar or what might be a stylized sea-horse; the bust is surrounded by cords resembling strings of pearls, ending in severed heads. The reverse shows a horse with a human head, being driven by a charioteer (in a chariot which in most cases, except occasionally for a wheel, has disappeared) holding over the horse a lash which ends in a fringed *vexillum* or standard; under the horse there is a recumbent winged figure.

While the above type slowly deteriorated in weight, metal content and workmanship, neighbouring tribes gradually borrowed certain aspects of the design for their own coinages. The first coins of the immediate neighbours of the Veneti to the north, the Osismii, might be crude copies of the coinage of the Veneti; we have, however, no actual proof that the coinage of the Veneti came first. The general theme of the coins of the Veneti, particularly of the reverse, appears on the coinage of the Coriosolites; both the Osismii and Coriosolites had borrowed the boar; the Redones the wheel; and so on.

*Fig. 7: Intermediate silver stater attributed to the Veneti.*
Cf C de B. Traité p 115 fig. 25.

Before treating in more detail with the Armorican tribes whose coins have been unearthed in the Channel Islands, I should emphasize my own contention that it would be impossible to describe any coin of the Armorican series, without using the word 'stylized'. Some years ago, possibly – and ironically – before certain 'modern art' forms had become universally recognized – if not entirely appreciated – the Armorican engraver was deemed to have been a creature of rather inferior ability. He was even thought – on occasion – to have been unable to understand the design that he was evidently copying; the result, it was held, was a disjointed and often unrecognizable imitation of the design of some coin which was probably descended from the stater of Philip of Macedon, or was perhaps a cross between that and some other imported Greek coin design.

It may be true to say that Philippic *staters* were imitated – not very accurately – in many parts of eastern and southern Gaul; on some imitations the word ΦΙΛΙΠΠΟΥ ('of Philip') was soon to become completely unintelligible. But it

*Fig. 8: Postumous gold stater of Philip II of Macedon.*
*c. 335 B.C. 8.61 g (Bank Leu auction 13, 29.4.1975; photo courtesy of the Numismatic Department of Bank Leu AG, Zurich).*

should be appreciated that the Armorican craftsmen appear to have reached the stage of *modifying* the design with their own art-forms in mind or – at worst – *improving* upon a design which may have been seriously debased before it ever reached Armorica. The fact that most of the coins are mute is, however, no proof of this, as the Armorican states maintained their identity longer than the rest of Gaul and would have resisted an alien (Latin or Greek or mixed) alphabet for a corresponding period. This theme will be enlarged upon, with particular reference to the Coriosolites, below.

## (i) The Coriosolites

Some 16,000 coins, attributed to this 'tribe', have been found in Jersey. The largest hoard of Armorican coins ever found (see below) consisted of some 12,000 coins, almost entirely Coriosolite. Coriosolite coins were the principal constituent of at least seven other hoards found in Jersey, and have occasionally been found singly.

The Coriosolite type consists of *'staters'*, generally in billon, of four main groups, (after Rybot) one of which (the least common) is further divided into three sub-groups or classes by some authorities. Twelve classes in all have been listed, including types not found in Jersey; however the latest thinking assigns the other six classes to the Veneti. *'Quarter-staters'* of most classes are also known. For the sake of simplicity, I have adhered to the four groups in the classification below.

The town of Corseul, some five miles north-west of Dinan, Côtes-du-Nord, has been linked with the capital of the Coriosolites, who were, incidentally, briefly mentioned four times by Julius Caesar.

## (ii) **Other Armorican Tribes**

Coins attributed to the Abrincatui, the Aulerci Cenomani, the Osismii and the Redones have been found in Jersey, always in hoards. Coins variously given to the Baiocasses and the Unelli have also come to light. Although the coins of the Veneti have not yet positively been identified, it is thought, following most recent theories (see above), that a small number of examples of their currency may also have been included in at least one hoard. In addition to the above, a number of extremely crude, diminutive types, which were found in one hoard in particular, are generally attributed to the Armorican area.

*Fig. 9: Examples of Coriosolite staters and quarter-staters in tentative chronological order, from the top.*

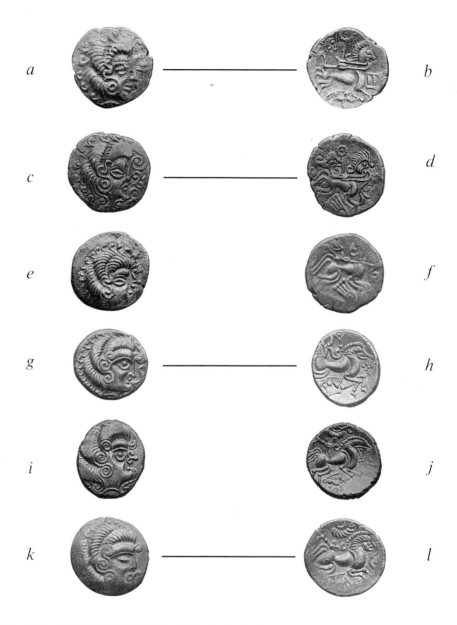

a, b: Rybot III 72, C de B VI, DLT –; 6.58 g (ex Lockett).
c, d: Rybot III 60, C de B V, DLT –; 6.55 g (ex Le Catillon, Jersey, 1957).
e: Rybot III 48, C de B IV, DLT –; 6.44 g.
f: Rybot III 48, C de B IV, DLT –; 6.34 g (ex La Marquanderie, Jersey, 1935).
g, h: Rybot II 32, C de B II, DLT cf J20; 6.45 g (ex Le Catillon, Jersey, 1957).
i: Rybot IV 80, C de B III, DLT cf J63; 6.29 g (ex Le Catillon, Jersey, 1957).
j: Rybot IV 75, C de B III, DLT J63; 6.16 g.
k, l: Rybot I 18, C de B I, DLT –; 6.59 g (ex La Marquanderie, Jersey, 1935).

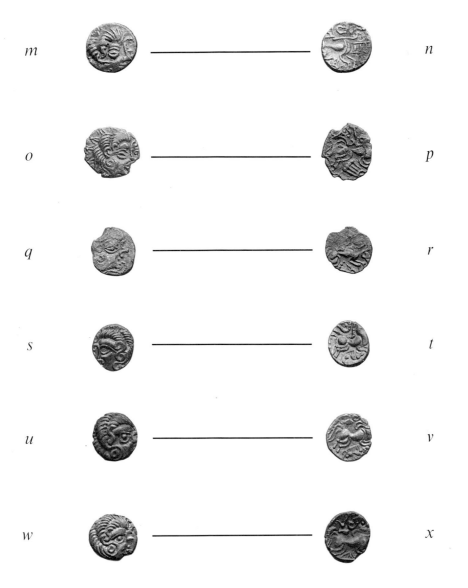

m, n:  Rybot –, C de B VI, DLT J30; 1.34 g.
o, p:  Rybot –, C de B V, DLT cf J36; 1.5 g (ex Le Catillon, Jersey, 1957).
q, r:  Rybot –, C de B IV, DLT –; 1.33 g.
s, t:  Rybot –, C de B II, Un 3e lot . . . p 53, 1570, DLT –; unique; 1.45 g (ex Le Catillon, Jersey, 1957).
u, v:  Rybot –, C de B III, DLT J26; 1.42 g (ex Le Catillon, Jersey, 1957).
w, x:  Rybot –, C de B I Le Trésor . . . 592-4, DLT cf J26; 1.45 g (ex Le Catillon, Jersey, 1957).

*Fig. 10; A selection of silver/billon coins of other Armorican peoples, neighbours of the Coriosolites; attributions are tentative.*

a: Baiocasses, DLT J23; 6.77 g (ex Le Catillon, Jersey, 1957).
b: Baiocasses, cf DLT 6967; 6,12 g (ex Le Catillon, Jersey, 1957).
c: Baiocasses, cf DLT J1, J33; 6.82 g (ex Le Catillon, Jersey, 1957).
d: Abrincatui, cf DLT J4; 6.32 g.
e: Abrincatui, cf J12; 6.45 g.
f: Osismii, DLT 6541; 6.7 g (ex Le Catillon, Jersey, 1957).
g: Redones, DLT 6783; 6.63 g.
h: Osismii, Blanchet, Traité p 314, fig. 215; 6.68 g.
i: Baiocasses, C de B, Un 3e lot . . . 1610; 0.9 g (ex Le Catillon, Jersey, 1957)? unique.

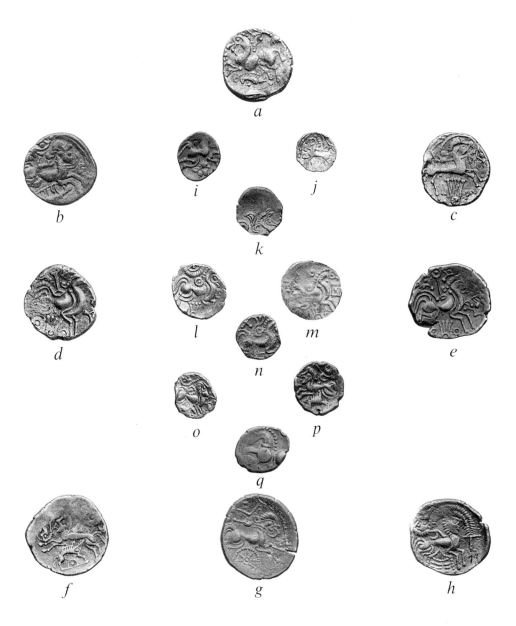

j: Baiocasses, C de B, Un 3e lot . . . VI, 1604; 0.8 g (ex Le Catillon, Jersey, 1957).
k: North West Gaul, DLT J59; 1.29 g.
l: Abrincatui, cf DLT J9; 1.45 g (ex Le Catillon, Jersey, 1957).
m: Abrincatui, cf DLT J11; 1.26 g.
n: Abrincatui, cf C de B, Un 3e lot . . . Pl. VI, 30; 1.72 g.
o: Osismii, obv. cf DLT 6543; 1.5 g.
p: Osismii, DLT 6543; 1.63 g.
q: North West Gaul, DLT J44; 1.64 g.

## B) Other Gaulish Types

Coins of many other tribes have been found in hoards in Jersey and Sark. Examples extend from the area of the Caletes and Veliocasses in the north through central Gaul to the area of Massilia (Marseille) in the south; one coin is believed to have been struck by the Helvetii. There are, however, practically no examples from south-west Gaul. The most common types have been assigned tentatively to the Sequani; among the other tribes represented, the Caletes, Bituriges Cubi, Santones, Aedui and Carnutes are (numerically) worthy of note. A few specimens from the hoard found in 1875 are the only ones of their type recorded.

*Fig. 11:* above: *obol of Massilia (Marseille) 4th century B.C. (enlarged).*
      below: *Gaulish imitation c. 100–50 B.C. (enlarged).*
*Cf DLT 580. The Greek colony of Massalia (later Massilia) struck silver obols between the 4th and 2nd centuries B.C. The first coin illustrated (weight: 0.71 g) dates from c 380 B.C. Over 30 000 such coins have been discovered in various finds of Gaulish coins not including one hoard found in 1366 near Toulon which is said to have weighed over 2 tons! The second coin (weight: 0.44 g) is a Gaulish imitation dated to 100–50 B.C. 25 worn obols of Massilia were found in Jersey–V.*

## C) British Coins

Celtic coins of the period of the Belgic migrations into Britain have been found in the Le Catillon hoard. Numerically they may not be significant – there are 21, of which 13 are of a Durotrigan type – but they will be seen to play an important chronological role.

# The Finds

In listing the Gaulish coin finds in the Channel Islands I have adhered for convenience to the chronological order in which the coins came to light, dealing first with the hoards and subsequently with the single coins finds. References are, unless otherwise stated, to plates in H. de la Tour, *'Atlas de monnaies gauloises'* (DLT). The implications and dating of the various finds will be dealt with in a later section. For conformity, and as a tribute to the enormous amount of work he has done in this subject, reference is also made to Dr J.-B. Colbert de Beaulieu's find-references as contained in his article *'Le trésor de Jersey-II et la numismatique celtique des deux Bretagnes'* (see Bibliography).

## Sark – I (1718)

In 1718, an iron-bound pot was turned up in Sark during the digging of a *'courtil'* (small enclosed plot) known as La Vauroque, which then belonged to a certain William Tanquerel. The pot and contents were subsequently directed to be surrendered to the Procureur of the Seigneur of Sark in an order dated 9th March 1718, in which the find was described as:

'Treize pièces baties en rond comme pourront etre des assiettes mais de différentes grandeur, et une en long, en figure d'un poisson et un petit lingot comme viron du poids de deux onches [ounces] qui était de coleur jaune et tout campé ['fine'] et dix huits petites pièces de paiyement . . .'

The hoard was duly handed in and for some 250 years nothing further was heard of it. Then, by a stroke of good fortune, six pages of engravings were turned up in the Library of the Society of Antiquaries which were to bear further witness to the hoard (see Allen: *'The Sark Hoard'*). The first engraving is of a large somewhat cracked bound pot inscribed:

GAULISH
ANTIQUITIES

Medals & silver Plates gilt
Found
in the Isle of Serck
in an Earthen Urn
Bound with an iron hoop
Anno
1719

In the background there is a seascape and a stylized island. Below, eighteen coins, obverse and reverse, are engraved. The second engraving is apparently of three views of a curious curved embossed silver object which has not yet been identified. The third, fourth and fifth engravings are of ten silver *phalerae* (ornamental disks), and the sixth of three more *phalerae* and one small unidentifiable gold-coloured object. It can be seen therefore that the *'treize pièces baties en rond..., et une en long..., et un petit lingot...'* are faithfully reproduced together with the *'dix huits petites pièces de paiyement...'*.

With one exception, all the identifiable coins are inscribed Gaulish types, the exception being a Roman Republican denarius of P. Crepusius which has been dated to 82–81 B.C. They are individually numbered on the engraving and have been identified as follows:

1. Roman Denarius – P. Crepusius. Die marks: obv. P. and turtle; rev. CCCCLVIII, Sydenham, *'The Coinage of the Roman Republic'* no. 738 A.
2. Gaulish silver coin – ATEVLA/VLATOS, DLT XXIX 7187
3.     do.        DLT XXIX 7191
4.     do.        DLT 7187
5.     do.        probably either DLT XXIX 7187 or 7191
6.     do.        ATPILLI F/ORGETIRIX, DLT XVI 4805
7.     do.        CUPINACIOS/VLATOS, DLT XXIX 7203
8.     do.        probably ATPILLI F/ORGETIRIX, DLT XVI 4805 or possibly SENODON/CALEDV, DLT XXIX 7174 or SOLIMA/COΛIMA, DLT XXXVII 9025
9.     do.        ARIVOS/SANTONO, DLT XIII 4525
10.–12. do.        probably all TOGIRIX/TOGIRIX, DLT XVI 5550
13.–16. do.        all uncertain
17.    do.        uncertain but compare DLT XXV 10400
18.    do.        apparently blank both sides.

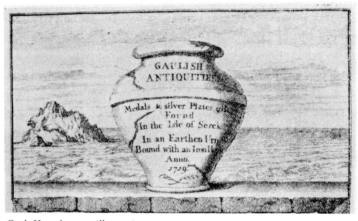

*Fig. 12: The Sark Hoard: cover illustration.*
From Allen, The Sark Hoard... p 38.

The coins themselves have never reappeared.

It is perhaps interesting to note that, until the engravings were discovered, and further examination became possible, this hoard was thought by some to have been Visigothic, dating from the beginning of the 5th Century A.D., as the coins were 'rudely engraved with a lion, the badge of the Visigothic dynasty'.

## Jersey – I (1787) – C de B 1

*'Dans des déblaiements [diggings] considérables qui eurent lieu de 1786 à 1787, pour établir une citadelle [later, Fort Regent], sur la hauteur qui domine la ville de Saint-Hélier, capitale de l'île de Jersey, on découvrit un grand nombre de médailles gauloises armoricaines, en billon. Cette découverte eut lieu au milieu de beaucoup de tombeaux et près d'un dolmen' (Lambert p 159).*

There is an illustration of one of the coins found at this site in 1787 with many others. The coin is shown to be of the type assigned to the Coriosolites, group III. By implication the other coins in the hoard may also have been of the Coriosolite type.

As to the fate of the hoard, the same source records: *'M. Fall, alors bibliothécaire de Jersey, remit un certain nombre de ces pièces à M. Duchevreuil, de Cherbourg, qui voulut bien nous en donner un exemplaire, en l'année 1825'.*

I understand that for many years, up to a time within the memory of the then Librarian, with whom I talked some years ago, a considerable number of Gaulish coins were lying loosely on an upper floor of the Public Library in St. Helier. It is possible that these were from this hoard. Their fate has not been definitely established.

## Jersey – II (1795) – C de B 2

There are eight Coriosolite type coins in the British Museum which are recorded as having been discovered in Jersey in 1795; these may possibly have come from a larger hoard.

24 other Armorican coins including two quarter staters were presented by P. R. Lemprière to the British Museum in 1846; these were said to have been found about fifty years before 'in an iron pot in a field near the great harbour, Jersey'. The total number of coins in this hoard is given variously as about 200 or about 2000 (the latter being the original entry in the Museum records). Both this and the previous lot of eight coins may have come from the same hoard.

Of the combined lots 29 coins are Coriosolite *staters* (all the groups represented, but only one example of group I), two are Coriosolite billon *quarter staters,* (the head on one of which faces to the left) and one coin has been assigned to the Baiocasses.

## Jersey – III (c. 1807) – C de B 3

In the preface (dated 1827) of his manuscript 'Catalogue', now in the Public Library, St. Helier, P. Mauger wrote: 'A few Celtic and Roman coins having been picked up here about twenty years ago...'; and later: '... Celtic coins were found in great abundance in the north part of Jersey several years ago but were unfortunately very much dispersed before any person here had turned his thoughts to collecting'. He may have been referring to JERSEY – IV (see below). Subsequently (apparently some five years later) he wrote: 'A considerable quantity of them (i.e. 'Celtic Medals') were found together in an old earthen vase near the harbour of Rozel in this island, about 25 years ago'.

Although it is possible that this hoard may have been confused with JERSEY – II, it has been pointed out a) that JERSEY II was found in an iron pot, and that this hoard was found in an earthenware pot, and b) that Rozel cannot be considered to have been the 'great harbour'. Although these points are debatable, it is perhaps worth mentioning that Rozel pier was built in 1829, i.e. during the period that Mauger was writing his 'Catalogue'.

Mauger made drawings of eight coins, numbered 1–8; I have identified them as follows:

1. Coriosolite *stater* group II; illustration labelled 'AE'
2. Coriosolite *stater* group III
3. Osismii, *stater* 'tent' type
4. probably Unelli, *stater;* illustration labelled 'AR'
5. Coriosolite, *stater* group IV or I (*rev.* drawn only)
6. Coriosolite, *stater* group IV
7. Coriosolite, *quarter-stater;* labelled 'AE'
8. Coriosolite, *quarter-stater*

After his reference to this Rozel hoard Mauger continued: 'occasionally also a few have been picked up in the country. I have not the least doubt but that this was the coin of the Island, and of course also of Gaul, before the invasion of the Romans'.

## Jersey – IV (1820) – C de B 5

A cliff-fall somewhere on the coast of Jersey in the year 1820 brought to light a hoard of 982 Armorican coins, almost all of which were Coriosolite. The whole hoard was acquired by the Baron de Donop, who, happily for posterity, had illustrations made of 760 of the coins. The illustrations were published in a book dedicated to H. M. Adelaide, Queen of Great Britain, Ireland and Hanover, which also contains the most extraordinary – but very readable – historical concoctions written around the discovery of the hoard. The Baron was apparently so carried away by the archaeological importance of the hoard, '... *comme monument unique et inappréciable des tem[p]s les plus reculés de l'Europe occidentale'*, that regrettably, he neglected to give the find-spot. However the illustrations, which appear to be faithful, remain.

I give below the analysis of the coins illustrated which constituted some 77% of the hoard. The first column is my own analysis, the second and third columns show for the purpose of comparison the analyses of two well-known experts in this field, respectively the late D. F. Allen and Dr J. B. Colbert de Beaulieu.

|  | 1. | 2. | 3. |
|---|---|---|---|
| Coriosolites, group I *staters* | 112 | 119 | 112 |
| Coriosolites, group II *staters* | 375 | 380 | 409 |
| Coriosolites, group III *staters* | 117 | 116 | 111 |
| Coriosolites, group IV *staters* | 139 | 142 | 108 |
| Coriosolites, link coin (I, II) | 1 | – | – |
| Coriosolites, *quarter-staters* | 2 | – | – |
| Baiocasses | – | 3 | – |
| Unelli | 4 | – | 4 |
| Uncertain | 10 | – | 16 |
|  | 760 | 760 | 760 |

On a lighter note, the Baron de Donop's own classification – including only those coins with well preserved obverses – was:

| Head of Baal | 220–230 |
| Head of Krishna | 120–130 |
| Head of Ogmios | 270–280 |

Incidentally, a distant descendant of the Baron, Colonel Pelham Grenville von Donop, contributed to another great cause when, in 1881, he shared his christian names with his godson, P. G. Wodehouse.

## Jersey – V (1875–80) – C de B 6

On the headland between Bouley Bay and Rozel Bay in the north-east corner of Jersey there are the remains of an earthwork which seems at one time to have extended right across the promontory from bay to bay. Judging by the mass of the earthwork – it is still in parts some 20 feet high and some 30 feet thick – it is reasonable to suppose that the area north and east of the rampart, still called le Castel de Rozel, was an example of one of the series of promontory forts of the late Iron age characteristic of the coasts of Brittany, Normandy, Cornwall and Ireland.

After particularly heavy rain in the area in 1875, two or more Gaulish hoards were uncovered after land-slips near the earthwork, and other coins, either in lots or isolated examples, were found in the débris on several later occasions; the last find of this series was published in 1880. Something less than half of all the coins found at this spot have been published. The author of the principal record of this hoard wrote that he had been able to examine more than 700 pieces, but that there was *'une notable quantité, peut-être autant, ou même davantage, qui a été dispersée et perdue pour la science' (A. de Barthélemy: 'Etude... Jersey p 177)*. Some coins may still be contained in private Jersey collections.

The main hoard seems (by implication) to have consisted of a large variety of Gaulish coins – in general terms perhaps evenly divided between anepigraphic (not inscribed, Armorican) and epigraphic (inscribed, other Gaulish) specimens

– and a few Roman coins, perhaps intruders; it is however recorded in one place that there were found *'des centaines de pièces de monnaies, tant Gauloises que Romaines'*.

I have examined all references and illustrations of coins from this group of hoards, and the evidence suggests that there were some 990 Gaulish coins of all types found, and probably well over 1000. If however one accepts the statement (see above) that there was 'a significant quantity, perhaps as many again, or even more, which have been dispersed . . .', there are good grounds for believing that the hoard(s) may have consisted of up to 2000 pieces.

The following chart sets out the evidence, documentary and physical, for my above estimate of 990–1000 Gaulish pieces. Roman finds are also shown. Only circumstantial evidence supports my insertion of the final column. Some or all of the 225 Armorican coins in the Evans collection in the British Museum, recorded as having been found in Jersey, may have come from this hoard. I have examined the collection but there are few clues. The numbers given are based on my own interpretation of the collection as a whole (less those coins which are definitely marked as having come from other provenances, mostly in Brittany), and they do not include any Armorican *quarter-staters* of which there are a considerable number which may also have come from this hoard. However it is important that this source should be securely on record as, when further research is made on the subject of dies and die-links of the Armorican series, I feel sure that this collection will provide a useful field for study. Further – perhaps less circumstantial – evidence supports the mention of the Evans collection, inasmuch as two Roman *denarii* (see below) are said to have been found together with the Armorican coins from Jersey.

I have thought fit not to include in the chart the number of coins from these hoards preserved in the collection of the Bibliothèque Nationale, Paris, as the chart has been designed simply to ascertain a minimum total in the 1875 hoard(s) and there might be a danger of duplication.

| *Attribution* | *Atlas* | *Barthélemy* | *Cable* | *C de B* | *Soc. Jersiaise Museum* | *Belgium*** | *BM* |
|---|---|---|---|---|---|---|---|
| Coriosolites | 14 | – | 8 | 9 | 131 | 2 | ?69+ |
| Abrincatui | 16 | * | 3 | 18 | – | 1 | ?21+ |
| Abrincatui 1/4 stater | – | – | 1 | – | – | – | – |
| Osismii | 2 | * | 2 | – | – | – | ?1+ |
| Unelli | 10 | * | – | 3 | – | – | ?31+ |
| other Armorican? | 1 | * | – | – | – | – | – |
| Gaulish inscribed | } 37 | 585 | 8 | 7 | 8 | – | – |
| other Gaulish |  | 2 | 3 | 2 | 9 | – | – |
| Total | 80 | 587 | 25 | 39 | 138 | 3 | ?121+ |
| Roman | – | 14 | 6 | – | 14 | – | – |

\* An indeterminate number of Armorican pieces was also recorded
\*\* Collection of the Bibliothèque Royale de Belgique

As can be seen from the chart this was a very heterogeneous hoard. The most numerous (recorded) group from the hoard consisted of a very wide range of epigraphic specimens, which are listed below. The readings have on occasion been differently interpreted by some authorities but they are generally recognizable and a DLT reference is given in most cases for the purposes of comparison. Coins marked with an asterisk were found for the first time in this hoard; illustrations marked with two asterisks are of specimens actually found in the hoard.

| Inscriptions | Metal | No. found | DLT-ref. |
|---|---|---|---|
| ANDECOM/ANDECOMBO | AR | 28 | ?XIX–6342 |
| ARIVOS/SANTONOS | AR | 30 | XXV–10385** |
| | | | XIII–4525 |
| ATEVLA/VLATOS | AR | 50 | XXIX–7191 |
| ATEVLA/VLATOS | AR | 12 | XXIX–7187/6 |
| BELINOC | AR | 10 | – |
| CALEDV | AR | 10 | XXIX–7177 |
| CAM | AR | 5 | XIV–4139, 4143 |
| CASSISVRATOS/ . . . LANTOS | AR | 1 | XXV–10384** |
| CICUTANOS* | AE | 2 | XXV–10400** |
| CVPINACIOS/VLATOS | AR | 1 | XXIX–7203/4 |
| DIASVLOS | AR | 7 | ?XXIX–J18** |
| | | | XV–4871 |
| DVBNOREIX/DVBNOCOV | AR | 5 | XV–5044 |
| EPAD | AR | 11 | ?XII–3885 |
| ESVIOS* | AR | 8 | XXV–10380/1** |
| GAIV.IVL/ACEDOMAPATIS | AR | 5 | XXV–10412** |
| IƆOIωI/SAA (?IωIOCI) | AR | 5 | XVII–5639 |
| IVLIOS/DVRAT | AR | 4 | XIII–4478 |
| IVLIV/TOGIRI (X) | AR | 4 | XVII–5632 |
| ΚΑΛΕΤΕΔΟΥ | AR | 2 | XXXII–8291 |
| similar to the above but ΔΕ | AR | 4 | XXXII–8178 |
| LITAVICOS | AR | 4 | XV–5075/6 |
| MA (oboles of Massilia, very worn) | AR | 25 | e.g. II–581 |
| NERCOD/NERCOD | AR | 3 | XIII–4535 |
| NINNO/NINNO | AR | 1 | XXXVIII–9355 |
| ORCITIRIX/ATPILLI.F | AR | 38 | XV–4800 or 4805 |
| ORCITIRIX/COIOS | AR | 2 | XV–4819 |
| ORCOPRIL/SII ƨIIDI* | AR | 1 | XXV–10413** |
| . . . OCOVIRV* | Billon | 1 | XXV–10382** |
| . . . CAVCE/ . . . RA* | AR | 1 | XXV–10405** |
| AMMI/ECS* | Billon | 1 | LV–D36** |
| PENNILE/RVPIL . . . * | AR | 1 | XXVI–10383** |
| PETRVCORI/ACINCOVEPVS | AR | 1 | – |
| PIXTILOS | AR | 2 | XXVIII–cf 7070 |
| PIXTILOS | AR | 2 | XXVIII–7058 |
| Q.DOCI SAM F | AR | 40 | XVI–5405–5411 |
| SANTONOS | AR | 8 | XIII–4520 |
| SEGVSIAVS/ARVS | AR | 1 | VII–4622 |
| SENODON/CALEDV | AR | 5 | XXIX–7181/2 |
| CEπΠ . . . * | AR | 1 | XXVI–J43** |
| SEQVANOIOTVOS | AR | 1 | XVI–5351 |
| SOLIMA | AR | 42 | XIV–4196 |
| TOGIRIX/TOGIRIX | AR | 150 | XVI–5550 |
| VIIPOTAL | AR | 1 | XIII–4495 |
| VIIPOTAL | AR | 49 | XIII–4484 |

*Fig. 13: Examples of Gaulish* quinarii *enlarged, with legends such as were found in Jersey V.*

*The* reverses *show some interesting interpretations of the horse, a very popular motif at the time (for notes on illustrations see page 30).*

*a*

*b*

*c*

*d*

*e*

*f*

*g*

*h*

*i* *j*

*k* *l*

*m* *n*

*(Notes on illustrations on pages 28 and 29.)*

a: **DLT 4525, 10385** AR; *(ex Forrer fig. 215)*. ARIVOS/SAN[TONO]. This coin, attributed to the Santones, is believed to have been modelled on a Roman Consular denarius dated to 57 B.C. 30 such coins were found in Jersey V (weight: 1.86 g).

b: **DLT 7187/6, 7191** AR ATEVLA/VLATOS. Note the neck torque *and* wings on the obverse; &, *off flan*, above animal on reverse. This example consists of a copper core dipped in silver (weight: 1.55 g) – an early example of coiner's fraud. The coin has been dated by some authorities to 57 B.C., by others to post 52 B.C. One reading gives 'devotee to Mars' from AT VLAT (VLAT=MARS). The coin has also been attributed to Attila the Hun! 62 such coins were found in Jersey V.

c: **Muret 6378** AR. BIIIN[OC] (reading BELINOS); possibly connected with the god Belen (Roman Apollo). These coins, attributed by Blanchet to the Arverni, by Wüthrich to the Helvetii, circulated widely. The obverse *is copied from a Republican denarius of C. Calpurnius Piso struck c 64 B.C.* 10 such coins are recorded from Jersey V (weight: 1.35 g; ex Stroehlin, Sotheby, 1910 and Wüthrich collections).

d: **DLT 7177** AR. CAL[EDV]. Attributed by some to the Caletes, and by others to the Remi, this coin is dated to 52 B.C. This example is a 'brockage' (weight: 1.57 g). 10 such coins were found in Jersey V.

e: **DLT 4139** AR. CAM. Attributed to the Bituriges Cubi; dated to 53 B.C. (weight: 1.95 g).

f: *Cf* **DLT 8178** AR. ΔE. Probably related to ΚΑΛΕΤΕΔΟΥ types with head of Minerva. Attributed to the Aedui or Caletes or even the Leuci (reading ΛVK). Finds of these coins are widely spread – as far east as Bavaria and Solothurn in Switzerland. 4 were found in Jersey V (weight: 1.93 g).

g: **DLT 4871** AR. DIA[SV]LOS. Attributed to the Aedui, dated to 57 B.C. Note torque *around neck* (weight: 1.73 g). 7 found in Jersey V.

h: **DLT 4478** AR. [DVR]AT/IVIIOI (JULIOS). Attributed to the Pictones, post 56 B.C. Duratios was mentioned by Caesar (B.G. VIII 26-7) as an ally of Rome (weight: 1.99 g). 4 found in Jersey V.

i: **DLT 5075/6** AR. LITΛVICOϩ. Dated by some to the time of the Helvetic league i.e. 58-7 B.C.; attributed by others to the Aedui, post 121 B.C. and pre-Gallic war. The obverse is inspired by the Roman head of Diana on a coin of Gens Plaetoria. Litaviccos is mentioned 14 times by J. Caesar (B.G. VII); he was involved in the short-lived insurrection of 52 B.C. (weight: 1.96 g). 4 found in Jersey V.

j: **DLT 4800** AR. [ΛTPILI·F]/ORCETIRIX. Attributed by some to the Aedui and believed to be money of alliance with Orgetorix of the Helvetii (weight: 1.95 g). 38 such coins were found in Jersey V (ex Wüthrich).

k: **DLT 7081** CU PIXTILOS. A countermark of this chieftain on a Roman coin has been used to date this series to 27–12 B.C. The attribution is uncertain. 4 PIXTILOS coins (of two other coin-types) were found in Jersey V (weight: 3.67 g; ex Changarnier).

l: **DLT 5405–5411**. Q DO[CI]/[Q DOCI] SΛΛF. Attributed to the Sequani by DLT and others; found as far afield as the Languedoc. 40 such coins were found in Jersey V (weight: 1.96 g).

m: **Muret 4517**. SANTONO[S]. Attributed with some confidence to the Santones. 8 coins with this legend were found in Jersey V (weight: 1.94 g; ex Changarnier).

n: **DLT 9025**.[ϩOLIMA] / COΛIMA. Attributed to Solimarius of the Leuci, this piece shows an interesting example of transliteration with the use of both the Roman and the Greek alphabets. A fish of some sort appears below the horse. 42 coins of this type were found in Jersey V (weight: 1.88 g; ex Forrer fig. 197).


Judging by the evidence from contemporary records, it would appear that most of the coins represented by the above list, being generally of a small – sometimes minute – type, were all found in one place, together with some fragments of pottery, suggesting that they might have been at one time contained in a jar. *'Un*

*peu plus loin, dans un trou qui se trouvait sur la ligne du terrain primitif...,
étaient des monnaies de grand module* [presumably '*staters*'], *au type armoricain, ...' (Barthélemy p 179).* There may therefore have been two separate hoards. If one adheres faithfully to the above description of the find, one can assume that the *quarter-staters* in the Evans collection in the British Museum – if they came from Jersey at all – were found together with the other small (epigraphic) coins. In the discussion of the circumstances of the burial (see below) this assumption may be relevant, together with the fact that many of the coins of both large and small types, were apparently defaced by having been bent, in some cases nearly double.

In addition to the Gaulish coins found at Le Castel, a certain number of Roman coins are also known to have been found at the same location at the same time. These are listed in another section.

## Jersey – VI (1883) – C de B 7

In 1883 a small earthenware pot was found at Rozel, close to the site of the Jersey V discoveries. 'It contained both Gaulish and Roman coins – the former, both of billon and silver, being mainly of the smaller or more rare sort, and each weighing only from 18 to 28 grains' (Lowsley p 6). Except for a *denarius* of Marcus Antonius of the Triumvirate period, which was recorded, the total number and the nature of the coins of this hoard remain otherwise undetermined. The current contents of the pot appear to be coins from the La Marquanderie hoard (Jersey – VIII).

## Jersey – VII (pre-1897)

Lieutenant-Colonel B. Lowsley wrote (p 5):
'I have looked through a 'find' of more than 200 Jersey Gaulish coins, which are in the possession of R. R. Lemprière, Esq. They were turned up by the plough on his manor of Rozel; and whatever covering had enclosed them had either gone to decay, or become broken up, as they were quite loose. He had cleaned a few of them. Even to the eye the metallic composition varied greatly – some being of the colour of silver, and some lowering to that of copper. In this lot, there were but two of the smaller size of 25 grains, and I think that proportion may perhaps give some indication as to the relative rarity of the two coins; for at a rough estimate one seems to meet only about one in a hundred, which is of the smaller kind.'

The only inference to be drawn from the above record (from the choice of the phrase 'smaller kind') is that the coins were almost certainly of an Armorican Type, probably Coriosolite.

Nothing else is known of this hoard.

## Jersey – VIII (1935) – C de B 9

In April of 1935, while the foundations for a house were being prepared at a site on La Marquanderie Hill, St. Brelade, a workman unearthed what '... looked like a lot of old buttons.' The owner of the property subsequently showed some of the 'buttons' to his bankers who, it may be said, recognized them to be coins but '... suggested that they might be Turkish'. Happily the late Major Rybot was eventually consulted and it is largely thanks to him that a major part of this very important Armorican coin hoard has been preserved for study. A full account of this find can be found in Rybot's 'Armorican Art'.

It is estimated that there were well over eleven thousand coins in this hoard (all *staters*) making it by far the largest Armorican coin hoard ever found. Some 10,600 coins were presented to the Société Jersiaise by the owner of the land, who retained a further 500 coins. It has also been estimated that as many as 200 pieces may have been removed by unauthorized persons at the site shortly after the discovery of the hoard.

Beneath the mass of coins were found 'The oxidised remains of a thin bronze vessel...'

In March 1937, a count totalled 10,547 coins, classified as follows:

| | |
|---|---|
| Coriosolite group I | 1255 |
| Coriosolite group II | 6410 |
| Coriosolite group III | 859 |
| Coriosolite group IV | 1975 |
| Coriosolite link coins (II/IV) | 7 |
| Coriosolite link coins (III/IV) | 33 |
| Osismii/Unelli | 7 |
| Other 'intruder' | 1 |
| | 10 547 |

The above classification was confirmed two years later by another authority who, however, apparently included the Link coins or 'mules' under type I (totalling 1295) and made no mention of the other intruder assigned subsequently to the Abrincatui; (the grand total given was therefore 10,546).

In 1957, the Museum of the Société Jersiaise had 9180 coins from this hoard in its possession. A further classification was made of these together with another 74 coins which had been distributed to Museums and other entities (then totalling 9262 coins); the result was as follows:

| | |
|---|---|
| Coriosolite group I | 1335 |
| Coriosolite group II | 5033 |
| Coriosolite group III | 806 |
| Coriosolite group IV | 2080 |
| Osismii | 7 |
| Abrincatui | 1 |
| | 9262 |

The proportionate differences in classification in the above two tables are probably due to the fact that at the time of the first classification only about four thousand had been thoroughly cleaned and that some of the remaining 6000, after cleaning, were reassigned. It is of interest that no *quarter-staters* were found in this hoard.

*Fig. 14: A coin of the Coriosolites group II from the La Marquanderie hoard. The flan is unusually ragged.*
*Rybot II 36. 6.3 g.*

In 1974, I was allowed by the Curator of the Société Jersiaise Museum to examine the coins from this hoard. In view of the limited time available, I was only able to make a count per principle group. The result was as follows:

| | |
|---|---:|
| Coriosolite group I | 1460 |
| Coriosolite group II | 5579 |
| Coriosolite group III | 790 |
| Coriosolite group IV | 2065 |
| Unelli | 7 |
| Abrincatui | 1 |
| Links | 47 |
| Unidentified | 35 |
| | 9984 |

The return of a package of coins from France, after analysis, apparently accounted for the increase in the totals.

I recognize that the above is only a very brief summary of such an important hoard, and look forward with great interest to reading a definitive publication. As will be seen later, this hoard, in its volume, provides the opportunity to make a study of a comprehensive series of dies; and such a study would not only give us a valuable insight into late Iron-age metallurgical processes, but might also provide valuable pointers to the evolution of Armorican coinages as a whole. At the time of writing, the study of JERSEY – VIII is once more under way.

## Jersey – IX (1957, 1959) – C de B 11

In January 1957, a large boulder, for years a hazard to ploughs, was lifted from a field at Le Catillon de Haut, Grouville. Beneath the boulder, together with the fragments of three bronze *fibulae,* two small rings, some ten millimetres of metal braid and the remains of at least three earthenware pots, a mass of coins was found. The hoard, though consisting largely of coins of the Armorican series, contained a few other Gaulish coins and also a number of British types. This was the first time that British or 'Belgic' types have been found in the Channel Islands. This and the fact that a disproportionate number of gold (or electrum) coins was found will be seen to be significant (see below).

The promising circumstances of the find, initially published in the Evening Post of 25th January, 1957, were unfortunately marred by the fact that a large part of it was sold off before a complete analysis could be made. Luckily, however, for students of this subject, two experts in this field were afforded separate opportunities to study portions of the hoard. The two studies overlap to a certain extent – a possibility hardly to be avoided under the circumstances – but they nevertheless succeed in imparting a very valuable amount of information about a hoard which will be seen to be one of the most interesting and significant of those found in the Channel Islands.

There is one other complication: the first part – that which came to light in 1957 – consisted of two lots of coins, similar enough in content to have been judged as having come from the same hoard. A second part, also similar in content, was found apparently under another boulder near to the first site at the beginning of 1959. This second part was also placed on the numismatic market in London but, fortunately, an expert was once again consulted before sale and an inventory was made. The first part of the hoard consisted of at least 610 pieces and, later, at least a further 255, totalling 865. The second part contained at least 1621 coins.

For the reasons stated above, it has not been possible to analyse this find with any guarantee of great accuracy. However, the information which the two experts were able to make available under the circumstances is very valuable in that it constitutes the 'official' record of the hoard – and I will give a summary below. The attributions of each expert (Allen and Colbert de Beaulieu) are given when either the opinion or the number of coins involved comes into question. It will also be seen that the metal content often appears to be different; this distinction is largely due to an approximation on the one hand (where all items are said to be either of gold or of silver) and more detail on the other hand, and is therefore largely academic. For the purposes of simplification I have termed all the coins either *'staters'* or *'fractions'*, under which latter term I have included *'1/4 staters'*, *'1/8 staters'* and the so-called *'petits billons'*. For the purposes of comparison, references are provided where possible, and I have also indicated in which part of the hoard the relative coins were found: the first column represents the first lot found in 1957; the second represents the second lot found in the same year and the third represents the part discovered in 1959. References are from De La Tour and Mack.

# Armorican

*Fig. 15: Coriosolite AR stater group I from Le Catillon.*
*Rybot I 23. 6.21 g.*

|  | First Lot | Second Lot | Third Lot |
|---|---|---|---|
| **Coriosolites** (A lists metal as AR in all cases; B billon.) | | | |
| *Staters* Group I | 65 | 9 | 197 |
| *Staters* Group II | 348 | 118 | 929 |
| *Staters* Group III | 28 | 12 | 63 |
| *Staters* Group IV | 89 | 45 | 325 |
| *Staters* Uncertain | 13 | 12 | 17 |

*Fig. 16: Coriosolite billon ¼-stater of group I from Le Catillon.*
*1.27 g.*

| | | | |
|---|---|---|---|
| *Fractions* Group I | 3 | – | 3 |
| *Fractions* Group II | 1 | 3 | 4 |
| *Fractions* Group III | 8 | – | 15 |
| *Fractions* Group IV | – | – | 4 |

*Fig. 17: AU stater attributed to the Aulerci Cenomani, from Le Catillon.*
*DLT 6870. Illust. BSJ 17 I (1957) facing p 19; also C de B RBN (1957) VI 2. 7.22 g.*

**Aulerci Cenomani**

| | | | |
|---|---|---|---|
| *Staters* AU | 2 (6852, 6870) | 1 (6852) | – |

*Fig. 18: Billon stater of the Redones from Le Catillon.*
*DLT 6793, 10386; Roth 27. 6.92 g.*

**Redones** A specified AU; B billon
| | | | |
|---|---|---|---|
| Staters | 1 | 1 (6793) | – |
| Fractions AR | – | – | 2 |

*Fig. 19: Billon ¼-stater of the Osismii from Le Catillon.*
*Illust. C de B RBN (1957) 12; possibly a unique fraction of the 'Tent' type stater. 1.22 g.*

**Osismii**
| | | | | |
|---|---|---|---|---|
| Staters AU or El | 3 | ('tent' type) | AU 8 (6508)<br>AR 4 (6508) | – |
| Fractions { AU or El | 4 | ('tent type', fractions of 6533) | AU or El 18 (6584, J55, fractions of 6533, 6551, 6973) | El 2<br>Br 2 |
| { El | 3 | (6584, J55) | | |

*Fig. 20: AR stater attributed to the Baiocasses or the Unelli from Le Catillon.*
*Cf DLT 6985 but head l. 6.67 g.*

**Baiocasses or Unelli**
| | | | |
|---|---|---|---|
| Staters | AR 1 (6978) | (AU 1 (6967, 6978)<br>(AR 2 (6985, J33) | AR 7 (6969, 6985) |
| Fractions | Bil 5 (J3, 10402) | (AR 3 (10402)<br>(Bil 3 (J49) | AR 15 (6980) |

*Fig. 21:* AR stater *and billon ¼-stater attributed by some authorities to the Abrincatui, from Le Catillon.*
*DLT J5, cf Roth 46. 6.82 g. DLT J59. 1.3 g*

| | | | |
|---|---|---|---|
| **Abrincatui (?)** | | | |
| *Staters* | AR 25 (J4,5,6,12,13,14) | 3 (J4,5,6,13,14) | 22 (J4, 12, 13) |
| *Fractions* | AR 3 (J9,10,11) | 2 (J10, 11) | 4 (J9, 10, 22, 59) |
| **Veneti (?)** | | | |
| *Stater* | AR – | 1 (6667) | – |
| **Other Armorican** | | | |
| *Staters* | El 1 | AU 1 (6793) | – |
| *Fractions* | AU 3 (6584, J3)<br>AR 6 (10402) | AU 4 (6584, J3, 6793)<br>AR 7 (10402, 6584, J3) | Bil 1 |
| **Others (possibly Armorican)** | | | |
| (not identified) | Bil – | – | 6 |

# Other Gaulish

*Fig. 22: CU stater attributed to the Bituriges Cubi, from Le Catillon.*
*DLT 4072; see also C de B RBN (1957) p 71, 2045. 6.85 g.*

| | *First Lot* | *Second Lot* | *Third Lot* |
|---|---|---|---|
| **Aedui** | AR – | 1 (5252) | – |
| **Bituriges Cubi** | AR – | 1 (4072) | – |

*Fig. 23: Billion fraction of the Volcae Arecomici, dated to 90–77 B.C., from Le Catillon. Muret 2620; C de B RBN (1957) p 71, 246. 2.09 g.*

| | | | |
|---|---|---|---|
| **Volcae Arecomici** | AR – | 1 (2630, 2621) | – |
| **Perhaps Central Gaul** | AR 1 (cf 4867, 4858) | – | – |
| **Others** | AR – | 2 | – |

# British

**British 'B' (Chute type)**
*Stater*   AU –   1 (M32)   –

**Type between British 'O' (Sussex type) and Gallo-Belgic 'D'**
*Fraction*   AU –   1 (M41a, cf 6916)   –

*Fig. 24: Durotriges AR stater from Le Catillon and fraction.*
Mack 317, 319. Coins of the Durotriges, dating from 60 B.C., have been found mainly in Dorset, Wiltshire and Somerset. Some have seen a picture of a boat with oars on the obverse (inverted) of the quarter stater (weights: 5.96 g, 1.09 g; the stater is ex Mack and is illustrated in Allen, Origins..., pl XIII no. 7).

| | | | | |
|---|---|---|---|---|
| **Durotrigan** | | | | |
| *Stater* | AR 1 (cf 9507) | 6 | (between M41 & M319) | – |
| *Fractions* | AR 2 (M319) | 3 | | 1 (M319) |
| **Hengistbury type** | AR 2 (M321) | – | | 2 (M321) |
| **Possibly British** | AR 1 (cf M87) | – | | – |
| **Sussex type/Armorican hybrid (possibly struck in Britain)** | AR 1 (cf 8514) | – | | – |

## Single Coin Finds

(items b), c), d) and e) below may have come from hoards).

a) A Coriosolite *stater* in billon of group II was found 'in 1812 or later... at the seat of the Prince de Bouillon at Bagatelle', St. Saviour, Jersey. The coin, a very fine specimen, is preserved in the British Museum collection (C de B 4).
b) Another billon Coriosolite *stater* group II was 'found in the Royal Harbour Jersey' (also preserved in the British Museum).
c) A gold *stater,* attributed to the Aulerci Cenomani (DLT 6818) was 'found in Jersey' (also preserved in the British Museum).
d) A *fraction* of the Abrincatui (?) in billon (copper prevailing) and very crude (cf DLT J8), labelled *'découverte de Jersey',* is preserved in the British Museum.
e) Another, similar to d), (but cf DLT J10), also labelled *'découverte de Jersey',* is preserved in the British Museum.
f) There is a beautiful little Armorican gold *quarter-stater* (cf DLT 6963 – horse reversed) in the collection of the Schweizerische Landesmuseum in Zürich. The coin, from the celebrated Forrer collection is labelled *'Fund von Jersey'.*
g) A billon *stater* of the Coriosolites, group III (but horse to the left) is illustrated in the sixth annual bulletin of the Société Jersiaise. It was said to have been 'found in the Island'.
h) Towards 1900, a coin of the Coriosolites, group II, is said to have been found in a garden in David Place, St. Helier (Colbert de Beaulieu: 'Armorican Coin Hoards... p 203).
i) In 1935, a Coriosolite *stater* of group II was discovered during excavations on a Gallo-Roman site at the Pinnacle rock, St. Ouen, Jersey (C de B 10).

## Enigmatic Finds

1) Three Gaulish coins of brass are said to have been found at Le Couperon, 'by whom unknown' (C de B – *trouvaille perdue du Couperon*).
2) In 1847 the Comte de Kergariou indicated that a hoard of 900 billon coins of the Coriosolites were found in Jersey in 1833. The weight of informed opinion now holds that this reference, which was taken up by Cable, is a duplication of Jersey IV (1820), and should therefore be disregarded (C de B – *trouvaille apocryphe de 1833*).
3) There is no firm evidence that any Gaulish coins have ever been found in Guernsey, although there are eleven Coriosolite coins – seven *staters* and four *quarter-staters* – in the Lukis Museum, as well as a small number in private collections, which are said to have been found in Guernsey (see Bourde de la Rogerie). One authority has suggested that these coins may have come from the hoard found in Jersey in 1875 (Jersey V).
4) There is also no evidence that Coriosolite coins have been found on the Minquiers, in spite of a persistent rumour to that effect.

It is perhaps worth recording that an indeterminate number of other isolated coin finds appear to have been made in Jersey, '... *sans avoir été jugées dignes d'une communication* ...'.

**Implications of the Finds**

So much for the finds. Now, it may reasonably be asked: what do these finds mean? When were the hoards buried? Why? Sceptics, holding that this whole series should not be included in a study of Channel Islands currencies, may anyway have had some of their doubts dispelled by the pure volume of the finds; 15–20,000 coins found in one small Island is, after all, no mean amount. But let us look further.

Leaving aside the isolated finds (items a) to g) above) for the time being, it is immediately clear that there are at least three distinct types of hoard. For convenience a brief summary of the hoards is given below:

| | |
|---|---|
| Sark I | – heterogeneous, no Armorican |
| Jersey I | – possibly Armorican (? Coriosolite) |
| Jersey II | – probably Coriosolite |
| Jersey III | – possibly Armorican |
| Jersey IV | – Armorican, almost entirely Coriosolite |
| Jersey V | – Heterogeneous, possibly two hoards – one heterogeneous, one Armorican |
| Jersey VI | – Uncertain |
| Jersey VII | – possibly Armorican |
| Jersey VIII | – Armorican, almost entirely Coriosolite |
| Jersey IX | – Mixed – Armorican, other Gaulish, British; possibly two deposits. |

The types of hoard are firstly those which include only Armorican and principally Coriosolite types (e.g. Jersey IV, VIII and possibly I, II, V and VII) and secondly those which consist of a very heterogeneous selection of Gaulish coins, sometimes together with a smaller cross-section of Armorican types (e.g. Sark I and Jersey V). Jersey IX can be considered as a third type consisting, as it does, of a large majority of Armorican types, a small number of Gaulish types and a few other coins apparently from Britain.

*Fig. 25: Gauls portrayed on Roman Republican coins.*
*Sydenham 952, 953; CR 448/2a, 3. Heads of Vercingetorix (?) and Gallia on AR denarii of L. Hostilius Saserna, dated to 48 B.C. (Both coins ex Duke of Northumberland collection, Sotheby 4.11.1982.)*

After many years of obscurity a dating pattern for these hoards is at last beginning to emerge. In the past it has been the custom to assign all such finds rather vaguely to the epoch of the Roman invasion of Gaul. The most recently discovered hoard (Jersey IX) has however provided us with a *point de départ* for a dating sequence. The most significant factor is that there were over forty gold coins in this hoard. As it is recognized that the Roman incursions marked the end of the gold coinage of Gaul, it follows that the hoard must have been buried at some time between 56 B.C., when D. Brutus, Caesar's lieutenant, campaigned and defeated the Veneti and allied Armorican tribes in the famous naval battle, and 51 B.C., when Caesar brought his Gallic campaigns to a successful conclusion. It is worth noting that the discovery of British gold types in this hoard has also provided a *terminus ante quem* (i.e. latest circulation date) for a significant number of uninscribed types from Britain, hitherto uncertainly dated. Caesar himself names Britain as 'a country which has provided help to our enemies in nearly all the wars', referring to his Armorican campaign; the presence of these British coins should therefore not surprise us if this dating is correct.

With the above as a starting point, it is generally assumed that the period before the upheavals of Caesar's Gallic wars, must be characterized by hoards of a more homogeneous character, evidencing an interchange between neighbouring Armorican tribes. These hoards must have been buried at the first signs of danger, or perhaps after the first defeat of the Armorican allies grouped under Viridovix in 56 B.C., before there had been time for coin types from Central Gaul to intrude. Following this principle, Jersey IV, V (the Armorican part) and VIII can all be assigned to this date. There is further evidence to support the theory that these three hoards were in some way connected, and possibly all buried at the same time: it has been shown that the percentages of Coriosolite *stater* types in the three hoards are remarkably similar:

|  | *group I* | *group II* | *group III* | *group IV* |
|---|---|---|---|---|
| *Jersey IV (740 coins)* | 15.1% | 55.3% | 14.9% | 14.5% |
| *Jersey V (125 coins)* | 15.2% | 52.8% | 18.4% | 13.6% |
| *Jersey VIII (9254 coins)* | 14.4% | 54.4% | 8.6% | 22.5% |

It is also generally assumed that the period following the wars is characterized by hoards of an increasingly heterogeneous character. These hoards are evidence that the coins of Central Gaul had by now reached a much wider circulation and were later apparently imitated outside their areas of provenance. Classification has shown that this type of hoard must have been buried shortly after the battle of Alesia (52/51 B.C.) as a smaller selection of these mixed coin types was found on the site of the battle (excavated on the Emperor Napoleon's instructions), having apparently been dropped by combatants.

There is evidence, principally from Roman coins found together with the Gaulish types, that an increasingly varying and depreciating selection of Gaulish coins was in circulation for perhaps a generation after the Roman conquest. The heterogeneous part of Jersey V has been dated down to 39/38 B.C. by the presence

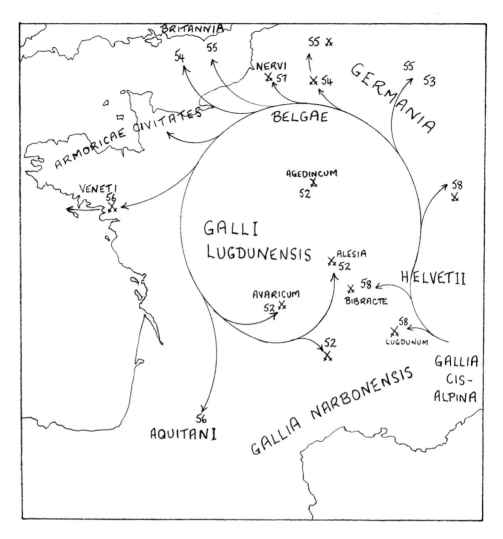

*Fig. 26: Caesar's conquest of Gaul.*
*Adapted from Deutscher Taschenbuch Verlag,* Atlas zur Weltgeschichte, *Munich, 1969.*

of at least two coins of Mark Antony of about this date. Other authorities feel that this type of hoard could be dated as late as 20 B.C. This latter theory is also supported in the case of Jersey V by the discovery of a coin of Caesar Augustus which could be dated to c. 20 B.C. The coin of the Emperor Trajan Decius is clearly an intruder.

Sark I has been dated to 40–30 B.C. through its similarity in content to Jersey V. The one Roman coin in this hoard, dated to 82/1 B.C., was certainly the oldest coin in the hoard. To summarize, burial dates of hoards found in the Channel Islands are, tentatively, as follows:

| | |
|---|---|
| Sark I | 40–30 B.C. |
| Jersey I | ? 56 B.C. |
| Jersey II | ? 56 B.C. |
| Jersey III | ? 56 B.C. |
| Jersey IV | 56 B.C. |
| Jersey V | part 1: 56 B.C. – part 2: 40–20 B.C. |
| Jersey VI | ? |
| Jersey VII | ? 56 B.C. |
| Jersey VIII | 56 B.C. |
| Jersey IX | 56–50 B.C. |

This is not the place to go into the reasons for the dating sequence of Gaulish coin hoards in general. It would however be in order to mention two factors which illustrate the above sequence, each of which occurs in a Jersey hoard.

Firstly, *'petits billons'* (or Armorican *'minimi'*) have been found in at least two Jersey hoards. These tiny coins, notably of the Osismii, have, to date, only been found in heterogeneous hoards in North-West France and the Channel Islands – never in homogeneous Armorican hoards. The presence of these coins, small, crude and of a poor alloy, only in heterogeneous hoards, would seem to fit very well into the theory set out above – that heterogeneous hoards were buried later. The dictum of Gresham's Law – bad money drives out good – could perhaps be cited. However it is more suitable to suppose that coins became so short towards the end of Caesar's campaign that inferior copies were accepted. A good parallel is the use of *'minimi'* and *'minimissimi'* in Imperial Britain some 450 years later, when the Romans themselves were under pressure.

The second factor which seems to have a bearing on the dating sequence was the practice of defacing the coins, by cutting, hammering or bending, in order, apparently, to ascertain the content and quality of the metal alloy. This practice was first thought by numismatists to have been an act of consecration, or even a symbol of demonetization – though it remains to be seen why coins should be ostentatiously demonetized at a time of shortage. Over the years it was noticed that this mutilation was applied more to coins which had circulated outside their areas of origin, this seeming to imply that people were inclined to test 'foreign' coins, when they received them in payment. This is the basis of the theory that such coins must have been in circulation longer (in order to reach these foreign regions) and were therefore probably buried at a later date. They are more common in heterogeneous hoards than they are in homogeneous hoards. In this connection it has been pointed out that less than a handful of marked coins were found in Jersey VIII, whereas no less than 28% of the Coriosolite staters in Jersey IX had been tested in some way. One doubt remains: unless some ancient 'clearing' operation had taken place, it is difficult to understand why tested Coriosolite coins were found in Coriosolite territory.

Any conclusions drawn about the circumstances of burial of any of these hoards must of course be qualified with due caution. In early 1971, the then Curator of the Jersey Museum asked me to look at a 'hoard' of some 1000 base (mostly bronze) coins which had just been dug up in a private garden in the Island. The coins represented an enormous geographic spectrum of the late 19th and early 20th centuries from Ireland to French Indo-China, and must have been buried shortly after the most recent coin in the hoard (a 1946 penny of the Irish Free State) was struck. One wonders what an archaeologist would have made of the hoard, 2000 years hence.

## The Single Coin Finds

Nearly all the isolated coin finds in Jersey were Coriosolite types. It is not definitely known that these were originally isolated finds; so many hoards have been found in the Island that it is quite probably that some of the coins were dropped centuries later by the finders. The fact remains however that the Coriosolites are well represented among these single finds. It is therefore, on the basis of the hoards and single finds, not rash to suggest that Jersey was occupied by the Coriosolites, at least in the middle of the 1st century B.C. The absence of burial places has been drawn on to indicate only a short – perhaps fleeting – occupation of Jersey by this people. However a map of all Coriosolite find-spots suggests that Jersey – if not the focal point – was certainly near the centre of Coriosolite territory. In addition to this, the very vastness of Jersey VIII suggests that these were the coins of an entire tribe – not of a mere family or individual. The coins were also struck only a short time before they were buried, and must therefore have been struck in or near the Island.

There is evidence of two waves of refugees in the Islands. The hill-fort at Rozel (see above) suggests that Jersey may have been part of the Coriosolite territory. They buried their treasury, apparently to prevent it falling into the hands of the Roman pursuers, and – to judge from the care with which many of the hoards were buried – they expected to come back for it. There is no evidence that the second wave (Sark I, Jersey V) was Armorican; it occurred up to a generation later. But it is significant that the two parts of Jersey V were found so close together inside the promontory fort. Did the second wave know where their predecessors had buried their money?

# The Coriosolites

As the Coriosolite series, and the largest Coriosolite hoard ever found (Jersey VIII), await definitive publication, I give below a few observations on this coinage. As will be seen, this section should not be read as reflecting a sequence of historical facts. It is hard to order this period between history and prehistory, and many deductions about it must be regarded with reserve.

*Fig. 27: Coriosolite hairstyles, groups I, II, III and IV (enlarged).*
*Rybot I– 6.28 g (ex Le Catillon); Rybot II 32 6.26 g; Rybot III 65 var. 6.75 g (ex Lockett 1955, lot 134); Rybot IV 75 6.82 g (ex Le Catillon).*

## Design

Notwithstanding the large number of different dies (still to be published in detail) of the four principal groups of the Coriosolite series, there are certain general features common to all of the coins. The style of the hair on the *obverse* is peculiar to the series, being arranged in three rolls or waves; from the forehead, and the two partings between these waves, separate hairs are carefully trained into an 'S' shape, and the waves themselves are clearly interlocked in an ornate double 'S' formation. The designs of the heads, which almost invariably face right, range from straightforward and clearly recognizable, through to the most imaginative and stylized of features which bring to mind in an uncanny way certain latter day 'modern art' forms. Sometimes lines of beading appear to issue from the mouth, usually in an S or double S formation.

*Fig. 28: A beautifully clear example of the S formation (enlarged).*
*Rybot II 32. 6.21 g.*

The *reverse* consists of a horse galloping (usually to the right) stylized and segmented but inevitably conserving a great deal of equine grace and movement. Above and behind the horse, there is a variety of curious but strangely balanced designs, usually taken to be the picture of the charioteer from some early Greek coin types, again stylized and strongly altered by additional artistic forms, but somehow not debased, even if they are at times almost entirely unrecognizable. Before the horse, there are puzzling devices, sometimes attached by lines to the charioteer, resembling alternatively flags, ladders, crosses or other curious curved objects. Underneath the horse there is either what is commonly taken to be a simplified lyre or what is clearly a stylized boar.

It is worthwhile briefly to study some features peculiar to these coins. As can be seen from the illustrations of the four principal groups, with the possible exception of group III, there is a certain tangible uniformity of design. Some authorities hold that there is little to support the attribution of group III to the Coriosolites at all. It is however a fact that coins of group III have always been found together with coins of the other three groups and in markedly consistent proportions to the other groups. Group III is now generally believed to be the oldest of the Coriosolite types (followed successively by groups I, IV and II). This theory is based upon the apparent process of development of the designs from the original gold prototypes and a certain refinement of the minting processes. The fact that each successive group is represented by a larger number of coins than the class before, is seen as lending weight to the theory that all four groups were issued from one mint; this view is not universally held.

One authority, Dr J.-B. Colbert de Beaulieu, who has divided the Coriosolite coins from Jersey into six classes, has used the study of characteristics of each

*Fig. 29: The horse, the 'lyre' and the boar of the Coriosolites (enlarged). Rybot III 68 var. 6.62 g; Rybot II 32. 6.21 g.*

die to determine the order of each class, and largely confirmed this order in a separate study of the silver content in the alloy; the sequence was as follows:

C de B Class VI  
C de B Class V     } Rybot Group III  
C de B Class IV  
C de B Class I        Rybot Group I  
C de B Class III      Rybot Group IV  
C de B Class II       Rybot Group II  

The positions of classes I and II were, after further studies by the same authority, reversed.

## Metallurgy

Whilst on the subject of minting processes, and before looking at the implications of the design, it might be useful briefly to touch upon the more earthy subject of metallurgy. The consensus of opinion is that Coriosolite coins – and indeed all coins of the Armorican *système* – were pressed while they were in a hot plastic state. It is further thought that one of the dies – usually the *obverse* – was made concave, so that the heated globule of metal would not fall off before it was 'struck'. It is not known what means our ancient Coriosolite coiners would have used to melt the metal and obtain the desired alloy, but charcoal, together with bellows, judiciously used, would generate enough heat to melt all the required metals, including gold. Next to nothing is known about the structure of Armorican dies, but a few other Gaulish dies – both upper and lower – have come to light and are often seen to consist of a bronze face set in an iron shaft, a design matching the most refined of early Roman Imperial dies.

This theory that Coriosolite coins were 'pressed' while soft, rather than struck, has been supported by analyses of the micro-structure of *'staters'* of this type. From these it would appear that changes in the micro-structure could only have been imparted while the metal was red-hot. The staters, which weigh around 100 grains (just over 6 grams) each, are made of an impressively consistent and hard billon alloy of approximately 80% copper, 14% silver and 4% tin, the balance being made up by natural mineral impurities which one would expect to find together with the above three metals. This alloy is so hard that, if struck cold, it would defeat even the most modern steel dies. It is, however, only fair to point out that of the dissenters to the above argument, some claim to have found evidence that the coins were not struck or 'pressed' but cast. In this respect, further analyses have recently been made (see Oddy: *Scientific Studies*...) and the results are worth summarizing.

The coins of group III (corresponding to C de B classes IV, V and VI) appear to have a much higher and more consistent silver content than those of groups I, II and IV. It seems that the 'ideal' metal content must have been copper 80%, silver 15% and tin 4%. Many coins – particularly of group III – come astonishingly close to this ideal, and show that the coiners had a remarkable understanding of the properties of alloys of this kind.

Metallurgical investigation has shown that coins of this series were first cast as blanks which were beaten flat while in a cold state. The blanks were subsequently reheated and then struck with the design. This sequence rests partly on the fact that many coins have an edge defect which might well have been caused when the blank was broken off the runner or funnel, through which the molten metal had entered the mould. Some coins – particularly of groups I, II and IV – have an uneven, 'bubbly' surface; others have drastic striking cracks: both these effects are believed to arise from overheating of the blank so that either the surface began to melt or the whole blank became unstable; impurities in the metal of these three classes may also have played a part.

Coins of group III (the rarest type) generally seem to have a greater silver content and a consistently higher weight than the other three groups. These coins, almost all of which have a lyre 'mintmark' (rather than a boar) are therefore thought to have been produced under different – more rigorously controlled – conditions from those under which the bulk of the hoards were produced. While recognizing that we must wait for the La Marquanderie hoard to be published before we obtain the most complete analysis, I give below – based on 56 Coriosolite *staters* in my own collection, 21 of which were found in Jersey – a more modest contribution to this study:

| *Rybot group* | *C de B class* | *Total coins* | *Av. weight* | *Weight variations* | *Coins weighing 6.20 gms or less* |
|---|---|---|---|---|---|
| I | I | 9 | 6.22 gm | 5.66–6.60 gm | 3 |
| II | II | 21 | 6.22 gm | 4.93–6.64 gm | 7 |
| III | IV | 6 | 6.39 gm | 6.27–6.65 gm | – |
| III | V | 9 | 6.54 gm | 5.12–6.92 gm | 1 |
| III | VI | 1 | (6.60 gm) | (6.60 gm) | – |
| IV | III | 10 | 6.27 gm | 5.75–6.81 gm | 3 |

The implications of die links in the hoard from La Marquanderie – albeit not yet fully published – are worth mentioning. Indications from silver content and weight (mentioned above), showing that there seem to be two categories of groups, i.e. Rybot I, II and IV on the one hand and Rybot III on the other, are borne out by die links between the first three groups. From a study of 1276 coins of these three groups from this hoard, it appears that the coins were struck from 53 *obverse* dies and 100 *reverse* dies, showing that wear and tear on the *reverse* die was almost twice as much as that on the *obverse* die.

The hand-held upper die, or 'trussel', had a flat or mushroom-shaped head to take the blows of the coining hammer. As the hammer destroyed the trussel twice as fast as the lower die, it was perhaps natural that the latter was reserved for the more difficult design, in this case the head. Many Coriosolite coins are 'dished', with a convex *obverse* and a concave *reverse,* and, although it would seem odd that a flat blank should be placed on to a slightly concave lower *(obverse)* die and smitten with a slightly convex *(reverse)* trussel, the 'dishing' could perhaps thus be explained.

# Interpretation of the Design

Returning now to a brief study of the implications of the design, it should be stressed that most of what follows is entirely hypothetical. Interpretations of the various aspects of the design are based, at best, on informed guesses. Even where the meaning of the original object (e.g. the boar standard) may be known, the reason for the use of such details as an integral part of Coriosolite coins design has not been firmly established. However, while examining these interpretations, it would be as well to keep in mind the theory that the designs as a whole are the results of an evolution from an older Greek type, tempered by the translation of most of the individual devices into an Armorican art form.

The treatment of the hair on the obverse of Coriosolite coins is unique, in its three interlocking waves of S-shaped curls. The 'S' symbol itself, however, is one of the oldest and commonest devices used throughout the Gaulish coinage systems. The symbol occurs as an integral part of the design – as in this case – or quite separately. Although it is believed by some to have been a development of the S-shaped serpents seen in the designs of some Greek coin types of the 2nd Century B.C., it is likely that the symbol had a distinct and significant meaning in Gaul – perhaps of a religious or superstitious nature. Some have seen a possible astrological meaning in it, citing the fact that on many coins the 'S' appears as two joined crescents (moons?); but there may also be a very simple, purely technical, reason for it.

*Fig. 30: A Gaulish bronze horse with S symbol (1:1).*

*Reproduced from Grivaud de la Vincelle,* Recveil de Monumens Antiques ... découverts dans l'ancienne Gaule, *Paris, 1817, pl IV.*

Lambert reproduces a curious little Gaulish bronze horse – apparently covered with devices associated with the cult of the sun – which rests its front right hoof on a large inverted 'S' – proof perhaps of an astrological significance.

I have tried to find a significance in the various combinations and distributions of curls on the *obverse* of Coriosolite coins as it seemed that the engravers had, where possible, avoided duplication. The meaning – if any – has so far eluded me but there might be some significance in the consistency of the total number of curls as related to the four mains groups (see figure A.) and the fact that of 54 combinations of curls published by Rybot, there seem to be only 10 combinations which are common to any two of the groups. (See figure B.)

**Figure A**

| No. of curls | I | II | III | IV |
|---|---|---|---|---|
| 8 | | | X | |
| 9 | | | X | |
| 10 | | | X | |
| 11 | | | X | |
| 12 | | | X | X |
| 13 | X | | X | |
| 14 | | | X | |
| 15 | X | | X | X |
| 16 | X | X | X | X |
| 17 | X | X | | X |
| 18 | X | X | | X |
| 19 | X | X | | |
| 20 | | | | |
| 21 | X | | | |

**Figure B**
(Groups I–IV together)

| No. of Curls | Combinations |
|---|---|
| 8 | 323  233 |
| 9 | 234  333  324 |
| 10 | 235  334  433  325  226  244 |
| 11 | 335  443  326  434  416  317 |
| 12 | 435  345  336 |
| 13 | 436  256  355  337 |
| 14 | 356  347  257  446 |
| 15 | 357  447  456  348 |
| 16 | 448  457  547  538  556  2410 |
| 17 | 458  467  557  647  539  548  449 |
| 18 | 468  648  567  549  4410  558 |
| 19 | 4510  658  748  (example: 21 curls, made up of 5, 8 and 8 curls in |
| 20 | each wave; combinations common to two or more |
| 21 | 588  groups are underlined) |

*Fig. 31: Parts of the design of Gaulish coins may have been influenced by ancient Greek types. Here (enlarged), a* tetradrachm *of Syracuse (317–310 B.C.) is flanked by two Coriosolite staters.*
*Rybot II 39/32. 6.40 g; Rybot II 41. 6.51 g (ex Le Catillon). The* tetradrachm *is attributed to Agathocles (317–289 B.C.) who claimed sovereignty over all Sicily.*

The lines of beading – 'S'-shaped or 'bracket'-shaped – sometimes issuing from the mouth and framing the head, appear to be direct – if simplified – descendants of the dolphins which framed many classical Greek coin obverses. But there may be another meaning (see below).

It is tempting to try to read some meaning into the distinctive ε-shaped nose of group IV, but probably more reasonable to treat it as a rationalization of former nose designs.

*Fig. 32: A Coriosolite* stater *of group IV and an enlargement of the unusual nose design.*
*Rybot IV 80, 6.36 g.*

There is no evidence of a Gaulish *pantheon,* analogous, say, to the Graeco-Roman model. From the earliest neolithic epoch of the cult of the stones, the Gaulish peoples worshipped in an enormous number of ways, essentially on a regional basis. The stone cult developed into a cult of rocks and of mountains. They held trees and forests sacred, as well as springs, streams, rivers, lakes and seas. There were divinities of the earth and 'goddess-mothers' of fertility; the list is endless. Many divinities were conceived in purely or partly animal form. Of these it is worth mentioning Kernunnos (see above) and Epona, represented on horseback in the later Gallo-Roman period and personified by a horse in earlier times.

*Fig. 33: One representation of the Coriosolite horse with its peculiar head (enlarged). Rybot I 18. 6.60 g.*

The horse on the *reverse* of Coriosolite coins, may be the personification of an Armorican divinity (based of course on the traditional horse and chariot design) – perhaps even the local edition of Epona. The horse's curious androcephalous head is peculiar to the Armorican region. An older view is that it could also be a type of Gaulish Pegasus, symbolic of the sun's course on the one hand, and of 'Good in general' on the other, portrayed – as it often is – leaping over an 'evil genius' (on one of the rarer classes of Coriosolite coins subsequently ascribed to the Veneti); but it is hard to see a bad influence in either the boar or the 'lyre', over which the Coriosolite horse more often leaps.

The boar, commonly called *'sus gallicus',* was also numbered among the animal divinities though it is not certain exactly what it represented. Figurines and amulets of this period have been discovered throughout modern day France and Switzerland, attesting to the religious significance of this beast, and it is one of the devices most commonly incorporated into Gaulish coin design. It is usually portrayed on a flat base which might have represented the upper part of a military standard; it was in fact a favourite army emblem and, later, graced the standard of a Roman Legion. Some authorities, however, believe this straight line to be a symbol of the earth, holding that the boar was revered as it partook of the fruit of the sacred oak. Tacitus, writing of a contemporary tribe in Northern Germany, tells us: 'They honour the mother of the gods; the symbols of this religion are figures of boars which they carry in their hands'.

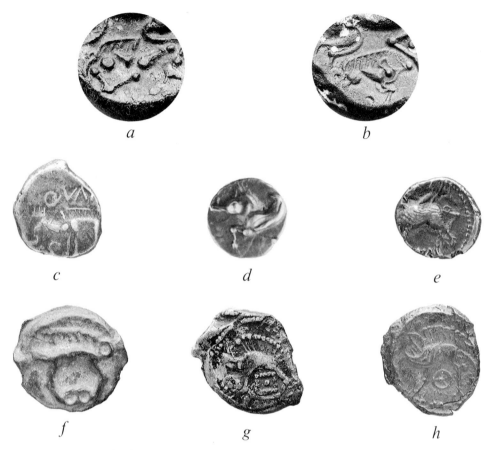

*Fig. 34: Two Coriosolite boars enlarged (top: groups II and IV) as compared to boars appearing on the coinage (also enlarged) of other Gaulish peoples. In the centre is a silver coin from the Auriol find (near Marseille) dating back to the 6th century B.C.*

a: Rybot II 32. 4.93 g.
b: Rybot IV 75. 6.36 g.
c: DLT 5351. AR *SEQVA[NOIOTVO]S*. The meaning of the legend is obscure but most authorities give this coin to the Sequani. One of these pieces was found in Jersey V.
d: DLT 221. 0.55 g. AR *fraction of the coinage of Clazomenae on the southern shore of the Gulf of Smyrna dated to 545–494 B.C. The badge of this city appears to have been a winged boar. Such coins, often apparently long in circulation, bear witness to the earlier cultural and trading connections between the Greek settlement in Massilia and those in Asia Minor.*
e: DLT 9355. 1.51 g. [NINMI] quinarius *of the Rauraci (Helvetii) from the Solothurn region of Switzerland. One similar coin, but with the inscription NINNO, was found in Jersey V.*
f: DLT 9078. 3.33 g. Cast coin of the Leuci in Potin *(an alloy of tin, copper, lead and zinc).*
g, h: DLT 7352,7333. 2.35 g, 2.1 g. CU coins attributed to the Veliocasses.

The so-called 'lyre' which seems to some extent interchangeable with the boar in the Armorican series, presents more difficulties. The lyre – rather more truly represented – does occur on many other Gaulish coinages, and it is therefore quite possible that this Armorican device is in fact a stylized lyre. To the Greeks, the sky was the lyre of God, and it was Apollo who tuned the chords. The Gauls may have had a similar concept but, if this symbol does have a deeper meaning, this may have had something to do with the worship of the sun. The whole of Brittany, in particular the area round Vannes, ancient capital of the Veneti, is thought to have been vital to the Gaulish pilgrims in its capacity as the land nearest to the 'temple of the setting sun'.

*Fig. 35: The 'lyre' of the Coriosolites. Rybot III 64. 6.89 g.*

If we accept that our Coriosolite forbears of two thousand years ago may well have been fascinated – if not obsessed – by the heavenly bodies, a periodic event such as the passing of a comet must have been of momentous importance. The returns to *perihelion* (closest approach to the sun) of what is now known as Halley's comet have been plotted back to 239 B.C., and most of the dates, which are separated by periods of approximately 77 years, have been correlated with contemporary records of observation. The Florentine master Giotto painted a dynamic comet rather than the traditional star of Bethlehem on his Adoration of the Magi; Halley's Comet which returned in October 1301 served as his model. The Bayeux Tapestry, commemorating the events of 1066, records the appearance of Halley's Comet in March of that year. The return of the Comet in A.D. 684 is recorded, on the page recounting the events of that year, in the Nuremberg Chronicles, published in 1493. Flavius Josephus, a Jewish historian of the 1st century A.D., referred in his writings to a comet, which was almost certainly Halley's Comet, on its return in A.D. 66.

The early Coriosolite silver / billon coins, i.e. group III with the 'lyre' mintmark, have been dated to the quarter century or so preceding the intervention of Julius Caesar in North-West Gaul. This would take us back to 85–80 B.C. on the basis that Caesar's activities began in 56 B.C. It is therefore tempting – and surely not unreasonable – to postulate that this is no lyre, but rather the first recorded representation of the return of Halley's Comet in B.C. 86.

**Returns to Perihelion of Halley's Comet**

| | | |
|---|---|---|
| B.C. | 239 | March 30 |
| | 163 | October 5 |
| | 86 | August 2 |
| | 11 | October 5 |
| A.D. | 66 | January 26 |
| | 141 | March 20 |
| | 218 | May 17 |
| | 295 | April 20 |
| | 374 | February 16 |
| | 451 | June 24 |
| | 530 | September 25 |
| | 607 | March 13 |
| | 684 | September 28 |
| | 760 | May 22 |
| | 837 | February 27 |
| | 912 | July 9 |
| | 989 | September 9 |
| | 1066 | March 23 |
| | 1145 | April 22 |
| | 1222 | October 1 |
| | 1301 | October 23 |
| | 1378 | November 9 |
| | 1456 | June 9 |
| | 1531 | August 25 |
| | 1607 | October 27 |
| | 1682 | September 15 |
| | 1759 | March 13 |
| | 1835 | November 16 |
| | 1910 | April 20 |
| | 1986 | February 9 |

Both the sun and the moon are known to have played an important part in Gaulish superstition and religion, and the wheel is thought to have symbolized the sun. Although possible parallels occur more in other types of Armorican coins (e.g. those of the Redones and perhaps the Abrincatui), there is one item on the reverse of Coriosolite coins of group II which should be examined in the light of a quotation of Maximus of Tyre, who wrote that the Paeonians, a people of Celtic origin who were living next to Macedonia, used to worship the sun of which the symbol was a little disc attached to a pole. Even today, albeit further afield, a solar disc and a lunar crescent still adorn the *stupa* which guards the approach to many a village in the Buddhist Himalaya.

*Fig. 36: The solar disc.*
*Rybot III 67. 6.87 g (ex Le Catillon, Jersey, 1957).*

There is possibly one other facet of the design of Coriosolite coins which should be touched upon. What appears to be a banner hanging before the horse's head on some coins of groups I and IV has traditionally been termed a *'peplum'*. This appears to have been based entirely upon the fact that the Ancient Greek πέπλος(veil) was white and sometimes (as on the coins) had a fringe. I feel bound to be sceptical about this explanation as I am convinced that this item, so carefully designed and often linked by cords to the hand of the 'charioteer' must have been an Armorican object. My own theory is that these designs may have represented peytrels, or breastplates, known to have been worn by horses at the time. An imposing example wrought in gold, now in the British Museum, was discovered at Mold, Flintshire, and was almost certainly decorative rather than functional. Alternatively the so-called *'peplum'* may, in fact represent the standard or the 'colours' of the tribe concerned. In ancient Indian Vedic society, a convenient exchange medium (according to contemporary literature) was called *nishka,* which may have been some kind of neck ornament. A *nishka* attached to a banner is on one occasion mentioned as the prize in a debating competition. Even now in Varanasi, India, during the month of Sravana, *Kavali* (singing) competitions are held. Each party which competes has its own flag, adorned with money (now currency notes), which is handed over to the victor as a trophy.

*Fig. 37: The Coriosolite* peplum.
*Rybot I 12. 6.17 g (ex La Marquanderie, Jersey 1935); Rybot IV, 80. 6.35 g*

All the above descriptions of facets of the design of Coriosolite coinage, and the calculated guesses about possible meanings of the devices used – all these may have advanced our own understanding of the people who minted these coins – but only minimally. We still know next to nothing about the real meaning of the designs chosen for the coins. Coins of later historical periods and modern pieces rarely do not include some reflection of contemporary life somewhere in their design – be it the likeness of the reigning sovereign, the symbol or name of the state, or the value. The careful consistency evident in the general aspects of the design of Coriosolite coins, might therefore reasonably indicate that these coins were no exception and must indeed – in some way – mirror the habits of the people who used them as currency. We may presume that the coins must have been recognizable to neighbour-peoples as being of the Coriosolites – although, if we have interpreted correctly the signs of 'testing' on some coins, these other peoples may not have been too confident about the quality of the alloy used.

Returning to the Channel Islands, one can only surmise that the hoards, described in detail above, were buried in an area which was regarded as safer than the average, and that Jersey, in particular, was probably considered to be an outpost of this same people, the Coriosolites. It is also reasonable to suppose that, judging by the apparent care with which these caches were buried, the owners intended to return when possible and collect them. It is possible that the fugitives – or so they appear to have been – returned eastwards or southwards to rejoin their countrymen in a last desperate and fatal fight against the invaders – the secret of the locations of the hoards dying with them. But there are known to have been other lands with which these Armoricans had, for centuries, had a cultural and commercial interchange.

# The Celtic Connection

Tacitus wrote that Hibernia appeared to be the focus of communications between Britain, Spain and Gaul. The spiral stone carvings of New Grange in Ireland, by their likeness in style to similar carvings throughout Brittany, attest to connections with Armorica dating from the earliest times. Continued connections are evidenced by the golden *torques* (see above) – similar to those found in Armorica – which have been turned up in Ireland, as well as Cornwall, Wales and Scotland on the western seaboard of Britannia. Among other finds, it is notable that certain types of Gaulish (La Tène style) pottery have come to light in the Dublin area, indicating that there was certainly a connection between the two regions and that Gaulish colonies might even have been established in Ireland at that time. Breton linguistic connections with parts of the West Country survive to this day – particularly with Wales where Breton onion-sellers are reputed still to be able to make themselves understood.

It is to Ireland that dedicated researchers have looked for traces of an Armorican influx 2000 years ago. Decorated stones, *torques* and pottery are the proof of an earlier connection with Armorica but there is unfortunately no such definable evidence concerning this later period. There are, however, other sources still open for study: those of the ancient Irish chroniclers. And these sources – covering as they do the nebulous periods somewhere between history and legend – may not only contain indications of the fate of the people who minted the coins subject of this study; they may also throw a glimmer of light on our understanding of the design.

Finds of Armorican coins in Britain are scattered in such a way as to suggest that most of these coins were dropped in the normal course of trade between the Armorican communities and coastal settlements in South and South-West England. There are single finds recorded in Yorkshire, Northumberland and Lanarkshire and there is one specimen in the Belfast Museum which might have been found in Ireland. In spite of a record in Strabo that the Veneti were the principal entrepreneurs in coastal trade, coin-finds suggest that it was the Coriosolites and not the Veneti who most actively traded along the coastlines of the area.

Certain evidence from the excavations at Maiden Castle, Dorset, suggests that Coriosolitan coins circulated in the area for a considerable time after they had ceased circulating in Armorican Gaul. And, in spite of the Belgic origins of the Durotrigan coinage in Southern England, strong trading ties are suggested by the associations of Durotrigan and Armorican coins found together in several hoards buried in the area. Recent excavations at Hengistbury Head have shown that the port – it has been called Britain's first international port – was flourishing in the early 1st century B.C. Evidence of contact with the St. Malo area of Brittany is prolific, and coins of the Abrincatui, Baiocasses and Osismii have been found.

Fig. 38: Finds of Coriosolite coins outline a trading area.

○ single coins
○ hoards
○ ,,

In the same way as the various Armorican coin types were the result of an interplay between certain Greek prototypes and patterns of strong local cultures in what we now call Normandy and Brittany, it is fair to speculate that such coin types – or the cultures which they represented – might themselves have had an influence on the cultures and coin-types of adjacent areas. There are, for example, grounds for believing that the base silver Armorican coins, which were brought by traders to the British Isles in the early part of the 1st century B.C., were instrumental in persuading the indigenous strikers of gold coins (from Belgic prototypes) that the same coins could in future be just as effectively struck in silver – particularly as silver could more easily be obtained from the mines in the Mendip Hills and elsewhere.

If we can take for granted that coins, in one way or another, reflect the culture or circumstances in which they are minted, it is surely reasonable to accept that knowledge of Armorican mores must have developed in those areas where Armorican seamen traded their wares. These coin-finds, then, testify to the existence in South-Western Britain of such knowledge about these Gaulish coastal communities, and their customs and beliefs.

It is also reasonable to suppose that certain of these customs and beliefs could be adopted by the 'receiving' communities in the same way as, for example, certain Greek symbols (such as the dolphins), which could have had very little meaning in isolation, were adopted by the Armorican coiners. At one remove we can speculate that, where proof of cultural development – such as is provided by coins – is lacking, one cannot automatically assume that cultural development did not take place; we cannot of course claim that it *did* take place, not, at least, until new evidence is at hand.

The background of the great Irish heroic epics is certainly older than the advent of Christianity to Ireland in the fifth century A.D. and is judged by some authorities to hail from the semi-barbarous period in the first century B.C., though these charmingly exaggerated stories were probably only first recorded in the eighth century A.D., having been passed down in word and song through at least forty generations.

Standing-stone monuments and funerary circles, from the earliest times, are still in evidence from Ireland to Iberia. And spiral decorations of striking similarity have been found cut into stone monuments as far apart as Leinster, Morbihan and Malta, though recent radiocarbon and tree-ring dating tests suggest that the stone structures of Brittany pre-date those in Malta by some 1000 years, and those at New Grange by as much as 2000. Finds of later precious metal objects, such as gold *torques* and crescents, again of very similar style, are as common in Scotland, Wales and Ireland as they are in the Côtes-du-Nord, Manche and Vendée and one splendid example (see above) has been found in Jersey.

Judging by the practically non-existent finds of coins of the first and second centuries B.C. in Ireland, one can reasonably suppose that the emerald isle was a cash-less society at that time. There are, however, in Irish heroic literature, certain descriptions which are strikingly similar to particular designs on Armorican coins, themselves dated to the first and early second centuries B.C. It is my view that, where it would be risky to draw any definite conclusions from these similarities, they should be seen to complement the generally accepted view that cultural and trading links did exist between Ireland and Armorica.

There have been many attempts to build up a convincing argument that the origins of Irish epic literature must have been contemporary – and at times directly connected – with Armorican cultures, at least as they are portrayed on the coins of the region. There are in this literature several references to Gaul and, more specifically, to Armorica. As an illustration, one Irish hero, Labraid Loingsech, returned home on one occasion with two thousand Gaulish mercenaries.

The legends of Cuchulainn, nephew of the King of Ulster, and more particularly the so-called 'contorsions' of this Irish hero, have furnished us with some of the more remarkable parallels with certain Armorican coin designs.

– Cuchulainn was clean-shaven. This seems to have been the norm in Armorica at least as portrayed on most types of Armorican coins.

*Fig. 39: Tattoes on a silver stater of the Abrincatui. DLT J12. 6.26 g.*

– He had either three or four different coloured marks or tattoes on each cheek.

*Fig. 40: Coriosolite waves.*
*Rybot I 18 var. 6.31 g (ex Le Catillon, Jersey, 1957).*

– His hair was arranged in three waves.

Cuchulainn's mysterious contorsions are described at least three times and the main elements are as follows:

*Fig. 41: Distinct hairs on a silver fraction of the Abrincatui.*
*Cf DLT J11. 1.76 g.*

- The hairs of his head became more distinct and pointed as if 'each one... had been struck into his head with a hammer'.

*Fig. 42: Drops of blood?*
AR stater *of the Veneti. Cf C de B,* 'Traité' *p 115 fig. 25.*

- There were sparks (or drops of blood) on the end of each hair.

*Fig. 43: A disjointed Coriosolite profile.*
*Rybot III 67. 6.92 g (ex Le Catillon, Jersey, 1957)*

- One eye contracted and became buried in his head; the other expanded monstrously or became positioned on the middle of his cheek.
- The jaw bones were distended and the gullet appeared.

*Fig. 44: The 'hero's moon' on a stater of the Abrincatui.*
*Cf DLT J13. 6.44 g.*

- The 'hero's moon' rose from the top of his head 'as thick as a warrior's sharpening stone, as long as his nose'.
- His body became dislocated so much that from the waist down it was back to front.

*Fig. 45: Expression of vomit? Rybot I 27. 5.66 g.*

- He vomited fire.

*Fig. 46: Vapours and a spark on an Osismian stater. DLT 6508. 6.48 g.*

- Strange apparitions of vapours and sparks appeared around his head.

*Fig. 47: A jet of blood? DLT J5. 6.86 g. Stater of the Abrincatui (ex Le Catillon, Jersey, 1957).*

- A jet of blood spurted from the top of his head.

The theme of decapitation is not uncommon in Irish heroic literature and the luckless Cuchulainn suffered this fate at the hands of Lugaid. It is quite likely that the *obverses* of this series of Armorican coinage portray a severed head; this would fit in well to the theory that decapitation and collection of heads (particularly of enemies), as evidenced by details of many surviving Gaulish antiquities, was not uncommon in Armorica.

Although both Irish and Gaulish war chariots are thought to have been drawn by two horses, only one horse appears on the *reverse* of Armorican coins. In this context it is curious to note that Conall Cernach, the avenger of Cuchulainn, was assisted in his own combat with Lugaid by his horse Derg Druchtach, who is in turn said to have had the head of a dog.

Finally, of many strange parallels between Irish legend and Gaulish culture, one other subject is worth mentioning here. The shield of Cuchulainn was decorated with the image of a wild boar. Diodorus tells us that the Celts of the Continent carried animal figurines on their shields and such wild boar decorations have been found on shields dating to the end of the La Tène period.

There is an episode in Welsh legend, recorded in the Mabinogion, set down in writing in the early 14th century, which may be the distant echo of something which had happened one thousand years earlier in Welsh-Armorican tradition and was reflected in the coin designs of some of the Coriosolites' neighbours. The young hero Culhwch, anxious to wed Olwen, daughter of Ysbaddaden Chief Giant, rides to the mysterious King Arthur for help 'on a shell-hooved horse... Never a hair-tip stirred on him, so exceeding light was his steed's canter under him on his way to the gate of Arthur's court'.

*Fig. 48: The horse, the boar and the bird on a* stater *of the Osismii.*
*DLT 6555. 6.54 g.*

Later Arthur and his warriors discover the whereabouts of Olwen and her father demands the performance of a series of tasks including the hunting of the boar Twrch Trwyth. Arthur goes to Ireland then gathers together what warriors there are 'in the Three Realms of Britain... in France and Brittany and Normandy...' and what there are 'of picked dogs and horses of renown'. He explains to his men that the boar had once been a King whom God, for his wickedness, had transformed into a swine. The quarry is eventually located and Arthur sends Gwrhyr Interpreter to him in the form of a bird which alights above the lair of the boar and his seven piglets. Grugyn Silver Bristle, speaking for his father, refuses to give up the comb, razor and scissors between his ears (these were required by Ysbaddaden for his barbering on his daughter's wedding day).

The Boar and his family set out by sea towards Wales, and the hunt begins. Twrch Trwyth is at last overtaken and driven into the Severn Estuary. While still in the water, two warriors seize the razor and scissors. He escapes with the comb and Arthur chases him into Cornwall. The comb is eventually won from him and Twrch Trwyth is again driven into the sea and disappears. The imagery of a boar travelling over the water's back would not have been unusual in those distant days, just as the ocean would have been judged to have a soul of its own.

*Fig. 49: Gold* stater *of the Baiocasses found in Jersey.*
*C de B RBN (1957) p 70, 36. 7.06 g.*

# Part II

The Romans
The Merovingians
The Carolingians
Normandy
The *Tournois* Period
The Jersey Mint
The Century of Transition

> For good ye are and bad, and like to coins,
> Some true, some light, but every one of you
> Stamp'd with the image of the King.
>
> Alfred, Lord Tennyson
> *The Idylls of the King. The Holy Grail.* l. 25

# The Romans

The principal classes of Roman coinage have traditionally been classified as follows:

| | |
|---|---|
| Republican | 'Aes rude' cast down to c. 270 B.C. |
| Republican | 'Aes grave' cast 269–242 B.C. |
| Republican | silver, bronze struck 269–c. 80 B.C. |
| Imperatorial | gold, silver, bronze struck c. 80–27 B.C. |
| Imperial (pre-reform*) | gold, silver, bronze struck 27 B.C. – c. A.D. 286 |
| Imperial (post-reform*) | gold, silver, bronze struck c. 286–476 |

* this refers to the great coinage reform (revaluation) of Diocletian when the *aureus, argenteus* and *follis* were introduced. Constantine the Great (307–337) made further changes, though these were to debase the coinage again)

The following table shows the principal denominations in circulation in the western part of the Roman domain during five phases of Roman numismatic history, from the earliest times to the fall of Rome in the 5th century. The

| c. 250 B.C. | Early Empire | Late 3rd century A.D. | 4th century A.D. | 5th century A.D. |
|---|---|---|---|---|
| **(Southern Italy)** | | | | |
| | AU *aureus* | →AU (heavy) *aureus* | →AU *solidus* | →AU *solidus* →sou |
| | AU *quinarius* | | AU *quinarius* | |
| AR *didrachm* | | | AU *semissis* | AU *semissis* |
| ↳*quadrigatus* | | | AU 1½ *scripulum*→AU *tremissis*→thrymsa | |
| ↳*victoriatus* | | | AR *miliarense* | |
| ↳*drachma* | | | | |
| **(Rome, C. Italy)** | | | | |
| AR *denarius* →AR *denarius* | →AR *argenteus* | →AR *siliqua* | →AR *siliqua* | |
| | ↳AE *antoninianus* | AE *follis* AE *'radiate'* | AE *follis* | |
| AR *quinarius* | AR *quinarius* | | AE *'minimi'* | AE *'minimi'* |
| AR *Sesterius* | orichalcum *sestertius* | | | |
| | orichalcum *dupondius* | AE *denarius* | | |
| ⎡ *as* | →AE *as* | | | |
| ⎪ *semis* | orichalcum *semis* | | | |
| 'Aes ⎨ *triens* | | | | |
| grave'⎪ *quadrans* | AE *quadrans* | | | |
| ⎪ *sextans* | | | | |
| ⎣ *uncia* | | | | |

relationship between the various types is outside the scope of this study but the succession clearly shows the ancestry of the *sou (solidus)* and its fractions, which were to provide the basis for a currency medium during the Merovingian period. Denominations underlined have been found in the Channel Islands, mainly in Jersey.

Unfortunately, the Islands have little to show for the four hundred years which represent Roman supremacy in western Europe; only Jersey and Alderney possess any tangible signs of Roman, or more properly Romano-Celtic, habitation. On Longy Common in Alderney, a small settlement of stone houses with tiled roofs has been excavated; the number of burial remains discovered points to a well-established colony and a number of Roman coins of the 1st and 2nd centuries A.D. have been found in the area, the latest of which is a coin of the Emperor Commodus (177–192 A.D.). Coins of the 4th century, including some of Constantine the Great, are, however, also said to have been discovered in Alderney.

Jersey's remains, though unquestionably Roman, are limited to one small Roman building near Pinnacle Rock to the north of St. Ouen's Bay. Another *sestertius* of Commodus was found at this site. Romanised pottery has been found in Guernsey, though this, in itself, is not sufficient proof of prolonged habitation. It is perhaps worth mentioning here that salt-working industries in Guernsey and Herm were apparently established in the Roman period; the scale of the workings suggests that salt may have been traded with other areas at the time. Recent excavations at Hengistbury Head in Hampshire indicate that a trade route then existed between that area and a port near St. Malo with an intermediate stop at Guernsey.

Several hoards of Roman coins have been found in the Channel Islands, only a few of which have been properly documented. For 150 years or so, Roman coins have been uncovered in the earthwork known as Le Câtel (or Castel) de Rozel in St. Martin's Parish, Jersey. The same site has another name, La Petite Césarée, which is centuries old and recalls one of the Roman names for the Island – Caesarea. In his manuscript 'Catalogue' (mentioned above in connection with the Gaulish coin hoard JERSEY III), P. Mauger wrote:

> 'A few Celtic and Roman coins having been picked up here [i.e. near the harbour of Rozel] about twenty years ago ... Of these [Roman] Imperial Coins, I have reason to suppose from the manner in which I obtained them, that the greater number have been found in Jersey ...'

Another Gaulish hoard, JERSEY V (see above) included a number of Roman Republican pieces and, although only a few are still extant, it is reasonably certain that *denarii* of the following types were included in the hoard (references are to Sydenham's *'The Coinage of the Roman Republic')*; the list is based on Barthélemy's *Études* and Cable (see Bibliography).

1. *Obv.* Head of Roma, X behind; *rev.* Diana in *biga,*
   ROMA below 145–138 B.C. (S 376)
2., 3. P. Maenius Antiaticus (2 examples) 119–110 B.C. (S 492)
4. M. Sergius Silus 109–108 B.C. (S 544)

5. Appius Claudius and Titus Mallius 106 B.C. (S 570)
6. ? A. Postumius Albinus 92–91 B.C. (S 612)
7. L. Titurius L.f. Sabinus 88 B.C. (S 698)
8. C. Licinius L.f. Macer 83 B.C. (S 732)
9. Q. Cassius Longinus 76 B.C. or possibly L. Cassius Longinus 52–50 B.C. (S 935)

*Fig. 50:* Denarius *of the type of no. 10.*
*This coin is believed to honour Diana the huntress; the* reverse *features a hunting dog.*

10. C. Postumius 74–73 B.C. (S 785)
11. M. Aemilius Scaurus and P. Plautius Hypsaeus 58 B.C. ( S 913)
12. L. Scribonius Libo 55 B.C. (S 928)

*Fig. 51:* Denarius *of P. Clodius.*
Obv. *laureate head of Apollo, lyre behind.* Rev. *Diana Lucifera holding two torches.*

13. P. Clodius 41 B.C. (S 1117)

Some Imperatorial coins were also found, including a *denarius* of Marcus Antonius and Octavianus of 40–39 B.C., and at least three other later *denarii* of Marcus Antonius, one a legionary issue (LEG. XII). The latest coins recorded as having been found in this hoard are two copper *asses* of Caesar Augustus, dated to 10 B.C. A sestertius of the Emperor Trajan Decius of A.D. 250, said to have been found at the same time, is probably an 'intruder'.

*Fig. 52: Republican* denarius *similar to that found in Sark in 1718.*
Obv. *laureate head of Apollo.* Rev. *horseman P. CREPVSI (S 738).*

The only other Roman Republican coin found in the Islands was a *denarius* of P. Crepusius, dated to 82–81 B.C., which was found in the Sark Gaulish coin hoard dug up in 1718 (see above). One very worn Republican *denarius,* recorded as having been found in Jersey, may have come from Rozel and another equally worn legionary *denarius* (?) of Marcus Antonius is also recorded.

*Fig. 53: Gorey Castle – site of many Roman and later coin finds (from a Jersey £1 note). See JN250.*

The 1st century A.D. is very poorly represented. A coin of Claudius I (41–54) was found with another Roman coin at Mont de la Ville (now Fort Regent) St. Helier, during excavations in 1785–6; a dupondius of Vespasian, dated to 72 A.D., was found at Gorey Castle. The 2nd century is only slightly better represented in Jersey; three denominations of the Emperor Trajan (98–117) were discovered: a *sestertius,* dated to 100 A.D., at Gorey Castle; a silver *tetradrachm* (minted 103–111) also found at Gorey Castle; and a *dupondius* found in the Parish of St. Clement. At least one *as* of Hadrian and *sestertii* of Faustina II and Commodus have also turned up. Twenty coins, mostly of the 2nd century, and apparently from one hoard, were found in St. Sampson's harbour Guernsey; they encompassed the reigns of Trajan, Antoninus Pius, Faustina, Marcus Aurelius and Commodus, i.e. the period 98–192 A.D.

*Fig. 54: St. Sampson's harbour where 20 2nd century Roman coins were found (from a Guernsey £1 note). See GN49.*

No coins of the first half of the 3rd century have yet been discovered in the Islands. The years between 200 and 260 A.D. showed the sharpest debasement of the Roman silver currency during the first three centuries of the Christian era. During the next forty years, that is during the period immediately preceding the reforms of Diocletian, Roman coinage apparently began circulating in the area again, and a hoard of 18 *antoniniani,* dating from 253 to 268 A.D., found at the site of previous excavations at the Ile Agois (see above), bears witness to this. Another 'barbaric' issue of Postumus (259–268) was found not far from the hoard. Two earlier *antoniniani* of Philip I ('the Arabian') may have been found in Jersey, and another coin of the same denomination of the Emperor Aurelian (270–275) is reported to come from Guernsey.

The largest hoard of Roman imperial coins found in the Channel Islands belongs to the early 4th century. The hoard, said to have originally numbered over 400 bronze coins, was found in a 'coarse earthenware jar' at the Quenvais (or les Quennevais), Jersey, in 1848. 357 of the coins were identified (by Emperor and Mint) by the Keeper of Coins at the British Museum in 1922; his summary was as follows (see Rybot, *Note,* 1922):

| | Londinium | Treviri | Lugdunum | Arelate | Ticinum | Ostia | Rome | Siscia | Thessalonica | Cyzicus | Heraclea | Uncertain | Totals |
|---|---|---|---|---|---|---|---|---|---|---|---|---|---|
| Diocletian (284–305) | | | | | | | | | | | | 1 | 1 |
| Maximianus (286–310) | 6 | | | | 1 | | | | | | | 3 | 10 |
| Constantius I (305–306) | 7 | 2 | | | 1 | | | | | | | 1 | 11 |
| Galerius (305–311) | | 4 | | | | | 1 | | | | | 1 | 6 |
| Maximinius II (309–313) | 5 | 11 | | | | | | | | 1 | | | 17 |
| Maxentius (306–312) | | | | | 4 | | 4 | | | | | 3 | 11 |
| Licinius I (308–324) | 32 | 42 | | 5 | 1 | 2 | | 2 | | | 1 | | 85 |
| Constantine I (307–337) | 86 | 39 | 23 | 23 | 9 | 4 | 4 | | 1 | | | 17 | 206 |
| Crispus (317–326) | | | | | | | | | | 1 | | | 1 |
| Constantine II (337–340) | | | | | | | | | | | | 1 | 1 |
| 'Constantinopolis' (330–346) | | | | | | | | | | | | 1 | 1 |
| Constantius II (337–361) | | | | | | | | 1 | 1 | | | 1 | 3 |
| Uncertain | | | | | | | | | | | | 4 | 4 |
| Totals | 136 | 98 | 23 | 28 | 16 | 6 | 9 | 3 | 2 | 2 | 1 | 33 | 357 |

As can be seen from the table, western mints prevail, and there may well have been an association with England, if due weight is given to the large number struck at Londinium; Triers, Lyons and Arles are, however, also well represented. Those coins given to Constantine I were assigned to the early part of his reign, i.e. up to 317 A.D. If this is correct, it would be reasonable to assume that the later coins were intruders, and that the hoard must have been buried shortly after 317 A.D. 337 coins survive.

*Fig. 55: Follis of Constantius I minted in Treviri (Triers).*
Obv. *CONSTANTIVS NOBIL C* round bearded laureate head. Rev. *GENIO POPVLI ROMANI PTR (Treviri)* round Genius standing (R.I.C. IIa).

To date, one other hoard, this time of the late 4th century, has been found in the Islands. In 1973, during drainage work being undertaken near the General Hospital, St. Helier, a group of 12 bronze coins – apparently from one hoard – was discovered. They range in date from 337 A.D. (one URBS ROMA Constantinian Commemorative) to c. 390 (coins of Theodosius I, 379–395); Eastern mints prevail. Various single 4th century finds have been made in the Islands; with the exception of one *follis* of Licinius I found at Gorey Castle, they have, unfortunately, been inadequately documented. No Roman coins of the 5th century are known.

The meaning of the above Roman coin finds is elusive. With few exceptions (e.g. at Longy Common, Alderney), there are no associations with other Roman remains and they can only be seen to show that there was from time to time a kind of Roman presence in the area. Almost certainly the Romans would have considered the Islands as of only transitory value and it has, in this connection, been pointed out that all recorded finds in Jersey have been made on or near the coast-line. They must have been of some value as an *entrepôt* area on the coastal trade routes between Britannia and the Mediterranean and this may explain the presence of the Quenvais hoard, though circumstances of burial remain obscure.

# The Merovingians

Although Brittany almost certainly stood apart, politically, from Merovingian Gaul, there is every likelihood that the forces of commerce applied cohesively to the whole country. In any event, no study of Channel Island currencies would be complete without a bridge between the decline of the late Roman Empire and the rise of the Carolingians. Moreover it is evident that from the earliest times, the Islands maintained a strong cultural link with Normandy.

Some twelve hundred years after his burial in 481 A.D., the remains of Childeric, King of the Franks, son of Mérovée and father of Clovis, were excavated in Tournai. Together with his personal arms and jewellery, a purse was found containing over 90 golden *solidi* or *sous,* of which 58 had been struck by the Eastern Emperor Leo I (457–474), Childeric's contemporary. There could be no better example of the medium of exchange in circulation in the mid-fifth century A.D.

The limits of authority of Syagrius, the last Roman Governor of Gaul, are unclear. Bishop Gregory of Tours (538–594), the recognized contemporary authority on this period, once described him as 'King of the Romans', a curious title for the late Empire but one which may imply that the style of his rule graduated towards that which, in those days, was not uncommon in the western confines of Europe. In any event, this last representative of the Roman Empire was confronted – and defeated – by the Franks under Clovis I in 486 A.D. This date is generally accepted as the formal end of the Roman Empire in Western Europe.

During the 250 years following the retreat of the Romans from the western sea-board of Europe, locally made copies of the coins of the Eastern Empire, sometimes crude but generally of pure gold, circulated together with the genuine article. With time, these Frankish and Gaulish copies became prevalent but more degenerate. The medium continued to be the gold *solidus (sou)* together with one third and (more rarely) one half *fractions,* called, respectively, the *tremissis* or *triens (1/3 sou),* and the *semissis (1/2 sou).* A group of diminutive silver and bronze coins is also known; these are thought to have been modelled on the *siliqua* (and *fractions)* of the late Roman Empire. Another – the *denarius* or *denier* group – was struck by certain church bodies and a number of independent moneyers over the period.

The gold issues, principally *tremisses,* must be divided into four overlapping groups – a distinction made no easier by the turbulent progress of the Frankish Kingdom, whose unity was shaken periodically by war or by the Frankish custom of partitioning the territories after the death of the ruler.

## 'Pseudo-Imperial' Issues 450–600

One of the earliest references to the concurrent circulation of genuine and Gaulish gold *solidi* is in an edict of the Emperor Majorian (457–461) where it is decreed that 'no tax collector shall refuse to take a *solidus,* if it is of good weight, except the Gaulish *solidus* of which the gold is taxed at less value *(minore aestimatione)'.* In spite of this implication that Gaulish gold was of inferior quality, it must be stressed that no inferior specimens of the period (i.e. first half of the 5th century) have yet been discovered; moreover Majorian's edict is quite likely to have had a political slant to it as records show that he entered Gaul in the same year, and subsequently defeated the Visigoths near Arelate. It is known that Visigothic authority in Aquitania at the time stretched as far north as Tours; the Visigoths under Alaric III had their own series of gold coins, dating to A.D. 500.

While more or less pure – but less servile – imitations of imperial *solidi* and *tremisses* continued to be struck during the reigns of Maurice Tiberius (582–602), Phocas (602–610) and even Heraclius (610–641) the prototypes of Gaulish Merovingian coinage are believed to be copies, in pale gold and of cruder style, of *tremisses* of Justin I (518–527) and Justinian I (527–565), with Gaulish mintmarks; the two mints of Decize (near Nevers and still well-known for its metalworking industry) and Lyons are thought to have been identified. At the same time, Gondebaud (491–516) and Sigismond (516–523), Kings of Burgundy, issued *tremisses* in their own names; they were contemporaries of Anastasius I whose own coinage continued to be imitated in Gaul, and whose monetary

*Fig. 56: Gold solidus of Anastasius I, often imitated in Gaul.*
Obv. DN ANASTASIVS PP AVC round armed bust. Rev. VICTORIA AVCCC Θ CONOB round Victory with long cross (DOC 3h; R. 312).

reforms in A.D. 498 mark the termination of the Roman and the beginning of the Byzantine coinage eras. As a footnote to this first 'Pseudo-Imperial' section it is worth mentioning that Gondebaud himself echoed the plaint of the Emperor Majorian when he criticized the quality of the gold coins of Alaric II whom he defeated in battle at Vouillé in A.D. 507.

In a different theatre (at some date between 500 and 540 A.D.) it is believed that St. Sampson, fleeing from Cornwall, settled with a party of Christians in Guernsey; and a Belgian hermit and disciple of St. Marculf settled on the rock in Jersey where the Hermitage Chapel now stands. The hermit, martyred by vandals in 559 A.D., was named St. Helier. St. Marculf himself is said to have visited Jersey in the mid-6th century and established a religious community somewhere in the north of the Island. Most of the Island of Sark had – according to tradition – been given to St. Magloire, nephew of St. Sampson, by Loyescou an Armorican chieftain, in payment for a miraculous cure. After performing a further miracle, St. Magloire acquired a third of Guernsey and subsequently built a chapel in the Vale; he also set up religious seats in Herm and Jersey before returning to Sark where he died.

*Fig. 57: The Hermitage Chapel (from a 2 pence Jersey coin).*
*See J105.*

As is so often the case in the western world, the earliest records were generally compiled by church authorities, and the Channel Islands were no exception. Many of the earliest payments recorded (from the 11th century onwards) were dues payable to the Church in Normandy, which evidently owned large tracts in the Channel Islands. It is interesting to speculate for a moment that this practice may well have dated from the time that St. Sampson, St. Helier and St. Magloire received some sort of title to large areas of Guernsey, Jersey and Sark respectively, as a reward for services rendered.

## 'Royal' Issues c. 500–700

While stressing a conviction that the Merovingian period must be an integral part of any numismatic history of Gaul, the main area of this study (the Channel Islands) should, of course, not be lost in a welter of detail about Merovingian history in general. The objective at this stage is to preserve the continuity of the series – however tenuous – through the Merovingian and Carolingian periods, and certain other information is necessary in order to keep this objective in view.

Clovis I, mentioned above, reigned as King of the Franks from 481 to 511. He seems to have spent most of his reign fighting to unite the Kingdom; no coins are ascribed to him with any certainty. Nor is it certain if he succeeded in conquering Armorica; Gregory Bishop of Tours wrote that Clovis 'waged many wars and won victories'; there is also an obscure reference to the 'Arborici' (Armorici?) where it is implied that this tribe acquitted itself well while fighting against the Germans (the Alamanni of Southern Austrasia). On Clovis' death, the Kingdom was divided among his four sons, with Thierry taking Austrasia, Clodomir the region of Orleans (Neustria), Childebert I Paris, Orleans (on the death of Clodomir) and Burgundy, and Clotaire I the northern seaboard from Normany to Flanders.

No coins of this period have ever been found in the Channel Islands and one can only hazard a guess that the currencies of Neustria and Normandy played their part in the economic development of the Islands. Only one silver coin of Clotaire I of Normandy (511–561) is known, an ancestor perhaps of the *denarius* system (see below); one *tremissis* of Childebert I (511–558) of Neustria and another (minted in Paris c. 565) of Caribert I are the only coins of these monarchs which survive. *Tremisses* of Clotaire II, King of Neustria (584–613) and of all the Franks (613–627), are abundant, as well as a few gold *solidi (sous)* – both denominations struck in his own name. The figures XXI and VII are often to be seen respectively on the *solidus* and *tremissis* coins, and are believed to confirm the 3:1 relationship between the two denominations.

It appears that, during the 7th century, both gold coins were most commonly produced in the Provence area south of Burgundy, and it is clear that, politically and economically, Marseille enjoyed a special status in the constant struggle for power between West and East – Neustria and Austrasia. However it is worth mentioning that the first known Paris *tremissis* was struck under Dagobert I who, ruling a united Territory from 629–639, was the first to use the style REX FR[ANCORUM]; more important, perhaps, for this survey, is the discovery of another *tremissis* of this ruler struck in the Archbishopric of Tours, – a city which will be seen to play an increasingly important part in Channel Island numismatic history of the middle ages.

## Church Issues c. 570–700

Certain *tremisses,* dated to the latter part of the Royal period, appear to have been struck by Church authorities in Merovingian France. The earliest example is ascribed to the Church of Chalon, southern Burgundy, in the second half of the 6th century. These Church issues are only slightly less rare than the 'Royal' issues. In north-western France, surviving examples include one from Le Mans, believed to date from the 7th century at the earliest; one from Angers (Maine-et-Loire) dated to 629 A.D.; and several of the Abbey of St. Martin in Tours. One can assume that, in order to strike their own coins, Church authorities – with or without the sanction of the local monarch – must have wielded a certain amount of secular power at the time, and it is perhaps relevant to note that in 577 Pretextatus, Archbishop of Rouen, though he is not known to have struck any coins, was banished by Chilperic I, King of the Francs in Neustria (561–584), to Augia (Jersey). Pretextatus is thought to have been responsible for much of the earliest ecclesiastical organization in the Islands which then formed part of the diocese of Coutances.

# Moneyers' Issues

The most common gold coin surviving from the Merovingian period is the *1/3 solidus* known as the *triens* or *tremissis,* whereas the most common coin mentioned in contemporary texts was the gold *solidus* (or *aureus)* of which very few examples survive. It is surmised that the *solidus* was primarily a money of account while the *tremissis* constituted the principal denomination in circulation. By far the largest number of *tremisses* were minted by independent moneyers throughout Merovingian France. These *tremisses* which feature simply the name of a place and the name of a moneyer, were characterized by an immense variety of styles, qualities and weights. The rarity of the *solidi* coins of independent moneyers contrasts with the fairly common *tremisses,* and enhances the theory of the *solidus* as a money of account.

During the reign of the Byzantine Justin II, it is recorded that provincial moneyers debased the gold coinage from 21 *siliquae* to the *solidus* to 24 (and 7 *siliquae* to the *tremissis* to 8) supplying evidence for the 3:1 ratio mentioned above. Pope Gregory the Great was certainly referring to these debased *solidi* (*'solidi gallicani')* when he pronounced that they should not circulate in Italy. The number of mints in Gaul increased from four (Trèves, Arles, Lyons and Narbonne) under the Roman Empire, to several hundred during the 7th and 8th centuries, and it is important to stress that any semblance of order which may have resulted from the study of the small number of Merovingian gold coins in the Royal category, is dispelled by the study of coins struck by independent moneyers. Contemporary sales contracts spoke of payment in *solidi 'probes et pensantes'* (true and carefully weighed); and there are many instances where taxes and legal dues are seen to have been paid in ingots (by weight) rather than in coin.

Where the names of the moneyers mean very little to us twelve centuries later, the names of certain towns and cities are seen to assert themselves as centres of commerce and culture. For historic and numismatic reasons I have selected nine names where tremisses are known to have been minted; the first four, interestingly, recall the Armorican period almost one thousand years before and prove that, though the trail is difficult to follow, there was a measure of continuity in commerce and culture in those distant days. They are: ABRINKTAS (now Avranches), BAIOCAS (Bayeux), REDONIS (Rennes) and VENETUS (Vannes). There are coins with the mark of CUSTANCIA; the Channel Islands at the time formed part of the Archbishopric of Coutances; and it is not inconceivable that such coins – albeit struck by independent moneyers – circulated in the Islands.

The following four towns, where *tremisses* were minted in the Merovingian period, are of special significance, and set the scene for the subsequent one thousand years of Channel Island numismatic history. They are: ROTOMO (now Rouen), CENNOMANNIS (Le Mans), ANDECAVIS (Angers, ancient capital of Anjou) and – most important of all – TURONUS (Tours).

*Fig. 58: 7th century coin of the Abbaye de St. Martin, Tours (enlargement). Obv. MART... round head; Rev. + VNCTER (Prou 340).*

### Silver and Bronze Coins

The Roman *nummus* or *denarius* of the 5th century had become little more than a money of account of minimal value and the diminutive late Roman bronze series was merely a proof that bad money drives out good. By the 8th century, gold Merovingian coins of the types mentioned above had largely disappeared from circulation in payment for goods conveyed to Gaul by Italian, Greek and oriental merchants. Silver coins, called *denarii,* began to appear in the latter years of the Merovingian period. In about 600 A.D. Frankish moneyers established and worked a mint at Canterbury in Kent where so-called *'thrymsas' (tremisses)* of gold were struck. The designs and fineness of these coins deteriorated as Saxon moneyers took over and, soon after 700 A.D., the silver *sceat,* a contemporary with the silver *denarius* in Gaul, became the prevalent means of exchange in Britain.

It is known that the Merovingian gold *solidus,* of 3 *tremisses,* was worth 40 *denarii.* At the same time a silver *solidus* of 12 *deniers* was also current. But it is now generally accepted that this silver *solidus* (like the gold *solidus*) was in fact mainly a money of account. Once again the names Rouen, Le Mans and Tours figure among the list of towns where silver *denarii* are known to have been struck and issues of the Abbey of St. Martin at Tours are not uncommon. It is reasonable to suppose that these *denarii* or *deniers* were also the medium of exchange in the Channel Islands at the time, and that the *solidus* or *sou* was the money of account.

More important, historically, is the fact that the Merovingian period of coinage constituted a direct link between the period of the late Roman Empire – as defined in the Salic law of Clovis – and the Carolingian period. Where the ancient towns of Rouen, Le Mans, Angers and Tours had set the scene, Pepin the Short, in 754 or 755 A.D., set the course of the numismatic history of the region when he limited the number of *solidi* (S) to 22 to the silver *libra* or pound (L) and – by extension – the number of silver *denarii* (D) to 264. These were the roots of a system which survived as a money of account in the Channel Islands for eleven hundred years, and as a circulation medium in the U.K., Empire and Commonwealth (£SD) until decimalization.

# The Carolingians

Under the Carolingians, or 'second race' of France, coinage was – almost exclusively – made of silver. Gold had become a rarity and it seems that more and more silver was being mined in the region of Melle, inland from La Rochelle. The principal silver denominations were the *denarius,* which was common to all Carolingian rulers, and the half-unit or *obol,* which was much rarer.

A continuity of style from the Merovingian period is traceable on some pieces, and certain types of Pepin (751–768) recall a style of the late Roman Empire. Pepin 'the Short', whose coins were of a very crude style, was survived by his two sons, Carloman, who inherited the east and south of the Kingdom (broadly Austrasia and Burgundy) and Charlemagne, who took on the north and west (essentially Neustria and Aquitania). On the death of Carloman, Charlemagne inherited his brother's rule and became the first Emperor of the West (800–814). Where the coins of Carloman have not been satisfactorily distinguished from those of Charlemagne, it is known that coins of the latter were struck in his name at over one hundred locations throughout the Empire. Similar coins were struck – albeit from a smaller number of mints – by Louis the Pious (Emperor from 806–840), Lothaire I (sole Emperor 840–855), and Pippin I or Pippin II of Aquitaine (respectively 817–838 and 838–864).

*Fig. 59:* Deniers *of Charlemagne (left) and Louis the Pious (right).*
*Left:* Obv. *CAROLUS;* Rev. *METOLO (Melle). Right:* Obv. *HLVDOVVICVS IMP +;* Rev. *XPISTIANA PELIGIO (CHRISTIANA RELIGIO) (Dolley 18/16; –).*

While the *deniers* of Pepin the Short still appear to have had a direct relationship with the Roman *libra,* those *deniers* with the monogram of Charlemagne appear to coincide with a *libra* which had become heavier. It is of interest to note that in about 780 the *libra* (divided into 12 ounces weight) was made up of 20 *sols,* each of which was made up of 12 *deniers;* this £SD relationship was a more exact forerunner of the British currency system until 1971.

Under Charles the Bald (King of Aquitaine 839–855, King of the West Franks 840–877, King of the 'Middle Realm' 869–877, and Emperor 876–877) it was decreed in the Edict of Pitres (864) that new *deniers* should have the royal name in a circular legend on one side, with the monogramme in the field; and on the other side the name of the city where the coin was struck and in the field a cross. Fragments of five Carolingian coins were found at the Île Agois in Jersey in July 1925. Two of the coins have been identified as *deniers* of Charles le Chauve, struck in Rennes c. 870; the other fragments appear also to be *deniers* of the same period. In 1974–75 further excavations were made on the same site and, among other artefacts, a small hoard of Roman coins of the mid-3rd century A.D. were discovered (see above). It is felt that the site was used or occupied in the early Iron Age, late pre-Roman Iron Age and the early Medieval period. In 1932 the Société Jersiaise presented to the British Museum a *denier* of the same monarch, struck in Rennes; the find spot is unfortunately not recorded, but the coin may well have come from this site.

The coinage of Charles the Bald (by far the most common of the Carolingian series), was followed by that of Louis II (King of the West Franks 877–879), and Carloman who reigned jointly with his brother Louis III (Kings of Francia 879–882). Odo (888–898) used the title REX FRANCORUM and it was his brother Robert, Duke-Abbot of Saint Martin de Tours, who obtained confirmation of the privileges of the Abbey which included the striking of coins in its own right. This privilege enhanced the role which the city of Tours was to play from the early 11th century – a role which will be seen to have important consequences in the story of specie current in the Channel Islands.

*Fig. 60: Odo,* denier *of Tours (clipped).*
Obv. *MISERICORDIA D'I round Odo monogram;* Rev. *HTVR+NES CIVITAS (Dolley 215–223).*

In the 10th century, the easing of royal authority is illustrated by the growing number of coins issued by local *seigneuries* throughout France. Charles the Simple (893–923), in the treaty of St-Claire-sur-Epte in 911, ceded Normandy to one Rollo – of Norwegian ancestry, an important personage in Channel Island history – and some years later was defeated and dethroned by Hugh the Great, Count of Paris and Duke of France. In 933 the Cotentin and the Channel Islands were added to the Duchy of Normandy. The royal position was further weakened by Magyar attacks from the east, and continuing Viking intrusions in the west. While the Magyar attacks were ended in 955 at the battle of Lechfeld near Augsburg, much of western France was exposed to Viking activity for many years to come until the Vikings themselves became assimilated.

*Fig. 61: Episcopal billon* denier *of Hugues Capet with Archbishop Hervé of Beauvais.*
Obv. *HERVEVS HVGO REX;* Rev. *BELVACVS CIVITAS round monogram of CROLS [Carolus] (Ciani 13).*

# Normandy

*Fig. 62:* Denier *of Charles the Bald.*
Obv. *CARLVS REX FR[ANCORUM];* Rev. *METVLLO + (Dolley 170).*

In order to follow the trail of the early Norman coinage, we must return for a moment to Charles the Bald, whose *deniers* appear to have been crudely imitated, probably after his time, at Bayeux, Coutances, Evreux, Lisieux and Rouen. Rollo is not known to have struck any coins; however *deniers,* struck in Rouen, have been attributed to the next two Dukes of Normandy, William I 'Long-sword' (927–943) and Richard I 'the Fearless' (from 943). The *deniers* of Richard II 'the Good' (996–1026) appear to have been imitated, in increasingly debased forms, for the next one hundred years or so, while Richard III (1026–1028), Robert I (1028–1035) and William II (1035–1087), were busying themselves trying to drive Canute and his successors out of England; and it is no surprise that William II, when he finally became William I of England, allowed the well organized Saxon moneyers the freedom that he did to continue striking their own coins, though the manufacture of the dies was controlled by Normans.

*Fig. 63:* AR *Penny of William I struck in London, PAXS type.*
Obv. *PILLELM REX;* Rev. *IEPI ON LIINDN (BMC VIII, Seaby 1257).*

It is interesting to note that the first contemporary use of the name JERSOI was in a charter of Richard II. Robert I is recorded by Robert Wace the Jersey Poet (1120–1183) as having landed in the Island shortly after his accession, having been frustrated by a storm in his attempt to land in England and place Edward (later 'the Confessor') on the throne. In this paragraph of contemporary historical events, one should make mention of a charter of Robert I which was confirmed by William (c. 1060), and to which was added half of the revenues from eight Jersey Churches. In 1066, England and Normandy, including the Channel Islands, became united under the same monarch, until 1087 when Robert, eldest son of William, inherited the Duchy of Normandy, while his brother William Rufus became King of England.

*Fig. 64: Henry I penny of London.*
*Pellets in quatrefoil type:* Obv. *HENRICVS REX;* Rev. *WVLGAR ON LVNDE. (BMC XIV, Seaby 1275).*

Henry I of England (1100–1135), the youngest son of William I, took advantage of his brother Robert's frequent absences in the Holy Land and, after defeating him at the Battle of Tinchebrai (near Argenton) in 1106, once again took possession of Normandy.

In England at this time, the coinage had become almost as debased as the Norman coinage, and it was while Henry was in Normandy in 1124 that the Bishop of Durham, under the King's orders, had the right hands of no less than ninety-four moneyers cut off, in Winchester, to try to remedy the situation. For the first time, during the reign of Henry I of England, Norman moneyers' names appear on the silver pennies current. There was one final period when Normandy passed out of the hands of the English Crown: this time to Geoffrey of Anjou who ruled in the name of his own little son, Henry I's grandson. This period

*Fig. 65: Stephen, penny of Lincoln; mint names were commonly obliterated to protect the moneyer.*
*Watford type:* Obv. *[STIE]FNE [REX];* Rev. *[R]EINNALD O[N LINC] (BMC I, Seaby 1278).*

lasted during the reign of Stephen (1135–1154), and Normandy and England were once again reunited on Henry II's accession. Fifty years later, in 1204, when mainland Normandy was conquered by Philippe II of France, the Channel Islands remained true to the British Crown.

*Fig. 66: Henry II silver penny of London.*
*Short cross coinage:* Obv. *HENRICVS · REX;* Rev. *[FIL. A]IMER · ON · LVNDE (Class 1b, Seaby 1344).*

Just over one hundred years after the Islands were added to the Duchy of Normandy, references began to be made in contemporary records – principally concerning the exchange of contracts – to the currency medium in the area, and we find the *libra* and *solidus* most commonly referred to as the money of account. On occasion the type of money is mentioned (£SD of Anjou, Rouen, or Le Mans); and, perhaps most relevant to this study, the value (in *librae* or *solidi*) is recorded as being payable in *denarii* or *deniers*. A few examples are gives below:
 – c. 1048: In a document referring to the engagements of Néel II, Viscount of the Cotentin towards the monks of Marmoutier concerning lands in Guernsey confiscated by Duke William and given to the Abbey of Marmoutier after the defeat of Néel, the latter confirmed the grants and received as recompense *'quadraginta librarum'* (40 *libras* or pounds) (S. J. *Cartulaire* p 381)
 – c. 1048: In similar circumstances, Néel received *'triginta et quinque librarum'* (35 *libras*) (ibid. p 382)
 – c. 1060: In a confirmation of a similar agreement he received *'septem libras denariorum'* (seven *libras* in *deniers*) and . . . *'triginta denariorum libras'* (30 *libras* in *deniers*) (ibid. p 383)
 – c. 1060: The same Néel ceded land in Guernsey to the monks of Mont St. Michel for *'X libras rothomagensium denariorum'* (ten *libras* in *deniers* of Rouen) (ibid. p 228)
 – c. 1060 (recorded in a church charter drawn up some 300 years later): the Duke of Normandy conceded to the receiver of church taxes Guillaume de Vauville (who had himself ceded the Church in Alderney with its tithes and other lands in the Islands) *'duos porcos quinque solidorum in navitate Domini et viginti solidos in Pascha et secreto dimidiam decimam molendinorum suorum de Gerneroio'* (two pigs, five *solidi* at Christmas and 20 *solidi* at Easter and in addition the half of the tithes of his mills in Guernsey) (ibid. p 401)
 – Post 1087: a charter records losses suffered by the monks of Mont St. Michel following the confiscation by King William of certain possessions in Guernsey, Sark, Alderney and Herm for which they had paid *'Centum e Lta libras'* (150 *libras*) (ibid. p 230)
 – 1125: *'Septem libras Rothomagensium nove monete'* (seven *libras* of Rouen in new money) are recorded as being payable to the Abbey of Mont St. Michael by Philippe de Carteret, as well as *'unum auri Bizanteum'* (one besant or *sou d'or*) by his mother (ibid. p 51)

- c. 1140: the sum of *'quinque solidi Rotomagensium'* was recorded as being due to Orenge daughter of Pierre with the consent of Osanne des Isles, together with land on which she and her mother could live, after Pierre had become a monk and given his entire heritage in Guernsey to the Abbey of Mont St. Michel (ibid. p 186–7)
- c. 1140: Renaud mortgaged to the monks of Mont St. Michel his land in Guernsey for *'Centum solidis cenomannensium* (100 *solidi* of Le Mans) (ibid. p 187)
- 1150: in a tract concerning commerce and trade, Guernsey is mentioned as being on the trade route between Ireland and Rouen; each ship from Ireland would, after calling at Guernsey set sail for Rouen; on arrival at customs, payment of *'unum tymbrium de marturina aut decem libras Rothom-[agensium]'* (one bundle of marten skins or ten *libras* of Rouen) was due to the King (ibid. p 424)
- 1154: a charter of one Roger Wach grants to the Abbey of St.-Sauveur-le-Vicomte the revenue from properties in Jersey in an amount of *'solidos duos et dimidium Andegavensium'* (two and one half *solidi* of Anjou) (ibid. p 293)
- 1160: Robert de Barneville assigns to the Abbey of Montebourg *'viginti solidos de centum solidos'* (20 *solidi* of 100 *solidi*) to be received from Guillaume de Vernon in Sark – an interesting and very early example of an assignment which, even today, can be a complicated financial transaction (ibid. p 389)
- ante 1179: The Abbey of Mont St. Michel paid *'LX solidos And.'* (60 *solidi* of Anjou) for properties in Guernsey (ibid. p 220)
- 1182: a charter mentions the grant of land in Alderney by Willelmus Artifex (William the Engineer) to the Abbey of Ste. Marie du Voeu for *'duobus solidis andegavensium annuatim'* (two *solidi* of Anjou p.a.) (ibid. p 335)
- c. 1185: a deed addressed by Guillaume de Tournebu, vicar of Coutances to Robert Florie, priest of the Church of St. Mary in Jersey mentions annual payment of *'soixante solds angevins'* for rent (ibid. p 375)
- 1199: in a charter King John gives to Vital de Villa and his heirs *'quinquaginta libratas redditus Andegavenses'* (50 *livres rente* of Anjou) for two whales in the port of Biarritz, in exchange for *rente* which King Richard, his brother, had given regarding the right of drying fish in the Islands of Guernsey and Jersey (ibid. p 428)

*Fig. 67: John, silver penny of Winchester (in the name of Henry II). Short cross coinage:* Obv. **hENRICVS · REX**; Rev. *ADAM ON WINC (Class 5b, Seaby 1351).*

- 1200: in another charter, confirming an earlier one, King John gives permanent title to the Abbey of Bellosanne on receipt of *'viginti libras redditus'* (20 *livres rente*) for properties on Mount St. Helier, Jersey. There is also mention in the same charter of a payment of *'quindecim solidos novem denarios'* (15 *sous* and 9 *deniers*) and *'decim & septem solidos & quatuor denarios'* (17 *sous* and 4 *deniers*) (ibid. p 418)
- early 13th cent: in a document recording the state of the revenue of the Abbey of St. Saviour in Jersey, one of the items mentioned among the receipts is an amount of *'quindecim denarios cenomanensium'* (15 *deniers du Mans*) (ibid. p 262)

After the conquest of Normandy in 1204, the *denier d'Anjou* or *'angevin'*, which had succeeded the *denier* de Rouen and the *denier du Mans*, was itself replaced by the *denier tournois* (of Tours), to which the next stage of Channel Island numismatic history must be dedicated.

*Fig. 68: Early billon* denier *of the Abbey of St. Martin at Tours.*
Obv. *SCI MARTIN;* Rev. *TVRONVS CIVI ( P.d'A. 1646, B. 185).*

# The Tournois Period

*Fig. 69: Henry III penny of Canterbury.*
*Long cross coinage:* Obv. HENRICVS REX III; Rev. WILLEM ON CANT *(Class Vb, Seaby 1368).*

The Channel Islands possessed certain privileges and freedoms before the reign of King John of England. These were confirmed by King John and endorsed by his son King Henry III. In 1284 Henry instituted an enquiry into the laws and customs of the Islands in an order addressed to Drogo de Barentin, Warden of the Islands. It was subsequently declared that the 'people of the Island (probably Guernsey) owe annually, as an aid, the sum of 70 *livres tournois,* in consideration of which they are free, as they have been free in the times of the King's predecessors, from all military service (outside the Island), taxes, and impositions *(de omnibus exercitibus tailliagiis, greveriis, et aliis occasionibus),* except, however, when they shall accompany the Duke of Normandy, when necessary, to recover possession of England *(ad Angliam recuperandum)*'.

These freedoms, which were endorsed and re-endorsed by latter monarchs, served as a foundation for the trading privileges of the Channel Islands, which were of great strategic value in the 13th century, lying, as they did, on the trade routes between England and Aquitaine.

Britain's first recorded exports were slaves. In the late 6th century, Pope Gregory is recorded to have given instructions for the purchase of English slave boys in Gaul, in order to rear them in the Christian faith to convert their countrymen. Although we have no records that these slave boys were allowed to stretch their legs in Jersey or Guernsey, the Islands' subsequent importance as an entrepôt for cattle, hogs, suet, cheese, wolf-hounds and – very important – wool (and later wool cloth) from England is well recorded. In exchange, English merchants imported wine and blubberfish via the Channel Islands; wine trading, particularly in Guernsey, was important right down to the 19th century, and vestiges of these ancient privileges survive in the bottles of liquor and tobacco which tourists take home with them from the Islands even today. A currency medium for these commodities was imperative.

Under Philippe Auguste of France (1180–1223) two currency systems asserted themselves: the *tournois* system (which originated in Tours) and the *parisis* system; where the former was so important that it became an international currency, the latter was current only in the north and centre of the Kingdom of France and gradually became the medium in which only royal revenues were reckoned. Both systems became moneys of account, with the *parisis,* in theory, 25% more valuable than the *tournois.* The *parisis,* as such, had in fact originated under the rule of Hugh Capet (987–996) and was current, with many other types including the *angevin* (of Anjou), the *denier du Mans* and the *denier de Rouen,* during the reigns of Robert (996–1031), Henry I (1031–1060), Philippe I (1060–1108), Louis VI (1108–1137) and Louis VII (1137–1180). But under Philippe Auguste all regional issues except for the *tournois* began to die out.

During the excavation of a medieval house in Old Street, St. Helier in 1973, two fragmentary coins were found; one has been identified as an English cut halfpenny of Henry II, struck at York in the 1180's; the other, a fragment of a French regal *denier,* has been assigned 'very tentatively' to Louis VIII or Louis IX. The English coin was legal tender (in England) until shortly after 1247 when the 'long cross' coinage was issued by Henry III.

Under Louis VIII (1223–1226) only *parisis* and *tournois* were struck, and under 'Saint' Louis IX (1226–1270), monetary reforms were carried out which, as well as being extremely important in themselves, enhanced the nature of both *denier* systems as moneys of account.

The following references in contemporary documents are relevant:

**Current Money:** A communication of 1208 from the Evêque de Coutances to the clerk of the churches of St. Martin le Vieux and Ste. Marie in Jersey mentioned annual payments of *'sept livres dix solds en monnaye aiant cours . . .'* (S.J. *Cartulaire* p 377)

**Lease of a Ship:** An order of King John of 25.3.1208 directs the Exchequer to reckon to the bailiffs of Southampton *20 sols* which they paid for a ship in which Stephen de Oxford sailed to Guernsey and Jersey by order of the King. (Le Quesne, *Const. Hist.* p 476)

**Fortifications:** Another order from King John of 11.11.1212 directs that the Treasury should pay to Philippe l'Albigny going to the Island of Jersey, of which Hasculfus de Soligny was Governor, *40 marks* for fortifying the Island (ibid. p 476)

**Payment in Kind:** 1219 – Guillaume d'Ouville cedes to the monks of St. Saviour a pair of boots which they 'paid' annually to him as well as *15 solidi.* (S.J. *Cartulaire* p 305)

**Garrison Dues:** In 1224 King Henry III ordered the Treasury to deliver to the Governor of Jersey, Galpidus de Lucy, *400 livres* for the payment of eight Knights, each Knight to receive *2 solidos per diem;* 35 cavalry officers, each to receive *12 deniers per diem;* and 60 foot soldiers, each to receive *7 deniers per diem (Le Quesne p 476)*

| | |
|---|---|
| **Alderney:** | An Act of 1238 mentions the renouncing of rights of land-owners in Alderney on payment of *'decem libris sterlingorum'* by the King (ibid. p 405) |
| **The Vagaries of Accounting:** | In a document of c. 1240, concerning the state of the Island of Alderney (then owned part by Henry III and part by the Chapitre de Coutances), among other items due, (the Chapter) *'habet summam denariorum, videlicet* [i.e.] *quatuor libras turonenses, vel eo circo* [or thereabouts]' (ibid. p 398) |
| **Monks' Pocket Money:** | In a letter of 1254 from Henry III to the Bailiff of Jersey and Guernsey, asking what the Monks of Mont St. Michel receive, the answer mentions (among other rights) payment of *4L 10s* due from Jersey. Incidentally the rights of the seas around Guernsey, Lihou and Jethou (i.e. flotsam) excluded gold, unworked silk, and uncut scarlet, which were for the King! (ibid. p 26) |

Although the Channel Islands had opted to stay under the aegis of the British crown, their proximity to the French coast brought with it a natural day-to-day commercial contact. At the same time, the coinage under King John and King Henry III of Britain – at least until the 'Long Cross' coinage was first issued in 1247 – had become very debased; and it is therefore not surprising that the French *tournois* system, which prevailed in Normandy after the French conquest, was adopted in the Islands. Moreover the reforms of Louis IX preceded those of Edward I of Britain by some thirty years (the idea for the first British groat or 4d

*Fig. 70:* AR gros tournois *of Louis IX, model for the first British groat.*
Obv. **BÑDICTV̄ː SITː NOMĒː DÑIː NR̄Iː DEIː IHV. XPĪ** + *round LVDOVICVS REX;*
Rev. *TVRONVS CIVIS round* Châtel tournois, *12* lis: *worth 12 deniers (Ciani 180).*

piece was almost certainly copied from the *gros tournois* of Louis IX). However it is important to stress that the *tournois* system was adopted as a money of account, in which the value of all other French (and foreign) coins were reckoned until well into the 18th century. French coins of all types remained, in fact, the principal medium of exchange in the Islands until the 19th century, and a review of the French coinage over the period is not out of place.

It was Louis IX who introduced the first gold coin of the 'Third Race' or Capetian dynasty of France. The *écu* or gold *denier* was valued at 10 *sols tournois*. At the same time he introduced the *gros tournois* of silver, valued at 12 *deniers*. Both these coin types were continued through the reign of Philippe III 'Le Hardi' (1270–1285) together with the *deniers* which had long been made of billon. Although Philippe IV 'Le Bel' (1285–1314) ran up considerable expenses in his

*Fig. 71:* AR double tournois *of Philippe IV.*
Obv. *PHILLIPUS· REX;* Rev. *MON· DVPLEX· REGAL (Ciani 218).*

war against the English in Flanders, the only coins which appear to have suffered were the billon series which became smaller, poorer in metal, and cruder in style; these were referred to derogatively as *'nummi'* in a document relating to Guernsey of 1289. Against this Philippe issued three new gold coins; the *chaise d'or,* worth 20 *sols parisis* – almost exactly twice the *'petit royal'* (successor of the *écu*), now worth 11 *sols parisis,* the *masse* or *royale dur* (hard because it was of poorer gold), and the *agnel d'or* (valued at 16 *sols parisis* or 20 *tournois).*

The gold *agnel* and the silver *gros* were continued through the reigns of Louis X (1314–1316) and Philippe V 'le Long' (1316–1322), with the *deniers* and *fractions* being reproduced in large quantities and deplorable style. Louis X's *agnel* had sunk in value to 12 ½ *sols tournois* and his *gros* to 12 *deniers tournois,* whereas Philippe V's *agnel* was stronger at 15 *sols tournois* and his *gros* at 15 *deniers tournois*. All the coins of Charles IV 'Le Bel' (1322–1328) suffered as a result of the war against England and Flanders; the circulation of 'black' money, of appalling quality, increased while manufacture of the *gros* was halted. Value of the *gros* increased from 12 *deniers parisis* in 1323 to 20 *deniers* in 1328. The *agnel* and *royal* (at 15 *sols tournois*) continued to be struck and a *demi-royal* was introduced. Small base silver coins of both Philip IV and Charles IV have been found in Jersey and there are two cut halfpennies of Edward II of England (1307–1327) in the Gorey Castle Museum. A *denier* of Arthur II of Brittany (1304–1312), still to be fully published, has recently been found at Mont Orgueil, as well as several other French coins of the 16th–17th centuries.

*Fig. 72:* Base silver *maille blanche of Charles IV.*
*Legend as Fig. 70 except for KAROLVS; 10 lis only (Ciani 256).*

Up to the end of the 13th century, with very few exceptions, properties were sold in the Islands for an annual rent in perpetuity of so many quarters, bushels, *cabots* or *sixtonniers* of wheat, usually payable on Michaelmas Day of each year. These *'rentes'* or rents could be sold by the owners for a sum of money. In the early 14th century purchases of property seem to have been made for amounts in *livres tournois;* and from about 1360 contracts were measured in *francs* (or *livres*), *sols* and *sous.* In an *'extente'* of 1331, 4 *livres tournois* were valued at £1 sterling, and 4 *deniers tournois* at 1 *'estellan'*. *'Esterling'* is mentioned in various documents concerning Jersey, Guernsey, Alderney and Lihou, in the 13th and 14th centuries (as is the *'Marc'* and *half-Marc* of silver). These *'esterlings'* were probably base continental imitations of the new English silver pennies of Edward I (1272–1302) known at the time as 'crocards' (the same root as crook), 'pollards' (from the 'polled' head characteristic of the coins of continental bishoprics), 'rosaries' (the head on some ecclesiastical coins wore a chaplet of roses), or *cocadones* (origin unknown). *Sterlingus* was medieval Latin for a penny, *obolus* for a halfpenny, and *ferlingus* for a farthing.

*Fig. 73: Anglo-Gallic issue of Edward I of England:* denier *of Bordeaux.*
Obv. *EDVARDVS REX + round lion, AGL/E;* Rev. *DVX AQIT BVRD [for BVRDEGALE – Bordeau] (Anglo-French coinage Pl III, 15).*

## Moneyage

In 1682, Jean Poingdestre, Lieutenant Bailiff of Jersey, wrote the following 'Account of Moneyage':

> 'Anciently the Kings Revenue consisted
> principally of seven Manors, which had
> been the Patrimony of the Dukes of Normandy.
> Those Manors were by Henry the Second lett
> out in fee farme to divers tenants at
> the rate of 460 livers tournois per
> Annū; which pounds tournois weighed
> at that time as much as the pounds
> Sterling doe at present. Another part
> of ye sayd Revenue was a certaine
> Ducall Right called Fouage or Moneage,
> of old given to the Dukes of Normandy
> by theire subiects, to the end they
> should not alter the Curant coyne of

> That Dutchy; & it consisted of one shilling
> or sol tournois for every fire, to be payd
> once in 3 yeares: which was then
> a considerable sume, because
> The shilling tournois went then neere
> the value of ye nowe English shilling;
> but nowe is worth but one penny.'

This levy, otherwise called *'fouage'* or hearth money (parallel to the Scottish 'feu dues'), was confirmed in *extentes* for the Islands dated 1331; with a few exemptions, all tenants and residents in the Islands with property worth at least 20 *sols tournois,* had to pay a tax of 12 *deniers tournois* per hearth, which was levied once every three years, in lieu of all other ancient *rentes* due on their properties. The Islanders could hardly object to such a tax, payable, as it was, in debased continental *deniers;* but there were serious disturbances in 1330 when they were required to pay it in the new money of Philippe de Valois.

Philippe VI de Valois (1328–1350), nephew of Philippe Le Bel, kept up a long war against Edward III of England, who succeeded in establishing himself in

*Fig. 74: Pre-treaty silver penny of Edward III.*
Obv. *EDWARDVS · REX · ANGLI +;* Rev. *CIVITAS LONDON (Class C, Seaby 1584).*

Valois after Crécy in 1346. This war gave rise to the so-called Anglo-French coinage series. Philippe's own endeavours to continue the reforms initiated by his uncle proved fruitless and he decided instead to create totally new denominations. In such a situation the money of account, usually so difficult to understand, actually becomes useful – at least to the historian – and a form of continuity is possible. The old *gros tournois* which had appreciated to the value of over 20 *deniers parisis* in 1329 was decreed in 1330 to be worth *'12 bons tournois petits'* (i.e. new *deniers*) of Philippe de Valois. As well as the new *denier,* Philippe had struck a new *gros parisis* (valued at 1 *sol parisis*). Among gold coins issued, the *parisis* was minted between 1330 and 1336 and represented one livre (20 *sols parisis* or *25 sols tournois*). The *denier d'or* or *florin à l'écu* (issued at 20 *sols tournois* in 1337) was the most durable gold coin but was being minted in a sadly depreciated form by the end of the reign.

The introduction of this new system had been preceded in 1329 and 1330 by a two-stage devaluation of the existing specie by 50% and it is ironical that after such a courageous attempt at controlling the coinage, and with ample reserves of gold, the whole plan was to collapse within six years because of a shortage of silver which was necessary to finance not only the day-to-day economy, but also the stipends of the soldiers fighting a war against England which was to last one hundred years. It is also ironical that the well-meaning attempt of Philippe to upgrade the circulation medium can only have foundered under the conditions of the day, where moneys of account were already strongly established (both the *tournois* and the *parisis*) and where the situation was ripe for bad money to drive out good. The last good *gros tournois* was issued in 1343; but the money of account survived.

Documents dated to 1338–1345, reporting this period when attacks on the Islands were frequent, show that contemporary prices were given in pounds, shillings and pence – one of the earliest records of a link between the French and English systems, where the *'chelin'* or shilling (a money of account at the time) had been the equivalent of the French *sol*. Examples of payments were:

*60 chelins pour 3 arbalètes* [crossbows] *à tour*

*£ 4–10 pour 17 arbalètes à pied*

*12 chelins pour 12 courroies pour tirer les arbalètes* [bowstrings]

*30 chelins pour 30 arcs* [bows]

*116 chelins 8 pennys pour 100 gerbes* [quiverfuls] *de fleches*

Men-of-arms were paid 6d per day, crossbowmen 3d, and archers (longbowmen) 2d. (BSJ IX p 4)

*Fig. 75: Grosnez Castle, dating back to the 14th century, as portrayed on a modern 50p piece. See J208.*

The main medium of exchange however was the *denier tournois* and it is recorded that every French ship putting in at St. Peter Port had to pay 12 *d.t.* (small craft 6 *d.t.*) in harbour dues. (BSJ XI p 52)

Here are some more contemporary references:

**A Loan:** A letter of the Dean of Jersey of 1281 confirms repayment of a loan of 30 *livres tournois*. (S.J. *Cartulaire* p 62)

**Coined Money:** (1286–7) a letter from the Bailliff (and attorney of Otho de Granson, Gardien des Îles) confirms that the prévôté of Noirmont belongs to the Abbey of the Mont St. Michel and the Prior of St. Clement. It mentions payment of *'decem libras turonensium in pecunia numerata'*. (ibid. p 140)

**A Fishing Licence:** A letter of Edward I to the Bailliff of Guernsey mentions the taking by the King of 20 *deniers tournois* for each one thousand mackerel fished by the Abbey of Pleinmont (1289). (ibid. p 192)

| | |
|---|---|
| **Weak Money:** | In the same letter it is recorded that customs paid by the tenant of The Vale (Guernsey) rose in 1306 to '*4 libras debilis moneta*'. (ibid.) <br> In various other documents post 1306, concerning the '*Prix des Denrées*' for that year, the prices are measured in 'strong' and 'weak' money. |
| **Library Dues:** | A letter from the Dean of Jersey dated 1308 attests that Henri de St. Martin has admitted to borrowing a book '*Dygestum Vetus*' from Mont St. Michel. He must return the book or pay the value i.e. '*decem libras bonorum parvorum turonensium*'. (ibid. p 163) |
| **Overdue Rates:** | 6th September 1311 – The Ecclesiastical Court held by the Dean of Jersey at St. Peter's condemns Jourdan Horman to pay 150 *livres tournois* overdue to the Abbaye de St. Sauveur-le-Vicomte (for a portion of the tithe). (ibid. p 280) |
| **Conger Eels:** | A document of 1313 mentions the leasing of the '*esperqueries*' of Guernsey and Jersey for 5 years for 15 *sols tournois* for '*chaque centaine de congres*'. (ibid. p 234) |
| **Damages:** | A plea of 1324 addressed to Edward II mentions damages of '*xij livres de tornoiz*'. (ibid. p 197) |
| **An Account:** | In a list of payments (1325) of Brother Pierre Lucas, Gardien of Noirmont and St. Clement, the items included: <br> 15 *libras* for a mill-stone <br> 12 *solidos* for the fare <br> 5 *solidos pro scambio monete* [for mill-stone grit C.O.D.] <br> *16 quarteria frumenti Magistro Gaufrido de Karteret pro expensis quas fecimos in insulis preter 16 L.T.* <br> and *50 solidos* 'for our part of a very large jar of wine'. (ibid. p 47) |
| **A lot of Coins:** | A letter (c. 1327) of the Prior of the Vale to the Prior of Otterton, Devon, mentions *50 livres de tournois*. (ibid. p 112) |
| **An early Postmark:** | '*Pro expensis decem solidos*' is written on the back of a letter of 1327, concerning the Priory of St. Clement, Jersey. (ibid. p 108) |
| **Protection Money:** | A letter of the Abbey of Mont St. Michel (1335) names one Guillaume Le Loreur to maintain and defend the rights of the Monks and Prior of St. Clement (Jersey) for *4 libras annue*. (ibid. p 233) |

**Isolated Islands:** A bulle of Pope Benoit XII dated 13th July 1336 allows the Eveque of Avranches to change or sell all his dues in Jersey, Sark and Herm not exceeding 10 *livres tournois* in view of the inconveniences arising from the distances of the Islands and the perils of the sea.

**The Wars:** A declaration of revenues of the Abbey of Mont St. Michel (1337) from The Vale and St. Clement, Guernsey, mentions a sum of about eleven hundred *livres tournois* not received for three years because of the wars (with England). (ibid. p 44)

**Inflation:** Raoul de Hermesthorp (Lieutenant of Thomas de Ferriers, Gardien des Îles) declares in a letter of 1347 that it has been brought to his attention that the Prior of Lihou receives from the Prior of the Vale *XV livres tournois* p.a. – in his opinion an insufficient amount at that time. (ibid. p 201)

King John 'the Good' (1350–1364) presided over one of the saddest periods in French history, with the 100 years war taking heavy toll. The coinage of the time bears this out. Although John made a half-hearted attempt, at the beginning of his reign, to maintain the standard his father had dreamed about, the quality of all denominations soon began to deteriorate, either in weight or alloy or both. His gold coins included the *écu*, the *mouton* and *demi-mouton*, the *denier d'or*, the *royal* and the *franc-à-cheval* (issued in 1360 to pay the ransom for the King). His silver coins contained less and less silver but their poor quality was made up for by quantity, and the many denominations struck turn the period into a numismatist's maze; they included a 'strong' *gros tournois* (struck in the

*Fig. 76: 'Strong'* gros tournois *of Jean 'le Bon' dated to 1359. Legend as 70 except for IOHANNES (Ciani 401).*

Languedoc) and a *maille blanche* of good quality, as well as six types of *gros* (worth about 15 deniers tournois), over six types of *blanc* (worth about 8 *deniers tournois),* and for the first time the *double tournois* which was put into circulation originally at 2 *deniers tournois* but in a short time sank in value to one *obole tournois* (or one half *denier*); to complete the confusion the *double parisis* was also issued as were *deniers* of both systems and *oboles*.

England's fortunes at this time were happier than those of France. The English wool trade was developing, following the immigration of the Flemish weavers, and the ensuing rise in prosperity was reflected in the coinage. The silver groat was again struck. A document, dated to 1357 mentions the use of *'gros'* in the Channel Islands at the time, though these were probably *gros tournois*. An English gold coinage was also produced, inspired by the handsome French prototype. The fourth coinage of Edward III (1327–1377) began in 1351 and can be divided into pre-Treaty, Treaty and post-Treaty periods (referring to the Treaty of Bretigny of 1351 when Edward exchanged his claim to the French throne for new lands in Aquitaine, thereafter giving us the inscription REX ANGL DNS HYB Z AQT [et Aquitaine]). 18 years later, war resumed and Edward once again claimed to be REX ANGL Z FRANC. A very fine quarter noble of this King was found at Pontac, Jersey and is now in the Société Jersiaise Museum.

Both he and his son Edward, the Black Prince, struck gold and silver denominations for the English possessions in France and one silver half groat of the Black Prince (mint unkown) was found at Gorey, Jersey.

Under Charles V (1364–1380), who had been regent during his father's captivity in England, better fortunes in war coincided with – or led to – an improvement in the currency. Issues were limited to the *franc à cheval* (20 s.t.) and the *franc à pied* of the same value; the *gros tournois* (15 d.t.) and the *blanc au K* [for Karolus]; and the *deniers tournois* and *parisis* as well as *oboles* (the *obole* is mentioned in connection with Jersey in a document of 1381). Coins of the Dauphiné were also struck in Charles' name. This improvement however was not to last and when the 12 year old Charles VI (1380–1422) inherited the French throne, the time was ripe for a resurgence of the power of local Duchies in the Kingdom. A base silver coin of John V of Brittany was discovered some years ago in the grounds of Gorey Castle, Jersey, as well as a very fine *écu d'or* of Charles VI; these two finds symbolize well the confused state of the monetary medium at the time.

The Kings of England, since Edward III, had all claimed to be Kings of France at the same time, and the French title on the English coinage (REX ANGL Z FRANC) bears this out. Henry V of England (1413–1422) decided to reactivate

*Fig. 77: Base silver penny of Henry V, York.*
Obv. *HENRICVS REX [ANGLIE]*; Rev. *EBORACI CIVITAS (Class G, York; Seaby 1790).*

this claim to the French throne, and, taking advantage of the disintegration of France under Charles VI, landed in Normandy and proclaimed himself King of France. The chaos which ensued led to Agincourt in 1415 and the treaty which

Charles was forced to sign with Henry V in 1420. A *denier tournois* of Henry V minted at St. Lô in 1421–2 is preserved in the Gorey Castle Museum. In the latter part of Henry's reign, in addition to his own currency, coins were struck by John, Duke of Bourgogne, Charles the Dauphin (in the Dauphiné and Languedoc) and Henry V of England (in Normandy and Guyenne).

The historical phenomenon of French coinage persisted at this time, and, while gold issues continued to be of high quality and workmanship, the 'silver' issues were of a constantly low quality. Issue of the gold *écu* and *mouton* was continued and the *écu heaumé* (helmed) and *demi écu heaumé* were introduced; the *écu heaumé* was worth two *moutons*. A Jersey property contract dated 1399 mentions payment in gold *francs*. Another gold coin, the *salut*, (named after the Angels' greeting 'AVE' pictured on the obverse) appeared for the first time; and mention should also be made of the *'double'* or *'chaise'* (the King seated), the largest gold coin of all, issued by the Dauphin in 1420, and its *fraction* the *demi-chaise*. The silver coinage included the *blanc* (or *guénar*) and *fractions*, and the *gros;* a new *gros* or *'grossus'* was also introduced (at 20 *d.t.*). Various types of *doubles* and *deniers* made up the small change of the period.

*Fig. 78: Left: Silver* grossus *of Charles VI of France, created in 1413. Right: Anglo-Gallic billon* grand blanc *of Henry VI of England.*
Left: Obv. *(inner) KL : DI : G : FRACORV : REX, (outer) + SIT : NOMEN : DOMINI : BENEDICTVM;* Rev. *GROSVS : TVRONVS, 12* lis *(Ciani 520). Right: Obv. FRANCORVM : ET : ANGLIE : REX surrounding HERICVS over conjoined shields of France and England. Rev. SIT : NOMEN : DNI : BENEDICTV round HERICVS below lily, cross and lion; mintmark lion, both sides (Anglo-French coinage Pl VI, 83).*

Perhaps the most symbolic of the coins struck in Normandy by Henry V of England was the *blanc aux écus,* with the coats of arms of England and France on the obverse and the lion and the *lis* separated by a cross on the reverse. This coin is also attributed to his son, Henry VI (1422–1453) who was proclaimed King of France at the age of two. To a great extent history repeated itself and during Henry VI's reign, following factional fighting between the Yorkists and the Lancastrians in England, his position in France became more and more untenable until, in a drive inspired by Joan of Arc, the French finally repossessed all of the territory which had been lost during Charles VI's reign, with the exception of Calais which was finally recovered in 1558. Issues of the French coins of Henry VI contracted as English influence diminished, until only mints in Normandy, Picardy and Guyenne remained active. The Calais mint which had produced gold and silver coins in far greater quantities even than London was finally closed down in 1440.

It was the Dauphin Charles who took over the reins of power during the final stages of the 100 years war and became Charles VII King of France (1422–1461). His efforts to impose his rule on the issue of coinage were largely successful, and with the exception of the Duchy of Burgundy, all of France once again struck coins in the name of the sovereign. It is interesting to note that where the *écu, grand blanc, petit blanc, double, gros tournois, denier parisis*, and *denier tournois* were permitted as currency in Greater France, the same coins were current in Normandy at different rates in relation to the *tournois* money of account. (During this period the *écu d'or* seems to have been an important measure of value in Jersey property contracts.)

At the same time, coins of England, Flanders and Brittany were current, as well as others from more distant territories. I give (from le Blanc p 303) the full list of coins current in Normandy below, together with the rates in *tournois* in 1456:

| | | | |
|---|---|---|---|
| *Écus* | at 30 *s.t.* | | |
| *Demi Écus* | at 15 *s.t.* | | |
| *Gros d'Angleterre* (Groat) | at 3 *s.t.* | | |
| *Gros tournois* | at 2 *s.t.* | 9 *d.t.* | |
| *Plaques (Double Gros) de Flandres* | at | 15 *d.t.* | |
| *Gros du Pape* | at | 14 *d.t.* | |
| *Gros de Provence* | at | 14 *d.t.* | |
| *Gros de Milan* | at | 14 *d.t.* | |
| *Blancs de Bretagne à la Targe* (little shield) | at | 12 *d.t.* | |
| *Blancs* | at | 11 *d.t.* | |
| *Blancs Bretons au Chapelet* | at | 9 *d.t.* | |
| *Blancs de Bar* (Bearn) | at | 7 *d.t.* | 1 *obol* |
| *Blancs de Lorraine* | at | 7 *d.t.* | 1 *obol* |
| *Petits Blancs* | at | 5 *d.t.* | 1 *obol* |
| *Liards* (of Dauphiné) | at | 3 *d.t.* | |
| Morlans | at | 2 *d.t.* | 1 *obol* |

A final selection from contemporary documents, covering the period from the mid-14th to mid-15th centuries, would not be out of place here:

**Exchange Rates:** In a letter dated 1357 of the Royal Court, Jersey, it was stated that the '*maalle a la coue [maille à la queue* which was named after the 'latin' cross on the observe] *valoyt lan precedent* [1356] *vj deniers Tournes a Rouen et escu de Johan* [King John] *xiij s. iiij d.* [13 *sols* 4 *deniers tournois*] ... *et que nostre sire le Roy devoyt rechevoyr en la dite Isle auteylle* [at the same rate] *monnoye comme le duc de Normandie* ...' (S.J. Cartulaire p 449)

| | |
|---|---|
| **A Pension Incentive Scheme:** | A letter of the Abbé of Mont St. Michel (1368) grants a pension of 4 *livres tournois* p.a. to Guillaume le Breton, clerk, of St. Brelade (to be paid by the Prior of St. Clement) for him to be counsellor, to be increased by 20 *sols tournois* if he becomes Sénéchal de l'Abbaye in Jersey. (ibid. p 158) |
| **Rentes:** | In a book of Rentes owed to the Priory of St. Clement in 1381, payments of money and grain were mentioned together with other payments in kind: *caboteaulx; libvres, sols, deniers, ancerem, gallinas; ova; quarterium; carchonnier; franc; obol.* (ibid. pp 74–7) |
| **The Ecréhou:** | A document of the 15th century mentions rentes of 'Notre Dame de Escrehou en Gierresy', which include:<br>    *quartiers de froment*<br>    *caboteaulx de froment, demi caboteaulx*<br>    *sols, deniers*<br>    *boisseaulx de fourment*<br>    *1 couronne d'or* (ibid. p 420–1) |
| **The English Occupation:** | An entry of 1482 in the Books of Lessay referring to Grouville shows *rien reçu 'parce que les dites ysles sont detenues et occupees par les Angloys'.* (ibid. p 35 f) |

Louis XI (1461–1483) son of Charles VII annexed the Dauphiné in the first year of his reign and gradually extended his power over Perpignan, Roussillon, Normandy, and Guyenne. The deaths of the Duke of Burgundy and the Count of Maine endowed him finally with the territories of Burgundy, Picardy and Artois, in the north and east, and Maine in the west.

While the King was busy consolidating his rule, the spectrum of coinage current throughout the country widened to include various gold denominations from Flanders, the Rhinelands, Utrecht and, of course, England (e.g. the *Noble Henry* which was given a value of *63 sols 4 deniers tournois* in 1470), as well as various silver denominations struck by Flanders and Spain; the *'vierlinc'* of Flanders made its appearance at this time – styled *virelans* in French – at 12 *deniers* 1 *obol tournois* value; this coin is the ancestor of the mysterious *'freluque'* which is discussed later.

Charles VIII (1483–1498) married Duchess Anne of Brittany, thereby annexing this Duchy to the crown, and continued the same style of coinage as his father. An interesting coin which he introduced (in 1488) was the *karolus* or *dizain* (for 10 *d.t.*) which can be called a real coin of account. The separate development of the Franco-Italian series (following Charles VIII's march into Italy) should not concern us here.

*Fig. 79: Billon* Karolus *or* dizain *introduced by Charles VIII in 1488.*
Obv. *KAROLVS: FRANCORVM: REX round crowned K and two* lis; *Rev. SIT NOMEN etc. Struck in Rouen (Ciani 814).*

In the Cambridge University Library, there is a quarto manuscript handbook, put together by a certain Nicholas Tyery. It is largely a list of coins in circulation in France in the early 16th century, to which Tyery added an address to Henry VIII of England; he asks to be granted office to have struck *'au pays Dirhelande* [Ireland] *et en ses aultres isles hors du pays Dangleterre monnoyes dor et dargent selon les especes et pourtraictz* [portraits] *que ledict humble supplian a faict figurer et paindre pour presenter honorablement a la digne et magnifique ... Roy Dangleterre ...'.*

That Tyery was really one of Henry VIII's mint-masters is disputed. Whoever he was, he was the first to have the idea that Jersey should have a coinage of its own; after the figures for Tyery's proposed Irish coins, there follows a design for

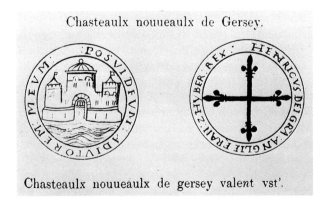

*Fig. 80: Jersey's earliest pattern piece.*

*The unfinished and confused quarto manuscript (Ff. 2. 22 in the University Library) was printed in Cambridge University Society Octavo Publications XXII; BNJ Vol 33 (1964). This illustration appears among those for Tyery's 'proposed coinage for Ireland'.*

a silver *'Chasteaulx nouveaulx de Gersey'* to be worth *'vst'* (presumably 5 *sous tournois*). This 'pattern', 3 centimetres in diameter, is described below:

*Obverse:* HENRICVS DEI GRA: ANGLIE FRAN: Z HYBER: REX:
round a large cross fleurdelysée
*Reverse:* POSVI DEVM: ADIVTOREM: MEVM:
round a stylized castle with a central keep and two towers, waves in foreground

It is not known if the address was ever received by the King and no coin has ever turned up with this design. One wonders if the design for the castle was not taken from Richard Popinjay's 'Platte of Jersey' of 1563, which featured a miniature drawing of Mont Orgeuil which might have served as the model.

On the death of Charles VIII of France, the throne passed to Louis d'Orléans who became Louis XII (1497–1515). After his coronation he separated from his first wife and married Charles' widow thereby finally integrating Brittany into France in 1499. His conquests in Italy resulted in a very extensive series of Franco-Italian coins which is interesting to the extent that the style of many of his coins was strongly influenced by the Renaissance. In France, the denominations were similar to those of previous reigns, with the *ludovicus* or *dizain* substituting the *karolus* of Charles VIII and the silver coinage in general acquiring a real intrinsic value rather than the nominated worth which it had had up to then. A *douzain* or *'grand blanc au porc-épic'* (porcupine) of this King has been found in Jersey. Day-to-day commercial transactions continued to be measured in *doubles* and *deniers tournois*.

When François I (1515–1547) came to the throne the only gold denominations which were struck were the *écu* and the *demi-écu;* these coins which are known to have circulated in the Channel Islands, were of many standards, weights and values. To control the issue better, the King instituted a new series of mint-marks (A = Paris, B = Rouen etc.) for the old 'secret' system (of dots, annulets, crescents etc., under or over letters). The only silver coins which this King issued were the *teston* and the *demi-teston;* the *blanc (douzain* and *dizain* – the former was mentioned as current in an Act of the Island of Jersey of 16.1.1537) and minor coins were made, as before, of a very poor billon, while the *hardi, liard, double tournois* and *denier tournois* were styled *'monnaie noire'.* Coins of previous reigns continued to circulate in the Islands and, in an order of the Royal Court of Guernsey dated 21.1.1537, the *carolusis (karolus or dizain)* of Charles VIII was assigned a value of 12 *deniers tournois;* it had the same value in Jersey. In the same order, the *vache,* a base silver coin of Béarn (of which the symbol was a cow), was valued at 3 *liards* (12 *deniers tournois* in the Islands); coins of this French Viscounty in the Pyrhenees are known to have circulated in the Islands at this time. In 1948 I was given one which had been ploughed up in St. Saviour's

*Fig. 81: Base silver* blanc *of Béarn, found in Jersey.*
*This is one of the series of coins struck by the Kings of Navarre, in this case Henri d'Albret, for Béarn; the legends are difficult to interpret. Two cows are just visible on the* obverse.

Parish, Jersey. There is also mention of *'les bons patacs'*; the *patac* was the *denier* of Provence. Two groats of Henry VIII of England, François I's contemporary, are preserved in the Gorey Castle Museum.

In an order of the Royal Court of Guernsey dated 21.3.1535 it was decreed that no one should coin *'freluques'* in future. The word *freluque* is enigmatic but is believed by some to have come from the medieval French word *'ferlin'* or *'frelin'* (from medieval Latin *ferlingus*), which is an etymological cousin of the Dutch *'vierlinc'* or farthing. Some billon *deniers* and *doubles* of Henry II were similar in style and size, and it is likely that the *'freluques'* being coined in Guernsey at this time were imitations of one of those coins – probably the double tournois. References to *freluques* in two later orders of 1619 and 1623 (see below) seem to confirm this. Frank le Maistre's *Dictionnaire Jersiais-Français* mentions the word in various forms: *ferluque* in old Jersey Texts; *freluque* more recently; and *furluque* used in the east of the Island. Other etymologists link the word *freluque* with *freluche,* meaning frivolous, an abbreviation of *franfreluche,* which came from the Italian *fanfaluca* apparently a corruption of the Greek πομφόλυξ, a bubble. The sense of frivolous, lightweight or bogus attached itself easily to a coin for which nobody had much respect; the same root provided *frelater* (to mix) and *frêle* (weak). In 16th century England the threehalfpence was nicknamed 'dandiprat' which had very much the same meaning. William Fleetwood elaborated: 'There were also little Pieces coined by Henry VII called Dandypratts, which, I suppose, were little and contemptible things, because that word has since been used to signifie small and worthless People'.

The short, violent reign of Henry II of France (1547–1559) is significant in that, while all the frontiers of the Kingdom were being defended against a plethora of enemies, a quiet revolution was going on at the Royal Mint in Paris: coins began to be struck by mechanical means. The machinery was installed in 1551 in the Monnaie du Moulin, one hundred years before Pierre Blondeau, a Frenchman, was to commence the new process at the Tower Mint in London. Very soon the style of French coinage was to improve beyond any comparison.

The *écus* of this King were valued at 45 *s.t.* and then, when the new issue featuring the King's head appeared, at 46 *s.t.*, with the *demi-écus* and *quarts-d'écus* at values pro rata. *Doubles-henris* (only known as *essais*) and *demi-henris* were also introduced with the *henri d'or*. Silver *testons* and *demi-testons* were issued and billon *gros de Nesle* (and *demi-gros de Nesle*) were named after the Hotel de Nesle where they were struck. The *douzain,* containing exactly 12 *deniers,* represented exactly one *sol tournois,* and *sixains* or *demi-sols* were also struck.

From 1549, both the *gros d'argent* and the English groat seem to have played an important part in the currency of the Channel Islands and the *'noble henry'* was mentioned frequently in contemporary documents. In 1551 the *teston* was valued in Jersey at 9 shillings and the gros *tournois* at 3 shillings; in England in 1553, 9 *deniers tournois* could be exchanged for one English penny. In January of the same year the Royal Court in Guernsey authorized one Collas de Guillemotte to strike *'enseignes de pallyn'* – coins (if they were coins) which

*Fig. 82: Anglo-Gallic jetton of the 15th century.*
Obv. + *ME · MEN · TO · DOMINE · MEI*; Rev. *AVEMARIA · GRASIA ·PENA [for PLENA]*
*(Feuardent,* Jetons et méreaux . . . 11548).

have hitherto defied identification. They may have been imitations of the continental jetton or *méreau;* the former was used for reckoning or gaming, the latter was employed in religious institutions. Both are believed to have circulated as currency in times of extreme shortage of change, between 1300 and 1600. Two such jettons were discovered in 1977 in a garden in St. Anne's High Street, Alderney. One was the work of Hans Krauwinckel of Nuremberg, one of the most prolific 16th century jetton manufacturers.

The short reign of François II (1559–1560) was significant for the fine Franco-Scottish coins following his marriage to Mary Stewart. His young brother Charles IX (1560–1574) was eleven years old when he assumed the throne and, as had happened so often before, the Regency – this time shared between his mother Catherine de Médicis and Antoine de Navarre – led to uneasiness in the realm, which was exacerbated by the beginnings of the strife between the Catholics and Protestants. The currency suffered accordingly and there were no innovations except for a *sol parisis* – an anachronism now that the *sol tournois* and *douzain* had become identical. The lower denominations of this reign were, largely, hand-struck. And the quality of all coins, compared to the previous reign,

*Fig. 83: Charles IX:* billon *gros de six blancs, 1569.*
*Ciani 1376; mintmark D = Lyon.*

left much to be desired. One of the few indications of the cost of living index in the Islands at this time was when the price of cider in Jersey was fixed at one *esterlin* the pot on 20.2.1561. A sixpence of Queen Elizabeth of England, found at Gorey, Jersey, provides evidence that English coins were also circulating at the time. A silver coin of Antoine de Bourbon and Jeanne d'Albret, King and Queen of Navarre, Duke and Duchess of Béarn (c. 1562) was also found at Gorey Castle; Antoine was to be the father of Henry IV of France.

Henry III (1574–1589), brother of Charles IX, was King of Poland when Charles died. He abandoned Poland and returned to a divided and chaotic country. While he was laying siege to Paris with Henry of Navarre, he was assassinated by a fanatical member of the Catholic League. During his reign the silver *franc* substituted the *teston* at 20 *s.t.*; *demi-francs* and *quarts de francs* were also struck as were *quarts d'écu* (at 15 *s.t.*) and *huitièmes d'écu* (at 7 *s.* 6 *d.*). For the first

*Fig. 84:* Double *and* denier tournois *of Henry III, the first issues in Copper.*
Ciani 1465, 1473.

time copper was employed for the *doubles* and *deniers tournois;* many copper coins of the period, both *doubles* and *deniers tournois,* have been discovered in the Islands.

*Fig. 85: Silver penny of Elizabeth I of England.*
Obv. R · DG · ROSA · SINE · SPINA *(a rose without a thorn);* Rev. CIVITAS LONDON; *mintmark: tun = 1592-5 (Seaby 2580).*

At Michaelmas time in the year 1581, the Royal Court in Guernsey ordered that 'Her Majesty's [Queen Elizabeth I] Receiver and others are to receive the coins named below at the values attached:

| | |
|---|---|
| French Crown | at 20 silver groats |
| Flemish Crown | at 19 ½ silver groats |
| *Pistole* | at 19 silver groats |
| Double Ducat | at 14 sols [shillings] sterling |
| *Double Millerays\** | at 14 sols sterling |

\* (There is some mystery about this coin as the larger denomination current in Portugal at the time was the *'São Vicente'* worth *1000 reais;* a countermarked gold *2000 reais* is known, dated 1582).
*Noble Henry* of France at 14 sols sterling
*Croizade* [Portuguese *cruzado* – little cross] at 20 ½ groats
Ditto cross *potence* [a slightly lighter coin] at 20 groats

Poll head [possibly a papal coin; base silver papal coins of the period are known to have been found in the Islands] at 15 groats
*Real* of Spain at 6½d sterling.'

A year later (Michaelmas 1582), the official values in Guernsey of the French Crown, the Flemish Crown, the *cruzado* and the *pistolet (pistole)* had all fallen by half a groat or two English pence. The values of coins current in Guernsey were again fixed by the Royal Court in January 1586 as follows:

'French Gold Crown at 19½ gros of silver
Flemish crown at 1 *sol tournois* less than the *Ecu au soleil*
Pistolet at 2 *sols tournois* less than the *Ecu au soleil*
Frank at 6 silver *gros* (if of full weight)
Half-Frank at 3 silver *gros*
Quarter crown at 4½ *gros*
Half-quarter crown at 2¼ *gros*
*Teston* of France at 17 *deniers*.'

Until quite recently the *pistole* was used as a money of account (10 *francs*) in Normandy. A Guernsey Ordinance of 21st January 1586, which also gave values in *tournois* of certain of the above coins, decreed that French money should continue current; the authorities had no alternative.

On his death-bed, Henry III had named Henry of Navarre as his successor. However, the Catholics would not recognize the new sovereign and Charles Cardinal de Bourbon (1589–1590) had the doubtful honour of being chosen as King and of having coins struck for him while in captivity. Effectively, he never ruled, but died while still in captivity one year after 'acceding'. Coins in his name (Charles X) were struck in Brittany for eight years after his death.

Recognized as King of France in 1589, Henry of Navarre had to reconquer practically the whole country before he became King in anything but name. Having re-established the civil peace he turned his attention to the religious turmoil and, in the Edict of Nantes of 1589, guaranteed the Protestants liberty of conscience in the whole country. After successfully reorganising many aspects of the economy, including monetary matters, he was assassinated while preparing a campaign against the Holy Roman Empire and Spain. At least one base silver coin of Pope Clement VIII of Avignon, dated to 1597, has been found in Jersey.

Henry's coinage was very similar to that of the previous reign and he continued the copper issues. While the gold, silver and billon coinages were hand-struck,

*Fig. 86: Machine-struck copper* double tournois *of Henry IV. Ciani 1576.*

the copper *doubles* and *deniers tournois* were struck in enormous quantities by machine. In 1605 it is recorded that French coins not worn out such as 1/2 crowns, 1/4 crowns, *testons* and *1/2 testons, francs* and *1/4 francs,* were to be received in Guernsey at the rate of 64 *sols* to the crown; Spanish *reals* were held to be worth 5 *deniers*. Incidentally, in 1604, two new copper denominations, the 'turner' and 'half-turner', were minted for Scotland, taking their name from the *tournois* system.

On 20.7.1607, following an approach by the Governor of Jersey, King James I appointed a Commission under Sir Robert Gardiner to determine (among other things) the different values of currency in the Island; the Commission also had scope as regards Guernsey.

*Fig. 87: Silver penny of James I of England.*
Obv. I · D · G · ROSA · SINE · SPINA ·; mintmark: thistle = 1603-4.

The first article of complaint by the Governor concerned the value of French coins. In those days there was little English coin in circulation and, strictly speaking, no fixed standard of value in Jersey. The *livre tournois* (as has been shown above) could scarcely be called a standard of value, and yet it was employed to measure the market price of all commodities important in the Island's economy. It was the currency in which accounts were kept. Current money was French and any variation in the value of this currency, compared to the *livre tournois,* would have to be regulated.

The States of Jersey, a few years before the arrival of the Commission, seeing that the King of France had altered and revalued his coins, established what they considered an equivalent value between the new coins and the money in Jersey current at the old rates. The difference was about 7%. The French crown was revalued by 4 *sous*, the *guardesen* from 15 to 16 *sous*, the *teston* from 14½ to 15½ *sous*, and the *franc* from 20 *sous* to 21 *sous* 4 *deniers tournois*. The only money in circulation was French and the Governor claimed the payments due to the Crown at the old rate.

The Commissioners were of a different opinion, claiming that it would be no prejudice to his Majesty or to the Governor if the moneys were received at the new rates; besides (said the Commissioners) it would be 'a great contentment' to the people of the Island to pay the same after the rate or value at which they had received it; but as the Commissioners considered that it was 'a prerogative of the Crown to diminish, alter or advance any moneys current among his own subjects', they ordered that the relative value of the moneys should continue as regulated by the States 'until His Majesty's pleasure be known what other course and order in times to come shall be held and kept therein'. This decision of the

Commissioners was confirmed by the Lords, but it is added in the order 'that in time to come, because it is a prerogative of His Majesty, and only appertaineth to royal right, to diminish alter or advance any moneys current among his subjects, we require that this be not until his Majesty's express consent be thereunto had and obtained' (see Le Quesne, p 225).

*Fig. 88: Above: liard of Henry IV of France. Below: contemporary imitation.*
*The official issue of this liard, called the 'Pied-Gailloux', is scarcely more presentable than the imitation (Ciani 1574).*

It was at this monetarily chaotic time, when there were countless different denominations circulating throughout Europe, in varying degrees of adulteration, that the paths of money and banking crossed. After many hundreds of years, weighing came back into vogue. The Bank of Amsterdam, set up in 1609 under the guarantee of that city, declared itself ready to receive all types of coin – however adulterate – at its *real intrinsic* value, and to give credit for the net value of the coin after deduction of coinage and management expenses. The example of the Bank of Amsterdam was emulated in other European centres and the standards of coinage steadily improved.

Louis XIII (1610–1643) – nine years old when he took on the throne of France – survived various intrigues before he enjoined Cardinal Richelieu to become his Prime Minister. Richelieu, a brilliant statesman, reformed many aspects of French life including the army, legislation, and finances. He was the creator of

*Fig. 89: The* denier *and* double tournois *(two types) of Louis XIII.*
*Doubles: Ciani 1718 (by Briot), Ciani 1724 (by Warin). Denier: Ciani 1725.*

the *Académie Française*. This marriage of authority and art under a liberal King, led to some beautiful coins being produced – many as *essai* pieces – by Nicholas Briot, Jean Warin and Guillaume Dupré. Many gold and silver coins continued to be struck by hand while the copper coins – in even greater quantities – were machine struck.

A new denomination, the *louis d'or,* was struck with a value of 10 *livres tournois;* one of these coins was discovered some years ago in St. Mary's Parish, Jersey, and is now in the Société Jersiaise Museum. A *double louis* and a *demi-louis* were also struck with pro rata values in *livres tournois*. Pieces of 4, 8 and 10 gold *louis* are also known. In 1641 the King ordered the production of a *louis d'argent* or *pièce de 60 sols (tournois),* known as the *écu blanc*. One such coin dated 1643, was found in a garden in St. Peter's Jersey in 1970. Similar silver pieces of *30, 15* and *5 sols* were also produced – the whole series being machine-struck. The *douzain* of billon continued to be produced as was the *sizain,* and *pièce de quinze deniers*. Copper *doubles* and *deniers tournois* were joined by *doubles lorrains*. The Franco-Spanish issues of Louis XIII are outside the scope of this study.

In 1619, many unauthorized persons in Guernsey having coined *freluques,* this practice was forbidden under pain of public whipping *'jusqu'à effusion de sang'*. Four years later, the Normans having sent to Guernsey a quantity of *deniers tournois,* which they were passing for *doubles,* the Governor was asked to appoint a person to coin *freluques;* this reference strongly suggests that the *freluques* were imitation *doubles tournois,* obviously in short supply in the Islands.

In an attempt to solve the mystery of the *freluque,* I have analysed a small group of sixteen early 17th century *doubles tournois* in my possession, six of which were found in Jersey at different times (marked J):

| No. | Minting authority | Date | Condition | Diameter mm | Weight gm |
| --- | --- | --- | --- | --- | --- |
| 1 | Louis XIII | 1612 | VF | 20.0 | 2.54 |
| 2 | Louis XIII | 1613 | VF | 20.0 | 3.33 |
| J 3 | Louis XIII | 1615 | Poor but legible | 19.8 | 2.34 |
| 4 | Louis XIII | 1616 | VF | 20.5 | 3.21 |
| 5 | Louis XIII | 1616 | VF | 20.3 | 2.64 |
| J 6 | Louis XIII | illegible | Poor | 19.4 | 2.45 |
| 7 | Louis XIII | 1621 | VF | 20.4 | 2.83 |
| 8 | Louis XIII (Warin head) | 1642 | VF | 19.1 | 2.51 |
| 9 | Louis XIII (Warin head) | 1643 | VF | 19.5 | 2.04 |
| 10 | Gaston de Dombes | 1641 | VF | 20.5 | 2.95 |
| J 11 | Gaston de Dombes | 1641 | Fair | 20.2 | 2.14 |
| 12 | Charles de Gonzague, Nevers | 1610 | F | 21.0 | 2.40 |
| J 13 | Fréderic Maurice, Sedan | c. 1623 | Fair (off centre) | 19.4 | 2.07 |
| 14 | Charles I, Arches (Charleville) | illegible | Poor | 20.0 | 2.40 |
| J 15 | ? imitation of Sedan or Arches | illegible | Poor | 17.7 | 0.99 |
| J 16 | illegible | illegible | Poor, bent | 18.6 | 1.27 |

The average weight of numbers 1–14 is 2.56 gm; numbers 15 and 16 are therefore significantly below the average. No 15 is of particular interest as part of the legend on one side (D)OUBLE D (... is clearly discernible). The only explanation for the elusive nature of the freluque, which was apparently so common, is that the type must be included among other clearly recognized types. Defective weight such as is the case with numbers 15 and 16 above is the most likely clue; and these two coins – particularly number 15 – seem to be reasonable 'candidates' in the identification parade.

In 1626 an Order of the Royal Court of Guernsey stated that 'the Island being flooded with foreign *doubles,* no one shall be compelled to take more of them then the value of 2 *sous tournois* per crown of the money to be paid to him'.

Two further Orders, this time of the States of Guernsey relate to this flood of light French coin. On 3.2.1640 it had been ordered that all such coins should pass for their nominal value without weighing. However this latter Order was followed closely by another dated 26.2.1640 to the effect that, contrary to the previous Order, the said coin should be weighed, 'as is done in Normandy'.

On 9.8.1646 the States of Guernsey complained that, whereas by their ancient customs they were allowed in Guernsey to pay all dues to the King in such money as was current in Normandy, the Governor and his Deputy had insisted on continuing to pay such French money as they had in their possession after it had been recalled, and would no longer pass in Normandy. Nothing more is known of the circumstances of this complaint but it should not be overlooked that Guernsey at that time – only a few months before Charles I was to lose his head – lost no opportunity to criticize his Royalist representatives in the Island. A more significant date in this study, however, was 4th January 1649, when the States of Guernsey ordained 'that the English shilling, being worth 12 pence sterling, shall go in this Island for 12 *sols tournois* in payment and receate [receipt], and other species of English money in proportion' – the first time that both currencies had officially circulated together, in theory if not in practice.

*Fig. 90: Charles I tower shilling.*
*Seaby 2785: type 3¹; mintmark: harp = 1632-3.*

According to Berry it maintained its value (i.e. 12 *sols tournois*) until the beginning of the 18th century. Berry also writes (p 117) that 'the old rentals, books of extent, and title-deeds, in Guernsey, mention the following ancient coins, viz.
–

| COIN. | Value in *Livres,* | *Sols,* | *Den.* |
|---|---|---|---|
| *Ecu monée* | 1 | 2 | 0 |
| *Noble ditto* | 2 | 4 | 0 |
| *Gros ditto* | 0 | 2 | 2 |
| *Vingt sols ditto* | 0 | 17 | 3 |
| *Sol ditto* | 0 | 0 | 10 |
| *Etelin* | 0 | 0 | 6 |
| *Noble sterling d'Angleterre* | 3 | 6 | 8 |
| *Ditto de Guernsey* | 3 | 1 | 6 |
| *Sou sterling d'Angleterre* | 0 | 10 | 6 |
| *Ditto de Guernsey* | 0 | 9 | 0 |
| *Gros sterling* or *gros d'argent sterling d'Angleterre* | 0 | 3 | 4 |
| *Gros d'argent, payement de Guernsey* | 0 | 3 | 0 |
| *Denier d'argent* or *denier sterling de Guernsey* | 0 | 1 | 9 |
| *Florin d'Hollande* | 1 | 0 | 0 |
| *Florin d'or d'Hollande* | 1 | 8 | 0 |
| *Denier de gros ditto* | 0 | 0 | 6 |
| *Sol de gros ditto* | 0 | 6 | 0 |
| *Livre de gros ditto* | 6 | 0 | 0 |
| *Franc d'or* | 1 | 2 | 0 |
| *Noble d'or* | 1 | 13 | 0 |
| *Ecu monée, rente seigneurialle* | 1 | 5 | 0 |
| *Denier sterling, payement d'Angleterre* | 0 | 1 | 0 |
| *Obolle* | 0 | 0 | 0½ |

'Besides these [Berry continues], the *noire maille, maille sterling, carolus monée,* and the *maille etling,* have been likewise current in the Island; but the exact value of each cannot now be correctly ascertained.'

In 1632 an early 'Treasure Trove' inquest in Jersey is recorded when

'... *quelques pièces d'or qui furent trouvées à Jersey, dans des murailles de la maison du Sieur Thomas Lemprière, en haut d'une fenestre, lui furent ajugées par la pluralité des opinions de la Cour Royale.*' (Le Geyt, chapter 'Du Thrésor Trouvé')

It is also recorded that a Royal Pardon was received for Maximilian and François Messervy who had been convicted in Jersey of forging *pistoles* and pieces-of-eight, sanction, perhaps, for illegal activities which alleviated the difficulties of the time, caused largely by the shortage of a circulating medium.

Louis XIV (1643–1715) succeeded his father when he was five years old, and, under the stewardship of Cardinal Mazarin, peace was maintained in Europe at large. However Mazarin was more of a diplomat than a statesman and, internally, France went through a difficult time. The consequent sufferings of the Royal Exchequer did not hinder Mazarin from making a considerable personal fortune. After Mazarin's death in 1661, Louis XIV began to rule in his own name – a reign characterized by the reinforcement of the royal 'absolutism' begun under Richelieu, the politics of glory, and grandiose constructions and events. Wars against Spain and Holland were entertained under the glorious guidance of Louis who had married Maria Theresia of Austria; battles were won and lost, territories were gained (e.g. Flanders) and surrendered (e.g. Newfoundland) and the Edict of Nantes was revoked, with appalling persecutions ensuing. The arts flourished, and names like Racine, Molière and La Rochefoucauld were born; Versailles was built.

Against this background, and under the guidance of Colbert, Controller General of Finance, perfect order was established at the 30 or so mints which struck coins for the King. During the reign the *écu d'or* was finally replaced by the *lis d'or* (of greater mass); the *louis d'or, double louis* and *demi louis* continued to be issued. Throughout the long reign the silver *écu* (worth 60 *sols* or 3 *livres tournois*) and its fractions survived, with varying designs. A new coin, the *lis d'argent* (worth one *livre tournois*) began to circulate with its own fractions the *demis-lis* and the *quart de lis*. Smaller denominations of four and two *sols* also circulated in addition to a few minor billon coins; copper coins consisted of the faithful *denier, double tournois, liard de trois deniers, quatre deniers,* and *six deniers* – the small change of the period.

The *liard,* whose value was diminished by one *denier* in 1658, became the successor of the *double*. Because of its value (2 *deniers*) it was referred to more often as a *'double'* than by its correct style. I have examined quite a number of *liards,* which are often discovered in the soil of the Channel Islands, having been the staple small currency for well over a hundred years. I have not yet seen any which were more deficient in weight than their generally poor condition would justify.

*Fig. 91:* Liard *of Louis XIV.*
*Ciani 2012.*

# The Jersey Mint

Perhaps the greatest enigma which faces students of Channel Island coinage is the documented but hitherto unsubstantiated story of the Royalist Mint which functioned in Jersey for some months in the mid-seventeenth century.

*Fig. 92: 'Adulterate money, halfecrowne-peices', a phrase from Sir Edward Hyde's letter. See Bibliography.*

The story is studded with famous names, such as Jersey's Lieutenant-Governor, George (later Sir George) Carteret, who plays a leading role with the Prince of Wales (later Charles II). The supporting cast includes Sir Edward Hyde (later Lord Clarendon), Royalist Chancellor of the Exchequer, Sir Edward Nicholas, Secretary of State, and John Ashburnham, Royalist Member of Parliament for Hastings, who became treasurer and paymaster of the King's army. John Digby, first Earl of Bristol, diplomatist, statesman, and a staunch Royalist, was in Exeter when that city capitulated to Fairfax in 1646, and arrived in Jersey on 27th April of that year, ten days after Prince Charles. Lord Culpeper (with whom Hyde always found time to quarrel) was Master of the Rolls.

Ralph, Lord Hopton was one of the King's most prominent supporters in the Commons, and an able military commander. He was appointed one of the councillors of the Prince of Wales when the latter was sent to the West Country; and it was intended that he should take up the post of Lieutenant-General of the Prince's army but this scheme fell through owing to a rival's intrigue. The unfortunate Hopton seems to have been particularly prone to intrigues throughout his career, and this may have prompted Hyde's remarks in the last paragraph of his letter (see below). In 1643, Sir Ralph had despatched a vessel to the Channel Islands to support and encourage the Royalist cause.

Star of the cast is a certain Colonel William Smyth, son of Robert Smyth (who died for the King in 1645). Though originally supporting the Parliamentarians, Colonel Smyth joined the Royalist cause in 1643 and was captured at Hillesden House near Oxford together with Sir Alexander Denton, whose daughter, Margaret, he married in 1644. According to the Verney Memoirs, Smyth escaped from his Roundhead captors and was not – as recorded by Hyde – exchanged for an unknown Irish Councillor.

Jean Chevalier, in his *'Journal et Receuil des Chosses les plus remarcables q se sont passes en ceste Isle de Jersey',* bequeathed us a firsthand account, in considerable detail, of the Island of Jersey as a Royalist stronghold in the mid-17th century. He provided us with valuable information of the life of 'Captain' George Carteret, and of the protection he afforded to the then Prince of Wales. Carteret had, previously, so distinguished himself that Charles I granted him in 1643 the Fiefs of the manors of Melesches, Grainville and Noirmont and various other rights, in return for an annual *rente* of £ 6–13–4 Jersey money, payable in equal amounts at the feast of St. Michael of the Archangel and the Annunciation of the Blessed Virgin Mary.

Twice in his *Journal,* Chevalier made mention of the brief and questionable career of a certain Colonel Smyth as Master of the Mint in Jersey. The Prince of Wales, having recently fled from the Scilly Isles to Jersey, had, wrote Chevalier, 'found fit with the advice of his court to have money of silver and gold coined . . . as they had great expenses in Jersey through the supplying of frigates in their charge, the frequent movement of men from one place to another, the victualling of many fighting men and the construction of forts and fortifications . . .' Evidently the Mint in Jersey was established for the same reasons as were the other Royalist emergency Mints of the 1640's. The Mints from York to Bristol and Shrewsbury to Oxford enabled Charles I to continue his war effort to the bitter end. The Jersey Mint has, however, never been listed among recognized Royalist Mints for want of anything better than documentary evidence that it ever existed.

Chevalier, in an entry between 9th and 14th June 1646, tells us that the house of a certain Michel le Guerdain, in Trinity Parish, was prepared and fitted out with furnaces 'to smelt silver and strike coins'. The house has been identified with the property called la Guerdainerie in Trinity Parish which the owner allowed me to visit some years ago.

*Fig. 93: La Guerdainerie, now 'The Old Mint', Jersey.*
*Photograph taken by the late E. Huelin in 1968.*

I was informed that extensive alterations had been undertaken some months before (early in 1967) in that part of the house where the Mint is supposed to have been sited, and the most likely location (the cellar) had subsequently been filled in and covered over with concrete. A workman did report that he had seen 'a beam studded with silver coins' before he buried it (but apparently, after he had learned the history of the building!) and a few 'copper blanks' had been found at various times but, unhappily, mislaid; (these, from their description, may have been well-worn examples of the *denier tournois,* often found in the Island).

It may or may not be a coincidence that Aaron Guerdain (Michel's eldest son) was appointed Master of the Mint by Parliament in London on 16th May, 1649. Guerdain held the post until 1660, having taken over from Sir Robert Harley, who had refused to remove King Charles' head from the coin of the realm. By 1662 he appears to have added the duties of 'Melter' to his official title of Master-Worker of the Monies. He died in 1676. Thomas Violet, a sometime commentator on Mint affairs, perhaps threw some light on Dr. Guerdain's qualifications when he wrote, 'it is beside the study of doctors of physic to be Mint Masters, and the State had better give them ten times as much salary and let them do nothing' – a comment, however, which brings us no closer to the reason why la Guerdainerie was selected for Smyth.

'The name of the Master of the Mint', wrote Chevalier, 'was Master Smyth'; and, in a later entry, he recorded that Colonel Smyth, Master of the Prince's Mint, had been a man of considerable means in England, a Privy Councillor of the King and then Colonel of a Company in the King's army. At some period during the Civil War he was made Master of one of the King's Mints, though, at this stage, we don't know which Mint Chevalier was referring to. After the defeat of the Kings's army Smyth left for France and thence came to Jersey.

Chevalier provides us with considerable details of the coins actually struck at the Jersey Mint: – 'They coined', we gather from his first entry, 'Halfcrown pieces of England, called St. Georges, which they put [into circulation] at 30 sous' – there was engraved on the one side the King on horseback with a sword in his hand, and on the other the harp, roses, fillets [fizez in the original French text], interlaced crosses, and the other devices on the King's coin; they [also] made a few shillings and some 20 shilling gold pieces – all legal tender in England'.

About a year later, Chevalier confirmed his first description in a second entry dated 20th May 1647: '[Colonel Smyth] minted money in Jersey such as English halfcrowns which they put [into circulation] in Jersey at 30 sous each; these were on the one side engraved with the same design as English coin, and on the other with a portrait of the King on horseback holding a sword in his hand; they also coined a few shillings and a good number of Jacobus before their departure for France . . .' The Jacobus was the gold sovereign or 'unite' (20 shilling piece) of James I, the value of which had risen to about 24 shillings in 1647.

Although it is difficult to guess at the designs of the shillings and 20 shillings pieces (we can only assume they were of a recognised type still current in England), Chevalier has given us a very adequate description of the halfcrowns minted. They were obviously similar to those issued at the Tower Mint under

King Charles and also to those issued at several emergency Mints, including York, Aberystwyth, Shrewsbury, Worcester, Chester, Truro and Exeter. The obverse design of the King on horseback is common to all such halfcrowns. On the reverse, 'the harp, ... fillets, interlaced crosses, and other devices' is a fair enough description; (the crosses, could either refer to the lines dividing and sub-dividing the shield, or to the cruceiform *fleurs-de-lis*).

The mention of roses, however, allows us to be more specific. Roses were only twice a feature of Charles I halfcrowns, each time as a mintmark: on those struck at the Tower Mint in the years 1631–2 and on those struck between 1642 and 1646 in Truro and Exeter; we may safely assume that Chevalier was not referring to the rose which appeared on the housings of the King's mount on some Tower halfcrowns, as he specifically stated that the roses appeared on the reverse.

Dr. Hoskins in his book 'Charles II in the Channel Islands', relates the story of Colonel Smyth in some detail, and gives an account of his departure for France after the mint had failed, apparently through mismanagement and scarcity of bullion. 'Smyth', he writes, '... was forced to dispose not only of his household goods, but the greater part of the machinery, reserving merely the dies he had brought with him'. It seems that Hoskins based his book to a large extent on Chevaliers' diary; but in the latter's account of Smyth's departure we read that 'they sold all their small utensils and the tools which they used, reserving only the dies which they took with them ('... *les quels ils en porterent'*). If we take it that Hoskins based his account on this very similar passage of Chevalier, it is apparent that he reached his assumption that Smyth had brought the dies with him to Jersey, through an unfortunate slip in his translation of the original French text. However, in the absence of any indication that the dies were engraved in Jersey, Hoskins' assumption was a reasonable one. Five years later Sir George Carteret himself shed some light on this subject when he wrote to a friend at the Hague (letter preserved in the Nicholas Papers): 'I know not what those false tongues in Holland mean by my keeping false-coiners' tools, for, having examined what they left in the island, I can learn but of a pair of bellows and two or three pieces of iron, which I think are of no use for that trade. I am little beholden, nor the King neither, to those that brought them to the island, and yet less to those that slander me with it'.

Perhaps the most important sentence in Chevalier's account occurs during his description of Smyth's departure: '... *ils fidrent* [entrusted or made] *de la monnos'*, he writes mysteriously, *'de quoy Je me tais'*. Is it too far-fetched to conclude that Chevalier, who had already given us an adequate description of one of the coins struck, was offended by something which went beyond purely technical problems such as mismanagement or scarcity of bullion? Can we assume that the technical difficulties mentioned were the real cause for the Mint's failure, or had there been some sort of fraudulent activity involving a betrayal of trust – betrayal perhaps of the Prince's trust? If this were the case, we could be sure that a contemporary diarist, such as Chevalier – a royalist to the core – would have given such a situation as little mention as was absolutely necessary to fulfil his duty as diarist, while avoiding damage to the Prince's cause through undue publicity. The passing of false money was incidentally by no means unknown in the Island; Chevalier had previously recorded that a certain Maximilian Messervy, already arrested and pardoned for such an offence, had subsequently been executed for disloyalty to the King.

To my knowledge the last person to deal in any detail with this subject was the late Helen Farquhar in her article 'A lost coinage in the Channel Islands'. Miss Farquhar quoted extensively from a letter of February 1646 from Sir Edward Hyde, then Chancellor of the Exchequer, to Sir Edward Nicholas, Secretary of State. Hyde had remained in Jersey after the departure of Prince Charles from Jersey in June 1646. The latter part of this letter throws much light on Chevalier's mysterious motives for 'keeping silent'. The letter which is dated 'Jerseye y$^e$ 24th of Febr 1646' deals, in the first instance, with many affairs of State and mutual friends, and continues

> '... I will tell you a Tale of w$^{ch}$ it may bee you may know somewt; if you doe not, take noe [now or new] notice of it from mee: When we were in Cornwall, Colonel Smyth (who was Sr. Alexander Denton's Sonne-in-Law, and taken in y$^e$ House) hauing obtayned his Liberty by J. Ashburnham's friendship upon such an Exchange (one of y$^e$ Councillo$^{rs}$ of Ireland) as would haue redeemed y$^e$ best man, came to us from y$^e$ King at Hereford. To mee hee brought a short perfunctory lre from my L$^d$ Digby, but from J.A. [John Ashburnham] to my L$^d$ Culpeper his dispatch was of weight, his buisinesse to erect a Mint: at Truro, w$^{ch}$ should yeild the King a vast profitt, Mr. Browne J.A.$^s$ man (who was long a Prysoner) w$^{th}$ him; The King's dues by a speciall Warrant (w$^{ch}$ I saw) to bee payd to Mr. Ashburnham; What hee did in Cornwall I know not, for you perceiue hee was to haue noe relacon or reference to mee, w$^{ch}$ if you had been Chancello$^r$ of the Excheq$^r$, you would haue taken unkindly; Shortly after the Prince came hither hee came to us, hauing left Cornwall a fortnight before wee did; you must imagine my L$^d$ Culpeper was forward to helpe him and here hee proposed to sett up his Mynt, and assured us, that hee had contracted w$^{th}$ Merchants at St. Malloe to bring in such a quantity of Bullyon as would make y$^e$ Revenue very considerable to y$^e$ Prince. We wondered why the Merchants of St. Malloe should desire to haue English money coyned, hee gaue us an answer y$^t$ appeared uery reasonable, that all y$^e$ Trade they droue w$^{th}$ the West Country for Tynne, ffish, or Wool, was driuen w$^{th}$ money, that therefore they sent ouer their Pistolls, and their livres, and peices of eight, in w$^{ch}$ they sustayned soe great a losse, that those Merchants had rather haue their Bullyon coyned into English money at 20 in the hundred [i.e. a loss of 20%], then [than] take y$^e$ other way; after seuall debates, in w$^{ch}$ (though there seemed noe convincing Argum$^t$ to exspect great profitt from it) there was not y$^e$ least suggestion of inconuenience, hee pretending y$^t$ hee had all Officers ready at St. Malloe, and such as belonged to y$^e$ King's Mynt, and likewise his Com$^n$ under y$^e$ great Seale (for hee $^p$duced only y$^e$ warrant under the Signe Manuall) The Prince writt a lre to y$^e$ Governo$^r$, Bayliffe, and Jurates to give him countenance, and to assigne him some convenient place to reside in; Shortly after the Prince went away, the Colonell proceedes, brings his Wife hither (who in truth is a sober woman) and takes a little house, remote from Neighbours, but pretended y$^t$ the Prince his remoue & other accidents had hindered the advance of y$^e$ seruice; but y$^t$ hee hoped hereafter to proceede in it. Here hee liued soberly and reseruedly, and after two or three moneths here was found adulterate money, halfecrowne-peices, w$^{ch}$ had been put off by people belonging to him; one only Officer hee hath, an old Catholique, one Vaughan, who is a good Graver, but his all. The Governo$^r$ (who is strangely ciuill to all men, but imoderately to such Gentlemen as haue seemed to serue the King in this Quarrell) was much perplexed, the ciuill Magistrates here taking notice of it, and sent him to speake w$^{th}$ him, told him y$^t$ hee beleiued his Educacon had not been to such Artifices, and y$^t$ hee might bee easily deceiued by the man hee trusted, who was not of crediit enough to beare y$^t$ burthen of such a trust, that if this Island fell into suspicon of such crafts, their Trade would bee undone, and therefore (hauing shewed him some peices of money) desired him by noe meanes to

proceede in y$^t$ designe, till satisfaction might bee giuen by the view of such Officers who were responsible for it; The Colonell denyed some of y$^e$ peices to bee of his coyning, but confessed others, and sayd it was by mistake too light; but I had forgott to tell you y$^t$ he had assured mee 2 or 3 dayes before that hee had yet coyned none; to conclude (though much troubled) hee promised y$^e$ Governo$^r$ not to proceede further in it; then hee came to mee; and told mee a long and untoward discourse of a great trust betweene y$^e$ King, Mr. Ashburnham and himselfe, and one more, w$^{ch}$ hee would not name, but let mee to beleiue it was Mr. A' freind at Paris, and y$^t$ the designe originally was to coyne Dollars, by w$^{ch}$ hee could gaine a vast advantage to y$^e$ King; hee found mee not soe ciuill as hee exspected, and therefore easily w$^{th}$drewe, and the same day attempted y$^e$ Governo$^r$ and offered him a strang Weekely Bribe (enough to keepe you and mee, and both our ffamilyes very gallantly) to coyne w$^{th}$ him, and assist him. his reception was not much better there, soe y$^t$ hee hath since procured a good stout l$\bar{\text{r}}$e from y$^e$ Prince, to com̄and y$^e$ Governo$^r$ Bayliffe, and Jurates to giue him all countenance, and to aduance y$^t$ seruice. This will put an end to it, for y$^e$ Governo$^r$ will deale freely w$^{th}$ the Prince, though upon the confidence wee haue still naughty new money, The reason of y$^e$ Governo$^r$ exceeding tendernesse in his duty to the King, to whom such a Com$^n$ (w$^{ch}$ indeede is a strang one) would draw much dishono$^r$. Tell me if you know anything of this, and whether you thinke your freind soe wise and carefull of his Masters hono$^r$ as hee should bee; but beyond this say nothing of it, except to my L$^d$ Hopton who can tell you how scurvy a thing it is.

    I will keepe you noe longer from invoying [unclear in ms] my Lord Hopton, who is as worthy a Man as liues, & hath been as unhansomely used, and yet I thinke is as ready for any gallant Action y$^t$ may aduance the King's seruice, as hee was y$^t$ first day. Pitty mee y$^t$ am now left alone. God of Heaven keepe you, and bring us againe well together.'

We note first from Hyde's letter that Smyth was originally empowered to erect a Mint at Truro.

In her very comprehensive article on 'The Royalist Mints of Truro and Exeter 1642–6' Mary Coate traced the story of first the Truro Mint then the Exeter Mint under the very able stewardship of Sir Richard Vyvyan, who was commissioned to coin money for King Charles I on November 14th, 1642. There is clear evidence of the existence of the Mint in Truro from that date until the capture of Exeter by the Royalists. Sir Richard was made a freeman of the city of Exeter on October 2nd, 1643 and immediately transferred his Mint there. The Mint remained in Exeter until the city was recaptured by Parliament in 1646. Miss Coate 'found no connexion between Vyvyan and Smyth or his graver Vaughan.' But we must keep in mind that Exeter surrendered to Parliament in April 1646, and that this confused period, during which Smyth appeared on the scene, may not have been too well documented. In view of this, perhaps we should not put too sinister an interpretation on Hyde's remark, 'what hee did in Cornwall I know not' . . . – while sympathizing with Hyde in that he, Chancellor of the Royalist Exchequer, was not being kept informed of a matter which so directly concerned him.

'Shortly after the Prince came hither', wrote Hyde from Jersey, 'he came to us, hauing left Cornwall a fortnight before wee did'. We know that the 15 year-old Prince of Wales arrived in Jersey from the Scilly Isles in the *Proud Black Eagle* on April 17th 1646 and can, therefore, safely surmise that Smyth followed him between, say, the end of April and the middle of May 1646 – a supposition which is endorsed by the date of Chevalier's first entry (between 9th and 14th June, 1646).

Was it pure coincidence that Smyth, who had been commissioned to erect – or re-erect – the Mint at Truro (which had been moved to Exeter through force of circumstance), arrived in Jersey so soon after the fall of Exeter?

The story of the merchants of St. Malo Hyde seems to have accepted as being perfectly feasible. Louis XIII of France had after all, planned five years before to convert all foreign monies current in France into coins with his own image; this measure had been designed expressly to counter the large-scale export of good French specie from the country. It was one thing, however, for the French to have such plans, but quite another to sanction such an activity in the name of King Charles I.

Smyth, meanwhile, pretended that 'hee had all Officers ready at St. Malloe, and such as belonged to y$^e$ King's Mynt' – those Officers, Hyde surely meant, who had fled some weeks before from the Mint at Exeter.

Hyde's description of the Colonel's setting up house in Jersey compares with Chevalier's, and sheds little new light on the subject; but the account of the appearance of 'adulterate money' – as poignant a description as Chevalier himself inferred by his silence – 'halfecrowne-peices', – this provides us with the valuable clue that some of the coins were of poor silver or of light weight. Smyth's elaborate plan to re-strike the French Merchants' 'Pistolls, and their livres, and peices of eight' would adequately explain this, as the debasement of continental coinages was a much publicised hazard of commerce in the mid-seventeenth century. Hyde made no mention of the few shillings or twenty shilling gold pieces mentioned by Chevalier; but it is quite possible that so few were struck as to have escaped his notice.

The identity of Smyth's Catholic graver, Vaughan, remains a mystery. There is no evidence that he was employed by Sir Richard Vyvyan, however tempting it is to attribute certain of the Truro and Exeter dies to his 'good Graver'. The spelling of proper names in those days was not too consistent: Samuel Pepys referred in his *Diary,* some fifteen years later, to two famous contemporary engravers, Thomas Simon and John Pottier, as 'Symons' and 'Potyr'. Here it is perhaps worth recalling that the most famous of a contemporary French family of engravers, Jean Warin, was appointed 'graveur général des monnaies' in Paris in 1646. Would it be entering too deeply into the realms of speculation to suggest that the 'good Graver', mentioned by Chevalier as being Smyth's only officer, might have been a Warin? The name Warin would, after all, have been pronounced in French in almost the same way as the name Vaughan, which Chevalier chose to record.

The reference to Lord Hopton, at the end of the letter is not so obscure. It is known that Hopton had been in Jersey and that, together with Hyde, Capel and Carteret he had signed an agreement for the defence of the Island against Lord Jermyn's supposed design of selling it – with Guernsey – to France for 200,000 *pistoles* and a French dukedom. But it may be of deeper significance that Sir Richard Vyvyan, in his original commission from Charles I to coin money, was charged '... to deliver the Bullyon and Plate, soe by you coyned from tyme to tyme, to our trusty Sir Ralph Hopton, Knight of the Bath, to whome we have given direcon for the same for our service'. Lord Jermyn was Governor of Jersey only in name, and is recorded as having visited the Island on only three occasions; George Carteret assumed all Jermyn's responsibilities in practice.

Although so much of Hyde's letter indicates that there may well have been some connection between the Jersey and Truro and Exeter mints, only more tangible evidence could substantiate this. Miss Coate held that Sir Richard Vyvyan administered his Mints with the highest standards of morality, keeping his books in minute detail – an opinion endorsed by Miss Farquhar who wrote: 'The mint at Exeter produced, as we know, some of the finest coins of the Civil War, and it is unthinkable that Sir Richard would have given his countenance to defective weight or workmanship at Truro'. It surely follows then, that, if we were to discover a coin struck from *dies* attributed to Truro or Exeter, but of markedly light weight or poor quality, there would be very strong evidence to suggest that the dies might have been appropriated from the Exeter mint and perhaps even used in Jersey.

Miss Farquhar was discouraged from this approach to the problem (which may have been suggested to her by Hoskins's misinterpretation of Chevalier's account) by Miss Coate who pointed out that the dies were all confiscated by the Parliamentarians when Exeter was captured. The list of items confiscated, which Miss Coate cites, includes 'Twenty three under Stamps' and 'Twenty three upper Stamps' – presumably of all denominations minted. The denominations which have been identified with the Truro and Exeter mints are the crown, halfcrown, shilling, sixpence, groat, halfgroat and penny. However, R. C. Lockett's comprehensive paper *Notes on the Mints of Truro and Exeter under Charles I* seems to suggest that not all Sir Richard's dies were confiscated; Lockett listed, by my reckoning, at least thirty-seven different reverse dies for the Truro / Exeter halfcrown – fourteen more than the total number of reverse dies confiscated. Many more have since come to light. What was the fate of the missing dies?

Some time after deciding that the solution must lie in the search for a halfcrown not of peculiar design, but rather of defective weight or low silver content, I was fortunate enough to find a Charles I halfcrown corresponding to Chevalier's description, with a rose mintmark on obverse and reverse. The coin is considerably lighter and narrower than the average halfcrown of the period, and has a base metal tinge to it, not unlike the colour of certain European debased 'silver' coins of the period. The diameter of the coin is not below the average but the perimeter is irregular. Its general appearance (i.e colour and shape) bears an uncanny resemblance to that of a debased silver *franc* of Henry III (dated 1586) also in my collection, but I can trace no other design on the halfcrown as might indicate that it was overstruck on such a coin.

The halfcrown was struck by dies listed by Lockett (no. 14, page 239 of his article) which he assigned to Exeter rather than Truro. The coin has almost exactly the same surface area (and general legible condition) as two similar Truro / Exeter halfcrowns in my collection, but, at 12.61 grams, is over 14% lighter than either of the other two coins which are manifestly of good silver. It is approximately 13% lighter than the average weight (14.41 grams) of 35 Truro /

Exeter halfcrowns in the British Museum, which I was allowed to examine some years ago; a similar light-weight coin of the same type in the British Museum collection weighed 13.57 grams while three others – apparently of the correct standard – weighed 14.67, 14.73 and 14.9 grams respectively. I have since learned that quite a number of Exeter halfcrowns weigh 13.5 grams or less.

*Fig. 94: Above: The light-weight half-crown. Below: another half-crown from the same dies but of full weight.*

*In March 1984, through the courtesy of Dr. H.-U. Nissen of the E.T.H. Laboratorium for Festkörperphysik in Zurich, the light-weight coin was analysed on the Faculty's JSM-840 scanning electron microscope, equipped with a Tracor Northern wavelength-dispersive X-ray microanalytical facility. The silver (Ka) content was found to be identical with that of the silver franc of Henry III mentioned above (Ciani 1434) and there were only minor variations between the two coins in the intensity of chlorine (Ka) and sulphur. This strengthens the theory that the light-weight coin might have been struck from a continental silver coin. It must be said, however, that the silver content was high in each case and cannot fairly be called 'debased'. The shape and varying thickness of the light-weight coin are typical characteristics of coins struck on the rocker press, in use at the time.*

There are no weight-remedy figures extant for the Civil War period and it is only fair to give due licence for the chaotic conditions prevalent at the time. However, it is worth recording that the short weight allowed for the first milled halfcrowns after the Restoration was one troy grain on each blank or about ½% (Royal Warrant of 5th February 1663 – *Mint Record Book IV* p 42). A coin weight in my possession for Charles I hammered halfcrowns (in fine condition, if slightly corroded) weighs 14.9 grams, i.e. the same as the heaviest example of Lockett no. 14 in the British Museum, mentioned above.

With two exceptions, the subject of this paper and the other in the British Museum (weighing 13.57 grams – see above), all the halfcrowns of this die-type appear to be of the correct weight and silver content; it would thus be over-ambitious to suggest, on the evidence set out here, that they may all have been struck in Jersey; it is however not inconceivable that the mysterious Vaughan may have executed the obverse die – which Lockett described as a 'monstrosity' – while the reverse die (possibly with others) was appropriated (according to Miss Coate) during 'the rifling of Sir Richard Vyvyan's house some weeks before the fall of Exeter on April 13th, 1646, at the orders of Sir John Berkeley', Governor of Exeter.

The significant fact remains, however, that the halfcrown is 'adulterate' and 'too light', and was minted with dies attributed to Exeter – a combination which Sir Richard Vyvyan clearly would not have countenanced.

Certain questions remain: no gold twenty shilling pieces are known of Truro or Exeter, and dies for such coins could not – in any event – have been used to strike the Jacobus of the previous reign of which, wrote Chevalier, they coined a good number. I once saw a very poor quality Charles I shilling in the stocks of a London coin dealer ascribed to the 'Jersey Mint'. It was weakly struck in debased silver and, at 5.1 grams, underweight. The mint-mark was scarcely distinguishable but can be described as a wedge rather than a lozenge. The dealer was not willing to part with it and was unable to provide me with any further information, such as a find spot, though the coin may have come from a north country collection. I am inclined to think that the attribution was spurious.

One must admit, though, having mentioned the subject of find spots, that none of Colonel Smyth's coins has been recorded as having been found in the Island. Such a find would certainly prove or disprove the theory set out above. Until then, if the theory only succeeds in exciting further interest in the mystery of the Prince's Mint in Jersey, it will have served its purpose.

\*\*\*

There is a post-script: nearly three years later, the self-styled Charles II sent Sir George Carteret a Commission dated 11th February 1649 to coin English money in Jersey. Possibly fearing a repetition of the events of 1646–7, the Lieutenant Governor apparently chose to ignore this Commission which is set out below:

> CHARLES by the grace of God, King of England, Scotland, France and Ireland, Defender of the faith, etc. To our trusty and welbeloved Sir George Carteret, Knight and Baronet, Lieutenant Governor of our Island of Jersey, and to all others to whom these presents shall come, Greeting. WHEREAS we conceive very necessary for our service and for the good of that our Island of Jersey that a Mint should be presently erected and established there for the making and coyning of such sortes and species of money as are by these presents hereafter specified. KNOW ye now, that we reposing trust and confidence in discretion, integrity, and good affection of you the said Sir George Carteret, Doe by these presents give you full power and authority to establish and erect a Mint in our said Isle of Jersey, in such place or part thereof as you shall thinke fitt AND to cause the severall species of Gold and Silver moneys hereafter mentioned to be minted, coyned, and stamped there; that is to say one peece of Gold of the value of Twenty Shillings Sterling; one piece of the value of ten Shillings Sterling; and one other piece of the value of five Shillings Sterling; and of Silver one piece of the value of five Shillings Sterling; one other piece of the value of two Shillings Sixpence Sterling; one other piece of the value of one Shilling or twelve Pence Sterling; and one other piece of six Pence Sterling. All the said several species to be of the same weight and fineness with the like species, usually heretofore coyned in England, that is to say the gold money, according to the weight and fineness of the same species usually heretofore made in England and of the silver

money every pound weight thereof to contain eleven ounces, two penny weight of fine silver, and eight teene penny weight of alloy; the said species above mentioned to be made and stamped with our image and inscription in such manner and forme as we have now sent the same unto you. Further heereby authorizing you to make choise of such Officers, Moneyers, and Workemen, as you shall conceive must necessarily be employed for the governing, ordering and directing the said Mint, and for the making and coyning the said severall species of Money above mentioned. Provided that for such gold and silver bullion, as shall not belong to Us, or to you the Lieutenant Governor for the use of the Garrison but shall be brough in by others to be coyned for their particular advantage such dues and rights of Signorage be made payable to Us upon the coining of the said moneys as shalbe just and reasonable. Giving you further power to doe, settle, and establish all such other things concerning the premisses, as shalbe necessary for our service, and for the good, and benefit of our Garrison, and other subjects in that Isle. Given at our Court in Jersey, the 11th day of february 1647. In the second yeare of our Reigne.

The commission was given eleven days after King Charles I had been executed on 30th January, and six days before Sir George had Prince Charles proclaimed King of England on 17th January. It is therefore not surprising that the thoughts of the Prince turned so quickly after his father's death to the vital subject of refuge; and where else but in the Island which had acted as a safe house for him three years previously? Protection meant a garrison and a garrison needed to be paid if it was to remain faithful; Charles had in fact been well advised on his previous visit to leave a large gratuity to be paid out to the soldiers. 'The second year of our Reigne' is better understood if one remembers that the New Year in those days commenced on March 15th. Charles was therefore almost into the second year of his reign when the Commission was penned.

None of the patterns mentioned in the letter (if patterns they were) have survived, and it is very unlikely that the terms of the Commission were implemented. Even after the young King's return to the Island, practically penniless, on 17th September 1649, the subject of a mint does not seem to have been further broached. As an alternative perhaps, following an Act of the States of 21st September 1649, the considerable sum of 5070 *écus* in *deniers* was collected, as a sign of *'l'Affection prompte et volontaire'* for His Majesty, and, after a previous loan was repaid, the balance was graciously accepted by the King.

Jean Chevalier, in an entry in his Journal dated 11th December 1649, recorded a 'Touching ceremony' which was conducted by the young King Charles II in the Island. Eleven persons, male and female, presented themselves to be cured of scrofula. It seems that those concerned, owing to the precarious state of the young King's finances, were obliged to furnish their own 'touch-pieces', some of which were 'angels' and others 'half-angels', almost certainly of James I, which were hung on pieces of ribbon aroung the patients' necks. A final touching ceremony took place on 10th February 1650.

One of the last acts of the King, before he left the Island on 13th February 1650 (as reported by Jean Chevalier) was to grant Sir George Carteret title to an island *'aux pres de viergines* [Virginia] *en la merique...',* together with some other islets nearby, with permission to take 300 souls to live there. The island was called at that time Smyth's island which was named after the English navigator John Smith who discovered it. (Smith, the husband of Pocahontas, was no relation of Colonel William Smyth). The island was later renamed New Jersey. As recognisance for this grant Sir George was to pay to the King the sum of six pounds sterling per annum. This island, in Chesapeake Bay, had no connection with the present State of New Jersey, formerly the colony of Nova Caesarea which Sir George Carteret founded fifteen years later.

*Fig. 95: New Jersey cent dated 1787.*
*By authority dated 1st June 1787, Walter Mould, Thomas Goadsby and Albion Cox obtained the right to strike the first New Jersey coins of the weight of six pennyweight and six grains each.*

With the departure of the King and his retinue for the continent, the enigmatic story of the Jersey Mint is concluded.

# The Century of Transition (1700–1800)

The interlude of the Jersey Mint marks the beginning of the decline of the surprisingly smooth-running economies of the Channel Islands. During the latter part of the reign of Louis XIV, it became more and more difficult to obtain any denominations greater than the *liard* and this hampered trade still further. The period 1700–1800 can be termed the century of transition, as the authorities in Jersey and Guernsey were forced by external circumstances to look at the advantages and disadvantages of their very ancient money of account systems, based on the *livre tournois*. The problem was exacerbated by the chaotic conditions of their traditional (French) currency medium.

Problems caused by the arrival in Guernsey of worn English coin were followed, not by the banning of such coin, but by an Act (dated 16th June 1696) which described the degree of wear which was to be allowed. An Act of the States of Jersey of 3rd October 1701 forbade the export from the Island of any gold, silver or other coin in an amount larger than the equivalent of 30 *livres tournois* at a time, on pain of confiscation of the coin, besides a fine, confiscation of the vessel involved and imprisonment of the master and crew. In 1720, the maximum amount of coin which could be exported was reduced to the equivalent of 5 *livres tournois*. In the same year it became evident that there was no longer any gold or silver money in circulation in the Island. There are, incidentally, 5 circular slate 'counters' in a show-case at Mont Orgeuil Castle, Jersey, three to four inches in diameter, one of them dated 1711. Their use is not known but they possibly have served as some sort of token or tally.

The situation in Guernsey was no different, as regards the gold and silver coin, but was worse in one other respect. Following the excessive import of *deniers,* and the coinage, locally, of *liards* and *double tournois,* an inflationary situation developed, to the extent that on 22nd April 1723 the *sol tournois* was ordered to be worth 16 *deniers,* as against 14 previously; the situation worsened fast and a rate of 20 *deniers* to the *sol* became official as at 2nd December of the same year. Jersey resorted to desperate measures which were doomed to failure. Resolving that the only solution was to create money – particularly in view of the pressure they were under to pay for half-completed contracts such as the harbour works – they decided to print a series of notes denominated in the old money of account to a total value of 50.000 *livres tournois;* denominations were as follows:

2000 notes of   20 *sous* (1 *livre*) *tournois*
1000 notes of   30 *sous* (1 ½ *livres*) tournois
1000 notes of   60 *sous* (3 *livres*) *tournois*
1000 notes of 100 *sous* (5 *livres*) *tournois*
 750 notes of   10 *livres tournois*
 500 notes of   20 *livres tournois*
 300 notes of   30 *livres tournois*
 240 notes of   50 *livres tournois*

The notes, which bore the Arms of the Island as a seal, were each individually signed by Philippe Dumaresq, representing the judiciary, François Le Couteur, jnr., as Rector of St. Helier and Jacques Lemprière as Constable of St. Helier. Not one of these notes, to my knowledge, has survived.

One should not forget that the Channel Islands could expect little economic or financial assistance at that time from England which had just suffered the disastrous consequences of a series of financial projects whereby the State was to sell certain trading monopolies in the south seas in exchange for a sum of money to pay off the National Debt. The South Sea Bubble burst in England at the same time as John Law's 'system' collapsed in France.

The *Banque Générale,* France's first 'bank of issue', had been set up under the management of Law in 1716. In spite of severe opposition from the Council of Finance, Philippe d'Orléans, the Regent (Louis XV was six years old at the time), provided the necessary letters patent for the Bank's establishment, with the right to issue notes for twenty years. In 1718 the *Banque Générale* was converted into the *Banque Royale,* with the young king as the sole proprietor. The *Compagnie des Indes* was formed in 1719 as a 'front' for the Royal interests which had become the first concern of the *Banque Royale.* In addition to monopolistic trading privileges, the company was permitted to purchase the management of the *Monnaie* and the right to issue coin for nine years.

Later that year the company made a massive loan to the King which was to pay off the State debt – the same motive though not quite the same method as was being used in England. This – and other projects – was financed by frequent share issues at a heavy premium against payment in *Banque Royale* notes, financed in turn by deposits of silver and gold (mainly the former). Speculation was so intense that *Banque Royale* notes became the only circulating medium and the word *millionaire* was born.

Just before the French 'bubble' burst, Law, having first limited the amount of gold and silver in circulation, was forced, finally, to demonetise coin altogether. Under these circumstances, one can easily imagine the difficulties which faced the Channel Islands at the time.

Now in total confusion, having banned the export of *liards* and *deniers* – the only money in circulation – the States of Jersey on 21st December 1725 banned its import. This confusion went on until, by an Act dated 19th September 1726, the free trade in *liards* was again permitted. On the same day they appointed a committee to prepare a representation to his Majesty in Council, on the relative value of the coins in circulation in the Island. Charles le Quesne takes up the story *(Constitutional History of Jersey,* p 421):

> 'This representation was adopted by the States on the 25th of November 1726. The ulterior sanction by Council of the recommendation of the States was the occasion of serious commotions and discontent in the Island. The avowed object of the States in their request to the Crown was to prevent the exportation of gold and silver coin from the Island, and to encourage the exportation of liards to France, which they asserted passed in Jersey above their intrinsic value, and with which they were very much burdened – reasons among the very worst which could be given, or upon which a legislative enactment could be based.
> 
> An Order in Council, dated the 22nd of May 1729, was issued, approving of the proposed alterations in the currency by the States; and it was accordingly ordered: –
> 
> 'That the French silver coins be current in the said Island only according to their intrinsic value, in proportion to the British crown-piece.
> 
> 'That the British crown-piece do continue at seventy-one sols; the half-crown at thirty-five sols and a half; the shilling at fourteen sols; and the sixpence at seven sols.
> 
> 'That the French liards be reduced to their old value of two deniers each; and that the British halfpence be current for seven deniers; and the farthing for three and a half. And his Majesty doth hereby further order, that the said coins do pass in all manner of payment, according to the said rates; but that this order shall not take effect till the expiration of six calendar months from the date thereof; and to the end that no person may pretend ignorance hereof, the bailiff and jurats of her Majesty's said Island of Jersey are to cause this order to be forthwith published, and to take care that it be executed according to the tenor thereof.'
> 
> The act of the States and the Order in Council were, to say the least of them, highly injudicious. The only coin apparently in circulation was the liard, and the accounts were kept in livres and sous. The proportion between the sol and the livre remained unchanged; but it followed, from the new law, that if a person did not meet his liabilities within the specified time of six months, his debts were consequently increased fifty per cent, if he had to pay them in liards; and he could pay them apparently in no other coin. The value of the sol relative to the liard was raised fifty per cent; that is, six liards were to be estimated as equivalent to one sol, instead of four liards as heretofore. Now, on what ground could the States establish this great difference, when it did not exist in reality? We ascertain positively by an act of the States of the 21st December 1725, that the real exchangeable difference between the liards, at their estimated value of four to a sol, and gold and silver coin, was only twelve per cent in favour of the latter. The rate of exchange between countries is not dependent on or regulated by any legislative authority, however despotic or absolute

it may be, but is regulated by the real intrinsic relative value of the coins in circulation in the two countries: and hence the rate of exchange, compared with the par of exchange, will show the depreciation sustained by the circulating medium of a country; for the difference between the par and the rate of exchange should in ordinary circumstances not exceed the cost of transmission of the precious metals from one country to the other. Now, by an act of the States of the 21st December 1725, we learn that they were indebted to a merchant at St. Malo for the proceeds of the sale of a cargo of wheat, which had been taken possession of and sold to the people by the States, at a time of great scarcity in the Island. They had remitted a portion of the amount; but there remained a balance due of 3332 livres tournois, which Mr. Patriarche had engaged to remit to St. Malo. The States ordered that this amount should be paid to Mr. Patriarche by the deputy viscount in liards, thus incidentally proving that there was in reality no other coin in circulation; but as Mr. Patriarche had to pay the amount to the merchant at St. Malo in gold and silver, and as these bore a premium compared to liards, the loss, or rather the amount of the premium, had of course to be made good by the States; and they accordingly ordered that that difference, amounting to 416 livres ten sous, should be raised by rate of the parishes and placed in the hands of the deputy viscount, for payment to Mr. Patriarche. We are thus enabled satisfactorily to ascertain the real comparative difference between the value of the liard and other metallic currency, or, in other words, the premium which the latter bore compared with the copper currency, at the rate of four liards to the sol. By a calculation on the data thus furnished, we find the difference to be precisely twelve per cent. in favour of gold and silver; and we are also to bear in mind that the great scarcity of gold and silver would of course add to the premium. By the Order in Council the difference was to be established at fifty per cent.

The States soon perceived either that they had committed a great mistake, or that they must yield to public opinion, which was strongly and decidedly opposed to the change ordered. They accordingly on the 20th of December 1729, petitioned his Majesty in Council for the recall of the Order in Council, being apprehensive that the said regulations would not answer the ends they at first expected from them. The States, on the 24th of April 1730, named a deputy in support of their petition. Counsel were heard by the committee of the Privy Council for the States, and also for several members of the States and others who opposed the petition of the States; but the opinion of the committee was, that the Order in Council regulating the currency ought not to be suspended or revoked, but carried into execution. His Majesty in Council, therefore, on the 9th of July 1730, ordered 'that the said Order in Council of the 22nd of May 1729 be carried into execution: but that during the term of six months from the date hereof all creditors in the said Island do receive their debts, if tendered to them at the rate at which the coins went current immediately before making the aforesaid Order in Council; and, in case of refusal, that such creditors do forfeit one third of their debts to the benefit of the debtors.'

Although by the Order in Council six months were allowed to individuals to pay their liabilities at the old rate of currency, yet those who could not discharge their debts or bonds within that time were to have their liabilities raised fifty per cent. Order money, as it was called, was to be fifty per cent higher in value than the ordinary money in livres tournois. Such was the construction put upon the Order, which caused intense dissatisfaction among a large proportion of the people, who viewed the enactment as a legalised system of robbery of the poor. The exasperation felt led to a riot, in which Mr. le Geyt, the lieutenant-bailli, narrowly escaped with his life, and fled for refuge to Elizabeth Castle.'

**Subsequently the Lieutenant-Governor, Colonel Howard, was charged with having neglected to assist the authorities in putting into execution the Order in Council relative to the currency, and in suppressing the riots. Le Quesne continues:**

Although the excitement of the public had in some degree subsided, there existed a strong feeling against those persons who had been favourable to the Orders in Council relative to the currency. They were looked upon as the enemies of the poor, as persons who would not scruple to benefit themselves by legal spoliation and wrong. To some families the reproach of 'six au sol' has adhered even to very recent times.

The Orders in Council of 22nd May 1729 and 9th July 1730 were subsequently enshrined in the Code of Laws of the Island of Jersey of the 28th March 1771 in the reign of George III. Currency in the Island was effectively decreed to be that of the United Kingdom though the circulating medium was recognized to be the silver coins and *liards* of France.

In an Ordinance of 7th December 1723, it was decreed that *sols marqués* were not to pass current. Since the 13th century, the Channel Islands – particularly Guernsey – had served as entrepôts in the wine trade between England and 'English' Gascony. The outbreak of war between England and France in 1744 – which only terminated in 1815 – was bound to disrupt this trade, but during protracted periods of peace, traffic in wines and other goods flourished. The great advantage was the avoidance by the British merchant of dues payable in England and smuggling became a way of life in the Islands. Unfortunately small change was increasingly difficult to procure; what remained very soon left in payment for the day-to-day needs of the islanders. This led to improvisation and, of course, forgery.

In theory, all Louis XI's coins were legal tender in the Channel Islands. In practice, only the lowest denominations could be found in the Islands.

We read in an Ordinance of 3rd October 1763 that as great quantities of *liards* (commonly called *great doubles*) were constantly being sent out of Guernsey, small change was difficult to obtain. Such *liards* were in future to go at six to the *sol tournois* (since 1741 they had been valued at 13 for 2 *sols tournois*); but no-one needed to accept more than 7 *sols tournois* at each payment. This revaluation of the *liard* – in view of scarcity – is interesting. The mention however of the previous value, from an Ordinance of June 1741, in terms of '2 *sols tournois*' – suggesting that 2 *sols tournois* was a denomination in itself – is equally significant. In February 1879, over one hundred years later, some 3000 forged 2 *sol* pieces (sometimes called *'marqués'*) were dug up in a field in St. Saviour, Jersey. Many years ago, I was given several of these 'coins' which are well-made in a base alloy;

*Fig. 96: Billon* double sol *or* marqué, *one of 3000 found in Jersey.*
*According to an edict of October 1738, such coins were struck for the French colonies; they were made current in Canada at 24* deniers *(cf Ciani 2138, Breton 508).*

there are several minor die varieties but all bear the 'H' mint mark of La Rochelle and a star in the obverse legend; although they compare favourably with the genuine article, they are on average 25% lighter. Were they perhaps fabricated in the Islands to alleviate the short change problem?

Ironically, while the economists, financiers and speculators were ruining the state of France, some very beautiful coins were being engraved by the Roettiers family who reigned at *La Monnaie* from 1704 to 1772. The constantly high quality of design of the higher denominations must have contributed to the return of France to economic sanity after Law's desperate demonetization measures. These machine-struck coins were modelled on those of previous reigns; various types of *double louis, louis* and *demi louis d'or,* were complemented by the silver *écu* and its many *fractions* (down to *1/20 écu*). The ill-fated *livre de la Compagnie des Indes* – worth 20 *sols* – is worth mentioning, with its distinctive JL device (for John Law). And, finally, the 24, 12 and 6 *sol* pieces were the 'two-bobs', 'bobs' and 'tanners' of the time. In fact the 24 and 12 *sols* became known in the Channel Islands as ten and five penny pieces and, for a century or so, played a very important currency role.

*Fig. 97: Left: Louis XIV écu aux insignes. Right: Louis XV écu aux lauriers. Ciani 1907, 2117. Decorated edge inscription on both coins: DOMINE SALVVM FAC REGEM.*

Louis XV's was the reign of the Royal Mistresses, and the names of Madame de Pompadour and Madame du Barry mixed uneasily with the house of Bourbon and Choiseul. India and Canada were lost, Corsica and Lorraine were won. Even now Louis XV is regarded as a monarch at the watershed of history.

Louis XVI was the grandson of Louis XV. The coins of his reign can be divided into two distinct series: the Royal series from his accession in 1774 to 1790, and the Constitutional series from April 1791 till the King's execution in January 1793. Where coins of the former were modelled on those of the previous reign, the King's title on the latter series was changed to *'Roi des François'*, and his reign was proclaimed the *'règne de la loi'*. New minor denominations of 30 and 15 *sols* were introduced together with the yellow copper coins of 2 *sols*, and 12, 6 and 3 *deniers* with the distinctive reverse *fasces* design and the revolutionary

*Fig. 98: Examples of late 18th century copper coinage which circulated in the Channel Islands. From the top: Louis XV demi sol d'Aix (Ciani 2145; mintmark &); contemporary fake halfpenny of George III (cf Seaby 3774); Louis XVI sol (Ciani 2194); George III 'cartwheel' penny (Seaby 3777).*

date. Quite frequently copper coins of this series are discovered in the soil of the Channel Islands and there is one very fine example of a *louis d'or* found at St. Aubin, in the museum of the Société Jersiaise.

In the late 18th century, England was suffering from an acute shortage of small change. During the first ten years of George III's reign no copper coins were struck at all owing to the high price of copper. As a result large numbers of crude forgeries of George II halfpennies appeared, usually light in weight and often with peculiar legends. For five years between 1770 and 1775, copper halfpennies and farthings were struck and then copper issues lapsed again until the famous 'cartwheel' pennies and two-penny pieces were struck by Matthew Bolton. These unwieldy coins together with the halfpennies and farthings which Bolton struck in 1799, are the first English coins which, judging by the numbers which are still turned up by the plough, circulated with any regularity in the Islands.

The price of silver was also high and only small amounts of Maundy coins were issued until 1787 when, after a sudden fall in the price of the metal, silver coins became – temporarily – quite plentiful. This dearth of small denominations was to some extent compensated by the issues of private tokens, although no such issues are known to have been made in the Channel Islands in the 18th century.

Little is known about the use of banknotes in the Islands at this time. The Bank of England had issued handwritten promissory notes and certificates of deposit since its foundation in 1694. By 1745 all denominations (from £ 20 to £ 1000) circulated freely throughout the United Kingdom, and it is hard to see how Jersey's and Guernsey's commerce could have survived the shortage of coin if such notes had not circulated there too.

In France, banknotes were far less respected, particularly since the disaster of John Law earlier in the century. The *Caisse d'Escompte* issued several denominations between 1776 and 1793, then, following the Revolution, the country was flooded with *'assignats'* in denominations down to 10 sous. These

*Fig. 99:* Assignat de dix sous.

*In a speech of 20th November 1789, Mirabeau declaimed: 'Qu'est-ce qui fait le crédit des billets de banque? la certitude qu'ils seront payés en argent, à présentation: toute autre doctrine est trompeuse'. In February 1796, when the plates for the* assignats *were finally destroyed, no less than 35 billion francs worth remained in circulation.*

notes certainly circulated in the Islands; in 1947 60 *assignats* of the *'Domaines Nationaux'*, of 5000 *livres* each dated 29th September 1790, were found in an attic in an old house in St. Lawrence, Jersey.

On the other hand, the economies of Jersey, Guernsey, Alderney and Sark were used to 'roughing it' and a contemporary writer tells us (of Jersey) that 'Tobacco is the chief commodity which the French purchase from the islanders, and that article and a few others supply them with the small sum of money which is necessary for the currency of the island.'

Occasionally, Russian coins of the late 18th century are found in Jersey and Guernsey; there is, for example, a copper 5 *kopek* coin of Catherine II dated 1790 in the Museum of the Société Jersiaise which is said to have been found at Grouville. In 1799, two divisions of Russian troops which had been engaged in the ill-fated expedition to Holland for the re-establishment of the Prince of Orange, landed in Guernsey and Jersey and were quartered in the Islands for over six months. This is certainly the explanation for the Russian coin finds; the Jersey contingent is known to have been quartered, in appalling conditions, on Grouville Common.

# Part III

1800–1830 Token Coinage
Philippe d'Auvergne's 5 *Franc* Piece
The Sir Isaac Brock Half Pennies
Channel Islands Paper Money
Guernsey and Jersey Coinages
The German Occupation
Commemoratives & Decimals
Medals, Checks and Other Curiosities
The Present
The Future

CECIL GRAHAM: What is a cynic?
LORD DARLINGTON: A man who knows the price of everything and the value of nothing.

Oscar Wilde. *Lady Windermere's Fan.*
Act III

# 1800–1830 – Token Coinage

The First Republic in France lasted from 1792 to 1804. The first period, the *Convention nationale,* was followed by the notorious *Directoire,* which began on the *'5 Brumaire an IV'* (27.10.1795) and ended on the *'18 Brumaire an VIII'* (9.11.1799). Financial crisis was a natural result of the tribulations of the times, the early symbol of which was the guillotine, first used in 1792. Wars against the Emperor, in Italy, and the King of England, in Egypt, once again drained the country of credit and small change, and it is perhaps ironical that the momentous decision to decimalize the currency was taken at this chaotic time. The last coins of the duodecimal system (the gold 24 *livres,* the silver *écus* of 6 and 3 *livres,* and the billon and copper *sou* and *half-sou*) were substituted by gold 40 and 20 *franc* denominations, silver coins of 5, 2, 1, ½ and ¼ *francs,* and copper *fractions:* 2 *décimes* and 5 and 1 *centime* pieces.

Silver coins of the second period of that Republic, the *Consulat* (1799–1804), were of similar denominations, and it was at the commencement of the Consulate, on the *'16 nivôse an VIII'* (6.1.1800) that first mention was made of the projected statutes of the *Banque de France,* in which Napoleon Bonaparte was one of the original shareholders. The early fortunes of the bank were to follow the military fortunes of Bonaparte who became sole Consul (for life) in 1802 and Emperor in 1804. After Austerlitz (1805) a certain stability began, but the combined forces of the sixth coalition – England, Austria, Prussia, Russia, Spain, Naples and Sweden – were too much for the new Emperor, and the economy – as well as the *Banque de France* – met its first Waterloo. Napoleon's coins were similar to the first decimal issue, with the addition of billon and copper 10 *centime* pieces. At the same time, the *Banque de France* printed its own bank-notes, with the first issue slightly altered from the design of the earlier notes of the *Caisse des comptes-courants.*

The younger brother of Louis XVI returned to France in 1814 and became Louis XVIII (1814–1824); coins issued in his name were in the same denominations as those of his imperial predecessor. During his reign the *Banque de France* was again reformed and the last note-issuing *'comptoirs'* (at Lyon, Rouen and Lille) were suppressed. Another brother succeeded him as Charles X, who added the 100 and 10 gold *franc* denominations to those already in existence.

In England, during the first fifteen years of the 19th century, there was a dearth of metal of all kinds, and coins were in very short supply. Matthew Boulton's well-known 'cartwheel' pennies and two penny pieces – weighing one and two ounces respectively – were followed by halfpennies and farthings of slightly different style; and there were further copper issues in 1806 and 1807. However, by 1811, practically all official issues had been cast into cannon for the French wars, or were being hoarded by speculators.

Silver, too, was already scarce by 1800, and the only silver coins in circulation in the United Kingdom were countermarked eight *real* pieces or *'dollars'* of Spain. These were valued at 4s/9d, then revalued at 5/-. In 1804 the Bank of England overstruck these *dollars* with a completely new design. These coins were not strictly royal issues; they foreshadowed the era of the official token money, with an intrinsic worth which was below the face value. After the Napoleonic wars were over, metals became more plentiful, silver denominations were once again struck and the era of the 'gold standard' was born when the guinea was replaced by the sovereign in 1817.

During this period of shortage, private tokens of denominations between one shilling and one farthing filled the void and this habit seems also to have been adopted in the Channel Islands (see below).

George III's sixty year reign came to an end in 1820, and he was succeeded by his son George IV (1820–1830). Farthings were again coined in 1821 after a fourteen year break, pennies and halfpennies in 1825.

Although the privateering 'industries' of the Channel Islands received a temporary boost during the unsettled times of the Napoleonic wars, the shortage of currency became chronic and there are many references to this problem during the period. Coins of the French duodecimal system were utilized well into the 1830's, and English, Spanish and other foreign coins circulated whenever they became available. The most popular larger denominations seem to have been the French *écu* or six *livres* piece, given a value of five shillings and three pence in 1797, and the Spanish *dollar,* worth rather less. The faithful *liard,* called the *'double'* and now worth 1/8 of a penny sterling was used for smaller payments and the authorities seem to have turned a blind eye to false *liards,* though the States of Guernsey were prompted as early as 1797, by the large quantities of forgeries in circulation, to pass an Act which suggested that a coinage should be

*Fig. 100:* Louis XVI liard.
*Ciani 2197. Mintmark AA = Metz.*

devised for the Island. As time went on, even *liards* became scarce and various base substitutes were used. The passing of *deniers* and *centimes* for *liards* was banned by ordinance in 1803, and by 1828, wrote one contemporary authority, *liards* were 'formed of various sizes, thickness, and materials, some of them being old English farthings, some Dutch or Flemish, others French or Spanish, many of them only very thin pieces of plain copper, whilst a few of them [were] soldiers' buttons, beaten flat'.

As early as 1803, it seems – from a Guernsey ordinance prohibiting the practice – that *deniers* and the new *centime* coins were being passed as *liards*. Frequently, the export of silver and copper coins from the Islands was banned – apparently with little effect – and the small amount of (mainly) French change which remained was subject to wild fluctuations in value. In July 1816 in Guernsey, following an official complaint of the inconvenience caused by this fluctuation in the value of French money 'which has always been current in this island', the said coins were ordered to pass at their current value, but could be refused. The values were fixed as follows:

Pieces or Crowns of 6 Francs – 4/10d
Petits Ecus – 2/4d
Pieces of 24 sous – 10d
Pieces of 12 sous – 5d

The order was not to apply to worn-out or defaced coins, or to Irish shillings. (Incidentally one of the coins found during excavations at Mont Orgeuil Castle, Jersey, was a brass shilling of James II, minted for Ireland in 1689).

The silver tokens of three shillings and eighteen pence, struck by the Royal Mint for the States of Jersey, dated 1813, constituted the first official metal currency for any of the Channel Islands. On the authority of an Order in Council from the Committee on Coins dated 5th February 1813, an amount of £10,000 worth of the tokens was initially struck, followed by a further amount which brought the total to £13,620. The design, which is unpretentious but not ungraceful, was by Thomas Wyon, Junior, who personally engraved the dies. The coins appear as J1 and J2 in the catalogue section.

I have already made the point that the Bank of England dollars dated 1804 foreshadowed the era of the official token money, with an intrinsic worth which was below face value. There were in fact three classes of token coinage current in the Channel Islands in the early nineteenth century; the two silver tokens mentioned above, minted specifically for Jersey, make up the first class.

French coins still in circulation constituted the second class of token, and the 24 and 12 *sous (sols)* pieces were, for some years, actually called respectively ten penny and five penny tokens. It is quite possible that semi-official striking of French coins took place in the Islands. In December 1813, for example, the Treasurer of the States of Guernsey apparently anticipated being in possession of quantities of *liards,* and the public were requested to apply for the coins accordingly. A newspaper report of 12th October 1829 mentioned the prosecution of a forger who had silvered *liards* and passed them for five penny pieces. Tokens of 1 *grand-double,* 3 *grand-doubles* and 1 *sou,* planned by the States of Guernsey in 1813, have never been identified. The rarity of Channel Island copper tokens – the third class – has never been satisfactorily explained. While it is generally thought that the Prince of Wales plumes / JERSEY GUERNSEY AND ALDERNEY combination was the 'official' issue, nobody has yet succeeded in providing a credible *raison d'être* for the other – even rarer – issues.

*Fig. 101: 6, 12 and 24* sol *pieces of Louis XVI.*
*Ciani 2192, 2191 and 2190 respectively. The latter two were referred to as five and ten penny pieces in the Channel Islands. These coins, also known as $^1/_{20}$, $^1/_{10}$ and $^1/_5$ écu, were designed by Duvivier.*

In March 1813, the circulation of English private tokens was banned in the Island of Guernsey and it is quite conceivable that the tokens referred to were in fact some or all of this copper series. There are die-links with several other English private tokens, and the date of the ban would fit in well with the period during which it appears the Channel Islands copper tokens were struck (see below). Jersey and Guernsey were at the time – and still are to a large extent – two separate entities, and it seems unlikely that the legend JERSEY GUERNSEY AND ALDERNEY would have been agreed upon by the respective Island authorities. It might however easily have been chosen by a merchant from the Midlands, ignorant in the ways of the islanders but anxious to come up with a design suitable for general circulation.

*Fig. 102: JERSEY GUERNSEY AND ALDERNEY Copper one penny token.*
*See T6i.*

The comparative rarity of the tokens suggests that – with the possible exception of the pennies with the JERSEY GUERNSEY AND ALDERNEY / Prince of Wales plumes combination – the pieces were struck as patterns for the approval of the Island authorities or other local entities (e.g. Elias Neel, Jersey). In April 1813, the States of Guernsey resolved to apply to the Privy Council to have copper coins struck by Matthew Boulton, of one penny and one halfpenny; no definite link has been established between these planned pieces and the copper tokens which survive.

I am inclined to believe that the tokens in question were private issues which probably circulated in the Islands; they are classified, together with the rare Bank of Guernsey five shilling token, in likely date order, below. Several authorities have classified the four items T8 – T11 as mules; I have retained them in the series for several reasons – not least because one (T9) is known to have been struck over T3. I have never seen the token issued by Elias Neel. Its rarity may imply that it was issued as a pattern for a private banking institution or even for Neel in his capacity as public benefactor (i.e. provider of small change) – such grounds were not unknown in England at the time: Ruding reported that in September 1812, 'more than one hundred of the inhabitants and tradesmen of Reading returned thanks to J. B. Monck, esq., for the convenience afforded to them by the issue of his silver tokens, . . .'

King George III of England had been Prince of Wales, and the three plumes design, which graces some of the copper tokens, may have honoured him; perhaps, too, they recalled the memory of his ancestor who, as Prince of Wales, had swept through Jersey 150 years previously. Incidentally, the original Prince of Wales probably inherited this badge from his mother Philippa of Hainault. His nickname, the Black Prince, may well have originated from his Banner for Peace which was a black flag with three ostrich feathers shown separately on it. It is amusing to note that one of these tokens, now in the Alderney Museum, is recorded (1969) as having been 'discovered in the takings in the till of an Alderney shop quite recently'.

The Bishop de Jersey five shilling token of 1809 is perhaps the rarest – and most sought after – coin in the Channel Island series. There is a splendid example in the British Museum collection, struck over a Spanish *dollar* of Charles III dated 1794, and there are probably no more than six other genuine examples extant. There are several good – perhaps contemporary – electrotype copies about, and the collector should be on his guard. On some examples there are minute variations, such as a missing serif on the N of GUERNSEY on the reverse.

The firm Bishop de Jersey and Co. was originally a partnership of Charles Bishop and Henry de Jersey with Philip le Gros; the association was dissolved in 1804 and the new firm took over the business of the partnership, and lasted until 1811 when, following financial difficulties, it went into liquidation. The firm also issued notes and will be mentioned again in a later section. Waters writes: 'This token is of an early date that is some two years before the time of general issue of (English) tokens in the years 1811–1812. They were made by being struck on Spanish Dollars at the Soho Mint Birmingham, by Boulton & Watt – produced on the same principal as that adopted for making Bank of England dollars a few years earlier ... if these tokens were struck in any quantity, they must have been converted into bullion when tokens were prohibited.'

Prices for these rare pieces have shown staggering increases over the last 100 years, as is shown below:

    1888 (Leycester sale) a specimen (together with a Jersey 3 shilling token) fetched £3–10s
  c. 1895 Lowsley reported a 'higher price still'
    1922 (Sotheby Sale) Spink purchased a specimen for £42
    1930 (Hamer sale) a specimen fetched £50
    1950 (Lingford sale) a specimen fetched £105
    1954 (ex-King Farouk) a specimen fetched £125 (Egyptian)
    1970 an electrotype copy (offered to me as genuine) was priced at £1200
    1974 a specimen was priced at $8,000 by a Canadian dealer
    1978 Spink sold a specimen for £5,750

# Philippe d'Auvergne's 5 Franc Piece

The reader may recall from an earlier section that a Coriosolite billon stater was found 'in 1812 or later... at the seat of the Prince de Bouillon at Bagatelle', St. Saviour, Jersey, and may have wondered casually who the Prince de Bouillon was. This is perhaps a convenient juncture to give a very short account of a remarkable Jerseyman, Admiral Philippe d'Auvergne, Duke of Bouillon, who was born Philippe Dauvergne in 1754.

He entered the Navy at 16 and very soon became involved in a search for the 'North-East Passage', sailing in the *H.M.S. Racehorse* under Captain Phipps to a point closer to the North Pole than any ship had reached before. While serving against the 'Yankies', he was given his first command at the age of 23. Two years later he was captured in an engagement with a French frigate and taken to Carhaix in Brittany.

By a strange coincidence, there lived in Carhaix a young Breton soldier, Théophile Malo Corret, who by an extraordinary quirk of fate was to decide – to his own disadvantage – the destiny of Philippe Dauvergne. Corret's mother claimed descent from an illegitimate half-brother of Henri de la Tour d'Auvergne, Vicomte de Turenne, Marshal of France (1611–1675), and Corret himself was being groomed to be the adopted heir of the then Duke of Bouillon, Godefroy Charles Henri de la Tour d'Auvergne. The Duchy of Bouillon, only slightly larger than the Island of Jersey, lay on the border, sandwiched between the Champagne district of France and the Austrian Netherlands (now the Belgian Ardennes).

Godefroy's interest was on one occasion awakened by a casual remark of Corret that one of the English prisoners in Carhaix apparently had the same surname as he had; Philippe Dauvergne's release was subsequently secured, and he was returned to England.

After another series of adventures – one of which was his spending 15 months on the remote island of Trinidad in the South Atlantic (now a Brazilian possession) – Dauvergne was met in England by the Duke of Bouillon. The Duke had armed himself with a pedigree, termed a 'mere heraldic figment' by one authority, which professed to show that Dauvergne was an authentic relation and – more important – a suitable heir. In November 1788 the Duke proceeded to make a will which referred to Dauvergne as his adopted son.

Three years later the cause of Philippe Dauvergne – or, as he began to be known, d'Auvergne – was advanced still further when the old Duke made him Prince-successor; this affidavit, though it met with entrenched resistance from the Bouillon Assembly, was formally sanctioned by George III of Great Britain. In the same year political tensions in France increased inexorably and d'Auvergne once again returned to London. The defence of the Channel Islands became a priority for him in 1794 and, from that date until the turn of the century, at the behest of the British Government under Pitt, he lent support to various anti-Republican movements in Brittany from his base in Jersey. He became very familiar with the French coast and was on one occasion charged with landing false banknotes or *assignats* in Normandy. In 1802 he bought the property in Jersey known as Bagatelle, but according to contemporary records, spent many a day during the following decade dreaming of his dukedom in Bouillon.

In 1814, d'Auvergne took advantage of the first defeat of Napoleon to return to Paris where he formally assumed his title, returning to Jersey as 'His Serene Highness the Duke of Bouillon' later that year.

His life-long ambition was, however, not to be realized. His position became weaker as Napoleon reentered Paris and the neutrality of Bouillon was proclaimed; any residual hopes which he might have had were finally dashed when the Congress of Vienna gave Bouillon to the Dutch.

D'Auvergne died, broken-hearted and bankrupt, in 1816.

There exist a few examples of a 5 *franc* coin, dated 1815, commemorating this remarkable man. The coin itself is a bit of a mystery. Some, spurred on perhaps by the exhortation on the edge 'DOMINE SALVUM FAC DUCEM', believe it was struck by order of 'Philippe d'Auvergne, Duc Souverain de Bouillon' (his title on the coin), but the minting style seems somehow out of period.

The name of the engraver, C. H. Werdun, appears below the bust but no such name has been traced in contemporary records. A certain Charles Würden, born in 1849, is known to have engraved at the Brussels mint in the 1870's and both the coin's style and the Brussels mintmark ('A') have persuaded at least one authority that the d'Auvergne 5 Franc piece was in fact a Belgian product of the end of the 19th century.

Whatever its origin, the coin is a handsome – if exotic – addition to any Channel Island coin collection.

*Fig. 103: The enigmatic 5* franc *piece of Philippe d'Auvergne.*
*Mazard,* Histoire Monétaire . . . *no. 740.*

# The Sir Isaac Brock Half-Pennies

Sir Isaac Brock, 'Hero of Upper Canada', was born in St. Peter Port, Guernsey, on 6th October 1769, in the same year that gave birth to Wellington and Napoleon. While Acting Administrator at York – later Toronto – in Canada, he heard that an American force under General Hull had crossed the Detroit river into Canada, shortly after the American Congress had declared war against Great Britain, on 18th June 1812.

Brock lost no time in summoning the Provincial Parliament and troops were sent to meet the Americans, and, himself commanding one of the small contingents, called upon the American garrison in Fort Detroit to surrender, which – unexpectedly – they did. Two months later, on 13th October 1812, Brock fell heroically at the Battle of Queenston Heights, where the Niagara river enters Lake Ontario. His passing was honoured both by the British and the American forces.

*Fig. 104: Sir Isaac Brock portrayed on a Guernsey £10 note. See GN51.*

Upper Canada, four years later, commemorated Sir Isaac Brock with an issue of copper half-pennies; there are two types:

1. (Breton No. 723)
   *Obverse:* SUCCESS TO THE COMMERCE OF UPP<sup>R</sup> AND LOW<sup>R</sup> CANADA round a three masted ship in full sail
   *Reverse:* Inscription (in 9 lines): SIR ISAAC BROOK [sic] BAR<sup>T</sup> THE HERO OF UPPER CANADA, WHO FELL AT THE GLORIOUS BATTLE OF QUEENSTOWN HEIGHTS ON THE 13 OCT<sup>R</sup> 1812
2. (Breton No. 724)
   *Obverse:* S<sup>R</sup> ISAAC BROCK THE HERO OF UP<sup>R</sup> CANADA round a sepulchral urn on a pedestal on which is inscribed FELL OCT. 13 1812; two angels hover over the urn and crown it with a wreath of laurel
   *Reverse:* SUCCESS TO COMMERCE AND PEACE TO THE WORLD round the date 1816 between two ornamental stars

While these little copper coins are an unassuming memorial to another great Channel Islander, they are no less important than Philippe d'Auvergne's 5 franc piece. In 1980, Sir Isaac Brock's life was once again recalled – when his portrait appeared on the Guernsey £10 note.

# Channel Islands Paper Money

In 1817, shortly after the silver and copper tokens were struck, Plees wrote in his *'Account of the Island of Jersey'*:

> 'The coin current in Jersey was, until lately, chiefly that of France, with a small proportion of Spanish money. The usual amount of specie, in circulation, has been estimated at nearly £80,000 sterling. After the French revolution, the coin of England became more generally into use, until the increased value of gold and silver completely drained the island of all specie but copper, and even that became scarce. There were, at this period, three regular banking houses in the town of St. Helier. These, and a few mercantile men, were accustomed to issue notes, payable to the bearer on demand, for twenty-four livres French currency, or one pound sterling. So great, however, and so increasing were the inconveniences occasioned by the almost total disappearance of silver, that those houses were obliged to issue notes of five and ten shillings: this induced individuals to do the same; all having 'Jersey Bank' on their notes; until there were about eighty of these soi disant bankers. The island was soon inundated with notes, from the value of one pound down to that of one shilling; many of them issued by the lowest description of traders and publicans. Alarming as this undoubtedly was, necessity gave to these notes a general and ready circulation.
>
> Seriously aware of the ultimate consequences, likely to result from this unrestrained emission of paper money, the States resolved to have a silver coin struck: accordingly a quantity of tokens was issued bearing the value of three shillings, and of eighteen pence English, . . .'

The above is a very succinct paraphrase of the circumstances of the introduction of paper currency into the Islands, a subject which was studied in great detail by Lieut-Colonel W. Marshall-Fraser in his *'History of Banking in the Channel Islands'*. He wrote:

> 'Jersey at one time had some 100 banks, firms, parishes and individuals with note issues, but the States of Jersey have never issued notes with the exception of a £1 denomination by the Harbour Committee in 1874 and, of course, the Occupation issues.
>
> The States of Guernsey began their note issues in 1816 and so continued to the present day. It was this fact that probably accounted for the absence of the spate of emissions which took place in Jersey.'

This is an important point which goes some way to explaining the disparity in the numbers of note-issuing institutions in the two Islands. Consequently, I have arranged the list of such institutions alphabetically in the case of Jersey, but chronologically for Guernsey. Although both listings are exhaustive, I cannot but admit the likelihood that they are not complete, as the circumstances of the early 19th century were such that many individuals – honest and dishonest – must have been tempted to issue their own paper. I have here taken the liberty of quoting in full some articles from the 'Jersey Independent' newspaper of October, 1859 entitled THE REIGN OF RAGS, cited by Marshall-Fraser; the articles poignantly recall the conditions of the time.

Amongst numerous publications of the 'useful knowledge' order, the reader may remember to have seen, or at least seen advertised, 'Everyman his own Brewer,' 'Everyman his own Gardener,' and so on, through most of the callings into which the national industry is divided. We do not remember to have seen 'Everyman his own Banker.' But if anyone with a genius for bookmaking is inclined to try his hand at the production of such a work, we recommend him to spend a month or two of inquiry in this Island. In the course of that time the intending author will be very dull indeed if he does not pick up enough of 'useful knowledge,' not merely to write 'Everyman his own Banker,' but also to turn his acquired information to practical account, by going into the Banking business, or at least note issuing business, on what the Yankees term 'his own book.' Perhaps, fresh from the other side of the water, he may imagine that to issue currency it is essential to be possessed of either sundry bars of bullion, or a few thousands of coined sovereigns. A short residence in Jersey may satisfy anyone that such a condition is by no means essential in taking up the business of circulating paper money. Remembering Cobbett's detestation of 'rag-money,' we can imagine that he would have felt himself in purgatory had he been doomed to live in Jersey, to pass possibly half his time without the sight of a good, honest looking portrait of Her Majesty done in gold. Poets tell of the 'golden age.' That was a very long time ago; and must have come to an end much earlier in Jersey than in many parts of the world; the dearth of gold being an old local complaint, which has more than once within the last one hundred and fifty years taxed the legislative wisdom of the Jersey States. The imaginative gentlemen just alluded to tell us that the 'age of silver,' which followed the age of gold also died out, and was succeeded by the less happy times of the 'bronze' and 'iron' ages. Vestiges of 'the age of bronze' may still be found in the Royal Court, and very fine specimens too! The present period should, however, be distinguished rather as 'the age of rags,' of which the general symbol and representative is to be found in the 'notes' of all names and descriptions, with which the Island is flooded. Why anybody in Jersey should be in want of money, or at least, of a circulating medium, we do not understand, seeing that anyone is at liberty to start a paper-mint on his own account. We have no patience with people who acknowledge to be 'in difficulties,' when it is patent to the meanest capacity that one has only to purchase a few reams of 'flimsy' and engage the services of an engraver, to forthwith command the contribution of Baker, Butcher, Wine-Merchant, Landlord, etc., comprising all classes from the lordly merchant to the polisher of boots! Let us at once say that amongst the Jersey note issuers there are all sorts, or at least three sorts. First, good and substantial; second, so-so, and passable; third, decidedly questionable, if not intolerably bad. There are so many of the second-named, and the third category is so constantly increasing, that to persons who have given the least thought to the subject the danger is apparent enough of general mistrust taking the place of a too heedless security, to the injury of respectable parties as well as the overthrow of those who ought never to have been allowed to dabble into the currency of the Island.

There can be no question that the facility for issuing notes payable on demand, and backed by unquestionable security, has been productive of great public good. Probably more than half of the improvements of the Island are to be traced to that facility. But it is no new thing to find a power which has been well employed abused. And we think that the list we are about to give will show that the abuse of a paper currency has already attained such a height in Jersey as to call loudly for the law's intervention.

It is not the first time that the abuse we speak of assumed alarming proportions and occasioned the intervention of the law. Previous to the year 1813 the Island was inundated with most ridiculous specimens of paper-money. There were notes representing one shilling, two shillings, half-a-crown and a crown, besides one pound. Those under a pound had this peculiarity, that the bearer could not obtain payment in coin of any note of one shilling, two shillings, etc., unless he presented to the issuer a quantity equal to one pound. In those days the dabblers in paper currency did not put themselves to the expense of employing an engraver, the notes were simply printed; of course opening a fine field to unlimited forgery. The peculiarity attending the cashing of the notes just mentioned suggested to some native genius the following bit of privateering on a small scale: He took up and carried out the idea of issuing only nineteen notes of one shilling each and seven of half-a-crown. Of course the pound's worth of either was never presented to him in cash, for a very obvious reason.

The States, on the 8th May, 1813, passed a law forbidding for the future any issue of money of less value than one pound. The law was confirmed on the 10th of June following. In the preamble it is therein stated, 'That recently notes of various amounts from one pound to one shilling, payable to the bearer, have been put into circulation by a large number of individuals, and which are received by the public without any regard as to the solvency of the issuers; that this circulation of paper, particularly notes of small amount, has occasioned great inconvenience, loss and even frauds, to the injury of the poor and uneducated inhabitants, and the soldiers of the garrison: that it is of the highest importance to repress and prevent so manifest an abuse of public confidence and to maintain that good faith which should regulate all commercial operations, without which there can be no prosperity.

If in 1813 the Island was inundated with paper-money, it may safely be said that, although shilling and half-crown notes are unknown to the present generation, the flood of paper money, and that, too, of a very questionable character, has already risen to a height demanding the attention of the Press preparatory to more effective action on the part of those to whose hands the safety of the community is entrusted. Now, as in 1813, the public receive notes issued by 'Jack,' 'Tom,' and 'Harry', 'without any regard as to the solvency of the issuers,' and unless a remedy is provided in time there may yet be occasion to lament over great inconvenience and loss' arising from 'abuse of public confidence,' and the violation of that 'good faith which should regulate all commercial operations, without which there can be no prosperity.'

But let us, without further preface, come to the list above alluded to, which list the reader will find worthy of his perusal.

As regards the six 'Banks of Issue' at the head of the above list, the only Banks, properly speaking, in the Island, we are happy to observe that there are no Banks throughout the United Kingdom, not excepting the oldest and richest establishments in the Metropolis, that are more worthy of public confidence. We have never heard the whisper of suspicion in reference to any of the six, and for all the purposes of business and ordinary transactions between man and man, in the Island, the notes of the Old Bank, Commercial Bank, the Banking Company, the Mercantile Union Bank, the Jersey Joint Stock Bank, and the Channel Island Bank are just as safe and much more convenient than the notes of the Bank of England.

As regards the Parochial Notes in general, we have nothing to say derogatory to their security. We believe that one or two parishes, if not two or three, over-do the system, and that they are gradually accumulating a responsibility which a succeeding generation will find exceedingly unpleasant. It is a question which will probably engage the attention of the Commissioners, whether the present mode of 'raising the wind' to provide for parish wants is the best, or whether the more simple method of loans, repayable within a given time, would not be preferable. But into that question we will not enter. We will only say of the Parish Notes that the guarantee is sufficient to justify public confidence. The only complaint we shall make is that some of the notes of the country parishes, though circulating in the town, are not payable at any place in St. Helier. Moreover some of the notes, and this applies to the town parish, do not bear on the face of them where payable.

The next class is that of notes bearing Parochial titles, but issued under the guarantee of private individuals only. In presence of the system of parochial issue on which we have just commented, it is a question whether individuals should be permitted to issue notes bearing titles open, if not calculated, to mislead the public. An Englishman not long resident, aware that the parishes are in the habit of issuing notes, receives one bearing the inscription 'St. Peter's New Bank,' or 'St. Martin's Bank,' or 'St. John's Bank,' or 'St. Clement's Bank,' and naturally concludes that these notes are parish notes, and have the security of the parish guarantee. We say this should not be allowed, and we say this without wishing to cast a slur upon such notes in general. But we must be allowed a few words on this particular section. As regards one issue, bearing a parochial name, though not issued or guaranteed by the parish, we are assured on excellent authority that this private speculation has now in circulation double the number of notes compared with any one of the six banks of issue. It is not mentioned where the note alluded to is payable. We have seen specimens on which some grimly facetious individual has written payable 'nowhere' – a locality we cannot find in any of the Jersey Guide Books! The section under notice includes SIXTEEN separate issues, all bearing parochial names, though as we have already explained, issued by individuals, the parishes being not at all responsible. Any unsophisticated person must suppose

*Fig. 105: £1 note of St. Saviour's Bank, signed by George Collas, Chief of Police. See JN40.*

reading the title of 'Parish of St. Helier' that the note bearing such inscription was issued under the guarantee of the parish. Not so. The proprietors of the property in Belmont Road wishing that thoroughfare paved 'raised the wind' by the issue of a certain number of notes. We believe the security is excellent, but were it otherwise the public could not fall back upon the parish. The public must be content with the security of the proprietors. Lastly, to conclude with the section under notice, the reader will have observed that three of the issues are refused by the principal Bankers.

We now come to the avowed Private issues. In this section may be found very big names, such as 'Association,' etc., names applicable enough to banks of issue or banks of deposit; but rather too big when assumed by two or three small individuals. Of this category there are SEVENTEEN issues. Jersey Agriculture would seem to be in a flourishing state judging by the number of 'Agricultural Associations,' as many as five, all issuing their notes and exhibiting an extraordinary illustration of the principle of fraternity. Judging by the repetition of names, one must infer that brotherly love, or at least a very intense degree of friendship must prevail in these 'Agricultural Associations.' *It will be observed that THREE of the issues in this category are refused by the Bankers.* As our readers may not be acquainted with a number of these 'promises to pay,' we will copy two specimens for their edification:

FAMILY ASSOCIATION BANK,

No. 49      JERSEY.      No. 49

I promise to pay the Bearer on demand

ONE POUND BRITISH.

Value received, the 12th Nov., 1858.

For LE BLANCQ, DE GRUCHY & CO.

Ph. LE BLANCQ,

ONE

PAYABLE AT 60, KING STREET,

BRITISH STERLING

JERSEY UNION ASSOCIATION BANK.

NO. 112

JERSEY.      30th AUGUST, 1859.

We promise to pay the bearer on demand

ONE POUND BRITISH VALUE RECEIVED

payable at No. 1. Cross Street, for LE MONTAIS DOLBEL, DE LA PERELLE & CO.

ONE

Elie Le Montais.
E. De La Perrelle.
E. Dolbel.
P. Hacquoil.

BRITISH STERLING.

The 'Family Association Bank' bears the date of the 12th November, 1858, but we have reason for believing that the plate from which the note was printed is some forty years old. To this plate hangs a tale, but being rather too romantic for our utilitarian columns we forbear from entering into particulars. We will merely remark that the history of this resuscitated plate will be found recorded in the annals of a celebrated Highland clan!

The 'Jersey Union Association Bank' bears prominently a name which, if memory serves, we have met before. Three years ago we had occasion to call attention to a certain circular issued by 'Monsieur Elie Le Montais, No. 10, Bond-street' which set forth his titles and qualifications as follows: 'Legal adviser, Surveyor, Attorney, etc.' who continues 'to sell Ground Rents on Commission as well as Property as Agent, to take Inventories, affairs in difficulties, etc., etc., to make valuations divisions of property, make measurements, to send actions for the recovery of accounts, etc., to write out remonstrances, Agreements, Contracts, Wills, and to give advice concerning the proceedings and customs of the Royal Court and of the Laws in general (well understood) on most moderate terms.' At that time, three years ago, Le Montais was in labour with a couple of Assurance offices, and the assurance with which he set forth the grossest falsehoods shewed him admirably qualified to play the part of a *Jeremy Diddler*. We believe that Mr. Le Bailly, farmer, and William Gaudin, Esq., Solicitor, could speak to Mr. Le Montais' character. Without saying more of Mr. Le Montais at present, the next name on the note is that of Dolbel, the maiden name of Mrs. Le Montais! De La Perelle, we are informed, is a ship-carpenter at Clark's shipbuilding yard! Lastly, P. Hacquoil is a gentleman who on the 27th of August last obtained a white-washing in the Royal Court. A 'Décret' was ordered on that day on his property, and Mr. John Coutanche was the Ecrivain appointed by his creditors to carry out the proceedings before the Greffier. The above note of the 'Jersey Union Association Bank,' it will be seen, was issued on the 30th August, 1859. It follows, therefore, that three days after his appearance before the Court, Mr. Hacquoil changed the termination of his title from 'rupt' into 'er,' and by one harlequin-like jump passed from the condition of a *Bankrupt* to the state and dignity of a *Banker!* The note of Le Montais and Co. is made payable at 1, Cross-street; and let the reader not forget, has been payable there from the 30th of August last. But on the 30th of August last, and for a month ensuing, No. 1, Cross-street was an empty house. It was on quarter day last, or a day or two preceding, that the respectable firm of the 'Jersey Union Association Bank' moved into No. 1, and stored their bullion in the cellars! As a number of Imperialists have been lately on a visit to the Island and lodging at Madame Boisnet's, they doubtless have had an eye on the Cross-street establishment, and it may be anticipated that should the threatened invasion take place, the first rush of the Zouaves and Turcos will be to the iron chests and well lined cellars of No. 1.

Perhaps by this time the reader is satisfied of the accuracy of the assertion we set out with at the beginning, that capital is not at all necessary in Jersey to enable anyone to go into the 'Banking business.' Let no one suppose that the notes of the 'Jersey Union Association Bank' are not in circulation, the one above copied is numbered '112', and last week a friend of ours had three brought to him, two of them bearing the numbers '91' and '144' respectively!

The evil we have called attention to may be summed up in a sentence. There are in Jersey – including the six banks of issue – fifty-two different descriptions of paper currency circulating in the Island!

It is not enough to point out an evil; it is necessary to suggest a remedy. But this article is already so lengthy as to preclude us from entering upon the subject. Enough for a day or two. Enough for the moment to have called attention to a serious evil which of late years 'has increased, is increasing, and ought to be diminished.'

II.

Our exposure of the rag bag 'currency' in last Saturday's INDEPENDENT caused, we understand, no small flutter and consternation among the gentlemen who are so liberal in their 'promises to pay.' Maledictions, not loud, but deep, have been hurled at us for endangering the 'vested interests' of the patriots whose philanthropy compasses both land and sea, and who above insular prejudices, keep English and French paper mills going, whilst stuffing the pockets and cramming the purses of their own *concitoyens* with 'bank-notes.'

The small whisperings of bitterness issuing from the subjects of our scarification, should, perhaps, be regarded as another example of their virtues. Le Montais & Co. and all of the tribe of Le Montais, do good by stealth and blush to find it fame. Hence we can conceive their annoyance at finding their deeds, or rather their 'promises' blazoned in the INDEPENDENT. Hence, too, we can understand why although a week has passed since we first directed public attention to this subject, we have not received a line, or heard a word from the 'Family Association' or 'the Jersey Union Association.' The inherent modesty of Le Blancq, de Gruchy & Co., the unsurpassing bashfulness of Le Montais, Dolbel, De La Perrelle and Hacquoil, induce them to prefer the shade of obscurity to the noonday light of publicity. Hence, also, it frequently happens that so many of the persons whose names figure in the third and fourth sections of the list given in last Saturday's paper are, when wanted, 'not at home.' This has occurred, we hear, in several instances during the last seven days.

There are some persons, however, persons of little faith, and by nature inclined to ungenerous suspicions, who assign other reasons for the invisibility of the ragmen. These persons pretend, indeed, to believe that the promisers to pay require as much looking after as the members of the States, the 'promises' of the former being no more trustworthy than the 'pledges' of the latter. In support of the opinion they cite such stories as the following, the facts having occurred within the last two or three weeks:

No. 1. – A customer enters a baker's shop, selects a penny bun, and sets his teeth in it; then he puts down a 'note' for change. The baker looks at the note and does not like the look of it. 'All right,' says the customer. 'But I don't think it is all right' replies the baker, beginning to feel 'crusty'. 'I never heard of this Bank before. Who's Jeremy Diddler? 'It's quite good, I assure you,' rejoins the customer, 'I'm Mr. Diddler!' The 'banker' has no small change. The baker runs the risk, changes the note, and the 'banker' departs satisfied with his day's work!

No. 2. – The head of a financial 'Association,' anxious to unite with crowned heads and the élite of Europe in encouraging gymnastic talent, and desirous also of relaxing from the cares of a banking business by enjoying an evening at the Circus, casts about how he may raise the 'needful'; for although he is the master of rolls upon rolls and piles and piles of 'bank-notes' and doubtless of metallic wealth to correspond, still he is like his brother 'banker' mentioned above, deficient in change. The Circus performers would rather not, thank you, take Jersey notes; they are Cobbettites and prefer 'hard stuff.' This is unfortunate, for our 'banker's fresh supply of sovereigns from the Bank of England has not arrived. He requests an old woman, a neighbour, to oblige him with change for one of his own notes. After much persuasion the good dame's strong scruples are overcome and she yields, on condition that the note shall be taken back next morning and replaced by 'money of Great Britain,' or by some Jersey note enjoying her confidence. The 'banker' hies him to the Circus. Next morning the old lady is on the look-out for her expected visitor. He comes not. She sends to him. He is 'not at home.' The message is repeated with no better results. The dame, wise in her generation, makes a purchase in the neighbourhood and succeeds in cashing the note. Her triumph is but of brief duration. The shopkeeper takes alarm, insists upon the note being re-exchanged and it returns to the dame. She is no female Job, and, losing patience, she proceeds to storm the 'Bank,' uttering terrible threats of calling in the police. There is no help for it, somehow, somewhere, the 'banker' obtains and pays to the old lady real value to the amount of twenty shillings; he being left with his note and to his own reflections on the difficulties of banking in dealing with persons too ignorant to repose confidence in the solvency of his financial establishment.

These are no fables. Several of our readers are acquainted with the names of the heroes of the above paragraph.

With such examples, we may reasonably expect to see presently announced 'The Jersey Shoe Black Union Bank,' 'The St. Helier's Pier Rangers Association Bank,' etc., etc. For our own part, we declare, we would much rather take any number of notes bearing the signature of 'Jim Flynn,' the respectable improver and polisher of local understandings, than such notes as the following, many varieties of which are in circulation in this island:

The United Chiffoniers' Association Bank

No. 000                  No. 000

Jersey, April 1, 1859.

We promise to pay the Bearer on demand One Pound British value received.

For Dunup, La Flimsy, Hardup & Co.

Jeremy Le Diddler.

Payable at No. 101, Nowhere Street.

British Sterling (!!!)

Some of our readers, we hear, treat as 'a joke' our mention of shilling and half-crown notes in our former article on this question. We have before us the original of one of the half-crown notes, issued at the time; it will be perceived, when there were still Bank of England 'One Pound Notes.' Trois livres were of the value of 2s. 6d.

No.      JERSEY      No.

We promise to pay a Bank of England Note for 8 of these Notes.

3 LIVRES.     ST. HELIER's     day of 181 .

The above must have been in use within the years 1810–1813. In the latter year the law was passed forbidding any issue of notes under the value of One Pound each.

It is remarkable that not only are *all* the notes (52 issues) at present circulated in the Island engraved and printed in the *English Language;* but also as far back as 1813–1810 [sic], notes intended for circulation among the *people,* small notes of half-a-crown value, were also printed in *English.* 'Captain Cuttle' would say 'take a note of this for the Commissioners.'

The public and private issues of notes in Jersey are enormous, astounding considering that the population cannot at the utmost exceed 70,000 souls. Over and above the notes of the recognised regular banks, the Parochial notes and those issued by the Town Vingtaine, there are thirty-three private issues. Doubtless many of the issuers are respectable and thoroughly solvent persons; but many are doubtful as regards both qualities, and some are notoriously neither respectable nor solvent. The end of such a state of things it is not difficult to foresee, unless averted by the timely and judicious intervention of the Legislature. In looking down the list given in last Saturday's *Independent,* the reader doubtless observed that in several instances the persons who figure as 'securities' are dead, and a number of notes mention no names as 'sureties.' Some half-dozen of the issues are refused by the Banks. Let us add that we have before us a list of persons who having had notes in circulation have failed within the last twenty years. We mention only some six or eight of the most recent:

'Thomas Jarvis,' Vingtaine du Mont-au-Prêtre, Rue du Val.

'G. W. Le Geyt,' Postmaster.

'W. G. Le Gallais,' Jersey Bank.

'Thomas Le Gros,' Vingtaine du Mont-au-Prêtre.

'Jean Carré,

'John Burridge,' Parish of St. Heliers. This note was issued for the paving of New Street, Craig Street and Upper Don Street, but guaranteed only by the issuer.

'Philip Du Heaume,' St.Ouen's Bank. Mr. Du Heaume did not fail, but there was a *Bénéfice d'Inventaire* held on his property at his death. The Notes which were not registered in the *Bénéfice d'Inventaire* were lost.

'Elias Le Bas,' Mont-au-Prêtre.

We have already spoken of the law of 1813 which extinguished the shilling and half-crown notes. In the year 1831, on the 15th February, the States passed a Bill which had been introduced by Mr. Francis Godfray, the Constable of St. Helier. We give a summary of that measure, which, on the whole, did credit to its framer.

The Bill provided that every person wishing to issue paper money must seek the permission of the Court, which could be refused. The applicant was bound to produce two sureties responsible for the amount intended to be put into circulation. Before making an application to the Court the applicant had to announce his intention in the local newspapers during one month preceding. When permission was granted it was ordered that the act of the Court be registered against the property of the applicant and his two sureties. Failing compliance with this order the party incurred a fine of a thousand *livres*. The applicant was bound to inform the Court the number of notes he intended to issue. His two sureties had to present a statement of their property, the value of which over all liabilities had to be at least one third more than the amount of notes they proposed to guarantee. The sureties could not escape from their responsibility, but by giving three weeks' notice in the newspapers of their intention that in six months from the date of the publication they would withdraw their security, if not objected to. The issuer was compelled to have an office in Town and to be in attendance every day, except Sunday, from 10 to 4 to change his notes.

(This would be deemed an enormous grievance by the proprietor of the St. Peter's New Bank.)

The notes were not to be less than £1 and to state where payable. The issuer, if absent from his office during the hours above mentioned, to be liable to prosecution. (The proprietor of the 'Grouville Parish Bank' would deem this a most outrageous violation of the liberty of the subject).

Those who had notes in circulation previous to the passing of the law were allowed from the date of the passing of the act to the 1st of October following to recall their notes, or comply with the provisions of the law. Any person issuing more notes than he was permitted by the act of the Court was subject to a penalty of sixteen livres on every note over and above the amount permitted. The same penalty was incurred if two notes bore the same number. The issuer was bound to number his notes correctly. The notes of the Town Vingtaine, and those of the Parishes, were exempted from the provisions of the bill.

This was a good law, and why it was not made permanent by obtaining the Royal confirmation we do not understand. That course was not taken. Consequently at the end of three years the law lapsed and was never revived. What reasons Mr. Godfray had for being so indifferent to his own legislative offspring we do not profess to know. It is a pity that one good measure connected with that gentleman's legislative career was not made the permanent law of the Island.

With certain alterations, we would propose, in the interest of the public, the re-enactment of the law of 1831. One difference we would suggest should be that the permission should take the form of a yearly licence. We will not name any particular sum, as it is not within our province to propose a *projet* to the States. We are satisfied that respectable banking establishments would not object to a payment, which, sufficient to operate as a check upon needy speculators, would be felt as a mere featherweight tax by wealthy banking firms. The Parishes and the Town Vingtaine should not be exempted from the provisions of the law as was the case with Mr. Godfray's Bill; but the licence fee might be remitted. At the same time the Court should not grant the required permission without being satisfied that good grounds existed for the application. Several points of Mr. Godfray's law might be modified or improved, but into these matters, for the reason already assigned, it is not necessary we should enter.

The question we have raised, coming within the scope of the duties of the Commissioners, will probably engage their attention. If they can propose any better remedy than we have suggested we shall be happy to record and support it. Be the form of amendment what it may, the security of public credit and the protection of those who live by their labour, demand, imperatively demand, that some means should be adopted, enacted, and enforced as the law of the land, to restore the character of the local currency, to send the chiffoniers back to their legitimate occupation and terminate 'The REIGN OF RAGS.'

Although there appears to have been quite a number of *soi-disant* Jersey bankers whose intentions were not altogether honourable, the reason for this proliferation of private notes should not be forgotten. In the United Kingdom and Channel Islands, incompetent official handling of the currency problem since the 1750's had caused industrial and commercial circles to take the law into their own hands. In spite of the fears of the 'Jersey Independent', the problems caused by the likes of 'Jeremy Diddler' were in fact far outweighed by the beneficial effects which this largely private currency medium had during these financially anarchic times.

In view of the interdependence of official, semi-official and private bank-note issues for Jersey and Guernsey, I have produced one bank-note catalogue for each Island which runs from the origins until 1939. This dating is arbitrary and for convenience only. In fact, while Guernsey had more or less regular issues between 1900 and 1939, Jersey had to make do with Bank of England paper and the new Treasury notes, for one pound and ten shillings, first issued in August 1914, as local issues had all but disappeared. Listings of occupation and post-war note issues appear in later sections. It goes without saying that, after 1830, both notes and coin circulated concurrently in the Islands, and, while the emphasis in the next section on Channel Island coinages will be on the issues of copper and bronze, the importance of the complementary paper currency should not be understated.

# Guernsey and Jersey Coinages

On April 26th 1830, the Finance Committee of the States of Guernsey resolved to replace the very worn copper coinage with new *liards* or, as they were by then called, *'doubles'*. Later in the same year, the contract to supply these new copper coins, styled 'one double' and still worth one eighth of a penny sterling, went to the Soho Mint, Birmingham. Over 1.6 million coins of this one double denomination, together with over 650,000 of a new denomination of 4 doubles (or *'sou'* worth one halfpenny sterling) were minted between 1830 and 1839. The weight of the 4 doubles coin (10 grams) was actually four times that of the 1 double denomination. Guernsey was thus first to recognize the need to have its own coinage and to alleviate the shortage of small change.

*Fig. 106: The 4 doubles and 1 double coins of Guernsey, first of the Channel Island copper series. See G24 and G61.*

In 1834 the old French duodecimal silver coins ceased to be current and the States of Guernsey matched this with their first issue of an *8 doubles* piece, of which over 220,000 were minted during the period 1834–1839. In the same year (1834) it was decreed in Jersey that after 1st October, English money would be the sole legal tender, with 26 *livres* being counted for the value of one pound sterling. However British coin was apparently difficult to attract to the Island and it took a further five years before a Committee of the States of Jersey received Royal Sanction to have struck copper coins of 1/13th, 1/26th and 1/52nd of a shilling to an amount not exceeding £1000 sterling. One can be sure that when, after some delay, the new coins finally arrived aboard the steamer *Transit* on 12th November 1841 and were distributed from the Cohue Royale a few days later, the Island's commercial community must have been, at once, relieved by this long-overdue alleviation of the currency problem ('money that circulates accumulates' goes an old Jersey adage) and mystified by the fractions. The unusual denominations, which were to last until 1876, followed from the pound/livre parity (as decreed in 1834; see above). With 20 shillings to the pound and 20 *sous* to the *livre*, one shilling was worth 26 *sous*. The value of the Jersey penny or *'pièce de deux sous'* therefore became 1/13th of a shilling, the halfpenny or *'sou'* 1/26th of a shilling and the farthing, or *pièce de deux liards* 1/52nd of a shilling. Thirteen Jersey pennies weighed the same as twelve English pennies i.e. 1 lb. avoirdupois.

An early 'ready reckoner' is known, published by 'C.A.' in Jersey in 1854. The work is entitled *'Comparative value of English, Jersey, French and Livres Tournois Currency to which is added the value of Rentes in Jersey in four currencies'*. A sampling shows the following values:

    1d      British = 1 ½d Jersey = 10 $^{5}/_{12}$ centimes = 2 sous 2 deniers tournois
    1/-d    British = 1/1d Jersey = 1 Franc 25 centimes = 1 livre 6 sous tournois
    £1      British = £1–1–8d Jersey = 25 Francs = 26 livres tournois

This early copper coinage continued as legal tender until new bronze issues appeared – more in keeping with the size of the new British 'bun' penny first struck in 1860; Guernsey's copper coins were finally withdrawn from circulation in 1868, and Jersey's early in the following year.

Where the *obverse* of all Jersey coins has always featured the head of the reigning monarch – a Jersey toast is to *'La Reine, notre Duc'* – Guernsey's coinage has not. With the exception of a small number of recent commemorative issues, the design has always been made up of motifs which are strictly 'Guernesiais'. This essential difference between the two coinages provides the collector with a contrast which is very striking, and one is transported back to those trying times in the mid-17th century when – for their own very valid reasons – Jersey sided with the Royalists while Guernsey preferred the Commonwealth. It is worth mentioning that, where Jersey coins have always been struck at the Royal Mint (except on rare occasions when it was too busy to complete the order), Guernsey coins were, until 1956, always struck at private mints in Birmingham.

Although the Island currencies had to a large extent solved the day-to-day problems of the shortage of small change, there was in fact, in the late 19th century, a very complicated financial situation in the area, which now relied on four different coinages: French and English as well as the Jersey and Guernsey series – which themselves were not models of simplicity. In addition, following the continuing public demand for small change, other European bronze coins also circulated in Britain and the Channel Islands. Although the most constantly used were the French bronze 10 *centimes* and 5 *centimes* (almost identical, in weight and diameter, to the English bronze penny and halfpenny respectively), coins of Italy, Luxembourg and Spain were also in circulation. To compound the problem, many in the Islands still kept their accounts in *tournois,* with the *livre* still being counted as 20 *sous* and the *sou* as four *liards.*

It was natural that there should be pressure from the populace for a simplified currency system and there were moves in both Islands to reinforce the sterling standard. In 1870, following discussion in the Guernsey States of the possible assimilation of the Island's currency to the British standard, it was once again ordained that English coin should be legal tender with the English shilling worth

12½ pence locally (it had officially been worth 12¾ pence since 1848). Three years later, Bank of England notes were once again proclaimed legal tender.

Jersey merchants had long been dissatisfied with the inconvenience of dividing the shilling into 13, 26 and 52 parts, and a petition was *'logée au Greffe'* in January 1876, requiring that the English standard be adopted. This petition was swiftly followed by an Act (25.2.1876) that the coinage should in future be denominated as the 12th, 24th and 48th parts of a shilling.

Contemporary correspondence reveals that there was some doubt as to whether the beasts on the Jersey shield were leopards or lions. The then Bailiff eventually reassured the Royal Mint that the leopards on the previous Coinage had been a mistake and that lions were the order of the day. The Mint had wanted to model the new coinage on the Jersey shield which had appeared on the obverse of the Channel Island Exhibition medal of 1871 (see below). Half a century later, in 1923, this plan was realized when the 'spindlier' beasts appeared albeit no longer on a heater-shaped shield. The shields of arms of the Channel Islands are discussed in more detail below.

The new Jersey coinage dated 1877, corresponded in size – though not consistently in weight – to that of the English bronze series; it was in fact struck by a private firm, R. Heaton & Son of Birmingham, from dies prepared at the Royal Mint. The exchange rate was 12 new pennies for 13 old, 12 new halfpence for 13 old, and 48 new farthings for 13 old pence. For some reason, the new issues neglected the fact that Queen Victoria had been proclaimed Empress of India; this was only put right – albeit in English – when Edward VII was styled 'King and Emperor'. On his issues, however, both 'D.G.' and 'F.D.' were omitted.

One hundred years later, on 25th March 1977, the centenary of this currency reform was celebrated by the issue of four postage stamps, which featured various Jersey coin designs over the period.

During the Victorian era, coin-collecting became very popular on both sides of the Atlantic, and there was an enormous number of publications on the subject. Auction houses were flourishing and, among others, the 'valuable and choice collection of Roman Coins...' of one Charles de St. Croix of Jersey was offered for sale by S. Leigh Sotheby and John Wilkinson on 10th April 1851. The beauty of contemporary machine-struck pieces was extolled and some of the early 'classics' on the subject of Gaulish medals (as they were called), began to appear. In a wise little editorial, the Jersey Coin Journal (of Egg Harbor City, New Jersey) in its Volume I, No. 1 dated Jan. & Feb. 1878, proclaimed:

> 'The collecting of coins and curiosities, has been a favorite employment of antiquitarians [sic] for many years. It is very probable that, in Greek and Roman times, there were numismatic collections as numerous as in these latter ages. It is not improbable that many of the fine specimens adorning our modern collections, were at one time the adornment of similar collections in Egypt, Greece, or Rome, more than a thousand years ago.
>
> During the last few years, the mania for collecting coins and curiosities has extended to nearly every corner of America. But a few years ago there were not many collections of note in the United States; now, there are many hundred, and the number steadily increasing.

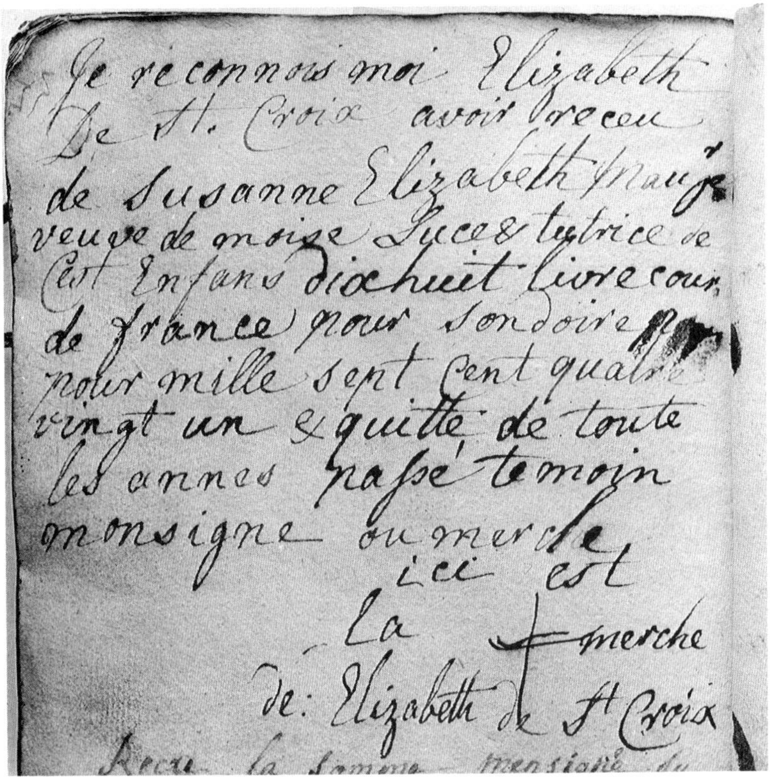

Je reconnois moi Elizabeth
De St. Croix avoir recu
de Susanne Elizabeth Mauger
veuve de moise Luce & tutrice de
Cest Enfans dixhuit livre cour
de france pour son doire
pour mille sept cent quatre
vingt un & quitte de toute
les annes passé temoin
mon signe ou merche
ici est
la + merche
de: Elizabeth de St Croix
Recu la somme mentioné

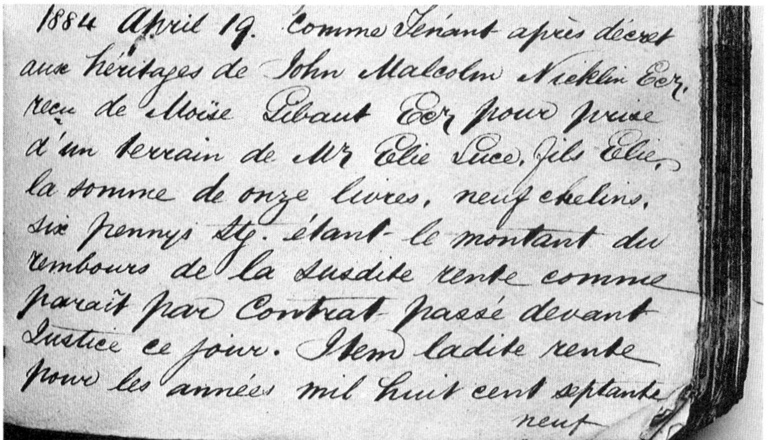

1884 April 19. Comme Tenant après décret
aux héritages de John Malcolm Nicklin Ecr,
reçu de Moïse Gibaut Ecr pour prise
d'un terrain de Mr Elie Luce, fils Elie,
la somme de onze livres, neuf chelins,
six pennys Stg. étant le montant du
rembours de la susdite rente comme
paraît par Contrat passé devant
Justice ce jour. Item ladite rente
pour les années mil huit cent septante
neuf

*Fig. 107: Extracts from a* Rente *receipt book in the author's possession, showing the change from French to English currency standards. French currency was finally withdrawn in the early 1920's. The first extract (top), dated 1781, the year of the Battle of Jersey, mentions 'dixhuit livre cour de france'; it is signed with a cross. The second (below), dated 1884, mentions 'la somme de onze livres, neuf chelins, six pennys Stg.'.*

Although manias are not to be encouraged, we know of none more pardonable than the coin mania; and the pursuit of coin collecting, within limits, is to be approved. It is of material advantage to the student, will help to fix dates and events in the memory, and prove a most important aid to historical research'.

In the catalogue section of the Journal, a Guernsey one double coin was offered, in good condition, for ten cents American. Incidentally, as far as I know, Guernsey and Jersey coins were first publicly offered for sale on the occasion of the auction of the Wellenheim collection (totalling some 45.000 lots!) in Vienna in 1845, during which a Guernsey penny of 1834 and Jersey three shillings and eighteen pence tokens were sold; the three items made, respectively, 17 kreuzers, 4 florins, and 2 florins 9 kreuzers. In the same sale, for comparison, a Pistrucci crown of George III dated 1818 made 2 florins 55 kreuzers. (In those days 60 Austrian kreuzers were equivalent to one florin – or gulden – and 2 florins to one thaler which in turn had a currency value approximately equal to one British crown.)

In the mid-19th century there was much talk of decimalization in England and some splendid pattern pieces were struck at the time. In 1900 a little book was published in Jersey which showed that the subject was still a matter for discussion. The book, written by Jurat A. Messervy, was entitled *'LSD versus £ – Florins – Parts or how to change our present complicated Monetary System to a System of Decimal Coinage within 48 hours and without changing one single coin'*. The system proposed was a variation on the £–mil system, where 100 parts were to equal one florin, and ten florins one pound. The idea was, needless to say, stillborn and the islanders had to wait another three generations before decimalization finally came.

From 1887 in Jersey and from 1902 in Guernsey, French bronze coins were no longer accepted as legal tender, though French gold and silver coins remained current for a few more years. During the period of the Great War, sovereigns and other gold coins disappeared from circulation and the price of silver rose to the extent that, for a few weeks in 1920, the value of silver in a coin was worth more than the coin's face value. To prevent hoarding, the issue of .925 silver coinage was suspended in England in 1920, and the question of whether or not French silver would also be withdrawn was of great concern to the Channel Islanders at the time. In fact all French silver coins were exchangeable for British coin with Banks in Guernsey until the end of April 1921 at the rate of 25.20 francs to the British pound. A certain number of French bronze coins also circulated in the Islands during the Great War years, in view of the shortage of local coin. These – some 500,000 coins – were withdrawn at the end of the war and were melted down and used in the second issue of Jersey pennies dated 1923, which are noticeably darker in colour.

The history of the associations of the currencies of France and the Channel Islands ends at this point although, even today, you may go into many a shop in St. Helier or St. Peter Port and obtain a very fine rate for your *francs*. The issue of a coinage expressed in 'doubles' continued in Guernsey until 1959 (proof 8 doubles and 4 doubles coins were struck as late as 1966) when the system was overtaken by decimalisation. However nothing can detract from the fascination shared by historians and numismatists at the unbroken connection of the Jersey 1/13th shilling and the Guernsey 1 double piece with a currency system which goes back two thousand years to the solidus and beyond.

..............................

A word on the shield of arms which graces the *reverses* of Jersey coins and the *obverses* of Guernsey coins would not go amiss. In 1279, in the same year as the first English groats were struck (see above), Edward I granted a seal which was for the use of both Bailiwicks. The seals for each Island were almost identical, differing only in the legends: *'S. Ballivie Insule de Gerseye'* for Jersey and *'S. Ballivie Insule de Gernseye'* for Guernsey. Each seal, at that time was surmounted by a branch, thought by some authorities to represent 'broom' or 'Plantagenista', King Edward's badge of rank; more recently, this feature has been seen as a branch of laurel or similar leaves in Guernsey. Centuries ago, it was dropped altogether from the Jersey arms and does not appear on Jersey coins.

The original seals bore the three lions of England, crowned; there is some doubt now whether they should represent lions or leopards, and the minute changes in the design of these *'luparts'* – as they are heraldically styled – is a study in itself. Several types of shield were used on the coinage of each Island. Jersey started with 'spade' shields on its silver eighteen pence and three shilling tokens (very similar, incidentally, to the shield on the rare Guernsey five shilling token). The first Jersey copper issues featured a square shield with an ornamented border and tincture lines; part of the ornament, above the shield, may have been designed to represent the missing sprig, though it has an uncanny resemblance to the Prince of Wales feathers.

In 1877 a 'heater-shaped' shield was introduced and this lasted until the second coinage of 1923 when the square shield was brought back, without the ornamented border, but with two ribbon scrolls containing the legend, above and below. This design was engraved by George Edward Kruger (later Kruger-Gray after he had added his wife's maiden name to his own) who was born and spent

*Fig. 108: Silver gilt medallion commemorating the Queen's visit to Alderney 1978. Also issued in sterling silver (5000), 9 ct gold sovereign size (1000) and 9 ct gold half sovereign size (1500); silver gilt issues numbered 2500. The royal yacht is shown superimposed on a map of Alderney (Pobjoy Mint).*

his childhood in Jersey. The rather heavy effect of the scrolls was not popular and, after only two issues (1923 and 1926), a plain square shield, again engraved by Kruger-Gray, was adopted for the rest of the series.

With the exception of the early 8 doubles, all Guernsey's copper and bronze coins bear a very plain square shield surmounted by a sprig. In fact, beyond some very minor – but very engaging – die varieties and, of course, the dates, the pre-war Guernsey series adhered more faithfully to its original design than any other series that I know of.

Alderney, with close economic links to Guernsey, has, to date, never had its own currency, though there has been discussion of the subject (the last time in 1976 when the issue of both distinctive postage stamps and currency notes was suggested). The Island has therefore seldom had a chance to show off its own seal: a lion rampant with a sprig in its paw. The design was however used on a series of official medallions issued in 1978 to commemorate the visit in that year of the Queen and the Duke of Edinburgh.

*Fig. 109: Medal, struck privately, to commemorate the fourth centenary of the Island of Sark. There are six medals (three gold and three silver) in each set, numbered 1–1000.*

Although a Sark shield, with two lions (or leopards) *passant gardant*, has official approval, the proper arms of the Island are those of the de Carteret family, a shield bearing four lozenges, surmounted by a crest consisting of a squirrel cracking a nut, and supported by two winged deer. The arms appear on the

*Fig. 110: Detail from Herm Island £1 coupon. The coupons, which are nominal, bear two signatures and are addressed to the Managers of five Herm establishments.*

obverse of a series of gold and silver medals struck privately to commemorate the fourth centenary of the grant of letters patent to Helier de Carteret; the reverse bears the arms of the well known Dame Sybil Hathaway who was Dame of Sark from 1927 until her death in 1974.

In the late 1950's, the tenant of Herm, Major Wood, issued £1 coupons for visitors; this was the closest the Island came to issuing its own currency. The badge of the Island, three friars (symbolizing the Augustinian community which flourished there in the middle ages) and two fish, in a diagonal pattern, appears on both sides of the coupon.

# The German Occupation

The German occupation of the Channel Islands lasted from July 1940 until May 1945. The German authorities were quick to extend to the Islands the orders which were already covering France; as a result the first exchange rate which was decreed was in terms of a currency which had not been legal tender for a generation. In the 'Journal Officiel no. 1' of 4th July 1940 (Art. IX), issued by the Military Governor in France, the exchange rate was fixed at:
'un franc français . . . = 0.05 Reichsmark'
At the same time (Art. X) it was decreed that the German troops *'payeront leurs achats et leurs commandes au comptant. Pour les sommes au delà des 500 Reichsmark (au lieu d'un payement au comptant) des certificats de livraisons seront délivrés. L'administration militaire allemande remboursera le montant.'*
Concurrently, the civil population of the Islands were introduced to *'Reichskreditkassenscheine'*, treasury notes of the third Reich which were used in numerous occupied countries. They came in denominations of 50, 20, 5, 2 and 1 Reichsmark as well as 50 Reichspfennig; the obverse of the 20 Reichsmark note featured *'der Bauermeister'* (the architect) by Albrecht Dürer.

*Fig. 111:*
*German 'Reichskredit-*
*kassenscheine'*
*(size reduced).*
Pick R135–140.

In the same month (8th July, 1940) the pound was devalued in the Islands to 8 *RM* – it had been worth 5 *RM*. The convenience, however, of the *RM* being worth exactly half-a-crown in terms of a one pound note was neutralized a few days later when the *RM* was revalued at 7 *RM* to the pound; for a short time in coinage terms, 1 *RM* was valued at 2 shillings and ten pence halfpenny. It held its value for two months until, on 3rd September, it was again devalued to 9.60 to the pound.

Very soon the situation became chaotic, with the following currency in circulation:
Notes: £1 notes of the Bank of England, which usually circulated at a premium
*Reichskassenscheine* (as above)
*Reichsbank* notes, mostly the RM 20 denomination

Guernsey notes – a few £1 and 10/–
Notes of the *Banque de France* – denominations: 5–5000 *francs*
Coins: British 'silver' and 'copper'
Jersey 1/12, 1/24 shilling
Guernsey 8, 4, 2 and 1 doubles
Various German denominations of the Weimar Republic (1919–1933) and the third Reich.
A quantity of French coins in denominations of 5 *centimes* to 20 *francs*

*Fig. 112: German coins which circulated during the occupation. Aluminium 50 Reichspfennig (obverse, Yeoman 92); zinc 10, 5, 1 Reichspfennig (reverses, Yeoman C92, B92, A92); bronze 2 Reichspfennig (reverse, Yeoman 89).*

In fact most of the above items – in small amounts – were still in circulation at the end of the war, in spite of several attempts by the German authorities to limit the medium to the *Reichskreditkassen* issues of notes and coin – at least until 26th November 1943. On that day it was decreed that the *Kreditkassenscheine* would be withdrawn and substituted by French notes on 1st December. On the 28th November, the order was rescinded as it was, apparently, impossible to implement.

In April 1944, a contemporary Jersey diarist recorded that owing to a change of currency in France, it was no longer possible to send *Reichsmarks* away to pay for purchases. As a result, an amount of some £ 1.5 million worth of *RM* notes and coin accumulated in Jersey alone. Although the exchange had been officially fixed at 9.36 *Reichsmarks* to the pound in September 1942, 15 *Marks* were being offered for one Bank of England £1 note by February 1943.

Under the circumstances, it was natural that barter should again have been practised and the plea 'For what?' was often heard in the markets and read in the classified columns of the local newspapers. The following is a small selection of advertisements from the Jersey 'Evening Post' of Friday June 12, 1942:
- LOST on Saturday by boy of thirteen, SEVEN SHILLINGS, half in marks...
- FOUND, CHILD'S SHOE; Also GENT'S SHOE...
- FOR SALE, RABBIT'S FOOD... 2/6 bag...
- COTTAGE to let, Havre-des-Pas, 4 rooms. Suit couple. 8/6 weekly...
- FOR SALE, LADY'S REAL CROCODILE DRESSING CASE, solid silver and ivory fittings. 500 marks...

- THREE GOLD SOVEREIGNS. What offers? . . .
- 60 FT. HALF-INCH GARDEN HOSE. What exchange? . . .
- EXCHANGE. FLOWER POTS (various sizes) for what?; also BED PAN AND AIR RING

While Guernsey had for many years had its own currency notes and was – at least to some extent – self-sufficient, this was not the case with Jersey. Thus it was that a special Currency Notes (Jersey) Law had to be passed when it became clear that the Jersey economy could not survive without such an exchange medium. Such a law was first passed as of the 29th April 1941 and by it the Finance Committee of the States were empowered to issue up to £5000 sterling in notes for two shillings. When it subsequently became clear that a two shillings denomination alone was not enough, an Amendment was passed (29th November 1941) which allowed the Finance Committee to issue notes of any denomination up to £1, to a total amount (all types) of £100,000. As a result, denominations of six pence, one shilling, two shillings (a second issue), ten shillings and one pound, engraved by the Jersey artist Edmund Blampied, were printed in the Island. The notes bore attractive Island motifs, in a style which, sadly only after his death, was to bring fame to the engraver.

*Fig. 113: The Rybot tokens:* – *above: common* obverse; *middle: shilling* reverses; *below: six pennies* reverse.
*Ex Pridmore and first published by him – see Bibliography.*

In addition to the £1 and ten shilling notes of the States of Guernsey, already in circulation, another set of rather plain style was issued, consisting of the following denominations: sixpence, one shilling, one shilling and threepence, two shillings and sixpence, five shillings, ten shillings and one pound. Unlike those of Jersey, these Guernsey issues were all dated and were printed by the Guernsey Press on various sorts of paper (including some blue French bank note paper which also served for certain of the Jersey postage stamps at the time). A five pound denomination was also printed for issue on the 1st January 1945.

At least one other attempt was made to alleviate the problems caused by the shortage of coin in 1942. The late Major N. V. L. Rybot submitted designs for sixpenny and one shilling tokens to the Jersey Treasury in that year. These coins were to be made of aluminium or some other base metal; one of the two 'shilling' designs incorporated a 'broken axis' motif. The project did not advance very far as such tokens would have to have been minted with the consent of the German authorities in Paris; in any event no metal was available. The shortage of silver coin is illustrated by the fact that a number of Jersey halfpennies were filed down to approximately the same diameter as shillings, for use in gas meters. Another set of imaginative brass uniface tokens, which included some ostensibly issued for the German Todt Organization, are spurious; they were produced in some numbers by an American entrepreneur in the 1970's.

*Fig. 114: Spurious occupation token. About ten such creations are known of various shapes and themes.*

Following the liberation of the Islands, German currency remained legal tender for a short term. The States of Guernsey, by proclamation of the Lieutenant Governor on 8th May 1945, were to accept *Reichskreditkassen* notes at the rate of two shillings per *Reichsmark;* exchange of these into States notes was restricted to £20 per person, with any amount in excess of this figure being credited to a bank account or exchanged for post-dated States warrants. The zinc ten and five *Pfennig* coins – nicknamed 'washers' because of the central hole in some of the earlier issues – stayed in circulation for the time being at rates of two pence halfpenny (20 doubles) and a penny farthing (10 doubles) respectively. As the situation returned to order and local and Bank of England notes became more plentiful, the earlier issues were gradually withdrawn. First to go, by ordinance of 26th May 1945, were the £1 and 10/– States issues previous to 9th March 1940; then, in July 1945, notes of the Bank of France as well as those issued to the

Allied Forces were recalled. Finally, by ordinance of 23rd March 1946, the emergency small denomination notes ceased to be legal tender after 31st May 1946.

Guernsey wartime notes, stamped 'WITHDRAWN FROM CIRCULATION' or 'CANCELLED' have found their way into several collections.

A series of Guernsey issues of 5 shillings, 10 shillings, 1 pound and 5 pounds notes has also been reported, which, ostensibly, was to cater for the situation at the end of the war. They are dated 1.1.1945 and are overprinted either 'BACKED WITH GUERNSEY NOTES' or 'BACKED BY BRITISH NOTES '. I have not been able to authenticate these issues.

In Jersey, a similar procedure was carried out. In the order for the restoration of Sterling of 15th May 1945, the rate of exchange during the period May 16th to May 18th was *RM* 9.36 to £1 (compared to *RM* 9.60 to the £1 in 1940). German currency was, after May 18th, no longer to be legal tender; in fact, as there was not enough Jersey or English money ready to substitute it, notes of the *Reichskreditkassen* and the despised 'washers' continued in circulation until the end of the month.

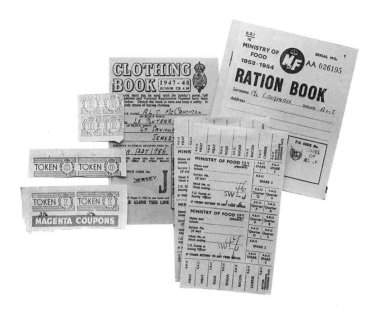

*Fig. 115: The author's ration books, a tiresome but necessary currency appendage in the post-war years.*

*In these prosperous days, it is hard to believe that such 'tokens' and 'coupons' were necessary for a period of time which was longer than the war itself.*

# Commemoratives & Decimals

## Commemoratives

After the restoration of the British coinage standard in 1945, the Islands carried on with their pre-war tradition. Coins of 8 doubles and 4 doubles denomination were struck for Guernsey to exactly the same specifications and design as the pre-war issues, in 1945, 1947 (8 doubles only) and 1949. Jersey had 1/12th and 1/24th coins minted in 1946 and 1947 which were also similar to earlier issues, but in 1949 they departed from tradition: in that year the 'Liberation penny' was issued, to commemorate the delivery of the Island from foreign occupation four years previously. Further issues of this penny, with the legend 'Liberated 1945' but otherwise undated, were made in 1950, 1952 and – with the obverse portrait of the new Queen – in 1954; while this commemorative coin was in fact for general circulation, it heralded a time when issues were to be made as collectors' items only.

1956 was an important year in Guernsey's numismatic history in that, for the first time, a coin was issued which implied official recognition of sterling currency as the circulating medium: this coin was a cupro-nickel three pence piece with a scalloped edge; it featured that most gentle Island inhabitant – the Guernsey cow. In the same year, completely newly designed 8 doubles and 4 doubles coins appeared, with the Guernsey lily on the reverse. A further issue of all three coins (with the three pence struck on a thick flan) was made in 1957. Jersey had issued its own 'one fourth shilling' in 1957, and a further issue was made in 1964.

In 1960, Jersey celebrated the 300th anniversary of the Restoration of Charles II on its pennies of that date and both Islands commemorated the 900th anniversary of the Norman conquest with sets of coins dated 1966. Of this latter series, while the Jersey 1/12th and 1/4th shilling coins circulated normally, and the distinctive Guernsey ten shilling piece was accepted as currency to a limited extent, the cumbersome Jersey five shilling piece hardly circulated at all. From then to the date of writing (1984), custom has dictated that, with one exception, there be two distinct types of legal tender coins; one which is designed to be accepted for general circulation, and another which is aimed purely at raising funds for the issuing body with no thought that the product should circulate, although – strictly speaking – the islanders could be legally obliged to accept the coins up to specific values. The only exception to the rule is the Jersey £1 coin issued in 1981 for general circulation which, at the same time, commemorated the 200th anniversary of the Battle of Jersey (see below).

The 'pure' commemorative coins have to date included the Jersey set, in silver and gold, in denominations from 50 pence to 50 pounds, celebrating the Royal 25th wedding anniversary in 1972, and Guernsey's more modest issue of a 25 pence coin in honour of the same event. In fact, Guernseymen have been more consistent in this field, limiting themselves to the issues of 25 pence pieces on all subsequent occasions which were:

1977 Silver Jubilee
1978 Royal Visit
1980 Queen Mother's 80th birthday
1981 Royal Wedding

Since its ambitious 1972 venture, Jersey has only celebrated one other event in this way: in 1981 a £2 coin was issued in honour of the Royal Wedding.

## Decimal Coinage

The Chinese were the first to recognize the convenience of a system based on the number of fingers on one pair of human hands. Some 3000 years later, in 1792, the first western country, the United States, decimalized its currency. One year later, as mentioned above, France followed suit and, during the Napoleonic war period, the idea was exported to other European countries.

In England, decimalization had been a subject of discussion for centuries, though there seems to have been no official consideration of the advantages. One of the most eminent proponents of the subject was Sir Christopher Wren who, in 1691, put forward a decimal currency based on a silver 'noble' divided into 10 'primes' and 100 'seconds'. One wonders if Jurat Messervy, 200 years later, was aware that he was in such select company.

One year after the Battle of Waterloo, a Tory M. P., John Croker, suggested during the second reading of the Silver Coinage Bill (7th June 1816) that Britain should follow France's example and issue a decimal currency. It will be remembered that England's currency was in a chaotic state at the time and Croker saw this as an ideal time for a reform. This was not to be, however, and, after years of debate, the first practical step towards such a system was taken only in 1851 when the first tenth of a pound piece, or florin, was introduced. And the country had to wait another 120 years for the final arrival of D-for-decimal-day, 15th February 1971.

The implementation of the new decimal system followed the same course in the Channel Islands as it did in Great Britain. In 1960 there were current in the United Kingdom, not counting sovereigns and half sovereigns, groats and Maundy pieces – by my reckoning – over 70 different coins, made up of several types of eight denominations of five monarchs. In the Channel Islands these were complemented by the local issues. Decimalization, when it finally came, not only implied the change to a new system; it was also a 'tidying up' operation; it was, in 1960, quite usual, for example, to find a very worn Victorian 'bun' penny in one's change, or a silver sixpence of the early issue of George V. By 1960, however, the falling value of the Pound sterling was already making itself felt, and the number of coin types in circulation was reduced by five during that year, when the faithful old farthing was demonetized.

Preparation for 'D'-day began in Jersey and Guernsey early in 1969, when new 5 and 10 new-pence pieces (dated 1968) were issued for each Island; they were identical in weight and dimension to the existing British two shillings and one shilling pieces, which they gradually substituted. Later in 1969, the heptagonal 50 new-pence coins were issued. All halfpenny coins were demonetized in August 1969 and halfcrowns in January of the following year. From November 1970, Jersey and Guernsey 10 shilling notes were slowly withdrawn. On 15th February 1971 – the necessary legislation having being passed the previous week – Jersey, Guernsey and the smaller islands made the switch and the new ½, 1 and 2 new-pence coins were issued. Six months later, the old penny was demonetized, as was the dodecagonal threepenny bit. The only coin of the old system which managed to survive – for nine more years – was the sixpence with the awkward value of 2½p; when this coin went, the change was complete, although old two shillings and one shilling pieces still crop up in change. Incidentally, Adam Smith in his *'Wealth of Nations'*, published in the early 19th century, reminds us that 'Among the ancient Saxons a shilling appears at one time to have contained five pennies...' So maybe the shilling will be allowed to remain in circulation together with the 5p piece! Until very recently (December 1981), the one shilling denomination – if only on paper – survived in Alderney. In that month, by dint of Section 15 (a) of The Alderney Road Traffic and Public Highways (Amendment) Ordinance, 1981, fees per passenger seat in public service vehicles – one shilling and five shillings until then – were raised to £1 and £5 respectively.

Jersey's new coinage is simple to describe, consisting of Arnold Machin's portrait of Queen Elizabeth on the *obverse,* and the Island's shield of arms and the value on the *reverse.* Guernsey's, however, has distinct reverse designs on each coin. The cow of the old threepenny piece was transposed to the 10NP and the Guernsey lily from the 1956 4 doubles to the 5NP. The 50NP features the Ducal Cap of the Duke of Normandy, while a picture of the Sark Mill on the 2NP and a gannet in flight on the 1NP remind us that Sark and Alderney (where a colony of gannets was established) are part of Guernsey's responsibilities. Full descriptions are given in the listing below.

While there have been complaints from the islanders that 'things are not as they were', the following vignettes, all taken from the Jersey Weekly Post during the 1970's, serve to show that *'plus ça change, plus c'est la même chose'.* The reader should not have much difficulty finding parallels for each report, in the history of Channel Island currencies on previous pages.

- 'JERSEY 10s. PIECE WORTH 8s.2d. AT ENGLISH BANKS
  The Worthing Chamber of Trade recently issued a warning to local shopkeepers to be on their guard against holidaymakers passing off 'foreign' coins – including the Jersey 10s piece, which apparently is worth only 8s.2d. at any mainland bank...' (JWP 16.7.1970)
- '10p PIECES FILED TO RESEMBLE 50p
  Guernsey police have warned shopkeepers that 10p pieces are being filed to resemble 50p coins...' (JWP 28.1.1971)

- 'JERSEY BANKNOTES EARN ISLAND £300,000 A YEAR
  Love them or curse them, those new Jersey banknotes are earning the Island money – as much as £300,000 a year... Every time a local £1 note is taken into circulation, it is, in effect, a loan to the States of Jersey.. In 1972, the 'JEP' [Jersey Evening Post] started something of a run on Jersey notes by publicising this as a means of raising money for work on the St. Helier Harbour car ferry berth' (JWP 26.8.1976)
- 'WHEN 32,000 COINS FELL OFF THE BACK OF A LORRY
  It seems that Guernsey have literally been throwing their money around lately, because some 32,000 Guernsey halfpennies were found scattered on the M4 motorway in Wales. The Royal Mint, suitably perplexed.. found out that, in fact, the money fell off the back of a lorry... Being Guernsey money it was totally valueless in the UK, though after the spillage was recovered, some 1.600 were missing...' (JWP 19.6.1977)
- 'FARMER'S BIG FIND
  A haul of Krugerrands and medals which were stolen from a house at La Robeline, St. Ouen, two months ago, have been found in a field...' (JWP 26.7.1979)

Guernsey had been issuing its own banknotes for many years, and the continuation of such a practice was quite natural. The first post-war series of 10/– and £1 notes was accordingly issued in late 1945 and continued until 1959 and 1966 respectively. A £5 note was also reintroduced from 1956 to 1966. Where the first two denomination featured the traditional view of Castle Cornet from St. Peter Port, the later £5 note preferred to show the Guernsey lily, which also appeared on the coinage for that year.

Jersey was a late starter in this field and only in 1963 did the first (undated) post-war series begin to appear; this was also in 10/–, £1 and £5 denominations, with pictures of St. Ouen's Manor, Mount Orgeuil Castle and St. Aubin's Fort, respectively, on their reverse sides. A £10 note, with the same picture of St. Ouen's Manor (the 10/– note had since been withdrawn) appeared in 1972. The first undated Guernsey series was printed for circulation in 1969; the £1, £5 and £10 notes of this series were produced by Bradbury, Wilkinson & Co. as opposed to previous issues which had been given to Perkins Bacon Ltd.

Each Island took advantage of the issue of the most recent set of notes to show off various aspects of Channel Island history. Jersey showed contemporary representations of various historical and architectural subjects after contemporary artists, while Guernsey featured famous Guernseymen. A denomination was added: the £20 note.

As usual Jersey's notes bear the sovereign's head, whereas Guernsey's do not. The scenes depicted on these notes, which are in circulation at the time of writing, are as follows:

JERSEY:   £1   Battle of Jersey: The death of Major Peirson, after John Singleton Copley
          £5   Elizabeth Castle, after George Woolfe

|              | £10 | Victoria College, after Felix Benoist |
|---|---|---|
|              | £20 | Gorey Castle, after Jean le Capelain |
| **GUERNSEY:** | £1  | Daniel de Lisle Brock, Bailiff of Guernsey 1762–1862 (background: Royal Court, St. Peter Port, 1840) |
|              | £5  | Thomas de la Rue, the Guernsey printer 1793–1866 (background: Fountain Street, St. Peter Port 1799) |
|              | £10 | Major General Sir Isaac Brock KB 1769–1812, Hero of Upper Canada (background: Battle of Queenston Heights) |
|              | £20 | Admiral Lord de Saumarez 1757–1836 (background: Gibraltar Bay: the British squadron on 12.7.1801 with five sail of the line and one frigate) |

In 1981, exactly 1500 years after the burial of Childeric and his golden solidi in Merovingian France (see above), one pound coins were struck for Jersey and Guernsey. Only the specimen collectors' pieces were struck in gold, it is true, but the reader will now perhaps be able to see that a link – albeit a tenuous one – exists. The Jersey pound and the Guernsey pound are quite different coins: Jersey borrowed the square design of the old Guernsey 10-shilling piece and simultaneously commemorated the Jersey Militia and the part it played in the Battle of Jersey 200 years ago when the French, under Baron de Rullecourt, landed their forces for the last time in the Island, but were defeated by the Militia and the garrison under the command of Major Peirson. Guernsey issued a sovereign-sized coin in a gold-coloured alloy intended essentially for circulation.

In 1982, a new twenty pence denomination was introduced in Jersey and Guernsey, a descendant of the double-florin of the Victorian Jubilee series – nicknamed the 'barmaid's grief' because of its similarity to the five-shilling piece. With its distinctive heptagonal shape there is little danger of confusion this time round. Jersey features Corbière Lighthouse on its coin, while Guernsey has chosen a traditional milk can as its motif.

At the time of writing (February 1984) the Jersey Finance and Economics Committee's plans for a new series of designs on the 1p, 2p, 5p, 10p and 50p denominations have just been realized; the themes on the coins, now in circulation, are the history and prehistory of the Island with the various ages represented respectively by a Jersey dolmen, St. Helier's Hermitage, Grosnez Castle arch, Seymour Tower and Le Hocq Tower. It is likely that the 'new' halfpenny coins of both Jersey and Guernsey will be withdrawn from circulation by the end of 1984. A new Jersey gold-coloured one pound coin, of the same size and thickness as that introduced in April 1983 in the U.K., features a smaller portrait of the Queen and the St. Helier's parish crest, first of a series. The Guernsey authorities have issued a new one pound coin featuring *HMS Crescent*, once commanded by another great Guernseyman, Captain James Saumarez.

While remembering the parallel development of the Channel Islands, one cannot forget that each is steeped in its own history and is determined to maintain its own character and traditions; the distinctive Channel Island currencies are a proof of this.

# Medals, Checks and Other Curiosities

To some, it may not seem logical to include a section here under the above heading. There is indeed no logical connection between coins and medals except, perhaps, the fact that the latter are substantially the same shape as the former. Also, mints often produce medals as well as coins.

A paragraph on tradesmen's checks and gaming tokens can perhaps more logically be appended to a study of currencies as they can be said, in a certain sense, to have circulated – albeit in limited circumstances – and to have constituted a token value for something (or receipt of the value for something), whether it was a sack of potatoes, an hour's billiards or a bottle of cider. In any event, such a chapter is a useful place to include all those items which could not more easily be alluded to in earlier sections.

## Commemorative Medals

Commemorative medals of Jersey and Guernsey celebrate, for the most part, Royal events. Guernsey honoured Queen Victoria's consort, Albert 'the Good', while Jersey celebrated the Royal visit in 1846 with an issue in silver and white metal. A commemorative medal was issued by St. Martin's Parish in Guernsey, celebrating the Queen's Diamond Jubilee in 1887, and another by the Bailiff of the Island to the same end. I know of at least four medals in bronze and white metal, two for each Island, which celebrated Edward VII's coronation. George V's coronation, his visit to the Islands in 1921, and 25 years of his reign in 1935, all these events were celebrated by both Jersey and Guernsey with white metal commemorative pieces, as was the coronation of his son, George VI.

After the war, the liberation was commemorated by each Island with issues of brass commemorative medals which were, in the usual way, handed out to school children. The Islands also celebrated the coronation of Elizabeth II in 1953.

Of the other Islands, Alderney has had one commemorative issue, in both silver and gilt, in honour of the Royal visit in 1978 while Sark saw a private series, in silver and gold, commemorating the 400th anniversary of the issuing of letters patent.

Of Guernsey stock, Lieutenant – later Captain – Philip Saumarez accompanied Captain George Anson in his circumnavigation of the world (1740–1744). Saumarez is perhaps, locally, better known as the officer who led the boarding party on the *Nuestra Señora de Cobadonga* treasure ship off Cape Espiritu Santo in the Philippines in June 1743, and was subsequently placed in command of the prize and its fabulous contents of gold and silver. His name appears, among those of the other Captains, on the reverse of the Anson medal which

173

Fig. 116: A selection of commemorative medals. (Sizes reduced)
a: Queen Victoria and Prince Albert: Visit to Jersey.
b: Queen Victoria: Diamond Jubilee (Guernsey).
c: Edward VII: Coronation (Jersey).
d: Edward VII: Coronation (Jersey – another type).
e: Edward VII and Queen Alexandra: Coronation (Guernsey).
f: Edward VII: Coronation (Guernsey).

  *i*
 *j*

  *k*
  *l*

  *m*
  *n*

  *o*

g: Edward VII: Coronation (Jersey, Guernsey, Sark, Alderney, Herm).
h: George V and Queen Mary: Coronation (Guernsey).
i: George V: Coronation (Jersey).
j: George V: Visit to Jersey.
k: George V and Queen Mary: Silver Jubilee (Jersey).
l: George VI and Queen Elizabeth: Coronation (Jersey).
m: Liberation (Guernsey).
n: Liberation (Jersey).
o: Elizabeth II: Coronation (Jersey).

*Fig. 117: Commemorative medallions. Above: Baron John Carteret. Below: Daniel de Lisle Brock.*

*The Carteret medallion is one of an extensive series by Dassier, commemorating prominent people; the Brock portrait was engraved by E. le Bas and struck by Thomas Halliday.*

commemorates Lord Anson's heroic voyage and the defeat of the French fleet off Finistère, in which Saumarez also took part; this happened shortly before his tragic death in another engagement in October 1747 at the age of thirty-four.

Other issues in this category must include a large bronze medallion by the Swiss engraver Jacques Antoine Dassier, commemorating Baron John Carteret, Earl Granville (1690–1763), great-grandson of Sir George Carteret of the Restoration. He was Seigneur of St. Ouen's and Bailiff of Jersey but, in British history, perhaps better known as a Whig Statesman and opponent, in the Lords, of Walpole and, later, Pitt. This piece, one of a series, was engraved at the Royal Mint, London, where Dassier was assistant engraver, but struck in Geneva.

One of the most distinguished Guernseyman, commemorated in the issues of at-least two medallions, was Daniel de Lisle Brock, Bailiff of Jersey and brother of Sir Isaac Brock, 'Hero of Upper Canada'. On one medallion Daniel is extolled for having defended the export privileges of the Channel Islands; on the other dated 1835, he receives the superlative accolade as someone 'whose devotion to his country's weal has obtained him a name more lasting and imperishable than all the honours which rank and titles could bestow'.

In January 1973, the Société Jersiaise celebrated its first 100 years as champion of Jersey's heritage and an attractive little medallet was struck to commemorate

*Fig. 118: Société Jersiaire centenary medal.*
The reverse *features the Chapel on La Hougue Bie, after a design by the late Major N.V.L. Rybot.*

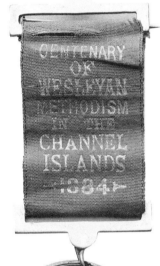
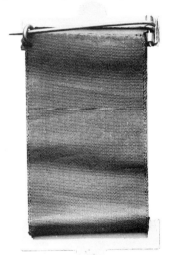

*Fig. 119: Wesleyan Methodism medal.*
*200 years after its introduction into the Channel Islands, Methodism is still an important ecclesiastical force.*

the event. In religious circles, another centenary was commemorated by the issue of a medal, nearly one hundred years ago: that of the centenary of the introduction of Wesleyan Methodism into the Channel Islands in 1784; these medals are not uncommon and can often be found still with their original ribbon and clasp.

## Medals for Personal Achievement (Militia, Schools etc.)

*Fig. 120: Jersey Militia gold medal.*
*Modelled by Joseph Shepard Wyon; edge inscription: PRIVATE JAMES ALEXANDRE I$^{ST}$ OR WEST REG.*

A splendid, though very rare, series of medals was issued in the 19th century for Royal Jersey Militia shooting prizes; awards, such as Long Service and Good Conduct medals, are also known to members of the various Militia regiments who later served in other forces. An example of the Efficiency Medal (Bar Jersey) which was awarded only to Militia members, has recently been presented to the Société Jersiaise. An early medal, also in the Société Jersiaise collection is that 'presented to Edward Touzel by the States of Jersey for his part in extinguishing a fire in the Powder Magazine on Fort Regent in 1804'. The Jersey Humane Society has, since its institution in 1865, presented over 50 silver and some 100 bronze medals to worthy recipients. Royal Guernsey Militia medals, particularly those of the "Challenge" series featuring three militiamen in full dress uniform, charging, resting and firing muzzle-loaders, are of special historical interest.

Early school medals of the Channel Islands are rare. One superbly engraved example in silver, from an institution of 'NOVI VICI [Newtown], SANCTI HELERII, CAESAREÆ INSULÆ', run in the early 19th century by one Charles Horlock, was presented in January 1830 to a certain William Verner, evidently in recognition of his talents in 'GRAMMATICA ARITHMETICA ET MATHEMATICA'.

*Fig. 121: Silver medal of the Humane Society of Jersey.*

Reverse *inscription: PRESENTED TO [RECIPIENT] FOR COURAGE AND HUMANITY.*

*Fig. 122: Early school medal of Jersey.*
*William J. Verner, the recipient of this splendid silver prize, was born in 1819, married one Mary Ann Rogers in 1850 and died in 1902.*

Both Victoria College in Jersey and Elizabeth College in Guernsey have, over the years, given out a good number of academic prizes in the form of medals, in gold, silver and bronze. There is a large Bronze medallion in the Jersey Museum inscribed to 'Auguste Lelong 1874' for the 'education de famille Jersey', which seems to be unique.

*Fig. 123: Victoria College gold medal (above), Elizabeth College bronze medal (below).*
The Victoria College medal was modelled by Allan Wyon, last of the Royal Mint Wyons; edge inscription on this medal: R.W. BENSON FOR MODERN LANGUAGES V.C.J. 29.7.08. The Elizabeth College medal is by Vaughton of Birmingham.

## Medals for Exhibitions and Competitions

The most attractive example of a medal in this category is the Prize Medal, issued both in Silver and Bronze, for the Channel Islands' Exhibition of 1871. I have calculated (from the *Official General Report and Financial Statement*) that 66 Silver and 176 Bronze medals were awarded altogether at a total cost to the organizers of £137–3–0. An example of one of these, with the conjoined shields of arms of Jersey and Guernsey, is a handsome addition to any collection. The background design on the obverse, incidentally, seems to have been borrowed from that of a British pattern florin, dated 1848.

Medals are also known of the following institutions (in no particular order):
Guernsey Horticultural Society
Jersey Trades & Industries Exhibition
Guernsey Electrical Exhibition
Jersey Eisteddford
Royal Jersey Golf Club
Concours Musical de Jersey 1910 (Souvenir pieces sponsored by Le Riches Stores Ltd.)

*Fig. 124: Channel Islands Exhibition silver medal together with reverse of pattern 'ONE CENTUM'. This medal was awarded to C.D.B. LARBALESTIER, NATURAL PRODUCTS Nº 10 (edge inscription). The 'centum' is an early decimal pattern by William Wyon.*

There are also some fine examples of medals awarded in the U.K. to Channel Island exhibitors, including some struck for the British Dairy Farmers' Association and – a favourite of mine – the Birmingham Jersey Show, the medals of which feature, in high relief, a beautiful Jersey bovine belle! (see Fig. 2 above)

## Gaming Tokens and other Checks; Counterstamps

Most Channel Island checks of the late 19th and early 20th centuries are 'gaming tokens' sometimes called 'games counters', or public house checks. Issuers were often hotels, the most common denomination being 1½. Below is a list, in alphabetical order, of those institutions whose counters most often turn up in collections; the list does not pretend to be complete:

Bagot Hotel Jersey, American Bowling Saloon
Brighton Hotel, Guernsey
Caesarean Billiard Bagatelle Table, Geo. Walters Proprietor, 1½
Grand Hotel Jersey, 3d
G. Hamon & Co., Guernsey, 1½d
Kings Arms / Geo Le Breton, 58 King St., 1½

Marine Hotel, Jersey, Threepence
The Oxford / James Pluck, New St., Jersey
Prince of Wales Hotel, J Sinel, 1½
St. Julien's Club, Guernsey, 1

*Fig. 125: Above: Sarnian Club check. Below: West of England Inn token (obverse and reverse).*

Sarnian Club, Guernsey; denominations: 1, 2 and 3 (2 varieties)
Victory Inn, Gorey, Jersey
Waysum's Albion Hotel, Guernsey
West of England Inn, Guernsey / 1½
P. Woods, Billiards and Bagatelle, Jersey, 1½

A few 'drink checks' or tavern tokens are also known; these include:
C. Brennan, 45 Bordage, Guernsey, Half Pint Whisky

*Fig. 126: Guernsey bottle tokens.*

H. Brenton, 22 Bordage St., Guernsey; 'half pint' and 'bottle' varieties
Auguste Bulteau, Cave de Bordeaux, Guernsey
Bertin Feuillerat, Caves de Bordeaux, Guernsey (in Nickel and Brass)

Tradesmen's checks, another category, also 'circulated' to an extent; the best known are:
Epicerie Française, denominations 20, 50; 25 for a shilling, and 50 for a shilling
J. Le Caudey, merchant, 59 Commercial St., Jersey, 6d
Maison de Paris, I Beghin . . ., (advertisement check), decagonal

*Fig. 127: Tradesmen's checks: John Terry of Jersey, S. Whitehouse of Guernsey.*

John Terry potato merchant, Jersey, 1s and 6d varieties

S. Whitehouse, Emporium Français, Commercial Arcade Guernsey (an interesting brass check with the young head of Victoria on one side and the date 1852; a law was passed in England in 1872 prohibiting the use of games counters in any way resembling outmoded regal coinage; this check was probably current in the 1880's and 1890's)

Oddly enough, no dairy tokens are recorded in the Channel Islands, although tokens for Jersey milk are not uncommon in Canada. 'Registered Jersey Farms' of British Columbia, for example, issued aluminium tokens which were 'GOOD FOR 1 PINT REGISTERED JERSEY MILK'. Brass and grey metal Guernsey tokens for 'FREE MILK ONE PINT MAX' are part of a spurious set produced in America in the 1970's.

Coins of the Channel Island copper and bronze series are not infrequently found with countermarks and names etched or stamped into them. These items – often, inaccurately, classed as 'love-tokens' – are difficult to categorize. Some were almost certainly intended as advertisement checks or 'truck tokens': 'W. GOSTICK' and 'W. MOLLET' are examples, stamped respectively into a Jersey 1/13th and Jersey 1/12th of a shilling. A more erudite example is that of a 'Devins and Bolton' counterstamp on a Guernsey 4 Doubles of 1830. Devins and Bolton was a drugstore which flourished in Montreal, Canada, as late as the 1870's.

*Fig. 128: Guernsey Town Hospital, possibly a queue check.*

I am unable to classify a St. Peter Port 1d token – perhaps a gaming token – and a check of the Town Hospital Guernsey. The latest check to be struck was by Cambria Products (a set of four) struck between 1969 and 1972. Some would

*Fig. 129: Alderney Steamer token.*

include here the only metallic transport tokens struck in the islands, which were 1st class and 2nd class oval tickets for the *Queen of the Isles* between Guernsey and Alderney (c. 1850–1860). At least one communion token (of St. Heliers Church dated 1853) is known, as well as a masonic penny of the 'Caesarian Lodge of M.M.M.' (Mark Master Masons), Jersey, and on this esoteric note this section must end.

# The Present

At the time of final proof correction (July 1984), new coins are being issued which it is too late to list in the 'Catalogue' section; hence the title of this addendum.

It is a useful moment, however, to remind the reader of the open numbering system designed for the decimal coinage section which begins for Jersey on page 287 and for Guernsey on page 336.

The most recent news is that the second one pound piece in the Jersey Parish Emblem series has been issued. The coin, similar in style to the previous issue (J230), will become J231 in the Catalogue. It features the Parish crest of St. Saviour – the three nails of the crucifix surrounded by the crown of thorns. Normal and inverted edge inscriptions are known. *AR* and *AU Proof* coins (J231A and J231B) are to be issued shortly. A similar set for St. Brelade (J232) will follow in the autumn.

On a sad note, the demise of the 1/2p – foreseen on page 187 – seems now very likely, as both Islands are preparing to follow the U.K.'s lead in withdrawing the coin by the end of 1984; if this happens there will never be a J68 or a G81. A new 10p coin the size of the old sixpence, albeit slightly thicker, is one of the options at present being considered by the Royal Mint.

# The Future

To the same extent that one can only speculate about the meaning of the motifs on the coins of ancient Armorica, one can only hazard a guess at the development of Channel Island currency in the future. There are four main themes:

## Parity

As we have seen, the tournois system endured as a standard in Jersey until 1834, and as late as 1921 in Guernsey and the other Islands. In 1834, 26 French livres (then the actual circulating medium, valued locally in livres tournois) were declared to be worth one gold sovereign, and a sterling standard was thereby initiated in Jersey. There had been 20 sous in the livre. Therefore:
as 26 livres equalled 20 shillings
then: $1\frac{3}{10}$ livres (or 26 sous or Jersey halfpence) equalled 1 shilling
and: 13 Jersey pence equalled 1 shilling

Accordingly, when the Island issued its own coins in 1841, there was a discrepancy between the British and the local denominations, which was compensated, as explained earlier, by making the Jersey coin slightly lighter than its British counterpart. Alignment between the two currencies took place in two stages: in 1866 when the new coinage was made of the same weight as the British series, and in 1877 when the Jersey 1/13th of a shilling became 1/12th of a shilling.

In Guernsey there was one short-lived attempt (between May 1848 and January 1850) to make British currency legal tender in the Island, motivated more by a dearth of French coin than by any real wish to introduce a British currency standard. A dual, French and British, standard was then sanctioned by an Ordinance of 3rd September, 1870 and this situation lasted until 1921 when the British currency standard prevailed. During this period, the gold sovereign was valued at 2016 Guernsey doubles (half-farthings) or 21 Guernsey shillings.

In 1877 and 1921, Jersey and Guernsey, respectively, in effect revalued their currencies against sterling to reach parity.

Five years ago, the Irish *punt* was allowed to float away from sterling in the hope that it would immediately show a premium. In the event, exactly the opposite happened and, at the time of writing, Irish currency has become nearly 30% cheaper than sterling. In February 1982, the Manx Treasury launched a study into the effects of leaving the sterling area, with an eye – at the time – on the possible reintroduction of U.K. exchange controls, and there was talk at the same time of the Channel Islands considering the same course.

The advantages of parity are not limited to convenience only. It has been calculated that Jersey and Guernsey would need reserves of £60–70 million each with which the respective Island central banking authorities could intervene, following any speculative outflow of funds, should parity be severed. Such funds would have to be borrowed – at a cost – on the Eurocurrency market. Difficult decisions would have to be taken about the exact amount of currency which would be borrowed as well as the currency in which the loan should be contracted, and the complexity of the subject would be compounded by local political and economic considerations. The advantages of a cheap Jersey and Guernsey pound (e.g. the easier promotion of tourism) would be lost in the wash. The advantages of a dear Channel Island pound would in practice be confined to the import sector, which is only one side of the coin.

If a decision were to be taken by Jersey or Guernsey to break away from sterling, a return towards a French or *tournois* standard would be out of the question. The Channel Island pound would stand alone with no automatic recourse to a lender of last resort, such as it has in effect had for the last 100 years or so. Such a small currency could become a victim of speculators or even of its own budget. New notes and coins would probably have to be designed. Who would finance this? The answer, of course, is – at the end of the line – the taxpayer, the very person who benefits from the prevailing situation i.e. a stable, civilized haven backed by a currency of world class, and taking comfort from unique circumstances in tax and customs dues. Why change?

## National Debt

The issue by the Channel Islands of their own currencies is a double-edged sword. As long as these issues were limited to coins in low denominations, for reasons of convenience, there was little danger that the 'national' debt of Jersey or Guernsey would suffer unduly. Since 1963, however, the States of Jersey has been issuing large numbers of notes of its own and has become indebted by the amount of issue of these notes. It is true to say that the *costs* of financing budgeted projects must be diminished by such issues, but there is a natural temptation to create too much money in this way. Local paper-issues not only aggravate inflation (particularly in an economy which relies so heavily on 'invisibles'), but also and more important, they cause national – i.e. States – debt to increase. The result of too large an issue, coupled, say, with a float away from sterling, and a subsequent analysis of the Island balance sheet could be disastrous.

Guernsey is no less exposed. The States has issued its own currency notes for the last 150 years and it is true to say that such issues have been limited (e.g. to about £1 per head of population from 1837 to 1895). However, since 1969 there seems to have been a marked increase in the use of States notes, now in denominations up to £20 – a far cry from the 8 doubles coins which were the staple currency until 1971. Inflation has of course taken its toll.

Early note issues in both Islands can be divided into three types: private, financial and currency issues. The danger now is that a financial motive is creeping into the concept which lies behind the issue of currency notes.

## Convenience

Nowadays, by convention, the smaller currency denominations are represented by metal coins and the larger by paper notes. Incidentally, to my knowledge, there is only one country – Greenland – which issued notes *before* it issued coins. In inflationary times this division is perhaps ironical, as the smaller denominations, which will be more quickly driven out of circulation (the 1/2p – value 1.2 old pence is a case in point) may have a life of up to 50 years, whereas the larger denominations (notes) have a life of as little as 3 months. However the public resists change.

Channel Island notes and coins – as is now universally the case – have no intrinsic value. The Royal Mint perpetually experiments with the utilitarian alloys involved in order to find the ideal mix, incorporating weight, hardness, colour and so on. Plastic coins have been a subject of discussion now for a quarter of a century: where cheapness and lightness would be obvious advantages, the absence of 'jingle' has seemed to be the most constant public objection. The Isle of Man Government has just issued a plastic one pound note. Coins have normally been circular, and departure from this norm – with the exception of the cleverly designed seven-sided 50p and 20p pieces – has never been generally accepted: for example, the Guernsey 10 shillings piece of 1966 or the Jersey 1 pound piece of 1981, although they were sought after as souvenirs, were never popular items of currency.

This mention of souvenirs brings us to an important theme. Commemorative coins, aimed at collectors rather than spenders, have become a fact of life in the last 30 years. The most extreme example in the Channel Islands was perhaps the Jersey set of coins in silver and gold, which celebrated the Royal 25th Wedding Anniversary in 1972. The economics of such an issue is simple: the States of Jersey or the States of Guernsey sanctions (and lends their name to) the issue of coins – more correctly the *sale* of coins – at a premium over their nominal value. This premium accrues – or should accrue – to the States. Often a precious metal (gold or silver) is used, and some or all of the coins are struck with polished dies and frosted finishes to improve the quality and the appearance of the issue. (Such issues are – erroneously as it happens – styled 'proofs'; they might be better described as 'special issues'). Although such money is, strictly speaking, legal tender, it is not intended that the States Treasury's tacit 'promise to pay' should be tested; and in any event, the intrinsic value of gold or silver coins is designed to make such a course unlikely. Finally, commemorative coins are often struck in limited editions to enhance their market value.

While in no way criticising such issues which have generally – though not always – contributed a useful amount of revenue to the respective Island Treasuries, a word of warning may not be out of place here.

John Kenneth Galbraith has pointed out that (in times of crisis) '... however desperately people want their money from a bank, when they are assured they can get it, they no longer want it'. Sir Thomas Gresham's 'law' that bad money always drives out good has been proved many times since the hoarding of good coin in Ancient Rome. 'Human nature may be an infinitely variant thing. But it has constants. One is that, given a choice, people keep what is the best for themselves, i.e. for those whom they love the most' (J. K. Galbraith again).

Treasuries should not lose sight of the fact that the 'man in the street' wants to have money in his pocket which is secure (i.e. not prone to fluctuation in value) and easily recognizable. If 'special issues' become too frequent, one runs the risk that the man in the street will become unsettled and muddled. The fact that such issues in gold and silver, are nowadays, so keenly accepted (to turn this argument on its head) may be a sign that Gresham's law is once again at work. A Royal visit to the Islands – all too infrequent – has been traditionally considered as an appropriate time for the issue of commemorative coins or medals. Such an occasion might still be deemed a good yard-stick in this debate, and one hopes that the occasion of the Queen Mother's visit to the Islands this year will be suitably commemorated.

## Electronic Money

The credit card is nothing less than a type of private token. It should not be contrasted to or compared with public issues of currency. It is evidence – to be accepted or declined – that a certain person is good for a certain sum of money which should accrue to the seller of the goods concerned at a later date. Credit cards are a substitute for cheques; they are not, strictly, a substitute for cash. That said, it is not unreasonable to accept that there have recently been scientific developments which may herald the beginnings of a cashless society, such as could as well become the case in the Channel Islands as anywhere else.

One new process – still being tested – is called 'electronic funds transfer at the point of sale' or 'EFT/POS' for short. 'EFT/POS' has become feasible through the reduction in size of certain standard electronic components, and a piece of plastic of the size of the (already traditional!) credit card can now incorporate a miniature electronic calculator as well as a microprocessor and a memory. This little gadget could, in principle, transfer funds from the client's account *at the moment of sale* – a sobering thought.

The answer to the question, 'what will happen in the future to our Channel Island currencies?' may be buried in the last few paragraphs. In any event it is to be hoped that invention and artistic talent will be allowed to flourish in some form, as they have done for the last 2000 years.

# Part IV

# CATALOGUE

Private Channel Island Tokens
Guernsey Banknotes
Jersey Banknotes
Jersey Coins
Guernsey Coins
Bibliography
Index

> Mr. Lely, I desire you would use all your skill to paint my picture truly like me, and not flatter me at all; but remark all these roughnesses, pimples, warts, and everything as you see me, otherwise I will never pay a farthing for it.
>
> Oliver Cromwell.
> *Remark, Walpole's Anecdotes of Painting.*
> ch. 12

# Note

- The token section consists of privately issued tokens, which circulated or were intended to circulate as currency, in tentative chronological order. The Three Shilling and Eighteen Pence tokens, being official issues, are listed in the Jersey Coin section.
- Guernsey Banknotes, both private and official, are listed in chronological order.
- Early Jersey Note issues are in alphabetical order; States of Jersey issues are listed chronologically.
- Jersey and Guernsey coins are listed by denomination and date. An allowance for up to twenty future issues has been made in the numbering of the decimal coins. The system allows for new coin varieties to be added as they are discovered.
- Abbreviations: 
  - *AU*   Gold
  - *AR*   Silver
  - *CU*   Copper
  - *l.*   left
  - *r.*   right
  - *obv.* obverse
  - *rev.* reverse
  - *GR*   Grained right
  - *GL*   Grained left
  - *EP*   Edge plain
  - *ND*   No date

# Private Tokens of the Channel Islands 1809–1814

**Silver**
**Guernsey Five Shillings**

T. = Total struck
M. = Mint
D. = Diameter
W. = Weight
E. = Edge

*T1*

T1    1809    *Obverse:* BISHOP DE JERSEY & CO. round the Arms of Jersey in a circle, a rose ornament below.

*Reverse:* TOKEN/OF FIVE/SHILLINGS in three lines within a wreath of oak;
legend: BANK OF GUERNSEY 1809.

Struck over Spanish dollars, details of which often show through the design.
Electrotype copies are known; on at least one example the upper serif on the N of GUERNSEY is defective.

See also GN 1.

T. Not known – perhaps six or seven genuine examples extant
M. Boulton & Watt, Soho Mint, Birmingham (dies by T. Wyon)
D. 42 mm
W. 26.97–27.02 g
E. 0=0=0 (traces from Spanish dollar) occasionally show through plain edge

**Copper**
**Pennies**

T2    1812    *Obverse:* JERSEY BANK TOKEN 1812 round a laureate profile of George III r.

*Reverse:* A BANK OF ENGLAND NOTE FOR 240 TOKENS round ELIAS NEEL JERSEY.

Of the highest rarity: Possibly a pattern. Note: A Parish of St. Helier note issue (for the paving of Belmont Road) which circulated between 1862 and 1879 was signed by one Elias Neel, Jnr., who also appears as guarantor on private notes of Jean Anthoine, (1836–1879) – see JN11.

T. Not known
M. Not known; however dies for this token are believed to have been engraved by Thomas Halliday of Birmingham
D.
W.
E.

T3

*T9 struck over T3; the back of George III's head can be seen quite clearly if the druid's head is inverted.*

| | | | |
|---|---|---|---|
| T3 | 1813 | *Obverse:* JERSEY BANK 1813 round a draped and laureate bust of George III, *r.*; small H upon bust (Halliday).<br><br>*Reverse:* ONE PENNY TOKEN round a robed female figure seated to *l.* on a bale, holding scales and cornucopia; a ship in the distance.<br><br>Very rare; possibly a pattern.<br><br>There are at least two die varieties. The token was perhaps never 'in circulation' as two other penny tokens are known to have been struck over it: T9 in this list (q.v.) and Davis Glos 16 – Plate A (20) of the Sedbury Iron Works Gloucestershire. The *reverse* occurs also in contemporary penny tokens from Burton, Sheffield and one of the 'Not Local' series. | T. Not known<br>M. Not known. Dies sunk by T. Halliday of Birmingham<br>D. 34.5 mm<br>W. 16.525 g<br>E. Probably plain, though traces of two previous strikings *GR/GL* leave herring-bone effect |
| T4 | 1813? | *Obverse:* Laureate and draped bust of George III *r.* within a wreath of oak; small H upon bust.<br><br>*Reverse:* JERSEY GUERNSEY AND ALDERNEY round ONE/PENNY/TOKEN in a circle.<br><br>Very rare; possibly a pattern.<br><br>The *obverse* was used on at least six other tokens of the 'Not Local' series, suggesting that this token was struck between 1812 and 1814. The (English) spelling of Guernsey suggests that no reference was made to the Islands before the token was produced. | T. Not known<br>M. Not known; dies sunk by T. Halliday of Birmingham<br>D.<br>W.<br>E. |

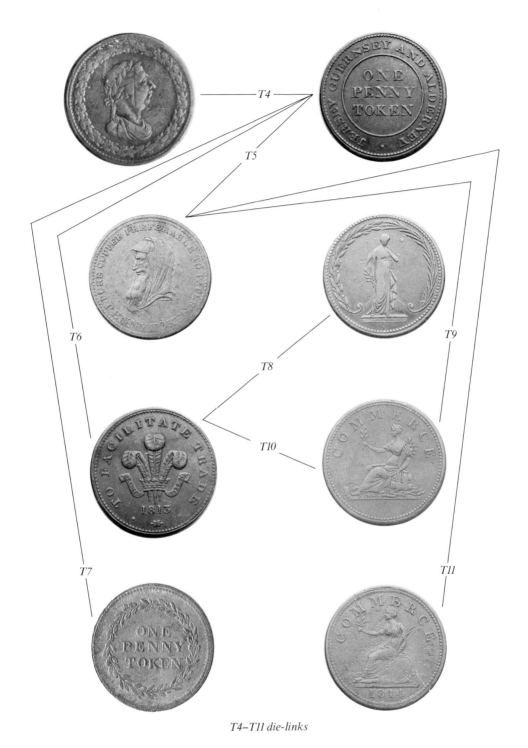

*T4–T11 die-links*

| T5 | 1814 | *Obverse:* PURE COPPER PREFERABLE TO PAPER round Druid's bust *l.*, PENNY TOKEN below in larger letters. | T. Not known |
| | | | M. Not known. Dies sunk by Turnpenny and Halliday |
| | | *Reverse: as reverse* of T4. Early die (see T7a). | D. 34 mm |
| | | Very rare; possibly a pattern. | W. 16.3–17.6 g |
| | | The legend mirrored the unpopularity of paper money which was perishable and often untrustworthy; copper was thought at the time to be 'a good investment'. The *obverse* die was used on a Burton penny token dated 1814. | E. *GR* over one, possibly two, previous strikings i.e. *GR/GR/GL* |

*T6i*     *T6ii*

*T6i*     *T6iii*     *T6iv*

| T6 | 1813 | *Obverse:* The Prince of Wales' feathers issuant from a coronet; motto on a ribbon ICH DIEN. Legend: TO FACILITATE TRADE. Below the crest: 1813 and an ornament ✱ | T. Not known |
| | | | M. Not known. Dies sunk by T. Halliday |
| | | *Reverse: as reverse* of T4 | D. (Average) |
| | | i  New dies; dies not inverted (a variety has dies inverted) Edge *GR* | i 34.1 mm |
| | | | ii 33.75 mm |
| | | | iii 33.65 mm |
| | | ii  Rusty *obverse* dies with rust also affecting JE of JERSEY and NEY of ALDERNEY. Edge as T6i but occasional traces of earlier strikes. Dies inverted. | iv 33.95 mm |
| | | | W. i 17.15–18.55 g |
| | | | ii 18.275–18.325 g |
| | | iii  As T6ii. Edge as T6ii but coarser graining. | iii 18.2–18.3 g |
| | | | iv 18.225–18.425 g |
| | | iv  As T6ii. Edge *GL* and incuse, with traces of earlier strikes. | E. i *GR* |
| | | | ii *GR* |
| | | This token is scarce but may well have been accepted for circulation in the Islands, albeit unofficially. | iii *GR* (coarser) |
| | | | iv *GL* (incuse) |
| | | *Obverse* and *reverse* dies occur muled with other dies of the English token series. The slogan 'TO FACILITATE TRADE' was meant to encourage circulation at a time when the shortage of change often caused merchants to charge a premium; the slogan also appears on other English, Canadian and Jamaican pieces. | |
| T7? | 1814? | *Obverse: as reverse* of T4 (there is evidence of a die link with the rusted varieties of T6 – hence this sequence). | T. Not known |
| | | | M. Not known. Dies sunk by Halliday |
| | | *Reverse:* ONE/PENNY/TOKEN in a continuous wreath of oak. | D. 34 mm |
| | | | W. 18.35 g |
| | | Very rare; possibly a pattern. | E. *GR* |

The *reverse* of this unimaginative coin is recorded by Davis on tokens of Sedbury (undated), Nottingham (1813), Burton (1814 and undated), Sheffield (undated), and Not Local (undated).

| | | | |
|---|---|---|---|
| T8 | 1813 | *Obverse:* as *obverse* of T6.<br><br>*Reverse:* a female figure (?Justice) standing on a pedestal holding a sprig of olive, between branches of laurel to the left and palm to the right. No legend.<br><br>Extremely rare; possibly a pattern; classified sometimes as a mule. | T. Not known<br>M. Not known. Dies sunk by T. Halliday<br>D. 33.9 mm<br>W. 17.25 g<br>E. *GR* |
| T9 | 1813? | *Obverse:* as *obverse* of T5.<br><br>*Reverse:* a robed female figure seated to left on a bale of merchandise, holding an olive branch and cornucopia; a ship in the distance; legend above: COMMERCE.<br><br>The edge is either plain or a weak *GR/GR;* on some examples the *GR* is over several previous strikings. The letters ... KEN of TOKEN and ... ER of PAPER appear to have been clumsily repaired at some stage.<br><br>This token is rare; it may have had no direct connection with the Channel Islands; however, at least two examples are known to have been struck over T3. Sometimes classified as a mule.<br><br>Similar *reverse* descriptions are recorded by Davis on 'Not Local' tokens 24 and 39 (undated) | T. Not known<br>M. Not known; dies sunk by Turnpenny and Halliday<br>D. 34.0–34.4 mm<br>W. 16.2–18.15 g<br>E. Normally *GR/GR* |
| T10 | 1813 | *Obverse:* as *obverse* of T6.<br><br>*Reverse:* as *reverse* of T9.<br><br>A rare mule token which may have had no direct connection with the Channel Islands.<br><br>Some ornate letters (e.g. in the word TRADE) suggest that the obverse die used on T6 may have deteriorated into plain letters – i.e. that this token may have preceded T6. On the other hand there is evidence of considerable wear to both dies, e.g. the base of the seated figure. | T. Not known<br>M. Not known; dies sunk by Halliday<br>D. (average) 34 mm<br>W. 16.75–19.5 g<br>E. *GR/GR/?GL* |
| T11 | 1814 | *Obverse:* as *obverse* of T5.<br><br>*Reverse:* a robed female figure seated to left, holding in her right hand a sprig of olive, and in her left a palm branch; a shield at her side; legend COMMERCE 1814.<br><br>  i Edge: *GR/GR*.<br>  ii Edge: *EP* over at least 3 earlier strikings – *GL/GL/GR*.<br><br>A rare token with no apparent connection with the Channel Islands; sometimes classified as a mule. | T. Not known<br>M. Not known: dies sunk by Turnpenny and Halliday<br>D. 33.85 mm<br>W. 18.25–19.1 g<br>E. i *GR/GR*<br>  ii *EP/GL/GL/GR* (incuse) |

# Halfpenny

*T12*

| | | | |
|---|---|---|---|
| T12 | 1813 | *Obverse:* as *obverse* of T6 but smaller; ornament below date rounder in style.<br><br>*Reverse:* as *reverse* of T6 but smaller; HALF/PENNY/TOKEN.<br><br>Extremely rare; possibly a pattern. After T1 this token is the most sought after in the series, though it may not be as rare as T2 and T3. | T. Not known<br>M. Not known; dies sunk by Halliday<br>D. 29 mm<br>W. 8.9 g<br>E. GR/GR |

# Early Guernsey Private £1 Note Issues

GN1

| | Name | Notes current | Examples known |
|---|---|---|---|
| GN 1 | Bishop, de Jersey & Co.<br>or Bank of Guernsey (established c. 1800, the Bank also issued 5 shilling silver tokens dated 1809; it failed in 1811). See also T1. | c. 1805–1811 | 1.9.1808,<br>5.1.1809 |

GN2

| | | | |
|---|---|---|---|
| GN 2 | Macculloch, Allaire, Bonamy & Co.<br>or The Guernsey Bank (Founded 1808, failed 1811). | 1808–1811 | 20.10.1808<br>5.1.1809<br>10.4.1809<br>1.8.1809<br>1.1.1811 |
| GN 3 | Richards & Co.<br>(Merchants, recorded as having lent their name to an amount of notes in excess of £2.000 to facilitate the exchange of worn British coin in 1817). | from 1817 | – |

GN4

GN4

| Name | Notes current | Examples known |
|---|---|---|
| GN 4 Priaulx, Le Marchant, Rougier & Co. or Guernsey Banking Company (later: Limited) or 'The Old Bank'. (Founded 1827, acquired by National Provincial in 1924) Watermark 'OLD BANK 1827' | 1827–1924 | 25.9.1828, 'Augt. 22$^{nd}$ 1861' (Specimen) 'May 1$^{st}$ 1863' 1866 'December 1$^{st}$ 1891' 1.9.1903 1.7.1906 (6 over 5) |

*GN5A*  *GN5*

| | | |
|---|---|---|
| GN 5 Guernsey Commercial Banking Company (Guernsey currency notes issued from 1835, date of establishment, until 1914 when right of issue ceased; British sterling notes from 1921 to 1923. The Bank was acquired by Westminster Bank on 1.1.1924). | 1835–1923 | 2.12.1868, 6.9.1869, undated |
| GN 5A Proof pull c. 1913 | | |
| GN 6 Southern District Banking Co., Isle of Wight, Guernsey Branch (Established 1838, failed 1840). | 1838–1840 | 28.6.1838 (unique) |

# Alderney

*AN1*

| | | |
|---|---|---|
| AN 1 Alderney Commercial Bank or Bank of Robilliard and Sanford. | c. 1810 | 26.12.1810 (unique?) |

# States of Guernsey Issues
# Financial Notes

|  | Denomination | Project | No. issued | Circulated | Examples known |
|---|---|---|---|---|---|
| GN 7 | £1 | Coastal preservation, Torteval Church and Jerbourg Monument (amortized £2750 in 1817, £1250 in 1818). | 4.000 | 1816–1818 | – |
| GN 8 | £1 | Market issue (Redeemable in 10 years from impôts). | 4.500 | 1820–1830 | 1.10.1820 |
| GN 9 | £1 | Further Market issue (same terms). | 5.000 | 1834–1844 | |
| GN 10 | £1 | Erection of Elizabeth College and certain parochial schools. | 6.500 | from 1826 | – |
| GN 11 | £5 | £8.000 issued, guaranteed by impôt of wines and spirits (of which £2.000 were for Sark). | 1.600 | from 1826 | – |
| GN 12 | £1 | Fountain Street. | 11.000 | from 1827 | 14.2.1829<br>10.7.1829<br>3.3.1830<br>7.1.1833 |
| GN 13 | £1 | Elizabeth College. | 8.500 | from 1827 | 21.11.1827 |
| GN 14 | £1 | Cholera prevention. | 1.000 | from 1834 | – |

# States of Guernsey Currency Notes

*GN15*

|  | Denomination | Series | Examples known |
|---|---|---|---|
| GN 15 | £1 | 1827–1837<br>(total issue £25.000 in 1827, increased to £55.000 then £15.000 withdrawn in 1837). | 21.11.1827<br>15.4.1828<br>10.7.1829<br>1.12.1829<br>1.10.1836 |

*GN16*

|  | Denomination | Series | Examples known |
|---|---|---|---|
| GN 16 | £1 | 1837–1895<br>(Total outstanding currency issues limited to £40.000 during the period). | 28.3.1857<br>4.1.1864<br>1867, 1874<br>16.12.1879<br>16.8.1889<br>22.5.1894 |

*GN17*

|  | Denomination | Series | Examples known |
|---|---|---|---|
| GN 17 | £1 | 1895 – 'Greenback' issue (Following a forgery attempt, all previous States notes were withdrawn). | 15.7.1895 |
| GN 18 | £1 | 1903–1914. | 25.3.1903. 3.4.1914 |
| GN 18A |  | Proof pull | 25.3.1903 |

*GN19*  *GN19*

|  |  |  |  |
|---|---|---|---|
| GN 19 | 5/– or 6 frs | 1914 (Emergency issue printed by the 'Star', Guernsey). | 5.8.1914 |
| GN 20 | 10/– or 12 frs | 1914 (Emergency issue printed by the 'Evening Press' Guernsey). | 7.8.1914 |

*GN21*

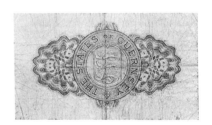

|  |  |  |  |
|---|---|---|---|
| GN 21 | 5/– or 6 frs | 1914–1921 (Printed by Perkins, Bacon & Co.). | 1.9.1914 |

*GN22*

|  | Denomination | Series | Examples known |
|---|---|---|---|
| GN 22 | 10/- or 12 frs | 1914–1921 (Printed by Perkins, Bacon & Co.). | 19.7.1919 |

*GN23*

|  | Denomination | Series | Examples known |
|---|---|---|---|
| GN 23 | £1 | 1914–1921 (Printed by Perkins, Bacon & Co.). | 3.4.1914<br>1.9.1916 |
| GN 24 | 5/- or 6 frs | AS GN 21 but overprinted 'BRITISH' in red (Issued April 1921). | 1.9.1914 |
| GN 25 | 10/- or 12 frs | As GN 22 but overprinted 'BRITISH' in red (Issued April 1921). | 1.9.1914 |

*GN26*

|  | Denomination | Series | Examples known |
|---|---|---|---|
| GN 26 | £1 | As GN 23 but overprinted 'BRITISH' in red (Issued April 1921). | 1.9.1914<br>1.8.1919 |
| GN 27 | 10/- | 1921–1932 Black and grey; no denomination in numerals in centre | 17.5.1924 |

*GN28*

|  | Denomination | Series | Examples known |
|---|---|---|---|
| GN 28 | £1 | 1921–1926 Black and grey on orange; no denomination in numerals in centre. | 1.3.1921<br>9.2.1924<br>17.5.1924 |

*GN29*

|  | Denomination | Series | Examples known |
|---|---|---|---|
| GN 29 | £1 | 1927–1932 Black and grey on red; '£1' in centre. | 6.12.1927<br>12.4.1928 |
| GN 30 | 10/– | 1933 Light blue and brown; '10/–' in centre; English wording on *rev.* | 18.11.1933 |
| GN 31 | £1 | 1933 Grey on red; as GN 29 but no 'ENTD'; English wording on *rev.* |  |

*GN32*

|  | Denomination | Series | Examples known |
|---|---|---|---|
| GN 32 | 10/– | From 1934 Light blue and orange; Guernsey seal on *rev.* in red | 29.3.1934,<br>5.6.1937 |

205

*GN33*

|  | Denomination | Series | Examples known |
|---|---|---|---|
| GN 33 | £1 | From 1934 Grey and red; seal on *rev.* in blue. | 29.3.1934, 9.6.1939 |
| GN 34 | £1 | 31.3.1940 – Last issue before the Occupation. | |

# States of Guernsey Note Issues from 1941

GN35

|  | Denomination | Dated | Description | No. printed | Size (cm) |
|---|---|---|---|---|---|
| GN 35 | 6d |  | *Obv.* Black lettering on blue/pink.<br>*Rev.* Mauve. | 180.000 | 9 x 6 |
|  | i | 16.10.1941 | A 'red overprint' variety has been reported. |  |  |
|  | ii | 1.1.1942 | Later issues printed on blue French banknote paper. |  |  |
|  | iii | 1.1.1943 |  |  |  |

GN36

|  | Denomination | Dated | Description | No. printed | Size (cm) |
|---|---|---|---|---|---|
| GN 36 | 1/–d |  | *Obv.* As GN 37 but overprinted 1/– in orange.<br>*Rev.* As GN 37. | 75.500 | 9 x 6 |
|  | i | 1.1.1942 | Printed on blue French banknote paper. |  |  |
|  | ii | 18.7.1942 | Printed on blue French banknote paper. |  |  |
|  | iii | 1.1.1943 |  |  |  |

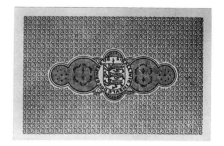

*GN37*

|  | Denomination | Dated | Description | No. printed | Size (cm) |
|---|---|---|---|---|---|
| GN 37 | 1/3d |  | Obv. Black and yellow.<br>Rev. Brown. | 25.500 | 9 x 6 |
|  |  | 16.10.1941 | A variety has a blank *reverse*. |  |  |
|  |  | 18.10.1942 |  |  |  |

*GN38*

| GN 38 | 2/6d |  | Obv. Blue on white, '2/6' in orange.<br>Rev. Blue on white. | 164.000 | 9 x 6 |
|---|---|---|---|---|---|
|  | i | 25.3.1941 |  |  |  |
|  | ii | 17.5.1941 |  |  |  |
|  | iii | 1.1.1942 | Printed on blue French banknote paper. |  |  |
|  | iv | 1.1.1943 |  |  |  |

*GN39*

|  | Deno-mination | Dated | Description | No. printed | Size (cm) |
|---|---|---|---|---|---|
| GN 39 | 5/–d | | *Obv.* Black on white, '5/–' in red.<br>*Rev.* Red on white. | 72.000 | 9.8 x 6.3 |
| | i | 25.3.1941 | | | |
| | ii | 17.5.1941 | A variety has central 5/– upside down. | | |
| | iii | 1.1.1942 | | | |
| | iv | 1.1.1943 | | | |

*GN40*

| GN 40 | 10/–d | 1.1.1943 | *Obv.* Blue on white, '10/–' in red<br>*Rev.* Red on white. | 88.000 | 13.5 x 8 |
|---|---|---|---|---|---|

*GN41*

| GN 41 | £1 | | *Obv.* Black on white, '£1' red centrepiece.<br>*Rev.* Blue on white. | 172.000 | 14.9 x 8.8 |
|---|---|---|---|---|---|
| | i | 1.1.1943 | | 160.000 | |
| | ii | 1.1.1945<br>(issued 9.5.1945) | Printed on blue French banknote paper. | 12.000 | |
| GN 42 | £5 | 1.1.1945<br>(issued 9.5.1945) | *Obv.* Green on green, red serial no.<br>*Rev.* Green on green. | 30.000 | 16.6 x 9.6 |

*GN43*

|  | Denomination | Dated | Description | No. printed | Size (cm) |
|---|---|---|---|---|---|
| GN 43 | 10/–d | 1945–1966 (various dates) | *Obv.* Lilac and green. *Rev.* Mauve. | Not published | 14.8 x 8.1 |

*GN44*

|  |  |  |  |  |  |
|---|---|---|---|---|---|
| GN 44 | £1 | 1945–1966 (various dates) | *Obv.* Violet and green. *Rev.* Green. | Not published | 15.4 x 8.7 |

*GN45*

|  |  |  |  |  |  |
|---|---|---|---|---|---|
| GN 45 | £5 | 1956–1966 (1.12.1956) | *Obv.* Green and blue. *Rev.* Green. | Not published | 15.6. x 8.9 |

*GN46*

|   | Denomination | Dated | Description | No. printed | Size (cm) |
|---|---|---|---|---|---|
| GN 46 | £1 | 1969–1975 (ND) | Obv. Olive green, yellow; arms. Rev. Olive green, Castle Cornet. | Not published | 13.5 x 7.3 |

*GN47*

| GN 47 | £5 | 1969–1975 (ND) | Obv. Mauve and gold; arms. Rev. Mauve and gold; sea-front. | Not published | 14.6 x 8.5 |
|---|---|---|---|---|---|

*GN48*

| GN 48 | £10 | 1975–1980 (ND) | Obv. Blue and green; Britannia, lion and arms. Rev. Blue; Battle of Queenston Heights. | Not published | 14.9 x 8.9 |
|---|---|---|---|---|---|

*GN49*

| GN 49 | £1 | From 1980 (ND) | Obv. Green/blue/yellow; market scene. Rev. Green; Daniel de Lisle Brock. | Not published | 13.5 x 6.7 |
|---|---|---|---|---|---|

*GN50*

|  | Denomination | Dated | Description | No. printed | Size (cm) |
|---|---|---|---|---|---|
| GN 50 | £5 | From 1980 (ND) | Obv. Multicoloured; fort. Rev. Brown; Thomas de la Rue. | Not published | 14.6 x 7.8 |

*GN51*

|  |  |  |  |  |  |
|---|---|---|---|---|---|
| GN 51 | £10 | From 1980 (ND) | Obv. Multicoloured; Castle Cornet. Rev. Blue; Sir Isaac Brock. | Not published | 15.2 x 8.5 |

*GN52*

|  |  |  |  |  |  |
|---|---|---|---|---|---|
| GN 52 | £20 | From 1980 (ND) | Obv. Mainly red; Saumarez Park. Rev. Red; Lord de Saumarez. | Not published | 16.1 x 9 |

# Early Jersey Note Issues

*JN1*

\* £1 unless otherwise stated  
\*\* see following list

|  | Name and address | Notes current | Examples known* | Paying agent** |
|---|---|---|---|---|
| JN1 | Ahier, Jean – St. Sauveur or St. Saviour's Bank, Jersey | 1836–41 | 1837 | 109, 123 |

*JN2*

|  | Name and address | Notes current | Examples known* | Paying agent** |
|---|---|---|---|---|
| JN2 | Ahier, Wm. Chas., Ph. le Capelain & Co. – Proche la Pompe de Haut (now Snow Hill; the public pump has since been removed) St. Helier | 1830–32 | 1830 | – |
| JN3 | Albion Bank | 1821–35 | – | 90 |
|  | Alexander & Co., – see Lowe, Alexander |  |  |  |
| JN4 | Alexander, John – Dove Street, St. Helier | 1817–18 | – | – |

*JN5*          *JN5*

|  | Name and address | Notes current | Examples known | Paying agent |
|---|---|---|---|---|
| JN5 | Alexandre, Matthew – St. Pierre or St. Peter's Jersey (some notes watermarked 'Jersey Bank' and are *'bon pour un louis'*) | 1817–73 | 18-- (Brown) | 93, 69, 57 |
| JN6 | Alexander, Matthew, Jnr. (some notes payable in Jersey Currency) | 1869–73 | – | – |

*JN7*

|  |  |  |  |  |
|---|---|---|---|---|
| JN7 | Amiraux et Cie. – Vieux Marché (between Burrard St. and Beresford St.) St. Helier or Amiraux, le Breton & Cie. or M. Amiraux & W. le Breton or Jersey Bank 1797 | 1797(?)–1832 | 1815 | – |
| JN8 | Amy & Hue (Constables) – Georgetown (on the border between St. Helier and St. Clement Parishes) | 1837–41 | – | – |
| JN9 | Amy, Ed. – En haut des Mielles (the area between Charing Cross and Gallows Hill on the outskirts of St. Helier) | 1819–20 | – | – |
| JN10 | Amy, Nicholas | 1820 | – | – |
|  | Ann Street Bank – see Journeaux, Philippe |  |  |  |

*JN11*

| | Name and address | Notes current | Examples known | Paying agent |
|---|---|---|---|---|
| JN11 | Anthoine, Jean – Commercial Buildings (on the 'Quai des Marchands' below Fort Regent) St. Helier or Jersey Union Bank | 1836–79 | undated | 81 |

*JN12*

*JN12*

*JN12*

*JN12*

| | | | | |
|---|---|---|---|---|
| JN12 | Arthur, de Carteret & Co. – Broad Street, St. Helier or Jersey Joint Stock Bank (Suspended payment & absorbed by Hampshire Banking Co. in 1873) | 1847–73 | 1860, 1867, 1869, 1871 and others, some unsigned | – |

*JN13*

| | Name and address | Notes current | Examples known | Paying agent |
|---|---|---|---|---|
| JN13 | Arthur, J., P. le Ruez, Elie de Carteret & Philip le Neveu<br>or Arthur, de Carteret, le Brock, Falle, Neel, le Neveu, Norman, le Bas & Co.<br>or Wesleyan Methodist Country Chapels Bank<br>(proof pulls, possibly reprints, exist*) | 1835–73 | 1835, 1850<br>*undated (Blue) | 56, 69 |
| | Arthur, N (& Jnr.) – see Le Couteur, Ph. | | | |
| JN14 | Arthur, Ph. – St. Aubin | 1820 | – | – |
| JN15 | Aubin, A., Jnr. | 1819 | – | 4 |
| JN16 | Aubin, Ab., Snr. | 1819–20 | – | 5, 4 |
| JN17 | Aubin, George – Grouville<br>(see also Parish of Grouville) | 1836–38 | – | 52, 125 |
| JN18 | Aubin, Josué | 1817 | – | 68 |
| JN19 | Averty, Jean – St. Clement<br>or St. Clement's Bank | 1836–69 | – | 116, 110, 126, 39, 92 |
| JN20 | Bailhache, Ch., ecr. – St. Helier and Mont-à-l'Abbé | 1817–20 | – | 47 |
| JN21 | Bank (nor further description) | ? | undated | – |
| | Banque de deux sous (see Jersey Bank) | | | |
| | Banque d'Epargnes – see Jersey Savings Bank | | | |

JN22

| Name and address | Notes current | Examples known | Paying agent |
|---|---|---|---|
| JN22 Baudains, Michel or Jersey Bank (£1, 5/–, 2/6 notes known) | 1813 | £1–1813, 1814, undated; 5/–, 2/6 1813 | – |
| Bertram, Amice – see Noel, Ph. | | | |

*JN23*

| | Name and address | Notes current | Examples known | Paying agent |
|---|---|---|---|---|
| JN23 | Bible Christians – Royal Crescent or Bible Christian Trust or Bible Christian Church* | 1872–84 | *undated | 23, 20 |
| JN24 | Bilot, Edward – Charing Cross and Mont-à-l'Abbé | 1817–18 | – | – |
| JN25 | Bisson, Fr. | 1821–32 | – | 98 |
| JN26 | Bisson, James – Rue de derrière (now King Street) | 1820 | – | – |
| JN27 | Bisson, Thomas – Rue de derrière | 1817 | – | – |
| JN28 | Blampied, Charles (& see Jersey Agricultural Assoc.) | 1859 | – | 57 |
| JN29 | Blampied, George – Charing Cross | 1817–20 | – | – |
| | Blampied, Peter (Guernsey) – see Union (Bank) | | | |
| JN30 | Blampied, Pierre – St. Pierre | 1817–20 | – | – |
| JN31 | Bosdet, G. J. – St. Brelade or St. Brelade's Association Bank | 1862–79 | – | 78, 92 |
| JN32 | Bricknell, Thomas – Rue de haut (now Hill Street) | 1817 | – | – |
| JN33 | British Bank | 1821–29 | – | 66 |

|  | Name and address | Notes current | Examples known | Paying agent |
|---|---|---|---|---|
| JN34 | Brohier, Madame – Rue des Vignes (Vine Street) | 1819 | – | – |
|  | Cabot, Jean Daniel – see Jersey Agricultural Assoc. | | | |
|  | Caesarea Bank – see De la Garde & Co. | | | |
|  | Caisse d'Epargnes – see Jersey Savings Bank | | | |
| JN35 | Carré, Jean – Rue des Trois Pigeons (now Hill Street) St. Helier | 1820 | – | – |
| JN36 | Carrel, John – Hill Street, St. Helier | 1817 | – | – |
| JN37 | Carrel, Philip – Rue de derrière, St. Helier | 1817–20 | – | – |
|  | Channel Islands Bank – see Hormon, Anthoine, Ahier, le Gros & Co. | | | |
|  | Chapelle Anglaise Wesleyenne – see Gorey English Wesleyan Methodist Chapel | | | |
| JN38 | Chevalier, J. – St. Ouen | 1817–20 | – | 15 |
| JN39 | Chevalier Jean – Rue de derrière, St. Helier (possibly the same as Chevalier, J.) | 1817–18 | – | – |
|  | Clement, Peter – see St. Lawrence Marsh or Common | | | |

JN40

| JN40 | Collas, George, Chief of Police or St. Saviour's Bank (Proof pulls exist*) | 1832 | *1832, 183– | 54 |
|---|---|---|---|---|
|  | Commercial & Exchange Bank – see Le Bas & Co. | | | |
| JN41 | Comptoir of Exchange – 7 Church St. (known also as Rue Trousse Cotillon; it was so dirty that ladies had to tuck up their skirts) | 1870–74 | – | – |

| | Name and address | Notes current | Examples known | Paying agent |
|---|---|---|---|---|
| | Corbel, Jean – see Lesbirel, Norman, Corbel, Le Sueur, Hocquard et Cie. | | | |
| | Corbel, Ph. – see Lesbirel, Norman, Corbel, Le Sueur, Hocquard et Cie. | | | |
| | Country Bank – see 1. Gibaut, Orange & Co. 2. Huelin, Ph. & Jean Syvret | | | |
| JN42 | Coutanche, Ed. – Colomberie, St. Helier | 1819 | – | – |
| JN43 | D'Auvergne, Frs., ecr, – Millbrook (on the boundary between St. Helier and St. Lawrence) | 1820 | – | 26 |
| JN44 | D'Auvergne, Philippe, ecr. – St. Ouen | 1817 | – | 26 |
| JN45 | Davis, William – Charing Cross, St. Helier | 1817–20 | – | – |
| JN46 | De Carteret | 1838–41 | – | 21 |
| | De Carteret, Charles, Jnr. – see Vingtaine du Mont-au-Prêtre | | | |
| | De Carteret, Elias – see 1. St. Lawrence Marsh or Common 2. Arthur, J., P. de Ruez et al. | | | |
| JN47 | De Gruchy – Queen St., St. Helier | 1817–20 | – | |

*JN48*

| | | | | |
|---|---|---|---|---|
| JN48 | De Gruchy, A., & Co. 11 and 17 Grande Rue (Broad St.) or Gosset, de Gruchy & Co. or Jersey Banking Company A.D. 1828 (early notes may have been issued by Nicolle, de Ste Croix etc.) (liquidated 1886) | 1828–86 | 1856, 1863, 1864 | – |

| | Name and address | Notes current | Examples known | Paying agent |
|---|---|---|---|---|
| JN49 | De la Garde & Co. – 19 Bond Street, St. Helier or Caesarea Bank (failed 1842) | 1836–42 | – | – |
| | De la Haye, Thomas – see Jersey Agricultural Assoc. | | | |
| | De la Perelle, E. – see 1. Hacquoil, de la Perelle & Co. 2. Elie le Montais et al. | | | |
| JN50 | De la Perrelle, J. – Au Coie, St. Helier | 1817–20 | – | 25 |
| JN51 | De la Taste et Wright – Grande Rue (Broad St.) | 1817–20 | – | – |
| JN52 | De la Taste, E. & T. – Vieux Marché, St. Helier | 1817–20 | – | – |
| JN53 | De Ste Croix, Josué – Rue des Sablons (Sand St.) St. Helier | 1817–20 | – | – |
| | De Ste Croix, Thos. – see St. Lawrence Marsh or Common | | | |
| JN54 | Deslandes, Josué – Ès Hemies (now Le Geyt St.) St. Helier (see also le Bailly & Deslandes) | 1817–20 | – | – |
| JN55 | Deslandes, Philip – Seale Street, St. Helier | 1819–20 | – | – |
| | Dolbel, George – see Le Montais, Elias, et al. | | | |
| | Dolbel, E. – see Le Montais, Elias, et al. | | | |
| JN56 | Dorey, Jean – Trinité (see also Jersey Agricultural Assoc.) | 1836–73 | – | 122, 39, 42, 40 |
| JN57 | Du Bois, Thomas – Charing Cross, St. Helier | 1817 | – | – |
| JN58 | Du Chemin, Pierre – Nouveau Marché (between Halkett Place and Halkett St) | 1817 | – | – |
| JN59 | Duhamel, T. & P. – Cross Street, St. Helier | 1821–41 | – | – |
| JN60 | Duheaume, Ed. – Ste. Marie | 1817–20 | – | 28 |
| JN61 | Duheaume, Philippe – St. Ouen or St. Owen's Bank | 1834–46 | 1834 | 107, 128, 78 |

*JN61*

|  | Name and address | Notes current | Examples known | Paying agent |
|---|---|---|---|---|
| JN62 | Dupré, Jean – Ste. Marie | 1817 | – | 43 |
|  | Durell, Charles – see<br>  Gorey English Wesleyan Methodist<br>  Chapel |  |  |  |
| JN63 | Durell, Elie, Jnr. – Hemery Row, St. Helier | 1817 | – | – |
|  | Duval, Ph. – see<br>  Union (Bank) |  |  |  |
|  | Economical Bank – see<br>  Péquin, P. |  |  |  |
|  | English & Jersey Union Bank – see<br>  Le Neveu, Sorel & Co. |  |  |  |
| JN64 | Ennis, James – Charing Cross, St. Helier | 1817–41 | – | – |
| JN65 | Esnouf, Dallain & Co. – St Jean<br>  or St. John's Bank | 1836–79 | – | 128, 117 |

*JN66*

| JN66 | Esplanade, The – St. Helier<br>('for the construction of a line of Quays<br>from the North Pier to Patriotic Place'<br>under guarantee of the States) | 1858 | 1858, 18--<br>some unsigned | – |

| | Name and address | Notes current | Examples known | Paying agent |
|---|---|---|---|---|
| JN67 | Falle & Orange – 56 Chemin Neuf (now Old St.) | 1837–46 | – | – |
| | Falle, G – see Le Bas, Elie | | | |
| JN68 | Falle, Thomas – Grouville | 1817 | – | – |
| | Family Association Bank – see Le Blancq, Ph. Farmers' Bank – see St. John's Farmers' Bank | | | |
| JN69 | Fauvel, Charles – Rue de derrière and Nouveau Marché, St. Helier | 1817–20 | – | – |
| JN70 | Fauvel, George – Rue de haut, St. Helier | 1817–20 | – | – |
| | Financial Agency – see Motref, Boulay & Cie. | | | |
| JN71 | Fixott, Charles – Nouveau Marché, St. Helier | 1817–20 | – | – |
| JN72 | Franche Ville Bank (Proof pulls exist*) | 1833–35 | *undated | 3 |
| | Friendly Association – see Péquin, Pierre | | | |
| JN73 | Gallichan, Matthieu – Rue de la Chaussée, St. Helier | 1817 | – | – |
| JN74 | Gallichan, Ph. – St. Sauveur | 1817–20 | – | 28 |
| | Gallichan, Thos. (Constable) – see Trinity Parish Church | | | |
| JN75 | Gaudin, D., Jnr. | 1817 | – | 31 |
| JN76 | Gaudin, E. or Jersey Bank | 1814–15 | 1815 | – |
| JN77 | Gibaut & Co. – New Street, St. Helier | 1833–35 | – | – |
| JN78 | Gibaut, Falla, Alexandre, Le Quesne & Co. | 1836–46 | – | 72 |
| JN79 | Gibaut, Orange, (Le Quesne) & Co. or Jersey Country Bank or Country Bank* (Proof pulls exist*) | 1834–79 | *undated | 12 |
| | Gibaut, Ph. – see St. Lawrence Marsh or Common | | | |
| JN80 | Giffard, François – Rue de derrière, St. Helier | 1817–20 | – | – |

|      | Name and address | Notes current | Examples known | Paying agent |
|------|------------------|---------------|----------------|--------------|
| JN81 | Godeau, Jean – Trinity (see also Jersey Agricultural Assoc.) | 1817–20, 1859(?) | – | 38, 57 |
| JN82 | Godfray & Orange – St. Aubin or Godfray, Orange & Herault or Ph. Godfray & John Herault | 1817–32 | – | 51 |

*JN83*

| JN83 | Godfray, Hugh, (Sons & Co.) – Hill St., St. Helier or Jersey (Old) Bank or Old Bank* Jersey 1797 or Godfray, Major & Godfray (Established 1797, amalgamated with Channel Islands Bank [q.v.] 1891) (an undated note* is watermarked 'British') (A note [unsigned] of the Old Bank dated 1901** is preserved in the Soc. Jersiaise Collection, suggesting that the Bank may have continued to issue its own notes after its amalgamation in 1891) | 1797–1891 | 18- *undated **1901 | – |
| JN84 | Gorey English Wesleyan Methodist Chapel or Wesleyan Bank (and many other permutations of this title) | 1817–79 | – | 98, 50, 14 |
|      | Gosset, de Gruchy & Co. – see A. de Gruchy & Co. | | | |
|      | Grandin, Jean – see Le Bas, Elias | | | |
|      | Grouville Parish Bank – see 1. Parish of Grouville 2. Noel, Ph. | | | |
|      | Grouville Union Bank – see Mallet, M. | | | |

| | Name and address | Notes current | Examples known | Paying agent |
|---|---|---|---|---|
| JN85 | Gruchy, Matthieu – St. Pierre | 1820 | – | – |
| | Guillot, Ann – see Vingtaine du Mont-au-Prêtre | | | |
| JN86 | Guiton & Perchard – 32 King Street, St. Helier | 1821–42 | – | 49 |

*JN87*

| | | | | |
|---|---|---|---|---|
| JN87 | Guiton (& Co.), John James – Grande Rue, St. Helier | 1817–20 | 181- | – |
| | Guiton, John – see Vingtaine du Mont-au-Prêtre | | | |

*JN88*

| | | | | |
|---|---|---|---|---|
| JN88 | Hacquoil, de la Perrelle & Co. or St. Ouen's Bank* (see also Jersey Union Assoc. Bank) | 1859–69 | *1859 (Blue) | – |
| JN89 | Hacquoil, Jean – St. Ouen | 1817 | – | 88 |
| | Hacquoil, Philippe – see 1. Hacquoil, de la Perrelle & Co. 2. Le Montais, Elie, etc. | | | |
| JN90 | Hamon, Ed. – St. Ouen | 1817–20 | – | 91 |
| JN91 | Hamon, Ph. or Jersey Bank | 1814–16 | 1814, 1815, 1816, 181- | – |

|  | Name and address | Notes current | Examples known | Paying agent |
|---|---|---|---|---|
| JN92 | Hamon, Samuel – Ste. Marie | 1817–20 | – | 30 |
|  | Hamptone, F. – see Vingtaine du Mont-au-Prêtre |  |  |  |
| JN93 | Hand-in-Hand Bank<br>Denominations: 5/–, 2/6<br>'Proof pulls', perhaps reprints,<br>in unusually good condition, exist* | 1813 | *181- | – |
| JN94 | Herault, M. – St. Aubin | 1821–29 | – | 51 |
|  | Hocquard, Charles – see Lesbirel, Norman etc. |  |  |  |
| JN95 | Hooper, Jean – Grouville | 1817–20 | – | 24 |

*JN96*

| JN96 | Horman, Anthoine, Ahier, Le Gros & Co.<br>or Channel Islands Bank<br>(Established 1858, taken over by<br>London & Midland Bank, Ltd., 1898) | 1858–98 | undated | – |
|---|---|---|---|---|
| JN97 | Hue, Philippe – Au Dicq, Havre des Pas<br>(see also Amy & Hue) | 1820 | – | – |
| JN98 | Huelin, Ph. and Jean Syvret<br>or Country Bank | 1854–79 | – | 78, 92 |

*JN99*

| JN99 | International Bank | 1865–68 | 1865 | – |
|---|---|---|---|---|

*JN100*

| | Name and address | Notes current | Examples known | Paying agent |
|---|---|---|---|---|
| JN100 | Janvrin, Durell, [de Veulle] & Company – Broad Street, St. Helier or Jersey Commercial Bank (Established 1808, failed and taken over by Robin Frères [Commercial Bank], 1879; Sterling and Jersey Currency Notes are known) | 1808–79 | 183-, 1856, 1862 | – |
| | Jarvis, Thos. – see Sorèl, Thomas | | | |
| JN101 | Jean, Ph. – St. Ouen and Rue de la Chaussée, St. Helier | 1817–20 | – | 28, 41 |
| JN102 | Jersey – British Sterling (no further description) (Proof pulls exist*) | ? | *undated | ? |

*JN103*

| | Name and address | Notes current | Examples known | Paying agent |
|---|---|---|---|---|
| JN103 | Jersey Agricultural Association or Trinity Bank or Le Masurier & Blampied (Signatories: Chas. Blampied, Jean Daniel Cabot, Jean Godeaux, Jean Dorey, Thomas de la Haye, George Larbalestier, Peter le Boutillier, Ph. Perchard, Philip Alexandre) | 1858–69 | 1835 | 42, 16, 29 |

JN104
(Unattributed)

JN104
(Unattributed; possibly G. Syvret, q.v.)

|  | Name and address | Notes current | Examples known | Paying agent |
|---|---|---|---|---|
| JN104 | Jersey Bank – see<br>  1. Gaudin, E.<br>  2. Hamon, Ph.<br>  3. Le Gallais, Wm. G.<br>  4. Syvrett, Geo.<br>  5. Baudains, Michel | | | |
| | Jersey Banking Co. – see<br>  1. De Gruchy, A., & Co.<br>  2. Nicolle, de Ste. Croix etc. | | | |
| | Jersey Caledonian Bank – see<br>  Le Cornu, Le Gresley & Co. | | | |
| | Jersey Commercial Bank – see<br>  Janvrin, Durell & Co. | | | |
| | Jersey Country Bank – see<br>  1. Gibaut, Orange etc.<br>  2. Huelin, Ph., & J. Syvret | | | |

JN105

| JN105 | Jersey Deposit Bank<br>  or G. & H. Challis Bros. & Co. | 1866–68 | 1866, undated | – |
| --- | --- | --- | --- | --- |
| | Jersey Economical Bank – see<br>  Péquin, P. | | | |

|  | Name and address | Notes current | Examples known | Paying agent |
|---|---|---|---|---|
|  | Jersey Joint Stock Bank – see<br>    Arthur, de Carteret & Co. | | | |
|  | Jersey Mercantile Union Bank – see<br>    1. Matthews, de Carteret & Co.<br>    2. Le Bailly, Deslandes & Co. | | | |
| JN106 | Jersey 1d Bank<br>    or Banque de Deux Sous | 1862 | – | – |
| JN107 | (Jersey) Savings Bank<br>    or Banque d'Epargnes<br>    or Caisse d'Epargnes | 1834–69 | – | – |
|  | Jersey Union Association Bank – see<br>    Le Montais, Elie et al. | | | |
|  | Jersey Union Bank – see<br>    1. Anthoine, Jean<br>    2. Noel, Ph. | | | |
|  | Jeune & le Quesne – see<br>    Vingtaine du Mont-au-Prêtre | | | |
| JN108 | Jeune, F. – Grande Rue, St. Helier | 1819 | – | – |
| JN109 | Jolin, Daniel – Vieux Marché, St. Helier | 1817 | – | – |
| JN110 | Jolin, David – Place Royale (Royal Square),<br>    St. Helier | 1820 | – | – |
| JN111 | Journeaux, Philippe – Ann Street, St. Helier<br>    or Ann Street Bank* | 1817–37 | *18-- | 47 |
| JN112 | Kingston, François – Dove Street, St. Helier | 1817–20 | – | – |
| JN113 | Langlois, H. | 1819 | – | 59 |
| JN114 | Larbalestier, Ch. – Trinité | 1817 | – | – |
| JN115 | Larbalestier, George<br>    (see also Jersey Agricultural Assoc.) | 1820 | – | – |

JN116

| | Name and address | Notes current | Examples known | Paying agent |
|---|---|---|---|---|
| JN116 | Le Bailly, Deslandes & Co., Don Street, St. Helier or Jersey Mercantile Union Bank* (suspended payments 1873, liquidated 1877) | 1822–77 | *1841, 1858, 1864, 1868, 18-- (Blue) | – |
| JN117 | Le Bas & Co. – Cross Street, St. Helier or Commercial & Exchange Bank (ceased 1852) | 1847–52 | – | – |

*JN118*

| | | | | |
|---|---|---|---|---|
| JN118 | Le Bas, Elie, & G. Falle or Mont-au-Prêtre Jersey Bank (see also Le Bas, Jean) | 1839–50 | 1839, 1850 (renewal), 183- | – |
| JN119 | Le Bas, Jean (& Elie le Bas & Jean Grandin*) – St. Brelade (1818–20) and Mont-au-Prêtre | 1818–20; 1836–53* | – | 93, 103, 106, 101 |
| JN120 | Le Blancq, Elie – St. Ouen | 1817 | – | 88 |
| JN121 | Le Blancq, Philip (for le Blancq, de Gruchy & Co.) or Family Association Bank* (Proof pulls exist*; defaced plate in Museum of Société Jersiaise. Banknotes of this bank were reported by The Jersey Independent newspaper of October 1858 to be not encashable) | 1858–69 | *18-- | 78, 95 |
| JN122 | Le Boutillier, Ch. – Trinité | 1817–20 | – | 13 |
| | Le Boutillier, Peter – see Jersey Agricultural Assoc. | | | |
| JN123 | Le Breton, Ch. – St. Sauveur | 1817–20 | – | – |

|  | Name and address | Notes current | Examples known | Paying agent |
|---|---|---|---|---|
| JN124 | Le Brocq, Ch. – St. Ouen | 1859 | – | – |
| JN125 | Le Brocq, Jacques – St. Ouen or St. Ouen's Leoville Bank | 1836–73 | – | 118, 123 |
| JN126 | Le Brun, Jean – St. Ouen | 1820 | – | 36 |
| JN127 | Le Brun, Ph. – St. Helier | 1817 | – | 124 |
| JN128 | Le Cappelain et Cie. | 1842–46 | – | 65 |
| JN129 | Le Cappelain, Philippe – Rue de derrière, St. Helier | 1830–32 | – | – |
| JN130 | Le Clercq, Josué – St. Clément or St. Clement's Bank* (signed also by Josué F. le Clercq, Jnr. Proof pulls exist*) | 1854–79 | *undated | 23, 99 |
|  | Le Coin Bank – see Lowe, Alexander |  |  |  |

*JN131*

| JN131 | Le Cornu, Le Gresley & Co. or Jersey Caledonian Bank | ? | undated | – |
|---|---|---|---|---|
|  | Le Couteur, Edouard – see Le Couteur, Jean |  |  |  |

*JN132*

| JN 132 | Le Couteur, Jas. – Colomberie, St. Helier | 1814–20 | 1814, 1815, 1816, 1817, 1818 | – |

*JN133*

| | Name and address | Notes current | Examples known | Paying agent |
|---|---|---|---|---|
| JN133 | Le Couteur, F. Jean (& Edouard G.) – Ste. Marie or St. John's Jersey (see also Le Couteur, Philip Fr.) | 1817–36 | 183-, 1836 | 46, 91 |
| JN134 | Le Couteur, Philip Fr. (N. Arthur, J. le Couteur et Cie.) or St. Peter's Windmill Association (other signatories: Philip le Feuvre, John Simon, Nicholas Arthur Jnr.) | 1817–91 | – | 28, 34, 119, 90, 85, 16, 59, 30, 36, 125, 94, 89, 16, 62 |
| JN135 | Le Feuvre, George – Chez Mr. Collyer, Grande Rue and Rue de la Chaussée, St. Helier (or possibly payable at these addresses) | 1817–20 | – | ? 19 |
| | Le Feuvre, Philip – see Le Couteur, Ph. Fr. | | | |
| JN136 | Le Gallais, Philippe – Rue de derrière, St. Helier | 1817–20 | – | – |
| JN137 | Le Gallais, Suson – Rue de Seale, (Seale St.), St. Helier | 1817–20 | – | – |

*JN138*

| | Name and address | Notes current | Examples known | Paying agent |
|---|---|---|---|---|
| JN138 | Le Gallais, William George – Rue de derrière, St. Helier or Jersey Bank* | 1817–20, 1843–46 | *1843 (Blue) | 65 |
| JN139 | Le Gros, Charles – Rue de derrière, St. Helier Le Gros, Edw. – see St. Lawrence Marsh or Common | 1830–32 | – | – |
| JN140 | Le Gros, George – Ès Hémies, St. Helier | 1817–20 | – | – |
| JN141 | Le Gros, Jean – Rue de derrière, St. Helier | 1817–20 | – | – |
| JN142 | Le Gros, Thomas – Rue des Sablons (Sand Street) St. Helier (see also St. Martin's & St. Peter's Association) | 1817–20 | – | – |
| JN143 | Le Hardy, Thomas (crown-size cardboard token, legend: 'I promise a pound banknote for 4 of these tokens') | 1812 | 1812 | – |
| JN144 | Le Maitre, Charles, ecr. – St. Ouen | 1817–20 | – | 47 |
| JN145 | Le Maitre, John – Rue de derrière, St. Helier | 1817 | – | – |

*JN146*

| | | | | |
|---|---|---|---|---|
| JN146 | Le Montais, Elie, E. Dolbel, George Dolbel, Mat. le Montais, E. de la Perrelle, P. Hacquoil (signatories) or Dolbel, le Montais & Co.* or St. Brelade's Parish Bank* or Jersey Union Association Bank (see also Lowe, Alexander. The notes of this group were described on more than one occasion as being 'payable nowhere') | 1859–69 | 1859; *undated | 105 |
| | Le Montais, Mat. – see Le Montais, Elie | | | |

| | Name and address | Notes current | Examples known | Paying agent |
|---|---|---|---|---|
| JN147 | Lemprière, Jean – Mont-au-Prêtre (on the Parish boundary between St. Helier and Trinity) | 1817 | – | 22 |
| | Le Neveu, P. – see Arthur, J. etc. | | | |

*JN148*

| | Name and address | Notes current | Examples known | Paying agent |
|---|---|---|---|---|
| JN148 | Le Neveu, Sorel & Co. – 5 Brook Street, St. Helier or English and Jersey Union Bank (taken over by Hampshire Banking Co. 1873) | 1860–73 | 1860, 1862, 1863 | – |
| JN149 | Le Quesne, Jean – St. Jean | 1819 | – | 8 |
| JN150 | Le Quesne, Richard, Chef de Police de St. Jean | 1821–32 | – | 4 |
| JN151 | Le Riche, Thomas – Vieux Chemin (now Old Street), St. Helier | 1817–20 | – | – |
| JN152 | Le Rossignol, Ed., Chief of Police – St. Ouen | 1830–32 | – | – |
| JN153 | Lerrier, John Francis or St. Clement's Bank | 1869–73 | – | – |
| | Le Ruez, P. – see Arthur, J. | | | |
| JN154 | Le Sauteur & Mourant – Queen Street, St. Helier | 1817 | – | – |
| JN155 | Le Sauteur, [Edward Elias] & [George] Sohier or St. Martin's Bank (see also St. Martin's & St. Peter's Assoc.) | 1847–79 | – | 92, 2, 62 |

|       | Name and address | Notes current | Examples known | Paying agent |
|-------|------------------|---------------|----------------|--------------|
| JN156 | Lesbirel, Norman, Corbel, le Sueur, Hocquard et Cie. or (St. John's) Farmers' Bank* (Signatories: Pierre Lesbirel, Ph. Norman, Jean Corbel, Ph. Corbel, Ph. le Sueur, Charles Hocquard & David Romeril) | 1836–73 | *undated | 69 |
|       | Lesbirel, Pierre – see Lesbirel, Norman etc. | | | |
| JN157 | Le Scelleur, Jean – St. Sauveur | 1819–20 | – | – |
| JN158 | Le Sueur, Charles – Cheapside and aux Mielles, St. Helier | 1817–20 | – | – |
| JN159 | Le Sueur, Clement – Aux Mielles, St. Helier | 1817–20 | – | – |
| JN160 | Le Sueur, Mrs. Elizabeth – Rue du Petit-Douet (now Brook Street) St. Helier | 1819–20 | – | – |
| JN161 | Le Sueur, Frs. – St. Sauveur | 1820 | – | 73 |
|       | Le Sueur, Ph. – see Lesbirel, Norman etc. | | | |

*JN162*

| JN162 | Lowe, Alexander and/or E. F. le Montais or Alexander & Co. or Le Coin Bank* | 1835–79 | *1835, undated | 78, 97, 92 |
|       | Malet de Carteret, E. C. – see St. Ouen's Church | | | |
| JN163 | Mallet, E. & E. – Rue de derrière, St. Helier | 1817–20 | – | – |
| JN164 | Mallet, Jean – Gorey | 1847–50 | – | – |
| JN165 | Mallet, M. or Grouville Union Bank* | 1847 | *1847 | 127 |
|       | Manuel, Jenny Luce – see Le Neveu, Sorel & Co. | | | |

| | Name and address | Notes current | Examples known | Paying agent |
|---|---|---|---|---|
| JN166 | Marett, Ed. – Vieux Chemin, St. Helier | 1820 | – | – |
| JN167 | Marrett & Jean – Derrière le Nouveau Marché, St. Helier | 1819 | – | – |

*JN168*

| | | | | |
|---|---|---|---|---|
| JN168 | Masonic Temple Company Limited (to build the Masonic Temple, Stopford Road; poor quality reprints exist*) | 1866–84 | *1844, 1866 | 76, 133 |

*Deposit-receipt*

*JN169*                                                    *cheque*

| | | | | |
|---|---|---|---|---|
| JN169 | Matthews, de Carteret & Co. – King Street, St. Helier or (Jersey) Mercantile Union Bank | 1836–65 | – | – |
| JN170 | Matthews, Charles – Vieux Chemin, St. Helier | 1817–20 | – | – |
| JN171 | Mauger, Ed. – St. Jean | 1819 | – | 9 |
| JN172 | Mauger, Philippe – Charing Cross, St. Helier | 1817–20 | – | – |
| | Mercantile Union Bank – see<br>  1. Le Bailly, Deslandes & Co.<br>  2. Matthews, de Carteret & Co. | | | |
| JN173 | Messervy, George – Rue de la Chaussée, St. Helier | 1817–20 | – | – |

|  | Name and address | Notes current | Examples known | Paying agent |
|---|---|---|---|---|
| JN174 | Millais, John – Vieux Chemin, St. Helier | 1817–20 | – | – |
|  | Mont-à-l'Abbé Bank – see Poingdestre, Charles | | | |
|  | Mont-au-Prêtre Jersey Bank – see Le Bas, Elie | | | |
| JN175 | Motref, Boulay & Cie. – 29/30 Grove Place, 7 Burrard St. and 7/9 New Street, St. Helier or Financial Agency, Office des Fonds Publiques or Soc. Générale Anglaise & Française Ltd. | 1893–1911 | – | – |
| JN176 | Mourant, Edouard – Rue de Haut, Mielles, St. Helier, and St. Clement (post 1818) | 1817–20 | – | – |
| JN177 | Much, William – Rue des Sablons, St. Helier | 1819 | – | – |

*JN178 Specimens*

JN178 Nicolle, de Ste. Croix, D'Auvergne, (le Quesne) & Co. – 23 Grande Rue, St. Helier
or Nicolle, de Ste. Croix, D'Auvergne & Co.
(notes marked 'British Sterling')

| Name and address | Notes current | Examples known | Paying agent |
|---|---|---|---|
| or Nicolle, de Ste. Croix, Bertram, (Malzard) & Co. ('Banking Company') or Nicolle, de Ste. Croix, Bertram & Co. £5* or Jersey Banking Company A.D. 1856 | 1821–63 | undated (specimens); *specimen £5 dated 1857 | – |
| JN179 Nicolle, Philippe, Thomas & Nicholas – Grande Rue, St. Helier | 1817–20 | – | – |
| JN180 Noel, D. – Rue de derrière, St. Helier | 1817 | – | – |
| JN181 Noel, Philippe (& Amice Bertram) or Noel & Co. | | | |
| or Grouville Parish Bank | 1847–79 | – | 127, 102, 114, 63, 33 |
| or Jersey Union Bank | 1854–79 | – | 50, 101 |
| Norman, Ph. – see Lesbirel, Norman etc. | | | |
| Office des Fonds Publiques – see Motref, Boulay & Cie. | | | |
| Old Bank – see Godfray, Hugh, & Co. | | | |
| JN182 Orange, Jean | 1820 | – | 82 |
| JN183 Parish of Grouville* or Grouville Parish Bank (signed by George Aubin, Constable q.v. Proof pulls exist*) | 1862–84 | *18-- | 130 |

JN184

| JN184 Parish of St. Brelade (signed by Geo. Philip Benest, Constable or J. A. Seale, Constable*) | 1842–1912 | *1886; 18-- | 131, 18, 75, 87, 1, 61 |

239

| | Name and address | Notes current | Examples known | Paying agent |
|---|---|---|---|---|
| JN185 | Parish of St. Clément<br>or St. Clement's Parish Bank<br>(signed by John le Neveu, Constable) | 1833–79 | – | 131, 78, 63 |

JN186,1

JN186,5

| | Name and address | Notes current | Examples known | Paying agent |
|---|---|---|---|---|
| JN186 | Parish of St. Helier<br>1. For paving Belmot Road<br>(signed by Elias Neel, Jnr., N. Westaway,<br>Thomas Gallichan or Thos. Duhamel)<br>2. For laying out Parade<br>3. For paving New St., Craig St. and<br>Upper Don St.<br>4. For paving Belmont Road, Halkett<br>Place and Beresford St.<br>5. Town and Parish of St. Helier<br>(signed by Ph. Aubin, Constable) | 1834–91 | 1. 18--<br>2. 1858<br>3. –<br>4. –<br>5. 1858<br>(unsigned) | 98, 55<br>–<br>133, 44, 32<br>133<br>96, 63, 134 |
| JN187 | Parish of St. Jean<br>or St. John's Bank<br>(signed by John Nicolle or Philip Gibaut,<br>Constables)<br>(A limited edition of 250 notes was printed<br>for the St. John's Fair in 1982 from the<br>original copper plate; the new notes are<br>embossed with the Parish Seal) | 1833–91 | 1836 | 131, 92, 46, 2, 6, 62 |
| JN188 | Parish of St. Lawrence<br>or St. Lawrence Parish (Bank)<br>(signed by John le Gros<br>or John le Gallais, Constables; Proof pulls<br>exist*) | 1857–91 | 1857; *18-- | 131 |

JN189

JN189

|  | Name and address | Notes current | Examples known | Paying agent |
|---|---|---|---|---|
| JN189 | Parish of St. Martin or St. Martin's Parish Bank ('BRITISH' overprinted in blue; signed by Ph. Godfray, Constable, George Sohier, Chief of Police or F. Richardson le Brun, Constable; some notes payable in Jersey Currency) (Proof pulls exist*) | 1821–1912 | 1831, 1897, *18-- | 131, 92, 2, 48, 84, 64, 85 |

JN190

JN190

| JN190 | Parish of St. Mary (Ste. Marie) or St. Mary's Parochial Bank (printed in black or blue; two varieties known; signed by J. L. C. la Cloche, Constable; at other times reportedly signed by J. L. C. le Gerche, J. L. C. la Gerche, J. L. S. la Gerche & J. C. la Cloche. Proof pulls exist*) | 1821–1912 | *18-- | 131, 62 |
|---|---|---|---|---|
| JN191 | Parish of St. Ouen or St. Ouen's Parochial Bank* (signed by Thomas le Cornu, John le Brocq, or Arthur le Cerf, Constables; some notes payable in Jersey Currency) (Proof pulls exist*) | 1814–1912 | 1815, 1859, *18-- | 131, 94, 70, 92, 132, 18, 75, 17 |

*JN192,1*

*JN192,2*

*JN192,2*

*JN192,3*

|  | Name and address | Notes current | Examples known | Paying agent |
|---|---|---|---|---|
| JN192 | Parish of St. Peter (Proof pulls exist**) |  | **189- |  |
|  | 1. Notes overprinted 'ONE' in orange or blue |  |  |  |
|  | 2. St. Peter's Parochial Bank (notes printed in black or orange; signed by John Simon, Constable, or by various Procureurs; some over-printed 'BEAUMONT ROAD'; one note dated 1827* termed 'bon pour un louis') | 1821–1912 | *1827, undated | 131, 62 |
|  | 3. St. Peter's Valley Road (signed by Phil. le Couteur, Constable) | 1828 | 1828 | 131 |

| | Name and address | Notes current | Examples known | Paying agent |
|---|---|---|---|---|
| JN193 | Parish of St. Saviour (signed by Constables) | 1832–46 | 1832 | 131 |
| JN194 | Parish of Trinity Trinity Parish Bank* (signed by Thomas Gallichan, Constable; some notes were issued for the paving of Rozel Road*, and of the streets in the Vingtaine du Mont-au-Prêtre [q.v.] Proof pulls exist*) | 1833–91 | *1836 | 131, 74, 62, 58 |
| JN195 | Patton, John – Derrière le Nouveau Marché, St. Helier | 1819–20 | – | – |
| JN196 | Patriarche, M. G. | 1822–29 | – | 35 |
| JN197 | Patriarche, William | 1826 | – | 35 |
| | Payn, Ph. – see St. Ouen's Church | | | |
| JN198 | Payne, Richard – Grouville | 1817–20 | – | – |
| JN199 | Pellier, Dan – St. Ouen and Trinity | 1817–20 | – | 113 |
| JN200 | Pellier, Ph. – St. Ouen | 1817 | – | 60 |
| JN201 | Penny Savings Bank – 6 Royal Square, St. Helier (no connection with National Penny Bank, U. K. which was established 1875 and liquidated 1914) | 1869 | – | – |
| JN202 | Péquin, Pierre – Rue des Sablons, St. Helier or Jersey Economical Bank (some notes signed by P. Péquin and Philip Perchard for the Friendly Association, to pay for the building of Don St. French Wesleyan Chapel) | 1821–73 | – | 49, 37 |
| | Perchard, Ph. – see 1. Jersey Agricultural Assoc. 2. Péquin, Pierre | | | |
| JN203 | Perret, Ab., & Huelin | 1852–53 | – | – |
| JN204 | Perrot, Rev. F. – Nouveau Marché, St. Helier | 1817 | – | – |
| JN205 | Picot, J. – Trinité | 1817 | – | 77 |
| | Pinel, Philip (Treasurer) – see United English Wesleyan Methodist Trust | | | |

|  | Name and address | Notes current | Examples known | Paying agent |
|---|---|---|---|---|
| JN206 | Pipon, Richard – St. Brelade | 1819 | – | – |
| JN207 | Pirouet, Elie – Ès Hémies, St. Helier | 1817–20 | – | – |
| JN208 | Poingdestre, A. – St. Jean | 1817–20 | – | 7 |
| JN209 | Poingdestre, Charles – Mont-à-l'Abbé or Mont-à-l'Abbé Bank* | 1858–73 | *undated | – |
| JN210 | Powell, (T.) & Clanalbin – Colomberie, St. Helier | 1821–41 | – | 79, (83) |
| JN211 | Primitive (Methodist) Trusts | 1869–79 | – | 133 |
| JN212 | Provincial Bank (Proof pulls exist*) | 1865 | *18-- | – |
| JN213 | Renouf, Josué – Derrière le Nouveau Marché, St. Helier | 1817–20 | – | – |
|  | Rive, Elie, Philip and Thos. – see St. Martin's & St. Peter's Association |  |  |  |
|  | Romeril, David – see Lesbirel, Norman etc. |  |  |  |
| JN214 | Romeril, Edward – Vauxhall, St. Helier | 1817–20 | – | – |
| JN215 | Roussell, Michael, & Son (notes signed by Michel Roussell, vis-à-vis Rue de Hue, or Michel Roussell Jnr., Rue des Sablons) | 1816–20 | 2/6, 5/– (undated) | 104 |

*JN216*

| JN216 | St. Aubin's Bank (Denominations known: £1, 5/–; Proof pulls, possibly reprints, exist*) or St. Aubin's Friendly Association (Bank) or Clement, le Feuvre, le Brocq & Co. | 1810 | 5/– 1810; *£1 18--, 1840 | – |

| Name and address | Notes current | Examples known | Paying agent |
|---|---|---|---|

St. Brelade's Association Bank – see
   Bosdet, G. J.

St. Brelade's Parish Bank – see
   Le Montais, Elias

St. Clement's Bank – see
   1. Le Clercq, Josué
   2. Averty, John
   3. Lerrier, John Francis

St. Clement's Parish Bank – see
   Parish of St. Clement

St. John's Jersey – see
   Le Couteur, F. Jean

St. John's Bank – see
   1. Parish of St. John
   2. Esnouf, Dallain & Co.

St. John's Farmers' Bank – see
   Lesbirel, Norman etc.

*JN217*

| | | | | |
|---|---|---|---|---|
| JN217 | St. John's Windmill | ? | 18-- | – |
| JN218 | St. Lawrence Marsh or Common (signed by Ph. Gibaut, Peter Clement, Elias de Carteret, Edw. le Gros and Thos. de Ste. Croix) | 1835 | 1835 | – |

St. Lawrence Parish (Bank) – see
   Parish of St. Lawrence

St. Martin's Bank – see
   Le Sauteur & Sohier

St. Martin's Parish Bank – see
   Parish of St. Martin

| | | | | |
|---|---|---|---|---|
| JN219 | St. Martin's & St. Peter's Association (signed by Thomas Sohier, Thos., Elie and Philip Rive, Thos. le Gros, and Edward E. le Sauteur). (Proof pulls exist*) | 1862–79 | *undated | 86 |

245

| | Name and address | Notes current | Examples known | Paying agent |
|---|---|---|---|---|
| | St. Mary's Parochial Bank – see Parish of St. Mary | | | |
| | St. Ouen's Bank – see 1. Syvrett, Geo. 2. Hacquoil, de la Perrelle & Co. | | | |
| JN220 | St. Ouen's Church (signed by E. C. Malet de Carteret, Ph. Payn & Frs. Vautier, Churchwardens) | 1892–97 | – | – |
| | St. Ouen's Leoville Bank – see Le Brocq, James | | | |
| | St. Ouen's Parish Bank – see Hacquoil, de la Perrelle & Co. | | | |
| | St. Ouen's Parochial Bank – see Parish of St. Ouen | | | |
| | St. Owen's Bank – see Duheaume, Philippe | | | |
| | St. Peter's (Jersey) – see Alexandre, Matthew | | | |
| | St. Peter's New Bank – see Simon, Duheaume & Co. | | | |
| | St. Peter's Parochial Bank – see Parish of St. Peter | | | |
| | St. Peter's Windmill Association – see Le Couteur, Ph. | | | |
| | St. Saviour's Bank – see 1. Ahier, Jean 2. Collas, George | | | |
| JN221 | St. Sauveur, Ab. | 1817 | – | 4 |
| JN222 | Simon, Duheaume & Co. – St. Pierre or St. Peter's New Bank (signed by the Constable, John Simon, in his own private name) | 1837–84 | – | 103, 83, 89 |
| | Simon, John – see 1. Simon, Duheaume & Co. 2. Le Couteur, Ph. Fr. | | | |
| JN223 | Sinel, John & George – St. Pierre or Union Bank | 1854–73 | – | 78, 100, 120 |
| | Société Générale Anglaise et Française – see Motref, Boulay & Cie. | | | |
| JN224 | Sohier, T. & Co. | 1838–46 | – | 121, 10 |
| | Sorel, John – see Sorel, Thomas | | | |

|  | Name and address | Notes current | Examples known | Paying agent |
|---|---|---|---|---|
| JN225 | Sorel, Thomas (& Thos Jarvis & John Sorel) – ès Hémies, St. Helier | 1830–32 | 1832 | – |
| JN226 | States Committee of Harbours (£1 notes issued by an Act dated 2.5.1874) | 1874–82 | – | – |

*JN227*

|  |  |  |  |  |
|---|---|---|---|---|
| JN227 | States of the Island of Jersey £5 Bearer Bond, carrying interest of ½d weekly, apparently circulated as a currency note. ('CORK' watermarked paper; signed and unsigned specimens known) | 1840–41 | 1840 | – |
| JN228 | Sullivan, Edouard – Rue de Seale, St. Helier | 1817–20 | – | – |

*JN229*  *JN229*

|  |  |  |  |  |
|---|---|---|---|---|
| JN229 | Syvret, George or Jersey Bank or St. Ouen's Bank | 1814–15 | 1815 | 43 |
| JN230 | Syvret, Jacques – St. Ouen | 1817–20 | – | 28 |
|  | Syvret, Jean – see Huelin, Ph. |  |  |  |
| JN231 | Syvret, Philip – St. Ouen | 1817–29 | – | 28, 45 |

*JN232*

|  | Name and address | Notes current | Examples known | Paying agent |
|---|---|---|---|---|
| JN232 | Temperance Society (signed by J. M. Nicklin, President, and others; some notes* were for building Temperance Hall) | 1847–79 | *18-- | 78, 27 |
|  | Town and Parish of St. Helier – see Parish of St. Helier |  |  |  |

*JN233*

|  | Name and address | Notes current | Examples known | Paying agent |
|---|---|---|---|---|
| JN233 | Town Vingtaine of St. Helier (notes and 'renewed' notes, some in Jersey Currency, were signed by various proprietors and Procureurs of the Vingtaine) | 1834–1912 | 1834, 18--, undated | 131, 133 |
|  | Trinity Bank – see Jersey Agricultural Assoc. |  |  |  |
|  | Trinity Parish Bank – see Parish of Trinity |  |  |  |
| JN234 | Trinity Parish Church (signed by T. Gallichan, Constable, Nicholas le Quesne, & John le Gros) | 1901–12 | – | 67 |

|  | Name and address | Notes current | Examples known | Paying agent |
|---|---|---|---|---|
| JN235 | Turner, Thomas & Thomas – Aux Mielles, St. Helier | 1817–20 | – | – |
| JN236 | Union (Bank) (signed by Peter Blampied of Guernsey, & Ph. Duval, the notes were issued to pay for the purchase of St. Peter's Dissenters' Cemetery & for building of the Wesleyan Chapel, Wesley Street, St. Helier) | 1862–79 | 18-- | 112 |
|  | Union Bank St. Peter – see Sinel, J. & G. |  |  |  |
| JN237 | United English Wesleyan Methodist Trusts (signed by Philip Pinel, Treasurer) | 1869–84 | – | 50 |
| JN238 | United Shipping Company's Bank (Proof pulls exist*) | 1867 | *undated | – |
|  | Vautier, Frs. – see St. Ouen's Church |  |  |  |
| JN239 | Vibert, Philippe | 1820 | – | – |

JN240,2

JN240,6

| JN240 | Vingtaine du Mont-au-Prêtre |  |  |
|---|---|---|---|
|  | 1. 'Issued from Charles Street' | 1. undated | – |
|  | 2. For the paving of Rue du Val, signed by Charles de Carteret, Jnr., Jeune & le Quesne or (?) Jones – (Proof pulls may exist*) | 2. *1834,1835 | 108, 71, 118 |
|  | 3. For the paving of Burrard, Union & le Geyt Streets, various signatories (Proof pulls may exist*) | 3. *18-- | 133, 34 |
|  | 4. For the paving of Burrard St. | 4. undated | – |
|  | 5. For the paving of Duhamel Place (signed by Ann Guillot) | 5. – | 80 |
|  | 6. 'Bath Street, St. Helier' (signed by G. le Geyt) | 6. 1838 | – |

| Name and address | Notes current | Examples known | Paying agent |
|---|---|---|---|

*JN241*                                               *JN241*

| | | | | |
|---|---|---|---|---|
| JN241 | Vingtaine du Rouge Bouillon | 1833–39 | 1833, 1838, 1839 | – |
| JN242 | Walch, M. – Rue de Haut, St. Helier | 1819 | – | – |
| | Wesleyan Bank – see   Gorey English Wesleyan Methodist   Chapel | | | |
| | Wesleyan Methodist Country Chapels Bank – see   Arthur, J., etc. | | | |

# Paying Agents

1. Alexandre, Capt. J. – High Street St. Aubin
2. Asplett, J. A. – Murier Lane
3. Aubin, George – Grouville
4. Aubin, Jean – Vieux Marché and Halkett Place
5. Aubin, Ph. – En haut de la Ville
6. Bailhache, Philip – Seaton Place, Sand St.
7. Bailleau, Miss – Rue de derrière
8. Barbet, Mrs. – Rue de derrière
9. Bigrel, Mrs. – Rue des Sablons
10. Bisson, Ph. – Charing Cross
11. Blampied Frères – 16 Esplanade
    Blampied & Laffoley – see Laffoley and Blampied
12. Briard & Orange – 7 and 4 Bond St.
13. Briard, Ch. – Rue de derrière
14. Bryant, Wm. – 6 Philip St. and Bath St.
15. Cabot, J. – Rue des Sablons
16. Cannings, Philip or Mrs. – Aurora Inn, 8 Castle St.
17. Capital & Counties Bank (q.v.)
18. Channel Islands Bank (q.v.)
19. Collyer, Mr. – Grande Rue and Rue de la Chaussée
    Commis Viscomte's office – see Simon, P. J.
20. Cory, John – 2 Oxford St. and 2 New Bath St.
21. De Gruchy, A. – King St.
22. De Gruchy, Mr. – Rue de derrière
23. De la Mare, A. (Baker) – 50 Colomberie
24. De la Taste, Edouard – Vieux Marché
25. De Quetteville, M.
26. De Ste. Croix, A., Ecr. – Grande Rue
27. De Ste. Croix, Philip, Jnr. – 9 Library Place
28. Deslandes, Josué – Ès Hémies
29. Dorey, Mr. – 18 Midvale Road
30. Du Bois, Capt. Thomas – Charing Cross
31. Du Chemin, Pierre – Nouveau Marché
32. Duhamel, Thomas – 16 Hill St.
33. Dumaresq, Messrs. – Old London House, King St.
34. Du Parcq, Richard (Procureur) – Grove Place
35. Dupré, Advocate – Place Royale, Dove St and Halkett Place
36. Ennis, James – Charing Cross
37. Falle & Sons – Beresford St.
38. Fauvel, C. – Rue de Haut
39. Gallichan, Edouard – 25 Place Royale
40. Gallichan, E. J. – Esplanade
41. Gallichan, J. – Charing Cross
42. Gallichan, John, (Jos.) – Place Royale
43. Gallichan, Matthieu – Bond St.
44. Gallichan, Thomas – 30 Great Union Road
45. Gallie, J. – Charing Cross
46. Gibaut, Moses – Royal Square
47. Giffard et Cie. (. . . et fils) – Rue de derrière
48. Guiton, P. – 13 Royal Square
49. Guiton & Clément (Perchard) – 32 Rue de derrière
50. Hamon & Vonberg (. . . & Fils) – 37, 39 and 60 King Street and 39 Ann St.
51. Hocquard, Mrs. – Dove St. ('Top of the Town')
52. Hotel des Trois Pigeons, Hill St.
53. Huelin, P. J. – 14 Royal Square
54. Huet, Ch. – 3 Halkett Place
55. Jersey Gas Light Co's office, Gas Lane (signatory Elias Neel Jnr. q.v.)
56. Jersey Joint Stock Bank q.v.
57. Laffoley & Blampied (. . . & le Masurier) – 15 Broad St.
58. Larbalestier, T., & Ogier (G. G. Larbalestier – Trinity Chambers), Hill St.
59. Le Bas, N. – Rue des Sablons
60. Le Boeuf, Matthieu
61. Le Boutillier, J. E. – St. Aubin
62. Le Brun, J. R. (butcher) – 30 & 31 Marché and 23 Hill St.
63. Le Cras, P. or Mrs. – 3 Bond St ('in the lane adjoining London Hotel') and 21 Place Royale
64. Le Feuvre, Ph. – 12 Hill St.
65. Le Gallais, Wm. George – Chemin Neuf, 'the Exchange Office'
66. Le Gros – British Warehouse
67. Le Gros. C. S. (solicitor) – 14 Hill St.
68. Le Maitre, Capt. – Vis-à-vis la Parade (Parade Place)
69. Le Masurier & Blampied – Charing Cross
70. Le Montais, P. – Brompton Villa, Great Union Road
71. Le Quesne, V. (jurat) – 49 Rouge Bouillon
72. Le Rossignol, N. – 15 Chemin Neuf
73. Le Sueur, Ch. – Aux Mielles
74. Le Sueur, P. & C. – 54 King St.
75. London (City) and Midland Bank
76. Malet de Carteret, E. C. – 14 Hill Street
77. Marett, M. E. – Rue de Haut

78. Métivier, James Temple – 60 and 62 King St.
79. Mourant, Ph. – Colomberie
    Neel, Elias, Jnr. – signatory of notes payable at Jersey Gas Light Co.'s office, q.v. (and guarantor on notes of Jean Anthoine q.v.). A certain Elias Neel, possibly Elias Neel senior, issued a copper 1d token in 1812; the token is extremely rare (see T2)
80. Nicolle, Ed. – 61 David Place
    Orange & Briard (. . . & Co.) – see Briard & Orange
    Perchard, Clément – see Guiton & Perchard
81. Pinel, Philip – Cheapside
82. Pirouet, Capt. – Proche la Pompe de Haut
83. Powell & Clanalbin – 3 Halkett Place
84. Richardson & Roissier
85. Richardson, P. M. (solicitor) – 10 Hill St.
86. Rive, Capt. Philip – 27 St. Saviour's Road
87. Seale, J. A. – 12 Hill St.
88. Simmoneaux, Mrs. – Rue de Seale and Rue des Sablons
89. Simon, (P.) John ('Commis Vicomte') and Thomas – 25 and 12 Hill St.
90. Sorel, Thomas – Ès Hémies or Charing Cross
91. Sullivan, Ed. – Rue de Seale
92. Syvret, George or Mrs. G. – 4, 20 and 13 Place Royale
93. Syvret, Jean – Grande Rue
94. Tarone, P. – 10 Queen St.
95. Vibert, John – Burrard St.
96. Voisin (Bisson) & Co. – King St.
97. Wellman, W. R. – 30 King St.
98. Westaway, Nathaniel (advocate) – 16 Don St. and office Royal Square
99. 8 Belmont Road
100. Beresford St.
101. 2 Bond St. (? Elias le Bas)
102. 3 Broad St.
103. 3 and 5 Caledonia Place
104. 14 Charing Cross
105. 1 Cross St. (Reported by the 'Jersey Independent' newspaper of October 1859 to have been empty premises)
106. 4 Cross St. (? Elie le Bas)
107. 8 and 9 Cross St.
108. 1 Devonshire Place
109. 2 Grove Place
110. 5 George Town
111. 30 Great Union Road
112. 47 Halkett Place
113. Hope St.
114. 8 King St.
115. 35 King St.
116. 71 King St.
117. 15 and 16 le Geyt St.
118. 6 Library Place
119. 3 New St.
120. 57 and 61 New St.
121. 7 Queen St.
122. 22 Place Royale
123. 26 Place Royale
124. Rue de derrière
125. 42 Sand St.
126. 47 Sand St.
127. 15 Union St.
128. 18 Union St.
129. 3 Val Plaisant
130. Windsor Road
131. – Residence or office of the relative Constable, or Procureur du Bien Public
132. – 'The Rector'
133. – Notes payable by the relative signatories (at their residences).
134. – Town Hall

# States of Jersey Notes Issues from 1941

*JN243*

| | Deno-<br>mination | Description | No. printed | Issued | Size (cm) |
|---|---|---|---|---|---|
| JN243 | 2/-d | *Obv.* Blue lettering on orange<br>*Rev.* Blue 2/– on orange | 50.000 | June 1941 *(ND)* | 10.3 x 7 |

*JN244*

*JN244*

| | | | | | |
|---|---|---|---|---|---|
| JN244 | 6d | *Obv.* Black lettering on orange | | | |
| | | *Rev.* 'six pence' in orange | 120.000 | April 1942 *(ND)* | |
| | | (Both numbered and unnum- | 120.000 | July 1942 *(ND)* | |
| | | bered notes of the series | 160.000 | January 1943 *(ND)* | |
| | | JN243–247 are known bearing | 200.000 | May 1943 *(ND)* | |
| | | the signature of E. Blampied | 200.000 | October 1943 *(ND)* | |
| | | and the date April 20 1942) | 40.000 | February 1945 *(ND)* | 10.7 x 6.9 |

| Denomination | Description | No. printed | Issued | Size (cm) |
|---|---|---|---|---|

JN244A  Unnumbered specimens are known

JN245

| JN245 | 1/-d | Obv. Brown lettering on grey Rev. Elderly Jersey couple (see note to JN244) | 100.000 100.000 | April 1942 *(ND)* June 1942 *(ND)* | 10.8 x 7 |

JN245A  Unnumbered specimens are known

JN246

| JN246 | 2/-d | Obv. Blue lettering on light blue Rev. Blue horse and cart (see note to JN244) | 50.000? (higher serial numbers known) | April 1942 *(ND)* | 10.8 x 7 |

JN246A  Unnumbered specimens are known

JN247

|  | Denomination | Description | No. printed | Issued | Size (cm) |
|---|---|---|---|---|---|
| JN247 | 10/-d | *Obv.* Green lettering on light green with lilac underprint *Rev.* Green farm girl and three Jersey cows (see note to JN244) | 20.000 6.000 | April 1942 *(ND)* June 1942 *(ND)* | 12.9 x 8.4 |
| JN247A |  | Trial with lilac underprint only on *obverse* |  |  |  |
| JN247B |  | Unnumbered specimens are known |  |  |  |

*JN248*

|  |  |  |  |  |  |
|---|---|---|---|---|---|
| JN248 | £1 | *Obv.* Mauve lettering on light green *Rev.* Mauve scene of *vraic* (seaweed) collecting (see note to JN244) | 7.000 4.000 | April 1942 *(ND)* June 1942 *(ND)* | 13 x 8.5 |
| JN248A |  | Unnumbered specimens are known |  |  |  |

*JN249*

|  |  |  |  |  |  |
|---|---|---|---|---|---|
| JN249 | 10/- | *Obv.* Queen Elizabeth, brown and green *Rev.* St. Ouen's Manor in brown | Not published | From 1963 *(ND)* | 14 x 7.1 |
| JN249A |  | SPECIMEN issue: thin black lettering |  |  |  |

*JN250*

| | Denomination | Description | No. printed | Issued | Size (cm) |
|---|---|---|---|---|---|
| JN250i | £1 | *Obv.* Queen Elizabeth, olive green<br>*Rev.* Mont Orgeuil Castle in green | Not published | From 1963 *(ND)* | 15.2 x 8.8 |
| JN250ii | | Variety with double signature (F. N. Padgham) | | | |
| JN250iii | | Variety without signature | | | |
| JN250A | | SPECIMEN issues: thin black, thin red, thick red lettering | | | |

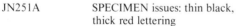

*JN251*

| JN251 | £5 | *Obv.* Queen Elizabeth in red<br>*Rev.* St. Aubin's Fort in red | Not published | From 1963 *(ND)* | 14 x 9.1 |
|---|---|---|---|---|---|
| JN251A | | SPECIMEN issues: thin black, thick red lettering | | | |

*JN252*

256

|  | Deno-mination | Description | No. printed | Issued | Size (cm) |
|---|---|---|---|---|---|
| JN252 | £10 | *Obv.* Queen Elizabeth, mauve and pink<br>*Rev.* St. Ouen's Manor in mauve | Not published | From 1963 *(ND)* | 15.1 x 8.6 |

*JN253*

|  |  |  |  |  |  |
|---|---|---|---|---|---|
| JN253 | £1 | *Obv.* Queen Elizabeth, mainly blue<br>*Rev.* Battle of Jersey, blue | Not published | From 1976 *(ND)* | 13.5 x 7.2 |

*JN254*

|  |  |  |  |  |  |
|---|---|---|---|---|---|
| JN254 | £5 | *Obv.* Queen Elizabeth, mainly brown<br>*Rev.* Elizabeth Castle, brown | Not published | From 1976 *(ND)* | 14.1 x 7.7 |
| JN254A | | SPECIMEN issue: thick red lettering | | | |

*JN255*

|  |  |  |  |  |  |
|---|---|---|---|---|---|
| JN255 | £10 | *Obv.* Queen Elizabeth, mainly green<br>*Rev.* Victoria College, green | Not published | From 1976 *(ND)* | 15.1 x 8.5 |

| Deno-mination | Description | No. printed | Issued | Size (cm) |
|---|---|---|---|---|
| JN255A | | SPECIMEN issue: thick red lettering | | |

 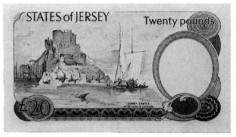

*JN256*

| JN256 | £20 | *Obv.* Queen Elizabeth, orange<br>*Rev.* Gorey Castle, orange | Not published | From 1976 *(ND)* | 16.1 x 9 |
|---|---|---|---|---|---|
| JN256A | | SPECIMEN issue: thick black lettering | | | |

# Jersey Coins

## Silver

## Three Shillings Token

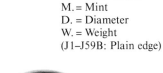

T. = Total struck
M. = Mint
D. = Diameter
W. = Weight
(J1–J59B: Plain edge)

J1

| | | | |
|---|---|---|---|
| J1 | 1813 | *Obverse:* STATES OF JERSEY. 1813 round arms of Jersey.<br>*Reverse:* THREE/SHILLINGS/TOKEN within a wreath of oak.<br>Although only one die has been traced, some minor details were repunched into the working matrix or the die and some minute differences are to be seen (e. g. spots on top leopard). In addition, some letters (e. g. T and K of TOKEN) seem to have been recut at some stage. On some finer specimens, striations caused by die-clashing are evident on the reverse. | T. Not known; total value of J1 and J2 together was £ 13.600.<br>£ 1.363–7–6 sterling (10%) were not accounted for when these tokens were recalled in 1834.<br>M. Royal Mint<br>D. 34.95 mm<br>W. Average 12.85 g |
| J1A | | *Proof* as J1. | |
| J1B | | *Proof* in copper as J1. | |

# Eighteen Pence Token

J2

| | | | |
|---|---|---|---|
| J2 | 1813 | *Obverse* as J1 but smaller.<br>*Reverse* as J1 but EIGHTEEN/PENCE/TOKEN. | T. see J1<br>M. Royal Mint<br>D. 26.5 mm |
| J2A | | *Proof* as J2. | W. Average 6.39 g |

## Copper

## One Thirteenth of a Shilling

J3      J3B

J3i    J3ii    J3Aii    J3B

| | | | |
|---|---|---|---|
| J3 | 1841 | *Obverse:* truncated head *l.* WW (William Wyon) incuse on truncation. VICTORIA D:G:BRITANNIAR: REGINA F:D:1841<br>*Reverse:* STATES OF JERSEY. $1/13$ OF A SHILLING round ornamented shield.<br>No die varieties traced, although one may exist (see J3A). Most specimens show evidence of a hair-line matrix-crack from the truncation across the V of VICTORIA; the same matrix was used in some of the issues dated 1844 and 1858 (q.v.). Serif of the J of JERSEY is defective, further evidence of die-link to J4 and J6. | T. 116,480<br>M. Royal Mint<br>D. 34.15 mm<br>W. Average 17.39 g |

     i   low 4 in date.

     ii   raised 4 in date.

J3Ai     *Proof* as J3i.

J3Aii     *Proof* as J3ii but with oblique final 1 of date; no hair-line crack is visible.

J3B     *Trial piece* (?) as J3i but with arms obliterated (? on die) and ¹/₁₃ missing; both 1's in date have pointed upper serifs.     W. 16.50 g (worn)

        J4i                         J4ii

J4    1844    Similar to J3 except for date.     T. 27.040  
               i   4–4 spacing 0.2 mm. Hair-line crack visible; colons repunched. There are signs of continuity of the *reverse* through to 1858, such as the weak – sometimes retouched – serif of the J in JERSEY;     M. Royal Mint   D. 34.1 mm   W. Average 17.54 g  
               ii   4–4 spacing 0.35 mm. No hair-line crack; colons and initial 1 of date repunched.

J4A     *Proof* as J4.

        J5i                         J5ii

J5    1851    Similar to J4 except for date.     T. 173.333  
               i   5–1 spacing 1.05 mm. 18 of date repunched. This die gradually collapsed and many characteristics of later coins are thicker and less sharp;     M. Royal Mint   D. Average 34.15 mm   W. Average 17.76 g    (17.54–17.98)  
               ii   5–1 spacing 0.95 mm. 8 and 5 of the date repunched; 5 appears taller. First I of VICTORIA also repunched. Striations sometimes visible on *obverse* due to die-clashing.

J5A     *Proof* as J5 (Recorded in B.N.J. Vol IV, 1970, p 354).

    J6i                    J6                  J6ii

| | | | |
|---|---|---|---|
| J6 | 1858 | Similar to J5 except for date. Although they should not strictly be classed as die varieties, the following variations are of interest: | T. 173.333<br>M. Royal Mint<br>D. Average 34.1 mm<br>W. Average 17.42 g<br>(17.25–17.83) |

      i Pronounced *obverse* matrix-crack (see J3);

      ii New die from new matrix with no crack. 1 of date repunched giving the impression that serif points upwards. Second 8 also repunched.

In both variations the top of the 3 in ¹⁄13 is crudely rounded.

J6A      *Proof,* similar to J6ii.

*J7i*            *J7ii*            *J7iii*            *J7iv*

| | | | |
|---|---|---|---|
| J7 | 1861 | Similar to J6 except for date. | T. 173.333<br>M. Royal Mint<br>D. Average 34.15 mm<br>W. Average 17.5 g<br>(17.27–17.61) |

      i 8–6 spacing 0.7 mm. 8 and many letters repunched;

      ii 8–6 spacing 0.5 mm NB $\frac{1}{13}$ (die fill);

      iii 8–6 spacing 0.45 mm. First 1 and many letters repunched;

      iv 8–6 spacing 0.3 mm; die-clash striations at neck.

J7A      *Proof* as J7iii.

*J8A*

| | | | |
|---|---|---|---|
| J8A | 1865 | *Proof* (no currency issue); similar to J7 but for date. | T. Not known<br>M. Royal Mint<br>D. 34.15 mm<br>W. 19.24 g |

# Bronze

## One Thirteenth of a Shilling

*J9*

*J9i*      *J9ii*      *J9A*

early L.C.W.     weak L.C.W.     repunched L.C.W.     no L.C.W. (J9B)

| | | | |
|---|---|---|---|
| J9 | 1866 | *New obverse:* truncated head *l.* wearing coronet. L.C.W. (Leonard Charles Wyon) on truncation; legend now divided by stops (not colons).<br>*Reverse* design similar to J8A but smaller; THIR-TEENTH now shown as a word instead of a fraction.<br><br>  i  6–6 spacing 0.9 mm. The incuse L.C.W. in time became very faint and was duly repunched – presumably on the working punch;<br><br>  ii  6.6 spacing 0.75 mm. | T. 173.333<br>M. Royal Mint<br>D. Average 29.35 mm<br>W. Average 9.37 g<br>    (9.21–9.45) |
| J9A | | *Proof* as J9; 6–6 spacing 0.65 mm. | |
| J9B | | *Proof* no L.C.W. date spacing as J9A. | |

*J10i*      *J10ii*

*J10iii*      *J10iv*      *J10v*

| | | | | |
|---|---|---|---|---|
| J10 | 1870 | Similar to J9 except for date. | | T. 173.333 |
| | | i Date spacing 8–7: 0.8 mm; 7–0: 0.8 mm; many items repunched; | | M. Royal Mint |
| | | | | D. 29.35 mm |
| | | ii Date spacing 8–7: 0.75 mm; 7–0: 0.9 mm; many items repunched; | | W. Average 9.36 g |
| | | | | (9.24–9.43) |
| | | iii Date spacing 8–7: 0.9 mm; 7–0: 0.8 mm; some items repunched; | | |
| | | iv Date spacing 8–7: 0.85 mm; 7–0; 0.7 mm; date repunched, some letters collapsing; | | |
| | | v Date spacing 8–7: 0.65 mm; 7–0; 0.7 mm; many items repunched. | | |
| J10A | | *Proof* as J10iv. | | W. 9.1 g |

*J11*       *J11*       *J11i*

*J11ii*

| | | | |
|---|---|---|---|
| J11 | 1871 | Similar to J10 except for date but incuse spots on leopards and shield redecorated | T. 173.333 |
| | | | M. Royal Mint |
| | | i Date spacing 7–1: 0.75 mm; | D. 29.35 mm |
| | | ii Date spacing 7–1: 1.0 mm. | W. Average 9.29 g |
| J11A | | *Proof* as J11i. | D. 29.25 mm |
| | | | W. 9.64 g |

# One Twelfth of a Shilling

*J12*

*J12i*  *J12ii*  *J12C*

| | | | |
|---|---|---|---|
| J12 | 1877H | New *obverse:* truncated head *l.*, similar to J11 but larger and with plain truncation; legend similar to J11 but date now on *reverse;* H (Heaton) and seven-pointed star below. New *reverse:* Arms of Jersey on a heater-shaped shield dividing date; similar legend except for TWELFTH.<br><br>  i Large H;<br><br>  ii Small H (thin right upright). | T. 240.000<br>M. Dies engraved at Royal Mint; coins struck by R. Heaton & Son, Birmingham<br>D. 30.7 mm<br>W. Average 9.33 g (9.13–9.54) |
| J12A | | *Proof* as J12ii. | W. Average 9.39 g (9.25–9.53) |
| J12B | | *Proof* in Nickel with H (Marshall – Fraser recorded [p 319] 'a cupronickel pattern of the 1d. with the 'H' in the cabinet of Mr. J. Wilfred du Pré, Jersey'). | |
| J12C | | *Proof* with H omitted. | D. 30.85 mm<br>W. 9.33 g |
| J12D | | *Proof* in nickel, H omitted? (Hocking, p. 253, 3121–2, records two such coins which are apparently not *proofs*). | |
| J12E | | *Proof* in aluminium, H omitted? (A pattern ¹/₁₂ shilling of 1877 struck in aluminium was recorded in Glendining's Sale of Coins and Medals, 16.12.1920, lot 86) | |
| J12F | | Pridmore recorded various *uniface* pieces (Pr. 55–58), cast in imitation of the early ¹/₁₂ of a shilling. They generally feature the Arms of Jersey within a Heater-shaped shield, with the legend STATES OF JERSEY above, and ONE TWELFTH OF A SHILLING below. One variety has the shield flanked by two roses; another (recorded by Marshall-Fraser) has the legend ONE TENTH OF A SHILLING. | |

*J12F*
*Uniface pieces, plain and enamelled (top and centre) used to decorate the handle of the Jersey cabbage walking stick (right); below, for comparison, is an example of J12, enamelled and decorated, turned into a brooch.*

I believe all these pieces (which are in copper, silver or aluminium) were used for decoration and were often enamelled. Typically, they adorned the handles of the Jersey cabbage walking sticks, very popular with tourists at the time; a Mr. Henry Gee of Beresford Street, St. Helier, was a leading manufacturer of these sticks from about 1870 to 1928. Similar imitations of the 1/48 of a shilling are known, one variety dated 1892 (see J59c).

| | | | |
|---|---|---|---|
| J13 | 1881 | As J12 (without H) except for date. | T. 81.380<br>M. Royal Mint (struck from metal from 249.760 farthings of 1877 withdrawn from circulation)<br>D. 30.85 mm<br>W. 9.5 g |

*J13*

*J14i*

*J14ii*

| | | | |
|---|---|---|---|
| J14 | 1888 | As J13 except for date.<br><br>   i Date spacing 8–8: 0.4 mm. Top left ray of star broken on most specimens (probably due to die-filling);<br><br>   ii Date spacing 8–8: 0.5 mm. | T. 195.000<br>M. Royal Mint<br>D. 30.85 mm<br>W. Average 9.56 g |

*J15i*       *J15ii*      *J15iii*      *J15A*

| | | | |
|---|---|---|---|
| J15 | 1894 | As J14 except for date.<br><br>   i Spacing 4-N of SHILLING: 0.55 mm;<br><br>   ii Spacing 4-N of SHILLING: 0.4 mm; 4 slightly raised, 9 repunched;<br><br>   iii Spacing 4-N of SHILLING: 0.4 mm; 4 repunched in lower position. | T. 180.000<br>M. Royal Mint<br>D. 30.9 mm<br>W. Average 9.4 g<br>(9.32–9.47) |
| J15A | | *Proof* as J15. Spacing 4-N of SHILLING: 0.35 mm. | |

*J16*

| | | | |
|---|---|---|---|
| J16 | 1909 | New *obverse:* Crowned bust *r.* DES (George William De Saulles) below. English legend: EDWARD VII KING & EMPEROR.<br>*Reverse* similar to J15 except for date. | T. 180.000<br>M. Royal Mint<br>D. 30.9 mm<br>W. 9.14 g |
| J17 | 1911 | New *obverse:* Crowned bust *l.* B.M. (Edgar Bertram Mackennal) on truncation; dot below bust. Latin legend: GEORGIVS V D.G. BRITT:OMN:REX F.D. IND:IMP: *Reverse* similar to J18 but for date.<br><br>   i Date spacing 1–9: 0.45 mm; 1–1: 1.2 mm;<br><br>   ii Date spacing 1–9: 0.5 mm; 1–1: 1.0 mm;<br><br>   iii Date spacing 1–9: 0.55 mm; 1–1: 1.05 mm;<br><br>   iv Date spacing 1–9: 0.8 mm; 1–1: 1.1 mm. | T. 204.000<br>M. Royal Mint<br>D. Average 30.85 mm<br>W. Average 9.46 g<br>(9.26–9.55) |

J17

J17i

J17ii

J17iii

J17iv

J18

| J18 | 1913 | As J17 but for date. | T. 204.000<br>M. Royal Mint<br>D. 30.9 mm<br>W. 9.46 g |

J19i

J19ii

J19iii

| J19 | 1923 | As J18 but for date.<br>  i Date spacing 1–9: 0.6 mm;<br>  ii Date spacing 1–9: 0.7 mm (commonest type);<br>  iii Date spacing 1–9: 0.75 mm. | T. 204.000<br>M. Royal Mint<br>D. 30.8 mm<br>W. Average 9.3 g<br>(9.21–9.52) |

J20

| | | | |
|---|---|---|---|
| J20 | 1923 | *Obverse* as J19.<br>New *reverse* by George Edward Kruger Gray: arms on squarer shield with legend STATES · OF · JERSEY · ONE · TWELFTH · OF · A · SHILLING on ribbon above and below. | T. 301.200<br>M. Royal Mint (struck from metal obtained from French coins withdrawn from circulation)<br>D. 30.8 mm<br>W. 9.33 g |

*J21*

| | | | |
|---|---|---|---|
| J21 | 1926 | As J20 except for date. | T. 82.800<br>M. Royal Mint<br>D. 30.8 mm<br>W. 9.42 g |

*J22*

| | | | |
|---|---|---|---|
| J22 | 1931 | *Obverse* as J21.<br>New *reverse* similar to J21 but without ribbons; initials KG (Kruger Gray); ◊ STATES ◊ OF ◊ JERSEY ◊ ONE · TWELFTH · OF · A · SHILLING. | T. 204.000<br>M. Royal Mint<br>D. 30.8 mm<br>W. 9.27 g |
| J22A | | *Proof* as J22. | |

*J23*

*J23i*     *J23ii*

| | | | |
|---|---|---|---|
| J23 | 1933 | As J22 except for date; *obverse* die varieties:<br>  i  176 teeth in rim; colon after IMP points to dot in rim; serif of F broken;<br>  ii  177 teeth in rim; colon after IMP points to space in rim; F has normal serif. | T. 204.000<br>M. Royal Mint<br>D. 30.8 mm<br>W. Average 9.43 g (9.33–9.54) |
| J23A | | *Proof* as J23i. | W. 9.55 g |

*J24i*

*J24ii*

| | | | |
|---|---|---|---|
| J24 | 1935 | As J23 except for date<br>i Date spacing $3 \genfrac{}{}{0pt}{}{\leftarrow 0.5\text{ mm} \rightarrow}{1.7\text{ mm}} 5$<br><br>ii Date spacing $3 \genfrac{}{}{0pt}{}{\leftarrow 0.3\text{ mm} \rightarrow}{1.55\text{ mm}} 5$ | T. 204.000<br>M. Royal Mint<br>D. 30.8 mm<br>W. Average 9.38 g |
| J24A | | *Proof* as J24. | |

*J25*

*J25i*  *J25ii*  *J25iii*  *J25iv*  *J25v*

| | | | |
|---|---|---|---|
| J25 | 1937 | New *obverse* crowned bust *l.*, initials PM (Percy Metcalfe) below in relief; legend: GEORGIVS VI D · G · BRITT · OMN · REX · F · D · IND · IMP:<br>*Reverse* as J24 except for date.<br>i Date spacing $3 \genfrac{}{}{0pt}{}{\leftarrow 0.5\text{ mm} \rightarrow}{2.05\text{ mm}} 7$<br><br>ii Date spacing $3 \genfrac{}{}{0pt}{}{\leftarrow 0.45\text{ mm} \rightarrow}{2.0\text{ mm}} 7$<br><br>iii Date spacing $3 \genfrac{}{}{0pt}{}{\leftarrow 0.5\text{ mm} \rightarrow}{2.1\text{ mm}} 7$<br>(upright of 7 appears almost perpendicular)<br>iv Date spacing $3 \genfrac{}{}{0pt}{}{\leftarrow 0.4\text{ mm} \rightarrow}{1.85\text{ mm}} 7$<br><br>v Date spacing $3 \genfrac{}{}{0pt}{}{\leftarrow 0.6\text{ mm} \rightarrow}{2.0\text{ mm}} 7$<br>(7 out of alignment). | T. 204.000<br>M. Royal Mint<br>D. 30.8 mm<br>W. Average 9.44 g<br>(9.38–9.59) |
| J25A | | *Proof* as J25v | W. 9.34 g |

*J26*

| | | | |
|---|---|---|---|
| J26 | 1946 | As J25 except for date. | T. 204.000<br>M. Royal Mint<br>D. 30.8 mm<br>W. 9.56 g |
| J26A | | *Proof* as J26. | |

*J27i*

*J27ii*

| | | | |
|---|---|---|---|
| J27 | 1947 | As J26 except for date.<br>  i Date spacing 4⎽7 1.1 mm (straight 7);<br>  ii Date spacing 4⎽7 0.9 mm (tilted 7). | T. 444.000<br>M. Royal Mint<br>D. 30.8 mm<br>W. Average 9.49 g<br>  (9.36–9.62) |
| J27A | | *Proof* as J27. | |

*J28*

*J28i*

*J28ii*

| | | |
|---|---|---|
| J28 | 'Liberation' issue (struck 1949, 1950, 1952)<br>*Obverse:* similar to J27 but legend now +GEORGIVS VI DEI GRA : BRITT : OMN : REX FID : DEF :<br>*Reverse:* Kruger Gray's arms of Jersey reduced, with denomination ONE TWELFTH OF A SHILLING round lower part; ◊ ISLAND ◊ OF ◊ JERSEY ◊ LIBERATED 1945. PM more spaced than in 1947 issue.<br>  i PM under uneven bust line;<br>  ii bust line straightened. | T. 1.200.000<br>M. Royal Mint<br>D. 30.8 mm<br>W. Average 9.53 g |
| J28A | *Proof* as J28ii. | |

*J29*

| | | | |
|---|---|---|---|
| J29 | | 'Liberation' issue (struck 1954).<br>New *obverse:* Crowned bust *r.;* legend clockwise from top right: QUEEN ELIZABETH THE SECOND.<br>*Reverse* as J28. | T. 720.000<br>M. Royal Mint<br>D. 30.8 mm<br>W. Average 9.37 g |
| J29A | | *Proof* as J29. | |

*J30*

| | | | |
|---|---|---|---|
| J30 | 1957 | *Obverse:* smaller crowned bust *r.;* legend as J29 but clockwise from bottom left.<br>*Reverse:* as J27 except for date and BAILIWICK for STATES. | T. 720.00<br>M. Royal Mint<br>D. 30.8 mm<br>W. Average 9.45 g<br>(9.38–9.53) |
| J30A | 1957 | *Proof* as J30. | |

*J31*

| | | | |
|---|---|---|---|
| J31 | 1960 | Charles II Commemorative.<br>*Obverse* as J30.<br>*Reverse:* Kruger Gray's arms of Jersey reduced, with CIIR 1660–1960 EIIR round lower half; otherwise legend as J30. | T. 1.200.000<br>M. Royal Mint<br>D. 30.8 mm<br>W. 9.52 g |
| J31A | | *Proof* as J31. | W. 9.71 g |
| J31B | | *Proof mule: obverse* of J29 with *reverse* of J31. | W. 9.52 g |

*J32*

| | | | |
|---|---|---|---|
| J32 | 1964 | *Obverse* as J31.<br>*Reverse* as J30 but for date. | T. 1.200.000<br>M. Royal Mint<br>D. 30.8 mm<br>W. 9.52 g |
| J32A | | *Proof* as J32 | W. 9.32 g |

*J33*

| | | | |
|---|---|---|---|
| J33 | 1966 | Norman Conquest Commemorative.<br>*Obverse* as J32<br>*Reverse* similar to J32 but smaller legend without stops;<br>1066 to left, 1966 to right of shield. | T. 1.200.000<br>M. Royal Mint<br>D. 30.8 mm<br>W. 9.11 g |
| J33A | | *Proof* as J33. | W. 9.4 g |

# Copper

## One Twenty-sixth of a Shilling

*J34*

*J34i*   *J34ii*   *J34*

| | | | |
|---|---|---|---|
| J34 | 1841 | *Obverse:* Similar to J3 but different hair-style and fillet;<br>date proportionally smaller.<br>*Reverse:* Similar to J3 but different positioning of leopards'<br>right fore-legs. $^{1}/_{26}$ of A SHILLING (ILL of SHILLING<br>out of line).<br>　　i Date spacing 4←→1 : 0.7 mm;<br>　　ii Date spacing 4←→1 : 0.6 mm (1 repunched). | T. 232.960<br>M. Royal Mint<br>D. 28.1 mm<br>W. Average 8.82 g<br>(8.77–8.87) |

| J34A | *Proof* as J34i (note: *obverse* die also used for Gibraltar proof 2 quarts 1841, and proof and currency issues for 1842. The head – though not the legend – appears to have originated from the Isle of Man halfpenny dated 1839). | W. 8.7 g |

*J35i*          *J35ii*          *J35*

| J35 | 1844 | As J34 but for date; ¹/₂₆ remodelled.<br>  i Date spacing 8 4 : 0.5 mm; die-clash striations.<br> ii Date spacing 8 4 : 0.75 mm. | T. 232.960<br>M. Royal Mint<br>D. 28.2 mm<br>W. Average 8.67 g<br>(8.51–8.83) |

*J36i*          *J36ii*          *J36iii*          *J36iv*

*J36i*                    *J36ii*

| J36 | 1851 | As J35 except for date: Many letters (e. g. H of SHILLING) badly repunched; Principal date variations:<br>   i Raised 5; (die clash striations); LL of SHILLING realigned;<br>  ii 8 doubly struck; LL of SHILLING very crooked;<br> iii All figures in date badly struck; LL as J36ii;<br> iv Date clear; LL as J36i. | T. 173.333<br>M. Royal Mint<br>D. Average 28.25 mm<br>W. Average 8.81 g<br>(8.59–8.97) |

*J37i*          *J37ii*          *J37iii*          *J37A*          *J37iii*

| J37 | 1858 | As J36 but for date; possible *reverse* die-link with J34 and J35.<br>   i Many letters repunched; date spacing 5 8 : 0.5 mm; striations at neck;<br>  ii Many letters repunched; date spacing 5 8 : 0.65 mm;<br> iii Many letters repunched; date spacing 5 8 : 0.7 mm; evidence of pronounced die-crack across 6 of ¹/₂₆ on reverse. | T. 173.33<br>M. Royal Mint<br>D. Average 28.15 mm<br>W. Average 8.58 g<br>(8.54–8.62) |
| J37A | | *Proof* as J37; date spacing 5 8 : 0.95 mm. | W. 8.59 g |

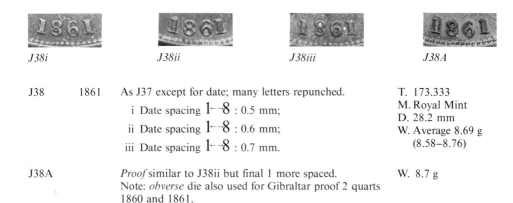

| | | | |
|---|---|---|---|
| J38i | J38ii | J38iii | J38A |

| | | | |
|---|---|---|---|
| J38 | 1861 | As J37 except for date; many letters repunched.<br>  i Date spacing 1--8 : 0.5 mm;<br>  ii Date spacing 1--8 : 0.6 mm;<br>  iii Date spacing 1--8 : 0.7 mm. | T. 173.333<br>M. Royal Mint<br>D. 28.2 mm<br>W. Average 8.69 g<br>(8.58–8.76) |
| J38A | | *Proof* similar to J38ii but final 1 more spaced.<br>Note: *obverse* die also used for Gibraltar proof 2 quarts 1860 and 1861. | W. 8.7 g |

## Bronze

## One Twenty-Sixth of a Shilling

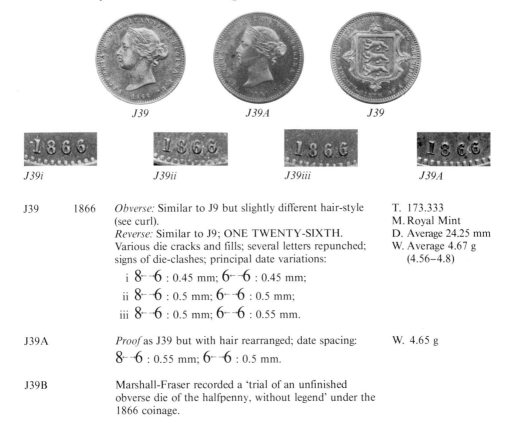

| | | | |
|---|---|---|---|
| J39i | J39ii | J39iii | J39A |

| | | | |
|---|---|---|---|
| J39 | 1866 | *Obverse:* Similar to J9 but slightly different hair-style (see curl).<br>*Reverse:* Similar to J9; ONE TWENTY-SIXTH.<br>Various die cracks and fills; several letters repunched; signs of die-clashes; principal date variations:<br>  i 8--6 : 0.45 mm; 6--6 : 0.45 mm;<br>  ii 8--6 : 0.5 mm; 6--6 : 0.5 mm;<br>  iii 8--6 : 0.5 mm; 6--6 : 0.55 mm. | T. 173.333<br>M. Royal Mint<br>D. Average 24.25 mm<br>W. Average 4.67 g<br>(4.56–4.8) |
| J39A | | *Proof* as J39 but with hair rearranged; date spacing:<br>8--6 : 0.55 mm; 6--6 : 0.5 mm. | W. 4.65 g |
| J39B | | Marshall-Fraser recorded a 'trial of an unfinished obverse die of the halfpenny, without legend' under the 1866 coinage. | |

J39C  A *pattern* ¹/₂₆ is known, as adopted issue but without *obverse* legend (Glendining's sale of Pridmore collection, 22ⁿᵈ September 1981, Lot 528).

*J40i*      *J40ii*      *J40iii*      *J40iii var.*      *J40iv*

| | | |
|---|---|---|
| J40 | 1870 | As J39; (including hair-style); principal date variations:<br>i 8←→7 : 0.8 mm;<br>ii 8←→7 : 0.7 mm;<br>iii 8←→7 : 0.6 mm (a variety has the date re-sunk);<br>iv 8←→7 : 0.5 mm. | T. 173.33<br>M. Royal Mint<br>D. Average 24.25 mm<br>W. Average 4.65 g<br>(4.6–4.7) |
| J40A | | *Proof* as J40iii. | W. 4.95 g |

*J41i*      *J41ii*      *J41iii*          *J41*

| | | | |
|---|---|---|---|
| J41 | 1871 | Similar to J40 but with incuse spots on leopards; most coins badly struck; principal date variations:<br>i 8←→7 : 0.7 mm;<br>ii 8←→7 : 0.6 mm;<br>iii 8←→7 : 0.5 mm. | T. 173.333<br>M. Royal Mint<br>D. 24.3 mm<br>W. Average 4.68 g<br>(4.63–4.74) |

## One Twenty-Fourth of a Shilling

*J42i*

*J42ii*

*J42i*      *J42iii*      *J42A*      *J42B*      *J42A*      *J42B*

| | | | |
|---|---|---|---|
| J42 | 1877H | *Obverse:* Similar to J12, slight differences in hairstyle (e. g. curl below bun).<br>*Reverse:* Similar to J12; ONE TWENTY-FOURTH (Note new style of U in FOURTH). | T. 336.000<br>M. Dies engraved at Royal Mint; coins struck by R. Heaton & Son, Birmingham<br>D. Average 25.57 mm<br>W. Average 5.66 g<br>(5.57–5.79) |

i *Obverse* legend badly aligned, e. g. BRITANNIAR, VICTORIA; star unclear; H nearer stop after D; die-clash striations.

ii Legend better aligned, otherwise as J42i but no striations

iii Star clear but not sharp; H midway between star and stop after D; die-clash striations; legend as J42ii.

J42A  *Proof* as J42iii but star sharper.

J42B  *Proof,* no H; very finely formed star; 77 of date realigned.

*J43i*  *J43ii*

| | | | |
|---|---|---|---|
| J43 | 1888 | i *Obverse* die link with J42i (e. g. BRITANNIAR VICTORIA); date spacing 88⇠⇢⌐ : 0.7 mm;<br>ii Legend better aligned; date spacing 88⇠⇢⌐ : 0.6 mm. | T. 130.000<br>M. Royal Mint<br>D. Average 25.57 mm<br>W. Average 5.68 g |

*J44i*  *J44ii*

| | | | |
|---|---|---|---|
| J44 | 1894 | As J43 except for date.<br>i Date spacing 9⇠⇢4 : 0.4 mm;<br>ii Date spacing 9⇠⇢4 : 0.25 mm; 9 very crudely cut. | T. 120.000<br>M. Royal Mint<br>D. Average 25.57 mm<br>W. Average 5.62 g |

J44A  *Proof* as J44 (Sotheby, Wilkinson & Hodge sale, 27th March – 1st April 1922, Lot 497).

*J45*

| | | | |
|---|---|---|---|
| J45 | 1909 | *Obverse* and *reverse* similar to J16 but ONE TWENTY-FOURTH; only 7 dots in line below orb in centre of crown. (Rev. die link with previous dates – see J⇠⇢ERSEY etc). | T. 120.000<br>M. Royal Mint<br>D. 25.55 mm<br>W. 5.74 g |

279

*J46*

| | | | |
|---|---|---|---|
| J46 | 1911 | *Obverse* as J17.<br>*Reverse* as J17; ONE TWENTY-FOURTH. Tiny dot visible on point of shield on finer specimens. | T. 72.000<br>M. Royal Mint<br>D. 25.55 mm<br>W. 5.70 g |

*J47*

| | | | |
|---|---|---|---|
| J47 | 1913 | Similar to J46 except for date; First E of JERSEY reset; E of ONE obliterated on some specimens due to die-filling, tail of top lion generally weak. | T. 72.000<br>M. Royal Mint<br>D. 25.55 mm<br>W. 5.55 g |

*J48*

| | | | |
|---|---|---|---|
| J48 | 1923 | As J47 except for date. | T. 72.000<br>M. Royal Mint<br>D. 25.55 mm<br>W. 5.80 g |

*J49*

| | | | |
|---|---|---|---|
| J49 | 1923 | New *reverse* as J20; ONE · TWENTYFOURTH. | T. 72.000<br>M. Royal Mint<br>(struck from metal obtained from French coins withdrawn from circulation)<br>D. 25.5 mm<br>W. 5.61 g |

*J50*

| | | | |
|---|---|---|---|
| J50 | 1926 | As J49 except for date. | T. 120.000<br>M. Royal Mint<br>D. 25.5 mm<br>W. 5.53 g |
| J50A | | *Proof* as J50. | |

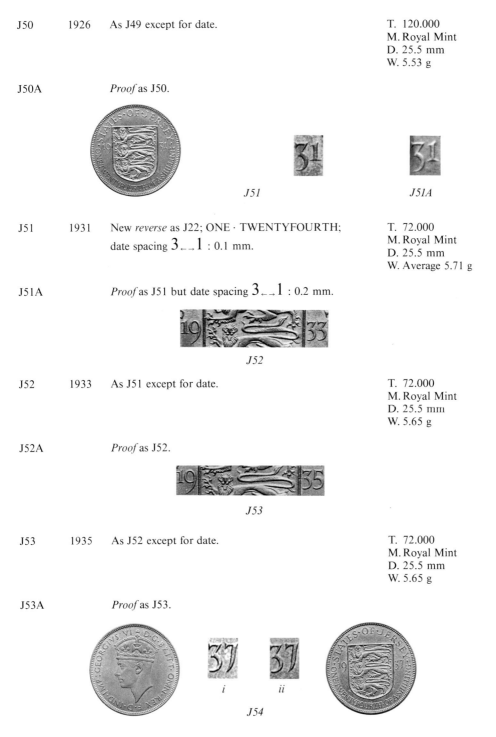

| | | | |
|---|---|---|---|
| J51 | 1931 | New *reverse* as J22; ONE · TWENTYFOURTH; date spacing $3 \leftarrow\rightarrow 1$ : 0.1 mm. | T. 72.000<br>M. Royal Mint<br>D. 25.5 mm<br>W. Average 5.71 g |
| J51A | | *Proof* as J51 but date spacing $3 \leftarrow\rightarrow 1$ : 0.2 mm. | |

*J52*

| | | | |
|---|---|---|---|
| J52 | 1933 | As J51 except for date. | T. 72.000<br>M. Royal Mint<br>D. 25.5 mm<br>W. 5.65 g |
| J52A | | *Proof* as J52. | |

*J53*

| | | | |
|---|---|---|---|
| J53 | 1935 | As J52 except for date. | T. 72.000<br>M. Royal Mint<br>D. 25.5 mm<br>W. 5.65 g |
| J53A | | *Proof* as J53. | |

*i* *ii*

*J54*

| | | | |
|---|---|---|---|
| J54 | 1937 | *Obverse* similar to J25.<br>*Reverse* as J53 except for date.<br>  i Low 7;<br>  ii High 7. | T. 72.000<br>M. Royal Mint<br>D. 25.55 mm<br>W. Average 5.71 g<br>   (5.61–5.77) |
| J54A | | *Proof* as J54i. | D. 25.5 mm |

J55

| | | | |
|---|---|---|---|
| J55 | 1946 | As J54 except for date. | T. 72.000<br>M. Royal Mint<br>D. 25.5 mm<br>W. 5.56 g |
| J55A | | *Proof* as J55. | |

J56

| | | | |
|---|---|---|---|
| J56 | 1947 | As J55 except for date. | T. 72.000<br>M. Royal Mint<br>D. 25.5 mm<br>W. 5.72 g |
| J56A | | *Proof* as J56. | |

# Copper

## One Fifty-Second of a Shilling

  i          ii          A

J57

| | | | |
|---|---|---|---|
| J57 | 1841 | *Obverse:* Design similar to J3 and J34 but hair-style differs slightly; plain fillet; larger bust in proportion to size of coin, intruding into legend between BRITANNIAR : and REGINA.<br>*Reverse:* Similar to J3 and J34 but several minute differences in design (e. g. shape and position of rectangle above centre of shield);<br>1⁄52 OF A SHILLING; Final 1 of date over 0. | T. 116.480<br>M. Royal Mint<br>D. 21.9 mm<br>W. Average 4.41 g<br>   (4.37–4.44) |

282

|  |  | i Date spacing 4←→1 : 0.7 mm;<br>ii Date spacing 4←→1 : 0.4 mm. |  |
|---|---|---|---|
| J57A |  | *Proof* as J57; date spacing 4←→1 : 0.5 mm.<br>Note: *Obverse* die also used for Gibraltar proof 1 quart 1841, and proof and currency issues for 1842. The head – though not the legend – appears to have originated from the Isle of Man farthing dated 1829. | W. 4.27 g |

*J58A*

| J58A | 1861 | Proof (no currency issue); as J57 but for date; signs of die-clashing on *obverse* and *reverse*.<br>Note: *obverse* die also used for Gibraltar proof 1 quart 1860 and 1861. | T. Not known<br>M. Royal Mint<br>D. 21.85 mm<br>W. 4.40 g |
|---|---|---|---|

# Bronze

## One Forty-Eight of a Shilling

*J59i*

*J59i*

*(enlarged)*
*J59ii*

*J59i*

| J59 | 1877H | *Obverse:* Similar to J12 and J42 but minute differences in hair-style (e. g. curl below bun)<br>*Reverse:* Similar to J12 and J42; ONE 48TH OF A SHILLING. Apparently only one matrix; dies however, show signs of progressive deterioration, e. g.<br>   i early *obverse* die;<br>   ii late *obverse* die (Note die filling). | T. 288.000 (249.760 later withdrawn – see J13)<br>M. Dies engraved at Royal Mint; coins struck by R. Heaton & Son, Birmingham<br>D. 20.3 mm<br>W. Average 2.85 g |
|---|---|---|---|
| J59A |  | Royal Mint *Proof* (No H) Note fine star. The RE of REGINA and ILL of SHILLING are out of line. | W. Average 2.82 g (2.81–2.83) |

| J59A | J59B | J59A | J59B |

*(enlargements)*

J59B      Heaton Mint *Proof.* Note Thick star. RE of REGINA and W. 2.85 g ILL of SHILLING have been adjusted.

*J59C: uniface (enlarged), napkin-ring and match-box.*

J59C      A *pattern* 1/48 shilling struck in brass has been reported, and another item has the standard 1/48 *reverse* with a plain laurel wreath and bow *obverse*. In addition a number of *uniface* imitations are known, decorating silver match-boxes, napkin-rings and other trinkets, popular with the Jersey tourist at the turn of the century. One variety is dated 1892. These 'coins' were, more often than not, enamelled.

## One Fourth Shilling – Nickel-Brass (Plain Edge)

*J60*

| | | | |
|---|---|---|---|
| J60 | 1957 | *Obverse* as J30 but smaller, with adjustments to legend, e. g. longer upper serif of E's. *Reverse* as J30 but legend below shield: ONE · FOURTH · OF · A · SHILLING. | T. 2.000.000 M. Royal Mint D. 21.05 mm W. 4.76 g |
| J60A | 1957 | *Proof* as J60; frosted relief. | T. 2.100 W. 4.81 g |

*J61A*

| | | | |
|---|---|---|---|
| J61A | 1960 | *Proof* only, as J60 except for date. | T. 4.200 M. Royal Mint D. 21.1 mm W. 4.90 g |

## One Fourth Shilling – Nickel-Brass (12-sided)

*J62*

| | | | |
|---|---|---|---|
| J62 | 1964 | As J60 except for date. | T. 1.200.000 M. Royal Mint D. 21.1 mm W. 6.81 g |
| J62A | 1964 | *Proof* as J62; frosted relief. | T. 20.000 W. 6.65 g |

*J63*

| | | | |
|---|---|---|---|
| J63 | 1966 | 900th Anniversary of the Norman Conquest.<br>*Obverse* as J62.<br>*Reverse* similar to J62 but no stops in legend;<br>1066 to *l.* and 1966 to *r.* of shield. | T. 1.200.000<br>M. Royal Mint<br>D. 21.15 mm<br>W. 6.81 g |
| J63A | 1966 | *Proof* as J63; frosted relief. | T. 30.000 |

## Five Shillings – Cupro-Nickel (Milled)

*J64*

| | | | |
|---|---|---|---|
| J64 | 1966 | Normal Conquest Commemorative.<br>*Obverse* as J63 but larger.<br>*Reverse* similar to J63 but FIVE SHILLINGS below shield. | T. 300.000<br>M. Royal Mint<br>D. 38.6 mm<br>W. 28.40 g |
| J64A | 1966 | *Proof* as J64; frosted relief. | T. 30.000<br>D. 38.5 mm<br>W. 28.20 g |

# Decimal – Bronze (Plain Edge)
## Half New Penny

*J65*

| | | | |
|---|---|---|---|
| J65 | 1971 | *Obverse:* QUEEN ELIZABETH THE SECOND round crowned bust *r*.<br>*Reverse:* BAILIWICK OF JERSEY HALF NEW PENNY 1971 round arms of Jersey.<br>Note: on all *reverses* of this series the lowest 'leopard' has a crooked right ear and the right hind claws of the middle 'leopard' are joined to the tail below.<br>*Obverse* bust designed by Arnold Machin. | T. 3.000.000<br>M. Royal Mint<br>D. 17.25 mm<br>W. 1.70 g |

*J66*

| | | | |
|---|---|---|---|
| J66 | 1980 | As J65 except for date. | T. 200.000<br>M. Royal Mint<br>D. 17.15 mm<br>W. 1.80 g |
| J66A | 1980 | *Proof* as J66, frosted relief. | T. 10.000 |

## Half Penny

*J67*

| | | | |
|---|---|---|---|
| J67 | 1981 | *Obverse* as J66<br>*Reverse* as J66 except HALF PENNY below shield which separates date 19 81<br>(note: cf *reverse* coin designs from 1877 to 1966; this new *reverse* was to have been introduced in 1980 and was struck after a test design of 1977) see also note to J65. | T. 50.000<br>M. Royal Mint<br>D. 17.10 mm<br>W. 1.78 g |
| J67A | 1981 | *Proof* as J67; frosted relief; wavy semi-circular markings on edge, as if lacquered, on some examples. | T. 15.000 |

# One New Penny

*J78*

| | | | | |
|---|---|---|---|---|
| J78 | 1971 | *Obverse:* QUEEN ELIZABETH THE SECOND round crowned bust *r*.<br>*Reverse:* BAILIWICK OF JERSEY ONE NEW PENNY 1971 round arms of Jersey.<br>(Reissued 1979); see note to J65. | T. 4.500.000<br>M. Royal Mint<br>D. 20.30 mm<br>W. 3.52 g |

*J79*

| | | | |
|---|---|---|---|
| J79 | 1980 | As J78 except for date. | T. 3.000.000<br>M. Royal Mint<br>D. 20.30 mm<br>W. 3.61 g |
| J79A | 1980 | *Proof* as J79; frosted relief. | T. 10.000<br>W. 3.55 g |

# One Penny

*J80*

| | | | |
|---|---|---|---|
| J80 | 1981 | *Obverse* as J79.<br>*Reverse* as J79 except ONE PENNY below shield which separates date 19 81; see note to J67. | T. 50.000<br>M. Royal Mint<br>D. 20.30 mm<br>W. 3.56 g |
| J80A | 1981 | *Proof* as J80; frosted relief; wavy edge markings as J67A. | T. 15.000 |

*J81*

| | | | |
|---|---|---|---|
| J81 | 1983 | *Obverse:* QUEEN ELIZABETH THE SECOND round crowned bust r., date 1983 below.<br>*Reverse:* Le Hocq Watch Tower, St. Clement; BAILIWICK OF JERSEY above, ONE PENNY below.<br>Note: the *obverse* of the new 1983 series was altered to avoid confusion with U.K coins: the bust is smaller than that of previous issues; the legend is larger and now accomodates the date; the hair-style is more detailed. It was first used on the 20p of 1982 (J172). | T.<br>M. Royal Mint<br>D. 20.30 mm<br>W. 3.56 g |
| J81A | 1983 | *AR Proof* as J81; frosted relief. | T. 5.000<br>W. 4.20 g |

## Two New Pence

 *J101*

| | | | |
|---|---|---|---|
| J101 | 1971 | *Obverse:* QUEEN ELIZABETH THE SECOND round crowned bust r.<br>*Reverse:* BAILIWICK OF JERSEY TWO NEW PENCE 1971 round arms of Jersey; see note to J65. | T. 2.225.000<br>M. Royal Mint<br>D. 25.90 mm<br>W. 7.20 g |

*J102*

| | | | |
|---|---|---|---|
| J102 | 1975 | As J101 except for date.<br>(Issued 1976; reissued 1979). | T. 3.250.000<br>M. Royal Mint<br>D. Average 25.95 mm<br>W. Average 7.27 g |

*J103*

| | | | |
|---|---|---|---|
| J103 | 1980 | As J102 except for date. | T. 2.000.000<br>M. Royal Mint<br>D. 25.90 mm<br>W. 7.02 g |
| J103A | 1980 | *Proof* as J103; frosted relief; wavy edge markings as J67A. | T. 10.000<br>D. 26.00 mm<br>W. 7.14 g |

## Two Pence

*J104*

| | | | |
|---|---|---|---|
| J104 | 1981 | *Obverse* as J103.<br>*Reverse* as J103 except TWO PENCE below shield which separates date 19 81; see note to J67. | T. 50.000<br>M. Royal Mint<br>D. 25.90 mm<br>W. 7.13 g |
| J104A | 1981 | *Proof* as J104; frosted relief, wavy edge markings as J67A. | T. 15.000<br>D. 26.00 mm<br>W. 7.25 g |

*J105*

| | | | |
|---|---|---|---|
| J105 | 1983 | *Obverse:* QUEEN ELIZABETH THE SECOND round crowned bust r., date 1983 below.<br>*Reverse:* L'Hermitage, St. Helier; BAILIWICK OF JERSEY above, TWO PENCE below.<br>See note to J81. | T.<br>M. Royal Mint<br>D. 25.90 mm<br>W. 7.13 g |
| J105A | 1983 | *AR Proof* as J105; frosted relief. | T. 5.000<br>W. 8.40 g |

# Decimal – Cupro-Nickel (Milled)

## Five New Pence

*J125*

| | | | |
|---|---|---|---|
| J125i | 1968 | *Obverse:* QUEEN ELIZABETH THE SECOND round crowned bust *r*.<br>*Reverse:* BAILIWICK OF JERSEY FIVE NEW PENCE 1968 round arms of Jersey see note to J65. | T. 3.600.000<br>M. Royal Mint<br>D. 23.6 mm<br>W. 5.65 g |
| J125ii | 1968 | (Reissued 1979) slightly thicker flan than J125i. | W. 5.67 g |

*J126*

| | | | |
|---|---|---|---|
| J126 | 1980 | As J125 except for date. | T. 800.000<br>M. Royal Mint<br>D. 23.6 mm<br>W. 5.70 g |
| J126A | 1980 | *Proof* as J126; frosted relief; parts of *obverse* (e.g. crown) indistinct; edge markings as J67A. | T. 10.000<br>D. 23.70 mm<br>W. 5.71 g |

## Five Pence

*J127*

| | | | |
|---|---|---|---|
| J127 | 1981 | *Obverse* as J126.<br>*Reverse* as J126 except FIVE PENCE below shield which separates date 19 81; see note to J67. | T. 50.000<br>M. Royal Mint<br>D. 23.60 mm<br>W. Average 5.70 g |
| J127A | 1981 | *Proof* as J127; frosted relief; edge markings as J67A. | T. 15.000<br>D. 23.5 mm<br>W. 5.70 g |

J128

| | | | |
|---|---|---|---|
| J128 | 1983 | *Obverse:* QUEEN ELIZABETH THE SECOND round crowned bust r., date 1983 below.<br>*Reverse:* Seymour Tower, Grouville bay; BAILIWICK OF JERSEY above, FIVE PENCE below.<br>See note to J81. | T.<br>M. Royal Mint<br>D. 23.60 mm<br>W. 5.66 g |
| J128A | 1983 | *AR Proof* as J128; frosted relief. | T. 5.000<br>W. 6.60 g |

## Ten New Pence

J148

| | | | |
|---|---|---|---|
| J148 | 1968 | *Obverse:* QUEEN ELIZABETH THE SECOND round crowned bust r.<br>*Reverse:* BAILIWICK OF JERSEY TEN NEW PENCE 1968 round arms of Jersey; see note to J65. | T. 1.500.000<br>M. Royal Mint<br>D. 28.50 mm<br>W. 11.00 g |

J149

| | | | |
|---|---|---|---|
| J149i | 1975 | As J148 except for date. | T. 1.022.000<br>M. Royal Mint<br>D. 28.55 mm<br>W. 11.32 g |
| J149ii | 1975 | (Reissued 1979) flan 0.1–0.2 mm thicker than J149i (this caused problems in telephone kiosks etc). | D. 28.5 mm<br>W. 11.45 g |

*J150*

| | | | |
|---|---|---|---|
| J150 | 1980 | As J149 except for date. | T. 1.000.000<br>M. Royal Mint<br>D. 28.5 mm<br>W. 11.36 g |
| J150A | 1980 | *Proof* as J150; frosted relief; edge markings as J67A. | T. 10.000<br>D. 28.55 mm<br>W. 11.45 g |

## Ten Pence

*J151*

| | | | |
|---|---|---|---|
| J151 | 1981 | *Obverse* as J150.<br>*Reverse* as J150 except TEN PENCE below shield which separates date 19 81; see note to J67. | T. 50.000<br>M. Royal Mint<br>D. 28.50 mm<br>W. official: 11.31 g<br>(but some as light as 11.14 g) |
| J151A | 1981 | *Proof* as J151; frosted relief; edge markings as J67A. | T. 15.000<br>W. 11.37 g |

*J152*

| | | | |
|---|---|---|---|
| J152 | 1983 | *Obverse:* QUEEN ELIZABETH THE SECOND round crowned bust *r.*, date 1983 below.<br>*Reverse:* Dolmen at Faldouet, St. Martin; BAILIWICK OF JERSEY above, TEN PENCE below.<br>See note to J81. | T.<br>M. Royal Mint<br>D. 28.50 mm<br>W. 11.31 g |
| J152A | 1983 | *AR Proof* as J152; frosted relief. | T. 5.000<br>W. 13.60 g |

# Twenty Pence (7-sided, Plain Edge)

J172

| | | | |
|---|---|---|---|
| J172 | 1982 | *Obverse:* QUEEN ELIZABETH THE SECOND round crowned bust *r.*,<br>*Reverse:* BAILIWICK OF JERSEY above, · TWENTY PENCE · below Corbière Lighthouse and the date 1982 incuse.<br>Note: *obverse* bust by Arnold Machin; *reverse* by Robert Lowe. | T.<br>M. Royal Mint<br>D. 21.40 mm<br>W. 5.90 g |
| J172A | 1982 | *AR Proof piedfort* as J172; frosted relief. | T. 1.500<br>W. 10.00 g |

J173

| | | | |
|---|---|---|---|
| J173 | 1983 | *Obverse* as J172 but bust smaller and legend larger; date 1983 below.<br>*Reverse* as J172 but no stops and no date.<br>See note to J81. | T.<br>M. Royal Mint<br>D. 21.40 mm<br>W. 5.90 g |
| J173A | 1983 | *AR Proof* as J173, frosted relief. | T. 5.000<br>W. 5.83 g |

# Twenty Five Pence

| | | | |
|---|---|---|---|
| J193 | 1977 | Silver Jubilee commemorative issue.<br>*Obverse:* QUEEN ELIZABETH THE SECOND 1952–1977 round (below) crowned bust *r.*<br>*Reverse:* BAILIWICK OF JERSEY above, TWENTY FIVE PENCE below, Mont Orgeuil Castle and Gorey Harbour with sailing boats in semi-circular design (by Bernard Sindall). | T. 255.510<br>M. Royal Mint<br>D. Average 38.63 mm<br>(official 38.61 mm)<br>W. Average 28.35 g<br>(official 28.276 g) |
| J193A | 1977 | *AR Proof* as J193; frosted relief, coarse milling. | T. 35.000<br>D. 38.70 mm<br>W. 28.00 g |

*J193*

## Fifty New Pence (7-sided)

*J204*

| | | | |
|---|---|---|---|
| J204 | 1969 | *Obverse:* QUEEN ELIZABETH THE SECOND round crowned bust *r.*<br>*Reverse:* BAILIWICK OF JERSEY FIFTY NEW PENCE 1969 round arms of Jersey; see note to J65. | T. 480.000<br>M. Royal Mint<br>D. 30.00 mm<br>W. 13.45 g |
| | | (Reissued 1979). | W. 13.50 g |

## Fifty Pence (Round, Milled)

| | | | |
|---|---|---|---|
| J205 | 1972 | AR 25th Wedding Anniversary Commemorative.<br>*Obverse:* QUEEN ELIZABETH THE SECOND – SILVER WEDDING 1972 round crowned bust *r.*<br>*Reverse:* BAILIWICK OF JERSEY above, FIFTY PENCE below, the Royal Mace of Jersey, superimposed on an outline of the Island (reverse designs of the 1972 set by Norman Sillman). | T. 23.500<br>M. York Stampings Ltd. Birmingham (Dies cut by H. B. Sale Ltd., Birmingham; blanks prepared by Sheffield Smelting Co. Ltd.)<br>D. 23.00 mm<br>W. 5.54 g<br>(official 5.42 g) |
| J205A | 1972 | *AR Proof* as J144; frosted relief. | T. 1.500<br>W. up to 5.97 g |

*J205*

## Fifty New Pence (7-sided)

*J206*

| | | | |
|---|---|---|---|
| J206 | 1980 | As J204 except for date. | T. 100.000<br>M. Royal Mint<br>D. 30.00 mm<br>W. 13.55 g |
| J206A | 1980 | *Proof* as J206; frosted relief; edge markings as J67A. | T. 10.000<br>W. 13.60 g |

## Fifty Pence

*J207*

| | | | |
|---|---|---|---|
| J207 | 1981 | *Obverse* as J206.<br>*Reverse* as J206 except FIFTY PENCE below shield which separates date 19 81; see note to J67. | T. 50.000<br>M. Royal Mint<br>D. 30.00 mm<br>W. 13.50 g |
| J207A | 1981 | *Proof* as J207; frosted relief; edge markings as J67A. | T. 15.000 |

*J208*

| | | | |
|---|---|---|---|
| J208 | 1983 | *Obverse:* QUEEN ELIZABETH THE SECOND round crowned bust *r.*, date 1983 below.<br>*Reverse:* Grosnez Castle gatehouse, St. Ouen; BAILIWICK OF JERSEY above, FIFTY PENCE below.<br>See note to J81. | T.<br>M. Royal Mint<br>D. 30.00 mm<br>W. 13.50 g |
| J208A | 1983 | *AR Proof* as J208; frosted relief. | T. 5.000<br>W. 15.66 g |

## Decimal Commemorative (Milled)

## One Pound

*J228*

| | | | |
|---|---|---|---|
| J228 | 1972 | *AR* 25th Wedding Anniversary Commemorative.<br>*Obverse* as J205 but larger.<br>*Reverse:* BAILIWICK OF JERSEY above, ONE POUND below, three florets of Jersey Lily (Amaryllis belladonna). | T. 23.500<br>M. see J144<br>D. 30.00 mm<br>W. up to 11.04 g<br>(official 10.84 g) |
| J228A | 1972 | *AR Proof* as J228; frosted relief. | T. 1.500<br>W. 11.58 g |

*J229*

| | | | |
|---|---|---|---|
| J229 | 1981 | Cupro-nickel square-shaped Battle of Jersey Commemorative.<br>*Obverse:* QUEEN ELIZABETH THE SECOND above, BAILIWICK OF JERSEY below crowned bust *r.*<br>*Reverse:* ONE POUND BICENTARY OF THE BATTLE OF JERSEY round badge of the Royal Jersey Militia which separates the dates 1781 1981. Straight edges milled; corners plain. | T. 200.000<br>M. Royal Mint<br>D. 29.70–25.40 mm<br>W. 9.00 g |
| J229A | 1981 | Cupro-nickel *Proof* as J229; frosted relief. Flan (edge) 0.2 mm thicker. | T. 15.000<br>W. 9.00 g |
| J229B | 1981 | *AR Proof* as J229A; coarse milling. | T. 10.000<br>D. 29.40–25.40 mm<br>W. 10.37 g |
| J229C | 1981 | *AU Proof* as J229. | T. 5.000<br>D. 29.40 x 25.40 mm<br>W. 17.57 g |

## One Pound (Nickel Brass)

*J230*

| | | | |
|---|---|---|---|
| J230 | 1983 | Parish Emblem Series No 1: Parish of St. Helier<br>*Obverse:* QUEEN ELIZABETH THE SECOND round crowned bust *r.*, date 1983 below.<br>*Reverse:* · BAILIWICK OF JERSEY · ONE POUND surrounding a crest heraldically described as 'azure, two axes in saltire, edges inwards, gold', PARISH OF above, St. HELIER below. INSULA CAESAREA incuse on milled edge.<br>  i Edge inscription normal;<br>  ii Edge inscription inverted. | T.<br>M. Royal Mint<br>D. 22.50 mm<br>W. 9.50 g |
| J230A | 1983 | *AR Proof* as J230; frosted relief. | T. 10.000<br>W. 11.68 g |
| J230B | 1983 | *AU Proof* as J230A. | T. 1.500<br>W. 19.65 g |

# Two Pounds

*J250*

| | | | |
|---|---|---|---|
| J250 | 1972 | *AR* 25th Wedding Anniversary Commemorative. *Obverse* as J228 but larger *Reverse:* BAILIWICK OF JERSEY above, TWO POUNDS, below the sailing ship Alexandra, built and registered in Jersey in 1865. | T. 23.500 M. see J144 D. 36.00 mm W. up to 21.92 g (official 21.64 g) |
| J250A | 1972 | *AR Proof* as J250; frosted relief. | T. 1.500 D. 36.10 mm W. 22.58 g |

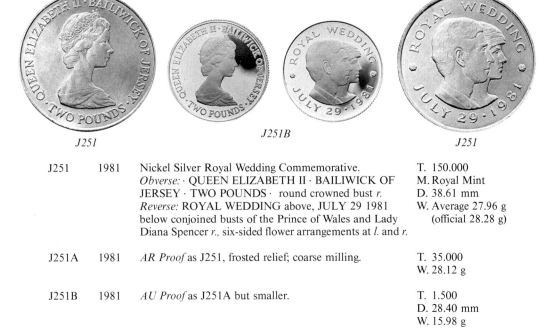

| | | | |
|---|---|---|---|
| J251 | 1981 | Nickel Silver Royal Wedding Commemorative. *Obverse:* · QUEEN ELIZABETH II · BAILIWICK OF JERSEY · TWO POUNDS ·  round crowned bust *r*. *Reverse:* ROYAL WEDDING above, JULY 29 1981 below conjoined busts of the Prince of Wales and Lady Diana Spencer *r*., six-sided flower arrangements at *l*. and *r*. | T. 150.000 M. Royal Mint D. 38.61 mm W. Average 27.96 g (official 28.28 g) |
| J251A | 1981 | *AR Proof* as J251, frosted relief; coarse milling. | T. 35.000 W. 28.12 g |
| J251B | 1981 | *AU Proof* as J251A but smaller. | T. 1.500 D. 28.40 mm W. 15.98 g |

# Two Pounds Fifty Pence

*J262*

| | | | |
|---|---|---|---|
| J262 | 1972 | *AR* 25th Wedding Anniversary Commemorative.<br>*Obverse* as J250 but larger.<br>*Reverse:* BAILIWICK OF JERSEY above, TWO POUNDS FIFTY PENCE below, a lobster (homarus vulcaris). | T. 23.500<br>M. see J144<br>D. 40.10 mm<br>W. up to 27.25 g<br>(official: 27.10 g) |
| J262A | 1972 | *AR Proof* as J262; frosted relief. | T. 1.500<br>W. 27.50 g |

# Five Pounds

*J273*

| | | | |
|---|---|---|---|
| J273 | 1972 | *AU* 25th Wedding Anniversary Commemorative.<br>*Obverse* as J262 except for size.<br>*Reverse:* BAILIWICK OF JERSEY above, FIVE POUNDS below, a lesser white toothed shrew (Crocidura Suaveolens), found in Jersey, Sark and the Scilly Islands. Die scratch across W of BAILIWICK. | T. 23.500<br>M. see J144<br>D. 14.5 mm<br>W. up to 2.69 g<br>(official: 2.62 g) |
| J273A | 1972 | *AU Proof* as J273; frosted relief. | T. 1.500<br>W. up to 3.08 g |

# Ten Pounds

  J284

| | | | |
|---|---|---|---|
| J284 | 1972 | *AU* 25th Wedding Anniversary Commemorative.<br>*Obverse* as J273 but larger.<br>*Reverse* BAILIWICK OF JERSEY above, TEN POUNDS below, the Bronze Age gold *torque* found in Jersey in 1889 with small description TORQUE CIRCA 1500 B. C. | T. 23.500<br>M. see J144<br>D. 18.00 mm<br>W. up to 4.77 g<br>(official 4.64 g) |
| J284A | 1972 | AU Proof as J284; frosted relief. | T. 1.500<br>W. up to 5.02 g |

# Twenty Pounds

  J295

| | | | |
|---|---|---|---|
| J295 | 1972 | *AU* 25th Wedding Anniversary Commemorative.<br>*Obverse* as J284 but larger.<br>*Reverse:* BAILIWICK OF JERSEY above, TWENTY POUNDS below, an Ormer (Haliotis Tuberculata), peculiar to the Channel Islands. | T. 23.500<br>M. see J144<br>D. 22.50 mm<br>W. up to 9.40 g<br>(official 9.26 g) |
| J295A | 1972 | *AU Proof* as J295; frosted relief. | T. 1.500<br>W. up to 9.84 g |

## Twenty Five Pounds

*J306*

| | | | | |
|---|---|---|---|---|
| J306 | 1972 | *AU* 25th Wedding Anniversary Commemorative. *Obverse* as J295 but larger. *Reverse:* BAILIWICK OF JERSEY above TWENTY FIVE POUNDS below, the Royal arms of Queen Elizabeth I, to be found in Elizabeth Castle, Jersey. | | T. 23.500 M. see J144 D. 25.00 mm W. up to 12.14 g (official 11.90 g) |
| J306A | 1972 | *AU Proof* as J306; frosted relief. | | T. 1.500 W. up to 12.40 g |

## Fifty Pounds

*J317*

| | | | |
|---|---|---|---|
| J317 | 1972 | *AU* 25th Wedding Anniversary Commemorative. *Obverse* as J306 but larger. *Reverse:* BAILIWICK OF JERSEY above, FIFTY POUNDS below, the arms of the Bailiwick. | T. 23.500 M. see J144 D. 31.00 mm W. up to 23.12 g (official: 22.63 g) |
| J317A | 1972 | *AU Proof* as J317, numbered on edge 1 to 1500; frosted relief. | T. 1.500 W. 22.82 g |

# Guernsey Coins

## Copper

### Eight Doubles

*G1*  *G1i*  *G1ii*  *G1*

(G1–G74: plain edge)

| | | | |
|---|---|---|---|
| G1 | 1834 | *Obverse:* GUERNESEY above arms between two laurel branches; *Reverse:* 8 / DOUBLES / 1834 between two laurel branches. Apparently only one matrix each for *obverse* and *reverse* but lower edge of right-hand leaf on sprig was fractionally adjusted at an early stage:<br><br>  i right leaf on sprig almost touching shield;<br>  ii separation more defined.<br><br>A die flaw is evident in milling at base of *reverse* on most specimens. Later examples are worn and die-fills common; earlier examples show distinct stem on *obverse* third berry left. | T. 221.760 (minted 1834–39)<br>M. Boulton Watt & Co., Soho Mint, Birmingham<br>D. 34.7 mm<br>W. Average 20.58 g (20.18–20.83) |
| G1Ai | | *Proof* as G1i. | |
| G1Aii | | *Proof* as G1ii. | |

*G2i*  *G2ii*  *G2i*  *G2ii*

| | | | |
|---|---|---|---|
| G2 | 1858 | As G1 but for date. | T. 111.469 |
| | | i The earlier and rarer coin: only 4 berries on left laurel branch on *obverse;* top of bow on *reverse* squashed down; | M. Henry Toy & Co., Birmingham<br>D. 34.8 mm<br>W. Average 18.34 |
| | | ii 5 berries on left laurel branch on *obverse;* different *reverse* die. | (17.87–18.81) |
| | | *Obverse* of ii with *reverse* of i may exist. | |
| G2A | | *Proof* as G2. | |
| G2B | | *Proof* struck on *oversize flan.* (Lot 734. Taffs sale. Glendining & Co. 1956.) | |

# Bronze

## Eight Doubles

(An 8 doubles date 1861 has been reported but it is generally doubted that such a coin ever existed. There is, however, an indication that a die might have been cut as the 4 in the date of G3iii appears to have been adapted from the figure 1.)

| | | | |
|---|---|---|---|
| G3 | 1864 | There are 5 *obverse* die varieties paired with 6 *reverse* dies as follows (based on Sealy's classification): | T. 284.736 (minted 1864–5) |
| | | *Obverse* dies: | M. Henry Toy & Co. |
| | | | D. Average 31.4 mm |
| | | 1. No berries at bow; wreath arranged – leaves 3-4-4, berries 2-2 both sides; bow deep; three leaves at top of shield spring from single stalk; lions tawnier. | (31.3–31.55)<br>W. i–ixa: av. 8.92 g<br>(8.68–9.16)<br>x: 8.35 g |
| | | 2. Wreath and berries as 1. Bow shallower; three leaves at top of shield have separate stalks. Trace of extra leaf on right to make 3-<u>5</u>-4 (?); lions thinner with smaller heads. | |
| | | 3. Two berries at right, one at left of bow; extra leaf in wreath at left; wreath arranged left – leaves 3-5-4, berries 2-2-1; right – leaves 3-4-4, berries 2-2-2; lions as 2. | |
| | | 3a. Variety of 3 lacking berry at left of bow, probably due to die-fill; wreath arranged left – leaves 3-5-4, berries 2-2; right – leaves 3-4-4, berries 2-2-2; lions as 2. | |
| | | 4. One berry each side of bow, twelve leaves in left half of wreath; wreath arranged left – leaves 3-5-4, berries 2-2-1, right – leaves 3-4-4, berries 2-2-1; lions as 1. | |
| | | 5. As 4 but eleven leaves in left half of wreath. Wreath arranged – leaves 3-4-4, berries 2-2-1 both sides; lions remodelled. | |

*Reverse* dies:

A. Centre leaf of triad (at right nearest S of DOUBLES) on top. Bar of 8 in date weak.

A*. Deteriorated state of die A, with blurred and irregular letters, particularly noticeable on BLE of DOUBLES. On some examples there is an excrescence on the lower margin of the top leaf at left. Bar of 8 in the date is generally missing. A* only occurs paired with obverse die 2, while the earlier die A occurs with 1 and 2. This fact establishes the order of this series. On some coins the 4 of the date seems to have been redesigned from a 1. (See note after G2B.)

B. Similar to A but left leaf of triad on top. Date is spaced; bar of the 8 is weak, base of the 4 is double.

C. Right leaf of triad is on top. Triad is irregular with the tip of the right-hand leaf out of line and lower than the others. Coins of this die are generally weakly struck.

D. Right-hand leaf of triad on top, and tips of all three leaves are at same level. The leaf immediately below S is well spaced from it.

D1. Right-hand leaf of triad on top and only slightly out of line. Bow is deep. Most berries and leaves are slightly repositioned.

E. As D but leaf immediately below S is almost touching it. Date is more closely spaced than on any other die.

The following die-pairings are recorded:

|   | Pridmore | M-Fraser |
|---|---|---|
| i 1 + A | 4a | 1 |
| ii 2 + A | 4b | 1 |
| iii 2 + A* | 4b | 1 |
| iv 2 + B | 4b | 1 |
| v 3 + B | 8 | 4 |
| vi 3 + C | 8 | 4 |
| vii 3a + C | – | – |
| viii 3 + D | 8 | 4 |
| ix 4 + D | 7 | 2 |
| ixa 4 + D1 (rarest) | – | – |
| x 5 + E (commonest) | 5 | 3 |

(All *reverse* dies are not inverted; axes of pairings i–iv are almost invariably off-centre). The above die-pairing sequence is taken to show that Henry Toy & Co., who is believed to have minted the coins for 1864, operated with only one press.

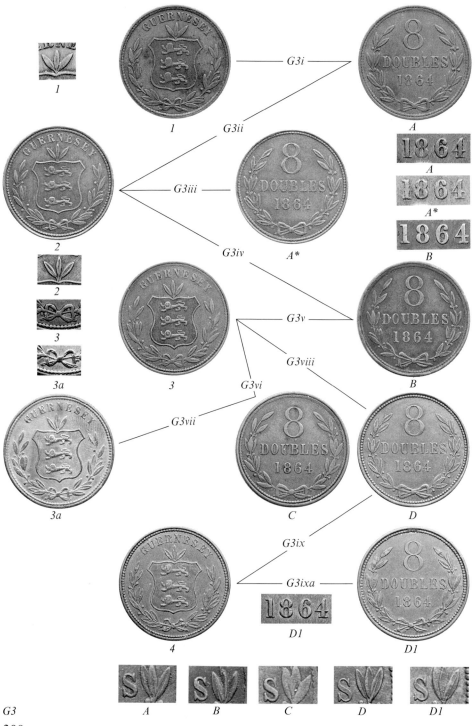

| G3A | | There is an example of G3ix in the British Museum which may be a *proof*.<br>(The catalogue of coins in the Royal Mint Museum, London, lists an 8 doubles for 1865. This may have been confused with the last issue of the coins dated 1864 – possibly G3x – reported to have been issued in 1865.) | |
|---|---|---|---|
| G4 | 1868 | Although as many as five types have been reported, I have been able to isolate only three; all *reverse* dies are inverted.<br><br>  i  11 leaves and 5 berries on left laurel branch on *obverse*;<br><br>  ii  As i but different *obverse* die;<br><br>  iii  12 leaves and 4 berries on left laurel branch on *obverse*; spray above shield redesigned; diameter 31.3 mm. On some examples, there is only a faint outline of the berry to the left of the bow on the *reverse*, perhaps due to die-filling. | T. 54.720<br>M. Partridge & Co., Birmingham<br>D. Average 31.7 mm (i, ii)<br>W. Average 9.17 g (8.9–9.4) |
| G5 | 1874 | New *obverse*: wider shield; *reverse* similar to G4. I have traced 2 *obverse* dies and 3 *reverse* dies. As in G3 and G4, faint traces of differently positioned leaves and berries probably account for several varieties reported by Marshall-Fraser.<br>*Reverse* dies are inverted. | T. 73.248<br>M. Partridge & Co.<br>D. Average 31.5 mm (31.1.–31.75)<br>W. Average 9.5 g (9.13–9.9) |

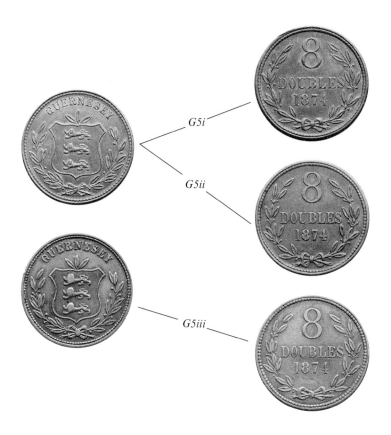

Combinations are:

  i *Obverse* left 12 leaves, 5 berries arranged 3-4-1-4, 2-1-1-1.
*Obverse* right 11 leaves, 5 berries arranged 2-1-4-4, 1-1-2-1.
*Reverse* left 13 leaves, 7 berries arranged 3-3-4-3, 2-2-2-1.
*Reverse* right 13 leaves, 7 berries arranged 3-3-3-4, 2-2-2-1.
(On most examples there is a trace of another leaf on the *obverse* left branch, which would, if separately classified, show leaves arranged 3-4-2-4.)
Date 1.85 cm long.

 ii *Obverse* as i
*Reverse* left arranged as i but in a slightly different position.
*Reverse* right 12 leaves, 7 berries arranged 3-3-3-3, 2-2-2-1.
Date 1.75 cm long.

iii *Obverse* left as i but in slightly different positions (no trace of extra leaf).
*Obverse* right 10 leaves, 5 berries arranged 2-1-4-4, 1-1-2-1, the tip of leaf 8 coincides with berry 4; on some examples the leaf is weak.
*Reverse* left arranged as i but again in slightly different positions.
*Reverse* right arranged as ii but in different positions. Date 1.85 cm long.

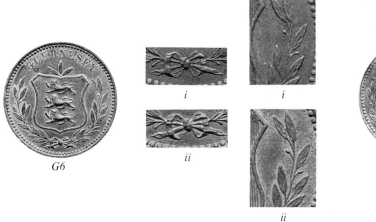

| | | |
|---|---|---|
| G6 | 1885H | *Obverse* again redesigned; base of shield less pointed, larger lions.<br>*Reverse* similar to G5; reverse dies inverted; minute varieties:<br><br>i narrow ribbon entering *obv.* bow lower left; *obv.* right third leaf joined to main stem.<br><br>ii die recut to show broader ribbon entering *obv.* bow lower left; *obv.* right third leaf joined to berry stem. | T. 69.696<br>M. R. Heaton & Sons, Birmingham<br>D. 31.7 mm<br>W. Average 9.66 g (9.36–10.08) |
| G6A | | *Proof* as G6ii. | |

G7

iii

iv

311

G7  1889H  As G6 except for date; reverse dies not inverted; varieties in date spacing:

    i spacing normal; 8←→9 : 0.5 mm;
    ii 9 slightly raised; 8←→9 : 0.4 mm;
    iii 9 slightly raised; 8←→9 : 0.25 mm;
    iv 9 markedly raised; 8←→9 : 0.55 mm.

T. 222.096 (minted 1889–90)
M. The Mint, Birmingham Limited (formerly R. Heaton & Sons)
D. Average 31.7 mm
W. Average 9.75 g (9.66–9.85)

G8      i      ii

G8  1893H  *Obverse:* lions redesigned, e.g. ends of tails now point upwards; *reverse* dies not inverted.

    i DOUBLES in large letters; date in large figures; the earlier die;
    ii DOUBLES in smaller letters; date in smaller figures; the *reverse* die is in fact redesigned and there are many minute differences.

T. 117.600
M. The Mint, Birmingham, Ltd.
D. 31.7 mm
W. 9.63 g

i      ii      G9      iii      iv

G9  1902H  Similar to G8 except for date; *reverse* dies inverted; the earlier style of *reverse* matrix (cf G8i) was again used. There are several constant faults on a seriously deteriorating obv. die, e.g. stalk below first two berries on left. Varieties in date spacing:

    i 9 slightly lower; 0←→2 : 0.8 mm;
    ii 02 lower; 0←→2 : 0.7 mm;
    iii 02 lower; 0←→2 : 0.5 mm;
    iv 902 lower; 0←→2 : 0.4 mm.

T. 235.200
M. The Mint, Birmingham, Ltd.
D. 31.75 mm
W. Average 9.72 g (9.63–9.88)

i      ii      G10      iii      iv

G10  1903H  As G9 except for date; *reverse* dies inverted; same deteriorated state of *obverse* die as G9 but attempt evident on G10iv to repair stalk; varieties in date spacing:

    i 9 raised; 9→0 : 0.7 mm;

    ii date regular; 9→0 : 0.6 mm;

    iii as ii but 0 lower; 9→0 : 0.6 mm;

    iv 0 raised; 9→0 : 0.5 mm.

T. 117.600
M. The Mint, Birmingham, Ltd.
D. 31.75 mm
W. Average 9.79 g (9.44–10.01)

*i*

*ii*

*i*

G11    *ii*

G11  1910H  As G10 except for date; *reverse* dies inverted. On the early coins of G11i the same *obverse* die fault is evident; on later coins the stalk has been re-sunk.

    i 1→0 : 1.3 mm; letters of GUERNESEY deteriorating;

    ii 1→0 : 1.2 mm; letters of GUERNESEY repaired.

T. 91.467
M. The Mint, Birmingham, Ltd.
D. 31.7 mm
W. Average 9.58 g (9.46–9.66)

*i*    G12    *ii*

G12  1911H  As G11 but for date; *reverse* dies inverted.

    i 1→1 : 2.0 mm; letters of GUERNESEY deteriorating (cf G11i);

    ii 1→1 : 2.3 mm; letters of GUERNESEY repaired (cf G11ii).

T. 78.400
M. The Mint, Birmingham, Ltd.
D. 31.7 mm
W. Average 9.59 g (9.45–9.73)

G13

| | | | |
|---|---|---|---|
| G13 | 1914H | *Obverse:* new shield and spray; laurel branches redesigned, bow smaller.<br>*Reverse* dies inverted. | T. 156.800<br>M. The Mint, Birmingham, Ltd.<br>D. 31.7 mm<br>W. Average 9.75 g (9.64–9.86) |

*i*

G14

*ii*

| | | | |
|---|---|---|---|
| G14 | 1918H | As G13 except for date; *reverse* dies inverted.<br>　i  1⃞8 : 1.3 mm;<br>　ii 1⃞8 : 1.6 mm. | T. 156.800<br>M. The Mint, Birmingham, Ltd.<br>D. 31.7 mm<br>W. 9.90 g |

*i*

G15

*ii*

| | | | |
|---|---|---|---|
| G15 | 1920H | As G14 except for date; *reverse* dies inverted.<br>　i  1⃞9 : 0.9 mm; 2 crooked;<br>　ii 1⃞9 : 1.2 mm; 0 raised. | T. 156.800<br>M. The Mint, Birmingham, Ltd.<br>D. 31.7 mm<br>W. 9.64 g |

*i*

G16

*ii*

| | | | |
|---|---|---|---|
| G16 | 1934H | As G15 except for date; *reverse* dies inverted.<br>　i Date spacing normal;<br>　ii 9 raised. | T. 123.600<br>M. The Mint, Birmingham, Ltd.<br>D. 31.7 mm<br>W. Average 9.77 g (9.68–9.80) |
| G16A | | 500 coins with a *burnished flan* were issued in 1935 to commemorate the silver jubilee of George V and the centenary of the first issue of Guernsey 8 doubles. These coins, from the same dies as G16ii are sometimes classed as *'Proofs'* (e. g. Glendining sale 2.10.1969, Lot 396). | T. 500 |

*i*

G17

*ii*

G17    1938H    As G16 except for date; *reverse* dies inverted.    T. 180.000
              i Date normal;    M. The Mint,
                    Birmingham, Ltd.
              ii 1 in date raised.    D. 31.6 mm
                    W. Average 9.66 g
                    (9.35–9.83)

G17A    *Proof* as G17ii.

*G18 var.*    *G18*    *G18 var.*

G18    1945H    As G17 except for date, figures of which are thicker.    T. 192.000
              *Reverse* dies inverted.    M. The Mint,
              Note: Coins of this date are known, struck in cupro-nickel    Birmingham, Ltd.
              with a central hole, apparently on contemporary British    D. 31.7 mm
              West Africa penny blanks, their authenticity has not been    W. 9.68 g
              established beyond doubt (see G42).

*G19*

*i*

*ii*    *iii*

G19    1947H    As G18. Figures of date finer;    T. 240.000
              *reverse* dies inverted; three stages of the same *obverse* die    M. The Mint,
              are evident:    Birmingham, Ltd.
                    D. 31.8 mm
              i normal;    W. Average 9.73 g
                    (9.66–9.85)
              ii wear at centre of shield;

              iii centre of shield clumsily repaired.

*G20*

G20   1949H   As G19 except for date; different style 1 and 9's in date; *reverse* dies inverted.   T. 230.400
M. The Mint, Birmingham, Ltd.
D. 31.9 mm
W. 9.83 g

*G21*

G21   1956   New *obverse* design, the Seal of the Bailiwick (from a 13$^{th}$ century Royal Seal): S'BALLIVIE INSVLE DE GERNE-REVE round arms surmounted by a spring of laurel. *Reverse:* single Guernsey lily, GUERNSEY above; 1956/EIGHT DOUBLES below. P.V. (Paul Vincze) to left of lily.
*Reverse* dies not inverted. At some stage part of the *obverse* die appears to have collapsed.
Note GUERNSEY spelling.   T. 494.600
M. The Mint, Birmingham, Ltd.
D. 30.9 mm
W. Average 9.77 g
(9.75–9.80)

G21A   1956   *Proof* as G21.   W. 9.55 g

*G22*

G22   1959   As G21 but for date; *reverse* dies not inverted.   T. 480.000
M. Royal Mint
D. 30.9 mm
W. 9.80 g

*G23A*

| G23A | 1966 | *Proof* only as G22 but for date; *obverse* die of poor quality. | T. 10.000<br>M. Royal Mint<br>D. 30.9 mm<br>W. 9.90 g |

## Copper

## Four Doubles

| G24 | 1830 | *Obverse:* arms of Guernsey in plain shield, GUERNESEY below.<br>*Reverse:* 4/DOUBLES/1830. *Reverse* dies inverted.<br>  i small beading;<br>  ii large (repunched) beading; 1, 3 and 0 of date restruck; tip of middle lion's tail remodelled; die axis on some examples marginally out of line;<br>  iii *Reverse* has also been reported with the *obverse* of G25. | T. 655.200 (minted 1830–39)<br>M. Boulton, Watt & Co., Soho Mint, Birmingham<br>D. 29.1 mm<br>W. Average 10.05 g (9.86–10.30) |

G24A    A small number of examples of the *reverse* of G24ii with    T. Not known
        the St. Helena halfpenny *obverse* of 1821 are known.        M. Not known
        This *'mule'* is a concoction dated to c 1850–60 (B.N.J.     D. 29.2 mm
        Vol. XVI, 1921–22, p 303).                                   W. 11.05 g

G24B    A *uniface* striking in lead has been reported (Lot 75.
        Brushfield Sale, Glendining & Co., 1945).

*i*          *i*    G25    *ii*          *ii*

G25    1858    Lions on shield redesigned (e. g. right forepaws point    T. 114.060
               upwards), *reverse* dies inverted; laurel sprig above shield    M. Henry Toy & Co.,
               less spread than G24.                                      Birmingham
                                                                         D. 28.9 mm
               i  sprig close to shield; figure 4 on reverse directly above    W. Average 9.03 g
                  B of DOUBLES; DOUBLES marginally more spread               (9.00–9.07)
                  than G25ii;

               ii lions remodelled, manes slightly shorter; figure 4
                  off-centre to right.

# Bronze

# Four Doubles

G26    1864    There are four *obverse* dies paired with two *reverse* dies    T. 212.976 (minted
               as follows:                                                      1864–5)
               *Obverse* dies:                                                 M. Henry Toy & Co.
                                                                               D. Average 26 mm
               1. 3 stems to sprig; tips of outside leaves 6.9 mm apart;         (25.75–26.1)
                  strong stem and weak stem varieties are known;              W. Average 4.85
                                                                                 (4.75–5.02)
               2. 1 stem to sprig; tips of outside leaves 6.7 mm apart;

               3. 2 stems to smaller sprig; tips of outside leaves 6.7 mm
                  apart; right leaf over centre leaf; lions redesigned;

               4. 1 stem to sprig; tips of outside leaves 6.9 mm apart.

               *Reverse* dies:

               A    Date 9 mm long;

               B    Date 8.7 mm long;

               B1   as B but evidence of rusty die.

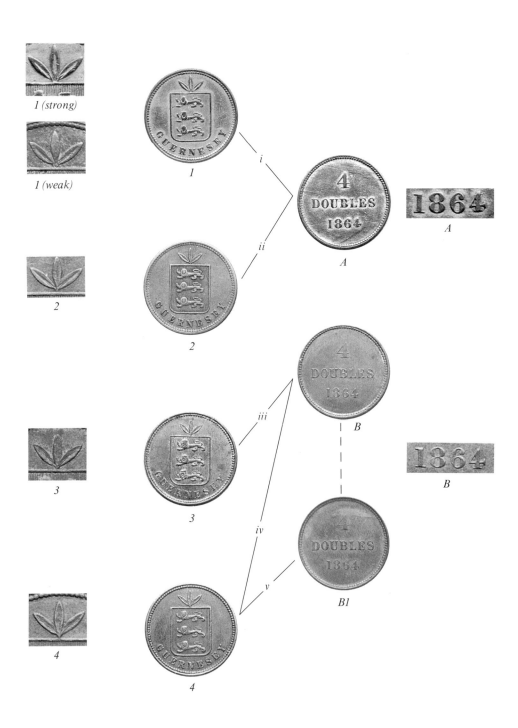

G26

The following die pairings exist:

i  1 + A (There are faint traces of a 3 under the 4 of the date on some finer examples);

ii  2 + A;

iii  3 + B;

iv  4 + B;

v  4 + B1.

All *reverses* are not inverted; axes of pairings iii, iv and v are off-centre. The above die sequence is further evidence that Henry Toy & Co. operated with only one machine (see G3).

G27

i
G27

i

i

ii
G27

ii

ii

| | | | |
|---|---|---|---|
| G27 | 1868 | New *obverse:* GUERNESEY less spread; hindquarters of middle lion slightly raised; *reverses* are inverted.<br><br>  i  3 stalks to sprig; date spacing 8⟵6 : 0.9 mm;<br>  ii  left stalk slightly apart; date spacing 8⟵6 : 0.6 mm; DOUBLES less spread. | T. 57.696<br>M. Partridge & Co., Birmingham<br>D. Average 26.1 mm (26.0–26.25)<br>W. 5.22 g |

G28

G28 1874 Lions now straight; GUERNESEY again more spread; left leaf of sprig repositioned; on most specimens there is a lump on the 8, caused by die pitting; *reverses* inverted.

T. 69.216
M. Partridge & Co.
D. 26.4 mm
W. Average 5.24 g
(5.07–5.41)

*G29*

G29 1885H *Obverse* redesigned – larger lions, sprig taller and more spread; legend and date on reverse larger. Some specimens were struck in a silvery metal.
*Reverses* inverted.

T. 69.696
M. R. Heaton & Sons, Birmingham
D. 26.35 mm
W. 4.90 g

G29A *Proof* as G29 (Sotheby, Wilkinson & Hodge Sale 11th–13th June, 1912, Lot 31).

*G30*

*i*

*iii*

*ii*

G30 1889H As G29 except for date; *reverses* not inverted.

Date spacing:
i 8⃪ 9⃫ : 0.4 mm; 9 raised;
ii 8⃪ 9⃫ : 0.5 mm;
iii 8⃪ 9⃫ : 0.7 mm.

T. 104.448 (minted 1889–90)
M. The Mint, Birmingham Ltd.
D. 26.35 mm
W. Average 4.81 g
(4.66–4.96)

G30A *Proof* as G30 struck on a *thick flan*.

W. 7.94 g

*G31*

| G31 | 1893H | *Obverse* recut: shield larger; lions slightly different e. g. shape of head and angle of tail (see G8); *reverse* dies not inverted. | T. 52.224<br>M. The Mint, Birmingham, Ltd.<br>D. 26.35 mm<br>W. 4.76 g |

*i*  *G32*  *ii*

| G32 | 1902H | As G31 except for date; *reverse* dies inverted.<br>i 9 of date slightly lower, 0 slightly higher;<br>ii 9 of date slightly higher, 0 slightly lower. | T. 104.534<br>M. The Mint, Birmingham, Ltd.<br>D. 26.35 mm<br>W. Average 4.89 g (4.85–4.93) |

*G33*

| G33 | 1903H | As G32 except for date; *reverse* dies inverted; some coins have been reported struck in a silvery metal. | T. 52.265<br>M. The Mint, Birmingham, Ltd.<br>D. 26.35 mm<br>W. 4.93 g |

*G34*

| G34 | 1906H | As G33 except for date; *reverse* dies inverted. | T. 52.266<br>M. The Mint, Birmingham, Ltd.<br>D. 26.35 mm<br>W. 4.83 g |

*G35*

G35    1908H    As G34 except for date; *reverse* dies inverted.    T. 25.760
M. The Mint, Birmingham, Ltd.
D. 26.4 mm
W. 4.92 g

*G36*

G36    1910H    As G35 except for date; *reverse* dies inverted.    T. 52.267
M. The Mint, Birmingham, Ltd.
D. 26.35 mm
W. 4.98 g

*i*

*ii*

*G37*

G37    1911H    As G36 except for date; *reverse* dies inverted.

       i   large H; date regular;

       ii   small H; 11 in date slightly raised.

T. 52.267
M. The Mint, Birmingham, Ltd.
D. 26.4 mm
W. Average 4.80 g
(4.73–4.87)

G37A    A *uniface trial* strike of the *obverse* has been reported; I have classified it tentatively under this date (see also G70A).

i

iii

G38

| G38 | 1914H | *Obverse* redesigned, shield almost identical to G13 but spray less spread.<br>*Reverse* as G37 but for date; *reverse* dies inverted.<br><br>Date spacing:<br>  i  1↤→4 : 1 mm;<br>  ii  Thick flan, date as G38i;<br>  iii  1↤→4 : 1.1 mm; second 1 in date slightly raised. | T. 209.067<br>M. The Mint,<br>    Birmingham, Ltd.<br>D. 26.4 mm<br>W. i, iii: average 4.77 g<br>    (4.72–4.82)<br>W. 6.59 g |
|---|---|---|---|

G39

| G39 | 1918H | As G38 except for date; *reverse* dies inverted. | T. 156.800<br>M. The Mint,<br>    Birmingham, Ltd.<br>D. 26.6 mm<br>W. 4.67 g |
|---|---|---|---|

i      G40      ii

| G40 | 1920H | As G39 except for date; *reverse* dies inverted; beading very weak.<br><br>Date spacing:<br>  i  2↤→0 : 1 mm;<br>  ii  2↤→0 : 0.8 mm. | T. 156.800<br>M. The Mint,<br>    Birmingham, Ltd.<br>D. 26.5 mm<br>W. Average 4.77 g<br>    (4.72–4.82) |
|---|---|---|---|

G41

| | | | |
|---|---|---|---|
| G41 | 1945H | Larger thicker date (cf G18); on later coins shield is indistinct; H always weak; *reverse* dies inverted. | T. 96.000<br>M. The Mint, Birmingham, Ltd.<br>D. 26.3 mm<br>W. 4.96 g |

*G42*

| | | | |
|---|---|---|---|
| G42 | 1949H | As G41 but date restyled (cf G20); *reverse* dies inverted.<br><br>Note: coins of this date are known, struck in cupro-nickel with a central hole, apparently on British West Africa ½d blanks; their authenticity has not been established beyond doubt (see G18). | T. 19.200<br>M. The Mint, Birmingham, Ltd.<br>D. 26.3 mm<br>W. 4.82 g |

*G43*

| | | | |
|---|---|---|---|
| G43 | 1956 | New *obverse* design as G21; Guernsey lily *reverse*; *reverse* dies not inverted. | T. 240.000<br>M. Royal Mint<br>D. 25.5 mm<br>W. 4.82 g |
| G43A | 1956 | *Proof* as G43 | W. 4.77 g |

*G44A*

| | | | |
|---|---|---|---|
| G44A | 1966 | *Proof* only, similar to G43 but for date. | T. 10.000<br>M. Royal Mint<br>D. 25.5 mm<br>W. 4.85 g |

## Copper

### Two Doubles

*G45*

| | | | |
|---|---|---|---|
| G45 | 1858 | *Obverse:* arms of Guernsey in plain shield, GUERNESEY below.<br>*Reverse:* 2/DOUBLES/1858.<br>*Reverse* dies inverted; only one die traced but there is evidence of alteration to it on some coins, e. g. in position of middle lion's tail. | T. 56.128<br>M. Henry Toy & Co., Birmingham<br>D. 22 mm<br>W. Average 4.52 g<br>(4.45–4.6) |

## Bronze

### Two Doubles

*G46*

*i*   *ii*   *iii*

G46  1868  Similar design to G45 but shield slightly larger; *reverse* dies inverted.

    i One stem to leaves;

    ii Same die but several items re-cut e. g. spines of leaves, top lion's tail;

    iii Different die: stem to each leaf; top lion lower, bottom lion higher.

T. 35.136
M. Partridge & Co., Birmingham
D. 22.2 mm
W. Average 3.80 g
(3.56–3.93)

i

G47

ii

| G47 | 1874 | Similar dies to G46iii but lions redesigned (e. g. thicker manes) and leaves taller; *reverse* dies inverted. | T. 45.216<br>M. Partridge & Co.<br>D. 22.3 mm<br>W. Average 366 g<br>(3.62–3.71) |
|---|---|---|---|
| | | i narrow *reverse* legend and date; | |
| | | ii wide *reverse* legend and date. | |

G48

| G48 | 1885 | *Obverse* and *reverse* dies redesigned (cf G29); *reverses* inverted. | T. 71.280<br>M. R. Heaton & Sons<br>D. 22.4 mm<br>W. 3.71 g |
|---|---|---|---|
| G48A | | *Proof* as G48. | D. 22.3 mm<br>W. 3.60 g |

i

G49

ii

| G49 | 1889H | As G48 but for date; *reverses* not inverted. | T. 35.616<br>M. The Mint,<br>Birmingham, Ltd.<br>D. 22.5 mm<br>W. 3.60 g |
|---|---|---|---|
| | | i 9 of date crooked; on later examples there is a die fill which obscures the three stalks on *obverse*. | |
| | | ii 9 straightened. | |

i

ii
G50

iii

| | | | |
|---|---|---|---|
| G50 | 1899H | As G49 but for date; *reverse* dies inverted; on all examples lower left serif of H is missing and right side of middle leaf on *obverse* is weak.<br><br>  i date spacing 9⁻⁻9 : 0.5 mm;<br>  ii date spacing 9⁻⁻9 : 0.6 mm; second 9 lower;<br>  iii date spacing 9⁻⁻9 : 0.8 mm. | T. 35.636<br>M. The Mint,<br>    Birmingham, Ltd.<br>D. 22.5 mm<br>W. Average 3.58 g<br>    (3.46–3.68) |

*G51*

| | | | |
|---|---|---|---|
| G51 | 1902H | Same characteristics of H and middle leaf as G50; *reverse* dies inverted. | T. 17.818<br>M. The Mint,<br>    Birmingham, Ltd.<br>D. 22.5 mm<br>W. 3.62 g |

*G52*

| | | | |
|---|---|---|---|
| G52 | 1903H | As G51 but for date; middle leaf tidied but still weak; H repunched; *reverse* dies inverted. | T. 17.818<br>M. The Mint,<br>    Birmingham, Ltd.<br>D. 22.5 mm<br>W. 3.52 g |

*G53*

| | | | |
|---|---|---|---|
| G53 | 1906H | *Obverse* as G52; *reverse* restruck e. g. smaller 2, spacing of DOUBLES different, H higher; *reverses* inverted. | T. 17.820<br>M. The Mint,<br>    Birmingham, Ltd.<br>D. 22.5 mm<br>W. 3.64 g |

*G54*

| | | | |
|---|---|---|---|
| G54 | 1908H | As G53 except for date; middle leaf on *obverse* clumsily repaired; *reverse* dies inverted. | T. 17.780<br>M. The Mint,<br>    Birmingham, Ltd.<br>D. 22.5 mm<br>W. 3.50 g |

*G55*

G55 1911H  As G54 except for date; also said to have been struck with new design (see G56) but no example traced; *reverse* dies inverted.  
T. 28.509  
M. The Mint, Birmingham, Ltd.  
D. 22.4 mm  
W. 3.59 g

*G56*

G56 1914H  New *obverse* design similar to G38 but smaller spray; *reverse* as G55 but for date. *Reverse* dies inverted.  
T. 28.509  
M. The Mint, Birmingham, Ltd.  
D. 22.6 mm  
W. Average 3.55 g

G56A  *Proof* as G56.

*i*  *G57*  *ii*

G57 1917H  As G56 but for date; the rarest of the 2 double series; *reverses* inverted.

i H centrally placed between 9 and 1 of date.

ii H nearer to 1 (a very rare variety, probably the earlier of the two).

T. 14.524  
M. The Mint, Birmingham, Ltd.  
D. 22.4 mm  
W. 3.54 g

*G58*

G58 1918H  As G57 but for date; *reverses* inverted.  
T. 57.018  
M. The Mint, Birmingham, Ltd.  
D. 22.4 mm  
W. 3.60 g

*G59*

| | | | |
|---|---|---|---|
| G59 | 1920H | As G58 except for date; H lower; *reverse* dies inverted. | T. 57.018<br>M. The Mint, Birmingham, Ltd.<br>D. 22.5 mm<br>W. 3.60 g |

*i*

G60

*ii*

| | | | |
|---|---|---|---|
| G60 | 1929H | As G59 except for date, first 9 of date larger than second 9; *reverse* dies inverted.<br>  i Date spacing about normal; H lower;<br> ii 29 of date lower; H raised. | T. 79.100<br>M. The Mint, Birmingham, Ltd.<br>D. 22.5 mm<br>W. Average 3.57 g (3.55–3.59) |

## Copper

## One Double

G61

*i*

*ii*

*iii*

| | | | |
|---|---|---|---|
| G61 | 1830 | The commonest of the series; I was told while on a recent visit to Guernsey that this coin was popular with farmers who found certain uses for it in their agricultural machinery up to quite recently; it is in fact often turned up by the plough in the Island. Design is similar to G 24 but 1 DOUBLE. *Reverse* dies inverted (except G61B, q. v.).<br>  i Date normal;<br> ii As G61i but dot (from die pitting) before 1 of date; possibly earlier than G61i; traces of a previous striking are evident on finer examples (see D of DOUBLES and all figures of date);<br> iii 0 of date slightly raised and turned clockwise. | T. 1.648.640<br>M. Boulton Watt & Co., Soho Mint, Birmingham<br>D. 18.8 mm<br>W. 2.50 g |
| G61A | 1830 | *Proof* as G61i. | D. 18.7 mm<br>W. 2.40 g |
| G61B | 1830 | *Proof* as G61A, but *reverse* die not inverted. | D. 18.7 mm<br>W. 2.04 g |

# Bronze

## One Double

*i*        *ii*        *i*        *ii*

*i*    G62    *ii*

| | | | |
|---|---|---|---|
| G62 | 1868 | Shield redesigned: lines coarser, lions larger; *reverses* inverted. | T. 64.368<br>M. Partridge & Co.<br>D. 18.65 mm<br>W. 2.25 g |

     i stalk to spray of five leaves on *obverse;* 1868 altered from 1830;

     ii no stalk to (different) spray on *obverse;* date normal; letters of DOUBLE more spaced.

A *'proof'* in brass without GUERNESEY was reported by Marshall-Fraser. Pridmore acquired 'undoubtedly the actual specimen from which Marshall-Fraser made his note' (apparently a 1 double 1868 with the legend erased); the existence of this *'proof'* is doubted.

G63        G63

G63    1877    Certain other pieces, ostensibly of this period, do not appear to have been official issues; although they may have been bona fide *patterns.* A *'pattern',* apparently of brass, dated 1877, with a markedly smaller shield, enclosed in an extra linear circle, has been reported. Other 1 double pieces, some dated 1877 (often enamelled) are known and the *obverse* or *reverse* motif has been employed for badges and charms. There are certain inconsistencies in the styles of these pieces – such as the spelling of GUERN(E)SEY and design of the sprig above the shield – which suggest strongly that they were struck unofficially. There is of course no proof that they did *not* circulate as currency (particularly those with designs consistent with official isues) and for reference purposes I am including them here.

*G64*      *G64*      *G64A*

G64    1885H    Shield again redesigned; three laurel leaves above; GUERNESEY larger; *reverse* legend and date larger; H slightly off-centre to the left; *reverse* dies inverted.    T. 56.016
M. R. Heaton & Sons
D. 18.75 mm
W. 2.30 g

G64A      *Proof* as G64 but H below mid-point of date.

*G65*      *i*      *ii*

G65    1889H    As G64 except for date; two dies traced but there may be others with minute differences; *reverse* dies not inverted.

     i large 9; $8\leftarrow\rightarrow 9$ : 0.5 mm;

     ii smaller raised 9; $8\leftarrow\rightarrow 9$ : 0.4 mm.

T. 112.032 (minted 1889–90)
M. The Mint, Birmingham, Ltd.
D. 18.8 mm
W. Average 2.32 g (2.30–2.35)

*G66*

G66    1893H    Lions redesigned (e. g. ears more prominent); otherwise as G65 except for date; H very weak.    T. 56.013
M. The Mint, Birmingham Ltd.
D. 18.9 mm
W. 2.30 g

*i*      *G67*      *ii*

G67    1899H    As G66 except for date; *reverses* inverted; date spacing:

     i $9\leftarrow\rightarrow 9$ : 0.4 mm;

     ii $9\leftarrow\rightarrow 9$ : 0.6 mm.

T. 56.000
M. The Mint, Birmingham, Ltd.
D. 18.85 mm
W. Average 2.30 g (2.22–2.37)

*G68*

G68  1902H  As G67 except for date; *reverses* inverted.  T. 84.000
M. The Mint, Birmingham, Ltd.
D. 18.8 mm
W. 2.31 g

*i*  *G69*  *ii*

G69  1903H  As G68 except for date; *reverses* inverted.
i date spacing 0⁻⁻3 : 0.6 mm; evidence of worn dies particularly on later issues;
ii date spacing 0⁻⁻3 : 0.3 mm.
T. 112.000
M. The Mint, Birmingham, Ltd.
D. 18.9 mm
W. Average 2.35 g (2.31–2.41)

*G70i*  *G70ii*  *G70A*

*G70i*  *G70ii*

G70  1911H  i As G69 except for date; *reverses* inverted; date spacing: 1⁻⁻9 : 0.8 mm.
T. 44.800
M. The Mint, Birmingham, Ltd.
D. 18.8 mm
W. 2.27 g

ii *Obverse* die redesigned (cf G38, G56); damage to *reverse* die (e. g. U and B of DOUBLE) repaired; date spacing: 1⁻⁻9 : 1.0 mm.
T. 89.600
D. 18.85 mm
W. 2.23 g

G70A  *Uniface trial* of new *obverse* die; different spray and top lion higher; fault on bottom lion's tail and other minor differences.
D. 19.2 mm
W. 3.5 g

*G71*

G71  1914H  As G70ii except for date; same defective *reverse* die; *reverses* inverted.
T. 44.800
M. The Mint, Birmingham, Ltd.
D. 18.8 mm
W. 2.31 g

| | | | |
|---|---|---|---|
| G71A | | *Proof* as G71. | D. 18.85 mm<br>W. 2.28 g |

*G72*

| | | | |
|---|---|---|---|
| G72 | 1929H | As G71 except for date; reverses inverted. | T. 79.100<br>M. The Mint, Birmingham, Ltd.<br>D. 18.8 mm<br>W. 2.25 g |

*G73*

| | | | |
|---|---|---|---|
| G73 | 1933H | Same defective *reverse* die as G69 (see U and B of DOUBLE); *reverses* inverted. | T. 96.000<br>M. The Mint, Birmingham, Ltd.<br>D. 18.85 mm<br>W. 2.27 g |

i        *G74*        ii

| | | | |
|---|---|---|---|
| G74 | 1938H | Similar to G73 except for date; repaired *reverse* die (see G70ii); *reverses* inverted.<br>  i 3←→8 : 0.3 mm; thick H;<br>  ii 3←→8 : 0.6 mm, BLE of DOUBLE repunched; thin H. | T. 96.000<br>M. The Mint, Birmingham, Ltd.<br>D. 19.0 mm<br>W. 2.25 g |

## Three Pence – Cupro-Nickel (scalloped Edge)

*G75*

| | | | |
|---|---|---|---|
| G75 | 1956 | *Obverse* as G21 but smaller.<br>*Reverse:* Guernsey cow standing r. in pasture; artist's initials P.V. (Paul Vincze) to right; GUERNSEY above; 1956 and THREE PENCE below. | T. 508.675<br>M. Royal Mint<br>D. 20.6 mm<br>W. 3.55 g |
| G75A | 1956 | *Proof* as G75; lightly frosted relief. | T. 3.100<br>W. 3.41 g |

*G76*

| | | | |
|---|---|---|---|
| G76 | 1959 | *Flan* almost twice as thick as previous issue (sheet join visible on edge of some examples) otherwise as G75 except for date. | T. 480.000<br>M. Royal Mint<br>D. 20.65 mm<br>W. 6.86 g |
| G76A | 1959 | *Proof* as G76; lightly frosted relief. | T. Unknown<br>W. 6.50 g |

*G77A*

| | | | |
|---|---|---|---|
| G77A | 1966 | *AR proof* only as G76A except for date. | T. 10.000<br>M. Royal Mint<br>D. 20.6 mm<br>W. 6.81 g |

## Ten Shillings – Cupro-Nickel (plain Edge)

*G78*

| | | | |
|---|---|---|---|
| G78 | 1966 | Norman Conquest Commemorative – square shaped.<br>*Obverse:* BAILIWICK OF GUERNSEY round crowned bust of Queen Elizabeth II *r.* 1966 below.<br>*Reverse:* WILLIAM I KING OF ENGLAND · 1066 · DUKE OF NORMANDY · TEN SHILLINGS round crowned bust of William I *r.*; crosses between legend and edge in each corner. | T. 300.000<br>M. Royal Mint<br>D. 25.7–30.25 mm<br>W. 11.40 g |
| G78A | 1966 | *AR proof* as G78; frosted relief. | T. 10.000<br>W. 11.34 g |

## Decimal – Bronze (plain Edge)

## Half New Penny

G79

| | | | | |
|---|---|---|---|---|
| G79 | 1971 | *Obverse* as G22 but smaller; line below each 'leopard's' belly missing or incomplete.<br>*Reverse:* ½ in centre, NEW PENNY above, · 1971 · below. | | T. 2.066.000<br>M. Royal Mint<br>D. 17.1 mm<br>W. 1.82 g |
| G79A | 1971 | *Proof* as G79. | | T. 10.000<br>D. 17.2 mm<br>W. 1.80 g |

## Half Penny

G80A

| | | | |
|---|---|---|---|
| G80A | 1979 | *Proof* only, obverse as G79A.<br>*Reverse:* ½ in centre, HALF PENNY above, · 1979 · below. | T. 20.000<br>M. Royal Mint<br>D. 17.25 mm<br>W. 1.80 g |

## One New Penny

G91

| | | | |
|---|---|---|---|
| G91 | 1971 | *Obverse* as G79 but larger.<br>*Reverse:* 1 separating NEW PENNY above a gannet in full flight (characteristic of the Island of Alderney); 1971 below. | T. 1.922.000<br>M. Royal Mint<br>D. 20.35 mm<br>W. 3.57 g |
| G91A | 1971 | *Proof* as G91; lines below leopards weak, cf G79A. | T. 10.000<br>W. 3.62 g |

# One Penny

*G92*

G92 1977 *Obverse* as G91.  
*Reverse:* 1 separating ONE PENNY above gannet; 1977 below.

T. 640.000  
M. Royal Mint  
D. 20.35 mm  
W. 3.57 g

*G93*

G93 1979 As G92 except for date.

T. 2.400.000  
M. Royal Mint  
D. 20.35 mm  
W. 3.57 g

G93A 1979 *Proof* as G93.

T. 20.000

# Two New Pence

*G114*

G114 1971 *Obverse* as G91 but larger.  
*Reverse:* 2 separating NEW PENCE above Sark Mill, built in 1571 (i. e. 400 years before issue of this coin) by Helier de Carteret; 1971 below.

T. 1.680.000  
M. Royal Mint  
D. 25.9 mm  
W. 7.09 g

G114A 1971 *Proof* as G114; lines below leopards weak, cf G91A.

T. 10.000  
W. 7.15 g

## Two Pence

*G115*

G115    1977    *Obverse* as G114  
                        *Reverse:* 2 separating TWO PENCE above Sark Mill; 1977 below.

T. 700.000  
M. Royal Mint  
D. 25.95 mm  
W. 7.08 g

*G116*

G116    1979    As G115 except for date.

T. 2.400.000  
M. Royal Mint  
D. 25.95 mm  
W. 7.08 g

G116A  1979    *Proof* as G116.

T. 20.000  
W. 7.12 g

## Decimal – Cupro-Nickel (milled)

## Five New Pence

*G137*

G137    1968    *Obverse* as G116 but smaller.  
                        *Reverse:* Guernsey lily design as used on G43 but centre pistil has been given a head (stigma), and designer's initials are omitted; 5 separating NEW PENCE above, 1968 below.

T. 800.000  
M. Royal Mint  
D. 23.6 mm  
W. 5.77 g

*G138A*

G138A    1971    *Proof* only, as G137 except for date but obverse and reverse weakly struck in parts, cf. G114A    T. 10.000
M. Royal Mint
D. 23.6 mm
W. 5.79 g

## Five Pence

*G139*

G139    1977    *Obverse* as G138A.
*Reverse:* 5 separating FIVE PENCE above Guernsey lily, new style date 1977 (e. g. thicker top to 7) below.    T. 250.000
M. Royal Mint
D. 23.6 mm
W. 5.70 g

*G140*

G140    1979    As G139 except for date; *flan* 0.2 mm thicker.    T. 600.000
M. Royal Mint
D. 23.6 mm
W. 5.70 g

G140A    1979    *Proof* as G140.    T. 20.000
D. 23.7 mm
W. 5.75 g

# Ten New Pence

*G161*

| | | | | |
|---|---|---|---|---|
| G161 | 1968 | *Obverse* as G140 but larger.<br>*Reverse:* Guernsey cow as G77A but without artist's initials; 10 above, 1968 and NEW PENCE below. | | T. 600.000<br>M. Royal Mint<br>D. 28.4 mm<br>W. 11.28 g |

*G162*

| | | | | |
|---|---|---|---|---|
| G162 | 1970 | As G161 except for date. | | T. 300.000<br>M. Royal Mint<br>D. 28.45 mm<br>W. 11.28 g |

*G163A*

| | | | | |
|---|---|---|---|---|
| G163A | 1971 | *Proof* only, as G162 except for date. | | G. 10.000<br>M. Royal Mint<br>D. 28.4 mm<br>W. 11.38 g |

# Ten Pence

*G164*

| | | | |
|---|---|---|---|
| G164 | 1977 | *Obverse* as G163A.<br>*Reverse* as G163A but TEN PENCE below 1977. | T. 480.000<br>M. Royal Mint<br>D. 28.45 mm<br>W. 11.23 g |

*G165*

| | | | |
|---|---|---|---|
| G165 | 1979 | As G164 except for date. | T. 659.000<br>M. Royal Mint<br>D. 28.5 mm<br>W. 11.32 g |
| G165A | 1979 | *Proof* as G165. | T. 20.000<br>D. 28.5 mm<br>W. 11.43 g |

# Twenty Pence (7-sided, plain Edge)

*G186*

| | | | |
|---|---|---|---|
| G186 | 1982 | *Obverse* as G235 but smaller.<br>*Reverse:* 20 separating TWENTY PENCE above a Guernsey milk can; 1982 below. | T.<br>M. Royal Mint<br>D. 21.4 mm<br>W. 5.0 g |

# Twenty Five Pence

*G207*

| | | | |
|---|---|---|---|
| G207 | 1972 | Silver Wedding Commemorative issue.<br>*Obverse:* Shield from the Bailiwick Seal, surmounted by a sprig of laurel, separating date 19 72; · BAILIWICK OF GUERNSEY · above; TWENTY FIVE PENCE below.<br>*Reverse:* Eros, the God of Love, tip-toe on Guernsey lily and rose design by Arnold Machin; inscription: ELIZABETH AND PHILIP·:· 1947 1972 ·:· ·:· ·:· | T. 56.250<br>M. Royal Mint<br>D. 38.5 mm<br>W. 28.35 g |
| G207A | 1972 | *AR Proof* as G207; frosted relief; coarse milling. | T. 15.000<br>D. 38.6 mm<br>W. 28.37 g |

*G208*

| | | | |
|---|---|---|---|
| G208 | 1977 | Silver Jubilee commemorative issue.<br>*Obverse:* QUEEN ELIZABETH THE SECOND 1952–1977 round (below) crowned bust *r*.<br>*Reverse:* Castle Cornet; BAILIWICK OF GUERNSEY above, TWENTY FIVE PENCE below (designer: Bernard Sindall). | T. 207.400<br>M. Royal Mint<br>D. 38.61 mm<br>(official)<br>W. 28.13 g<br>(official 28.276 g) |
| G208A | 1977 | *AR proof* as G208; frosted relief; coarse milling. | T. 25.000<br>W. 28.63 g |

*G209*

| | | | |
|---|---|---|---|
| G209 | 1978 | Royal visit commemorative issue.<br>*Obverse:* QUEEN ELIZABETH THE SECOND ·<br>TWENTY FIVE PENCE · round crowned bust *r.*<br>*Reverse:* Shield with sprig as *obverse* G207, date 19 78 to each side; BAILIWICK OF GUERNSEY above · ROYAL VISIT · below | T. 105.220<br>M. Royal Mint<br>D. 38.6 mm<br>W. 28.19 g |
| G209A | 1978 | *AR proof* as G209; frosted relief; coarse milling. | T. 25.000<br>W. 27.85 g |

*G210*

| | | | |
|---|---|---|---|
| G210 | 1980 | Queen Mother's 80th Birthday commemorative issue.<br>*Obverse:* QUEEN ELIZABETH II · BAILIWICK OF GUERNSEY · 25 PENCE · round crowned bust *r.*<br>*Reverse:* Crowned bust of Queen Mother *l.,* above a garland of flowers which includes the Guernsey lily and the Elizabeth of Glamis rose, designed by Franka Belsky; legend: QUEEN ELIZABETH THE QUEEN MOTHER 1900 · AUGUST 4 · 1980. | T. 150.000<br>M. Royal Mint<br>D. 38.6 mm<br>W. 29.35 g |
| G210 | 1980 | *AR Proof* as G210; frosted relief; coarse milling. | T. 25.000<br>W. 28.17g |

*G211*

343

| | | | | |
|---|---|---|---|---|
| G211 | 1981 | Royal Wedding commemorative. *Obverse* as G210. *Reverse:* heads of Prince Charles and Lady Diana Spencer to *l.* and *r.* of field; Prince of Wales feathers above; small shield from Bailiwick seal below, resting on 2 sprays of Guernsey lilies; legend: H.R.H. THE PRINCE OF WALES THE LADY DIANA SPENCER · 1981 · | | T. 100.000 M. Royal Mint D. 38.6 mm W. 28.45 g |
| G211 | 1981 | *AR proof* as G211; frosted relief; coarse milling. | | T. 35.000 D. 38.7 mm (official 38.61) W. 28.09 g |

## Fifty New Pence (7-sided)

*G232*

| | | | |
|---|---|---|---|
| G232 | 1969 | *Obverse* from same matrix as G161, set in seven-sided border. *Reverse:* the Ducal Cap of the Duke of Normandy; 50 dividing NEW PENCE above; 1969 below; designer: Sir Anthony Wagner. | T. 200.000 M. Royal Mint D. 30.0 mm W. 13.48 g |

*G233*

| | | | |
|---|---|---|---|
| G233 | 1970 | As G232 except for date. | T. 200.000 M. Royal Mint D. 30.0 mm W. 13.68 g |

*G234A*

| | | | |
|---|---|---|---|
| G234 | 1971 | *Proof* only, as G233 except for date. | T. 10.000<br>M. Royal Mint<br>D. 30.0 mm<br>W. 13.33 g |

# Fifty Pence (7-sided)

*G235A*

G235   1979   *Proof* only.  
              *Obverse* as G234A.  
              *Reverse:* 50 dividing FIFTY PENCE above Ducal Cap; 1979 below.

T. 20.000  
M. Royal Mint  
D. 30.0 mm  
W. 13.43 g

*G236*

G236   1981   As G235A except for date.

T.  
M. Royal Mint  
D. 30.0 mm  
W. 13.57 g

# One Pound (Nickel Silver)

*G257*

| | | | | |
|---|---|---|---|---|
| G257 | 1981 | *Obverse:* the Guernsey Arms based on the Bailiwick Seal (see G21). | | T. |
| | | | | M. Royal Mint |
| | | *Reverse:* a stem of Guernsey lilies; ONE POUND above, 1981 below. | | D. 22.1 mm |
| | | | | W. 8.08 g |
| | | BAILIWICK OF GUERNSEY incuse on milled edge; 2.85 mm thick. | | |

    i Edge inscription normal;
    ii Edge inscription inverted.

| | | | | |
|---|---|---|---|---|
| G257A | 1981 | *AU proof* as G257 but 1.6 mm thick; frosted relief; coarse milling; no incuse edge inscription. | | T. 4.500 |
| | | | | W. 8.02 g |

*G258*

| | | | | |
|---|---|---|---|---|
| G257B | 1981 | *AU proof Piefort* as G257 but 2.85 mm thick. | | T. 500 |
| | | | | W. 15.90 g |
| G258 | 1983 | *Obverse:* as G257 but shield and legend smaller and extra circle of beading. | | T. |
| | | | | M. Royal Mint |
| | | *Reverse: HMS Crescent;* ONE POUND above, 1983 below. | | D. 22.5 mm |
| | | | | W. 9.5 g |
| | | Edge as G257 but *flan* 3.25 mm thick. | | |

    i Edge inscription normal;
    ii Edge inscription inverted.

# Bibliography

**Ancient and Armorican**

| | |
|---|---|
| Akermann, J. Y. | *Ancient Coins... Hispania-Gallia-Britannia,* London, 1846 |
| Allen, D. F. | *The Origins of Coinage in Britain: A Reappraisal,* London, 1960; reprinted from *Problems of the Iron Age in Southern Britain,* ed. S. Frere, London, 1958 [re Le Catillon] |
| | *The La Marquanderie hoard of Armorican coins,* Num. Chron. 5th Series 5 (1939), pp 180–184 |
| | *The Sark Hoard of Celtic Coins and Phalerae,* Num. Chron. 7th Series 7 (1968), pp 37–54 |
| | *An Introduction to Celtic Coins,* British Museum Publications, 1978 |
| | *New Light on the Date of Early British Coins – Notes on the Le Catillon, Jersey, Hoard of Armorican Coins,* Num. Circ. Vol LXVI, 4 (April 1958) pp 85–87; also BSJ Vol 17 III (1959) pp 259–264 |
| | *The Coins of the Ancient Celts,* Edinburgh, 1980, ed. Daphne Nash |
| Barral, M. and others | *Quelques éléments de métallurgie monetaire gauloise,* in Journées de Paléometallurgie, 22–23 février 1983, Université de Compiègne |
| Barralis, J. see Barral M. | |
| Barthélemy, A. de | *Etudes sur les monnaies gauloises découvertes à Jersey en 1875,* RN III 2 (1884) pp 177–202 |
| | *Essai de classification chronologique de différents groupes de monnaies gauloises,* in CAIBL 4th Series XVIII (1890) pp 173–179 |
| | *Légendes des monnaies gauloises,* RC IX (1887) pp 26–35 |
| | *Le Monnayage du nord-ouest de la Gaule,* RC XII pp 309–316 |
| Betham, Sir W. | *The Gael and Cymbri...,* Dublin, 1834 |
| Blanchet, A. | *Traité des monnaies gauloises,* Paris, 1905; reprinted Bologna, 1971 |
| | *Chronique de numismatique celtique* [critique of Sir Cyril Brooke q. v.], EC I (1936), p 134 |
| Bourde de la Rogerie, A. | *Les monnaies gauloises des îles de la Manche,* SG Vol 9 (1917–25) pp 111–115 |
| Brooke, Sir C. | *The Philippus in the West and the Belgic Invasions of Britain,* Num. Chron. 5th Series XIII (1933) pp 88–138 |
| | *The Distribution of Gaulish and British Coins in Britain,* Antiquity, September 1933 |
| Burdo, C. | *Le Catillon Hoard* (Archaeological Report), BSJ Vol 17 II (1958) pp 121–123, Vol 17 III (1958) pp 211–213 |

| | |
|---|---|
| Cable, E. K. | *Report on Coins found at Rozel,* BSJ I, 2 (1876) pp 29–31 |
| | *Report on Coins found at Rozel Bay,* Jersey, BSJ I (1878) pp 85–88 |
| | *Gaulish, Roman and French Coins,* BSJ I (1880) pp 207–210 |
| | *Gaulish, Roman and Parthian Coins,* BSJ I (1881) pp 274–276 |
| | *Roman and Gaulish coins found at Rozel, Jersey,* BSJ I (1886) pp 119–123 |
| Callow, P. see McBurney, C.B.M. | |
| Castelin, K. | *Keltische Münzen, Katalog der Sammlung des Schweizerischen Landesmuseums Zürich I;* see also Forrer, R. |
| Chabouillet, A. see Muret, E. | |
| Colbert de Beaulieu, Dr. J. B. | *Le Trésor de Jersey–11 et la numismatique celtiques des deux Bretagnes,* RBN CIII (1957) pp 47–88 [re Le Catillon] |
| | *Trouvaille de Jersey–11 (2ᵉ lot),* Notices de numismatique armoricaine, AB 65 I (1958) pp 38–43 |
| | *Un 3ᵉ lot de la récolte de Jersey–11,* RBN CV (1959) pp 49–57 [re Le Catillon] |
| | *[Le Catillon],* Num. Circ. LXVI (April 1958) pp 85–87 |
| | *Armorican Coin Hoards in the Channel Islands,* PPS XXIV (1958) pp 201–210 |
| | *Les Monnaies Celtiques des Vénètes.* MSHAB XXXIII |
| | *La Trouvaille de Jersey–6 provient-elle d'un lot unique?,* AB LX 2 (1953) pp 326–328 |
| | *Un lot inédit de la trouvaille de Jersey–6,* AB LX 2 (1953) pp 323–8 |
| | *De la poterie néolithique à la monnaie celtique en Bretagne* [re. axes as currency], AB Vol 70 I (March 1963) pp 52–57 |
| | *Armorican coin hoards in the Channel Islands,* BSJ XVII (1958) pp 167–8 |
| | *Un monnayage celtique non attribué, isolé dans le nord-est de l'Armorique,* AB 59 I pp 81–93 |
| | *Traité de numismatique celtique I Méthodologie des ensembles,* Paris (Centre de Recherches d'Historie ancienne Vol 5 série numismatique), 1973 |
| | *Trésors de monnaies celtiques de l'île de Jersey et la circulation des monnaies gauloises,* BSNAF, 29.5.1957 |
| | *Les trouvailles de monnaies Osismiennes de l'île de Jersey,* Notices de numismatique celtique, AB 63 I (1956) pp 32–36 |
| | *Le Monnayage Coriosolite,* Num. Circ. (July 1951) pp 322–4; transcr. French Num. Soc. |
| | *La récolte de monnaies armoricaines de Jersey,* AB 65 I (1958) pp 44–53 |
| Cornwall, Dr. I. and Johnston D. E. | *A Short Provisional Account of Archaeology in Jersey. The Palaeolithic... to the Roman,* Société Jersiaise publication |
| Dalido, P. | *Jersey, île agricole anglo-normande,* Vannes, 1951 |

| | |
|---|---|
| de la Rogerie, B. | *Les Monnaies Gauloises des Îles de la Manche,* SG Vol IX pp 111–115 |
| de la Tour, H. | *Atlas de monnaies gauloises,* Paris, 1892; reprinted for Spink & Son 1965 |
| de la Vincelle, G. | *Receuil de Monumens Antiques... dans l'ancienne Gaule* I, II, Paris, 1817 |
| Donop, Baron de | *Les médailles Gallo-gaëliques, Description de la trouvaille de l'île de Jersey,* Hanover, 1838 |
| Duchalais, A. | *Description des médailles gauloises faisant partie des collections de la Bibliothèque Royale,* Paris, 1846 |
| Evans, J. | *The Coins of the Ancient Britons,* London, 1864 |
| Fillioux, A. | *... Monnaies de la Gaule,* Paris, 1867 |
| Forrer, R. | *Keltische Numismatik der Rhein- und Donaulande* (Strassburg, 1908), enlarged edition, revised by K. Castelin and others, Graz, 1968 |
| Gruel, K. | *Le Trésor de Trébry (Côtes du Nord)...,* Paris 1981; see also Barral, M. |
| Hawkes, J. | *The Archaeology of the Channel Islands II: The Bailiwick of Jersey,* London, 1937 |
| Head, B. V. | *Historia Numorum,* Oxford, 1911 |
| Higginbottom, R. W. | *Roman coin finds in Jersey,* Num. Circ. Vol 87, 2 (February 1979) pp 62–63 and Vol 88, 2 p 211 |
| Hucher, E. | *L'art gaulois ou les Gaulois d'après leurs médailles,* Paris, Le Mans, 1868 |
| Jeuffrain, A. | *Essai d'Interprétation des types de quelques médailles muettes émises par les Celtes-Gaulois,* Tours, 1846 |
| Johnston, D. E. see Cornwall, Dr. I | |
| Jones, Professors G. & T. (translators) | *The Mabinogion,* London, 1978 |
| Kendrick, T. D. | *The Archaeology of the Channel Islands I: The Bailiwick of Guernsey,* London, 1928 |
| Lambert, E. | *Essai sur la Numismatique gauloise du Nord-Ouest de la France,* Paris, Bayeux, 1844 |
| Lecoq-Kerneven, M. | *Carte Numismatique de la Péninsule Armoricaine,* Société de Numismatique et d'Archéologie, Paris, 1867 |
| Lowsley, Lieut.-Col.B. | *The Coinages of the Channel Islands* (pp 1–9), London, 1897 |
| Mack, R. P. | *The Coinage of Ancient Britain,* London (1953), 3rd edition 1975 |
| Mauger, P. | Manuscript *Catalogue of Roman, Greek and Celtic Coins,* deposited in the Public Library, St. Helier, Jersey. |
| McBurney, C.B.M. and Callow P. | *The Cambridge excavations at La Cotte de St. Brelade, Jersey–a preliminary report* PPS Vol 37 (1971) pp 162–207 |
| Muret, E. and Chabouillet A. | *Catalogue des Monnaies gauloises de la Bibliothèque nationale,* Paris, 1889 |

Nash, D. see Allen D. F.

Nasir, M. J. see Thompson, F. C.

Oberreiner, C. — *Les premiers habitants de Jersey,* BSJ Vol 9 I (1919) pp 15–17

Oddy, W. A. (Editor) — *Scientific Studies in Numismatics:* Occasional Paper No 18 pp 41–52, British Museum, 1980 [Analysis of Coriosolite coins]

Olson, R. J. M. — *Giotto's Portrait of Halley's Comet,* Scientific American (May 1979) Vol 240 No 5 pp 134–42

Pink, K. — *Einführung in die keltische Münzkunde,* Archaeologica Austriaca Beiheft 4, Vienna, 1960

Poste, B. — *Celtic Inscriptions on Gaulish and British Coins,* London, 1861

Renouf J. and Urry, J. — *The first farmers in the Channel Islands,* London, 1976

Roth, B. — *Ancient Gaulish Coins, including those of the Channel Islands,* London, 1913

Rybot, Major N. V. L. — *Armorican Art,* enlarged from an article first published in BSJ (1937)

*Note on the Gaulish & Roman Coins belonging to the Society,* BSJ IX 4 (1922) pp 367–368

*A note on the Rozel Hoards of Gaulish coins,* BSJ (1934) pp 321–327

*Some notes on the Le Catillon Hoard of Armorican Coins,* BSJ Vol 17 III (1959) p 269

Sahlins, M. — *Stone Age Economics,* London, 1974

Sjœstedt-Jonval, M.-L. — *Légendes Épiques irlandaises et monnaies gauloises – recherches sur la constitution de la légende de Cuchulainn,* EC V 13 (1939) pp 1–77

Stapleton, H. E. — *The Coinage of the Channel Islands,* Transactions of the International Numismatic Congress, London 30th June–6th July 1936

Thompson, F. C. and Nasir, M. J. — *The Manufacture of Celtic Coins from the La Marquanderie Hoard,* Num. Chron. 1972 pp 61–73

Urry, J. see Renouf, J.

Wheeler, Sir M. & K. M. — *Hill-Forts of Northern France* (pp 48–52), Oxford, 1957

Wymer, J. — *The Palaeolithic Age,* London, 1982

**The Jersey Mint**

| | |
|---|---|
| Balleine, Rev. G. R. | *All for the King – The Life Story of Sir George Carteret* (1609–1680), Société Jersiaise, Jersey, 1976 |
| Chevalier, Jean | *Journal . . .: Recueil des Chosses les plus remarcables $\bar{q}$ se sont passes en ceste Isle de Jersey . . .* [1643–1651], Société Jersiaise, Jersey, 1906–1914 |
| Coate, Mary | *The Royalist Mints of Truro and Exeter 1642-6,* Num. Chron, 5th Series Vol VIII pp 213–48 |
| Farquhar, Helen | *A Lost Coinage in the Channel Islands,* Num. Chron. 5th Series Vol VIII pp 119–212 |
| Fleetwood, William | *Chronicum preciosum, or an account of English money . . .,* London, 1707 |
| Hoskins, Dr. S. Elliott | *Charles II in the Channel Islands,* London, 1854 |
| Hyde, Sir Edward | *Letter to Sir Edward Nicholas,* no 2447 in the Calendar of State Papers at the Bodleian Library Vol I pp 362–3 (shelfmark MS Clarendon State Papers 29, folios 107, 108) |
| Lockett, R. C. | *Notes on the Mints of Truro and Exeter under Charles I,* BNJ XXII (1936-7) pp 227–46 |
| Royal Mint | *Records Book* IV p 42 etc [re short weight] |
| Saunders, A. C. | *Jean Chevalier and his Times,* Jersey, 1936 |
| Selby, Peter | *Provincial and Civil War Mints of Charles I – The West Country,* CM Vol 5 No 11 pp 610–11, 618 |
| Vaughan, Rice | *A Discourse of Coin and Coinage . . .,* London, 1675 |
| Violet, Thomas | *An humble declaration to the Lords . . . touching the transport of gold & silver . . .,* London, 1643 |
| | *Mysteries and Secrets of Trade and Mint-affairs,* London, 1653 |

**General**

| | |
|---|---|
| Anon | *An authentic narrative of the oppressions of the Islanders of Jersey,* Vol I, London, 1771 |
| Ansted, D. T. | *The Channel Islands,* London, 1862 |
| Balleine, G. R. | *A Biographical Dictionary of Jersey,* London, 1948 |
| Banyai, R. | *The German Military Occupation of the British Channel Islands (Jersey and Guernsey) and Occupation Monetary Policy, 1940–41,* IBNS Vol 10, 1 (September 1970) pp 42–4 |
| Berry, William | *A History of the Island of Guernsey . . .,* London, 1815 |
| Bigot, Alexis | *Essai sur les Monnaies du Royaume et Duché de Bretagne,* Paris, 1857 |
| Blanchet, A. and Dieudonné, A. | *Manuel de Numismatique française,* 4 vols, Paris 1912–1936 (Reprinted Bologna, 1969) |

| | |
|---|---|
| Blanchet, J.-A. | *Nouveau Manuel de numismatique du moyen âge et moderne*, 2 Vols., Paris, 1890 |
| Breton, P. N. | *Guide Populaire Illustré des Monnaies et Médailles Canadiennes etc*, Montreal, 1894 & 1912 (Reprinted 1963) |
| Buckley, R. F. | *Devins & Bolton Counterstamped Pieces Revisited,* Addenda and Errata, CNJ Vol 27 No 1 (January 1981) pp 8–10 |
| 'C. A.' | *Comparative value of English, Jersey, French and Livres Tournois Currency...,* Jersey, 1854 |
| Cable, Edwin K. | *Gaulish, Roman and French Coins,* BSJ I (1880) pp 207–10 |
| [Channel Islands' Exhibition 1871] | *Official General Report & Financial Statement,* Jersey, 1872 |
| Ciani, Louis | *Les Monnaies Royales Françaises de Hugues Capet à Louis XVI...,* Paris, 1926 |
| Coton, L. A. | *The Channel Islands – Part I, The States of Jersey,* ANS (May 1964) pp 187–94 |
| | *The Channel Islands – Part II, Guernsey,* ANS (June 1964) pp 211–13 |
| Craig, Sir John H. M. | *The Mint – a history...,* Cambridge, 1953 |
| Curtis, S. Carey | *The Currency of Guernsey in Historical Times,* SG Vol 9 (1917–25) pp 101–10 |
| Davis, W. J. | *Nineteenth Century Token Coinage...,* London, 1904 |
| de Gruchy, G. F. B. | *Medieval Land Tenures in Jersey,* Jersey, 1957 |
| de Sausmarez, Sir H., Bt | *The Extentes of Guernsey 1248 and 1331...,* Guernsey, 1934 |
| de Sausmarez, R. see Priaulx, T. F. | |
| Dieudonné, A. see Blanchet, A. | |
| Dolley, R. H. M. and Morrison, K. F. | *The Carolingian Coins in the British Museum,* London, 1966 |
| Duncan, J. | *History of Guernsey,* London, 1841 |
| Dupont, G. | *Histoire du Cotentin et de ses Îles,* Vol I & II, Caen, 1870 |
| Du Pré, J. W. | *Jersey's Copper Coins* BSJ, XV pp 399–410 |
| Du Quesne Bird | *A Catalogue of Original Documents relating to the Monetary History of Guernsey,* Num. Circ. LXXXIII, no 5 (May 1975) pp 201–2; no 6 (June 1975) pp 240–1; no 7–8 (July–August 1975) pp 286–7; no 10 (October 1975) pp 387–9 |
| | *A Catalogue of Original Documents relating to the Monetary History of Jersey,* Num. Circ. LXXXIV, no 3 (March 1976) pp 99–100; no 4 (April 1976) pp 145–6 |
| | *A Guernsey coinage of 1871,* Num. Circ. LXXXVII, 10 (October 1979) p 441 |
| Eastwood, S. K. | *Coins and Tokens of Jersey,* Numisma I, 1 (May 1939) pp 1–6 |
| Edmundson, J. | *The Decimals of the Islands,* MCB I, (July–August 1971) pp 3–4 |
| Exley, W. | *Guernsey Coinage,* Guernsey, 1968 |

| | |
|---|---|
| Falle, P. | *An account of the Isle of Jersey,* Jersey, 1734 |
| Falle, R. | Typescript notes re first copper currency of Jersey (deposited in Public Library, Jersey) |
| Finlaison, M. and Holdsworth P. | *Excavations on the Île Agois, Jersey,* BSJ XXII, 3 (1979) pp 322–346 |
| Forrer, L. | *A Biographical Dictionary of Medallists,* (8 Vol's), London, 1904–1930 |
| Galbraith, Professor J. K. | *MONEY. Whence it came, where it went,* New York, 1975 |
| Gibbs, J. | *Sir Isaac Brock and the Brock Half-Pennies,* CNJ Vol 10, 1 pp 13–15 (Reprinted from The Numismatist, 1902) |
| Greenwood, D. | *Channel Island coins trace history spanning 22 centuries,* 'Coins' no 95 (November 1971) pp 1394, 1396, 1400, 1402, 1404, 1406 |
| Grunthal, H. see Morrison, K. F. | |
| Haskins, C. H. | *Norman Institutions,* Harvard University Press, 1918 |
| Havet, J. | *Les Cours royales des Îles Normandes,* Paris, 1878 |
| Hawkins, R. N. P. | *Dictionary of Makers of British Nineteenth Century Metallic tickets and checks,* supplement I [re Henry Toy & Co.], SCMB no 620 Vol 4 (1970) p 127 |
| Hocking, W. J. | *Catalogue of the Coins, Tokens, Medals, Dies and Seals in the Museum of the Royal Mint,* Vol's I, II, London 1906, 1910 |
| Holdsworth, P. see Finlaison M. | |
| Holmes, U. T. Jnr | *Coins of old French Literature,* Speculum Vol 31, no 2 pp 316–20 |
| Howlett, C. J. | *History & Catalogue of Channel Island Coinages,* Guernsey, 1968 |
| Jacob, J. | *Annals of the Bailiwick of Guernsey,* Guernsey, 1830 |
| Josset, C. R. | *Money in Britain,* London, 1962 |
| Kromas, J. A. | *George Edward Kruger-Gray,* CNJ Vol 10, 4 (April 1965) pp 137–9, 144 |
| Le Blanc | *Traité Historique des Monnaies de France,* Paris, 1703 |
| Le Geyt, P. | *Les manuscrits de ... sur la Constitution etc.,* Jersey, 1846 |
| Le Maistre, F. | *Dictionnaire Jersiais-Français,* Don Balleine Trust, 1966 |
| Le Marchant, R. | *Paper Treasure of the Channel Islands,* Guernsey |
| [Le Quesne, C.] | *Observations on the Currency of the Island of Jersey by a Member of the Chamber of Commerce,* Jersey, 1845 |
| | *A Constitutional History of Jersey,* London, 1856 |
| Levesque, J. C. | *The Quality and Efficiency of Royal Mint Dies a Century ago,* CNJ Vol 23,8 (September 1978) pp 309–11 |
| Lowsley, Lieut-Col. B. | *The Coinages of the Channel Islands,* London, 1897 |

| | |
|---|---|
| Marshall-Fraser, Lieut-Col. W. | *The Coinages of the Channel Islands,* SG 1948 pp 298–332 |
| | *A History of Banking in the Channel Islands and a Record of Bank-Note Issues,* SG 1949 pp 378–443 |
| Messervy, A. | *LSD versus £-Florins-Parts,* Jersey, 1900 |
| [Messervy, D.] | *Journal de Daniel Messervy 1769–1772,* Jersey (Soc. Jersiaise), 1896 |
| Morrison, K. F. with Grunthal, H. | *Carolingian Coinage,* New York (The American Numismatic Society), 1967; see also Dolley R.H.M. |
| Nicolle, E. T. | *Mont Orgueil Castle,* Jersey, 1921 |
| | *L'Administration des Îles Normandes et leurs rapports avec le Cotentin,* Caen, 1925 |
| | *The Town of St. Helier,* Jersey, (2nd edition) 1972 |
| Ozeray, M. J. | *Histoire de la Ville et du Duché de Bouillon,* Luxemburg, 1827 |
| Plees, W. | *An account of the Island of Jersey,* Jersey, 1817 (pp 74–76) |
| Poingdestre, Jean | *Caesarea or A Discourse of the island of Jersey,* Jersey, 1682 |
| Priaulx, T. F. and de Sausmarez, R. | *The Guernsey Stocking Export Trade in the 17th Century,* SG XVII, 2 (1961) pp 210–22 |
| Pridmore, F. | *Coins of the British Commonwealth of Nations, Part I,* London (Spink & Son), 1960 |
| | *Notes on Colonial Coins. A suggested coinage for the Island of Jersey 1942,* Num. Circ. LXVIII, 7–8 (July–August 1960) p 161 |
| Prou, M. | *Les monnaies mérovingiennes,* Paris, 1896 (reprinted Graz, 1969) |
| Ramon, G. | *Histoire de la Banque de France . . .,* Paris, 1929 |
| Ruding, Rev. R. | *Annals of the Coinage of Great Britain . . .,* 3rd edition, 3 Vol's, London, 1840 |
| Rybot, Major N.V.L. | *A Report on the Excavations made in the North-East outer slopes of Mont Orgeuil Castle during the latter half of the year 1940,* BSJ XV, II (1950) pp 239–48 |
| | *Gorey Castle,* 5th edition, Jersey (States of Jersey), 1949 |
| [Seaby] | *New Guernsey Decimal Coinage,* SCMB Vol 9, 625 (1970) pp 310–11 |
| Seaby, P and Purvey, F. | *Standard Catalogue of British Coins, Vol 2, Coins of Scotland, Ireland & the Islands (Jersey, Guernsey, Man & Lundy),* London (Seaby Publications Ltd), 1984 |
| Sealy, D. L. F. | *The Guernsey Eight Doubles of 1864,* BNJ, 1964 pp 164–7; see also *Coin Varieties,* Coins (July 1968) p 609 |
| | *Coin Varieties* [re Guernsey 8 doubles 1893], CM Vol 3, 10 (October 1966) p 626 |
| | *Coin Varieties* [re Jersey 1/12 shilling 1933 etc], Coins Vol 8,3 (March 1971) pp 24–5 |
| Sear, D. R. | *Roman Coins and their values,* London (Seaby Publications Ltd) 1964 (revised 1970) |

| | |
|---|---|
| Sinel, L. P. | *The German Occupation of Jersey. A complete diary of events from June 1940 to June 1945,* Jersey (Evening Post) [1946] |
| Société Jersiaise | *Extente des Iles de Jersey, Guernsey, Aurigny et Serk... 1274. – Edouard I,* Jersey, 1877 |
| | *Rapport des Commissaires envoyés à Jersey. L'an 7 du Règne de Henri VIII,* Jersey, 1878 |
| | *Documents Historiques relatifs aux Iles de la Manche... 1199–1244,* Jersey, 1879 |
| | *Extente de l'Ile de Jersey 1668. – Charles II,* Jersey, 1882 |
| | *Extente de l'Ile de Jersey 1528. – Henry VIII,* Jersey, 1881. |
| | *Extente de l'Ile de Jersey 1668. – Charles II,* Jersey, 1882 |
| | *Extente de l'Ile de Jersey 1749. – George II,* Jersey, 1883 |
| | *Documents relatifs aux Iles de la Manche tirés des rôles des Lettres Closes... 1205–1327,* Parts 1 & 2, Jersey, 1891, 1893 |
| | *Ancient Petitions of the Chancery and the Exchequer...,* Jersey, 1902 |
| | *Rolls of the Assizes held in the Channel Islands in... 1309,* Jersey, 1903 |
| | *Cartulaire de Jersey, Guernesey, et les autres Iles Normandes: Recueil de Documents...,* Jersey, 1918–1924 |
| Sutherland, Dr. C. | *Jersey's Liberation Penny,* BSJ XV part IV (1952) p 464 |
| Sweeny, J. O. | *A Numismatic History of the Birmingham Mint,* Birmingham, 1981 |
| Sydenham, E. A. | *The Coinage of the Roman Republic,* London, 1952 |
| Tupper, F. B. | *The Chronicles of Castle Cornet...,* Guernsey, 1851 |
| | *History of Guernsey,* 2nd edition, Guernsey, 1876 |
| Unwin, G. | *Finance and Trade under Edward III,* Manchester University Press, 1918 |
| White, M. | *The Carteret Priaulx Papers (The Influence of the Napoleonic Wars on Guernsey),* SG XVII, part IV (1963) pp 447–88 |
| Wilkinson, R. L. | *A Brief History of Jersey's Coinage,* ANS XXXII (September, 1967) pp 23–6 |
| Willey, R. C. | *Slogans found on Canadian Colonial Tokens,* CNJ Vol 16 no. 2 (February 1971) pp 38–42 |
| Williams, T. | *The Importance of the Channel Islands in British relations with the Continent during the Thirteenth and Fourteenth Centuries; a study in Historical Geography,* BSJ XI (1928), pp XVII–XVIII and 1–89 |
| Wilson, J. S. G. | *French Banking Structure and Credit Policy,* London, 1957 |

**Publications**

| | |
|---|---|
| AB | *Annales de Bretagne* (Faculté des lettres de Rennes) |
| ANS | *Report of the Australian Numismatic Society* |
| BNJ | *British Numismatic Journal* (British Numismatic Society) |
| BSJ | *Bulletin of the Société Jersiaise* |
| BSNAF | *Bulletin de la Société nationale des Antiquaires de France* |
| CAIBL | *Comtes rendus de l'Académie des Inscriptions et Belles Lettres* |
| CM | *Coins and Medals* |
| CNJ | *Canadian Numismatic Journal* |
| EC | *Études Celtiques* |
| IBNS | *International Bank Note Society* |
| MCB | *Modern Coins & Banknotes* |
| MSHAB | *Mémoires de la Société Historique et Archéologique de Bretagne* |
| Num. Chron. | *Numismatic Chronicle* (Royal Numismatic Society) |
| Num. Circ. | *Spink's Numismatic Circular* |
| PPS | *Proceeds of the Prehistoric Society* |
| RBN | *Revue belge de Numismatique* |
| RC | *Revue Celtique* |
| RN | *Revue Numismatique* |
| SCMB | *Seaby's Coin & Medal Bulletin* |
| SG | *Société Guernesiaise, Report and Transactions* |

# General Index

A. Postumius Albinus  71
Abbey of Montebourg  86
Abbey of Pleinmont  94
Abbey of St. Saviour  87
Aberystwyth  116
Abrincatui  15, *18, 19*, 26, 33, 39, 56, 59, *62, 63, 64*
*Académie Française*  109
Aedui  20, *30*, 37
*Aes grave*  7, 69
*Aes rude*  7, 69
Agathocles  *52*
Agincourt  97
Alamanni  77
Alaric II  76
Alaric III  76
Albert 'the Good'  173, *174*
Alderney  70, 85, 90, 92, 104, 132, 137, 138, 139, *160*, 170, 173, *200*, 326, *336, 337*
Alesia  41
Alexandra  174
*Alexandra* (sailing ship)  *299*
Allen, D.F.  21, 24, 34 f.
Allia  10
Amber  9
Anastasius I  *76*
Angers  78, 79, 80
Anjou  79, 85 f.
Anne, Duchess of Brittany  100
Anson, Captain George  173, 176
Antoine de Bourbon  104
Antoine de Navarre  104
Antonius Pius  72
Appius Claudius  71
Aquitaine  76, 81, 97
Arborici  77
Arelate  73, 76
Arles  79
Arthur  65, 66
Arthur II  91
Arverni  12, *30*
Ashburnham, John  113, 117, 118
*Assignats*  *131,* 142
Augia  78
Aurelian  72
Aulerci Cenomani  15, *35, 37,* 39
Auriol  *54*
Austerlitz  135
Austrasia  77, 78, 81

Avranches  79
Axeheads  7

Bagatelle  39
Bagot Hotel  181
Baiocasses  15, *18, 19,* 23, *36,* 59, *66*
Bank of Amsterdam  108
Bank of England  131, 136, 137, 147, 163
Bank of Guernsey  131, 191, *199*
*Banque de France*  135
*Banque Générale*  125
*Banque Royale*  125, 126
Barthélemy, A. de  26, 70
Battle of Jersey  171, 172, *257, 297,* 298
Bavaria  30
Bayeux  55, 79, 83
Béarn  99, *102,* 104
Belfast Museum  59
Belgic coin types  34, 60
Belgic migrations  20
Bellosanne  87
Benoit XII  96
Berkeley, Sir John  122
Berry, William  110, 111
Bibliography  349 f.
*Bibliothèque Nationale*  26
*Bibliothèque Royale de Belgique*  26
Birmingham Jersey Show  *6,* 181
Bishop de Jersey  139, 140, 199
Bishop of Durham  84
Bituriges Cubi  20, *30,* 37
Blampied, Edmund  165, 253 f.
Blanchet, A.  30
Blondeau, Pierre  103
Bolton, Matthew  131, 135, 139
Bouillon  141
Bouley Bay  25
Bourbon  129
Bourde de la Rogerie  39
Bradbury, Wilkinson & Co.  171
Brennan, C.  182
Brennus  10
Brenton, H.  182
Bretigny  97
Brighton Hotel  181
Briot, Nicholas  109
Bristol  114
British 'B', 'O' coin types  38
British Dairy Farmers' Assoc.  181

British Museum   23, 26, 39, 57, 73, 82, 121, 309
British West Africa   315
Brock, Daniel de Lisle   172, *176, 211*
Brock, Sir Isaac   143, 144, 172, *211, 212*
Bulteau, Auguste   182
Burgundy   9, 76, 78, 81, 99

C. Licinius Macer   71
C. Postumius   *71*
Cable   26, 70
Caesar   9, 12, 14, *30*, 41, *42*, 55, 71
Caesarean Billiards   181
*Caisse d'Escompte*   131
*Caisse des comptes courants*   135
Calais   98, 99
Caletes   20, *30*
Cambria Products   183
Cambridge University   101
Canada   129, 143, 144
Canterbury   80
Canute   83
Capel   119
Caribert I   78
Carloman   81, 82
Carnutes   20
Carolingians   81 f.
Carteret, Baron John   *176*
Carteret, Sir George   113 f.
Castel de Rozel   25 f., 44, 70
Castle Cornet   171, *210, 342*
Catherine II   132
Catherine de Medicis   104
Chalon   78
Changarnier   30
Channel Islands Exhibition   157, 180, *181*
Charlemagne   *181*
Charles I   *110*, 119, 121, 122, 123
Charles I of Arches   109
Charles II   113, 122, *274*
Charles IV 'le Bel'   *191*
Charles V   97
Charles VI   97, *98*
Charles VII   99, 100
Charles VIII   100, 102
Charles IX   *104,* 105
Charles X   135
Charles, Cardinal de Bourbon   106
Charles de Gonzague   109
Charles 'the Bold'   81, 82, *83*
Charles 'the Simple'   82
Checks   181 f.
Chester   116
Chevalier, Jean   113 f.
Childebert I   77, 78
Childeric   75, 172

Chilperic I   78
Chinese currencies   7
Choiseul   129
Cholera   201
Claudius I   72
Clazomenae   54
Clement VIII (Pope) of Avignon   106
Clodomir   77, 78
Clotaire I   78
Clovis   75, 80
Coate, Mary   118, 120, 122
Colbert   112
Colbert de Beaulieu   21, 24, 34 f., 39, 46
Collas de Guillemotte   103
Commemorative coins   168 f.
Commodus   70, 72
Communion token   184
*Compagnie des Indes*   125, 126, 129
*Comptoirs*   135
Comte de Kergariou   39
*Concours Musical de Jersey*   180
Constantine   69, 70, 73, 74
Constantine II   73
Constantinopolis   73
Constantius I   *73*
Constantius II   73
*Consulat*   135
Convenience   187
*Convention nationale*   135
Conway   5
Corbière Lighthouse   *294*
Coriosolites   10, 13 f., 26, 31, 32, 33, 35, 39, 40 f., 50 f., 60 f.
Cornwall   66, 117, 118
Corseul   14
Corsica   129
Côtes-du-Nord   7, 14, 61
Coutances   78, 79, 83, 86, 89, 90
Crécy   93
Croker, John   169
Cuchulainn   62 f.
Culhwch   65
Culpeper   113, 117
Cyzicus   73

Dagobert I   78
Dairy tokens   183
Danube   9, 10
Dassier, Jacques Antoine   176
Dauphiné   97
D'Auvergne, Philippe   141, *142*
David Place   39
Decimalization   159, 169 f., 287 f.
Decize   76
De la Rue, Thomas   172, *212*

De la Tour   10, 21, 26, 34 f.
Denier   75 f.
Denton, Sir A.   113, 117
Derg Druchtach   65
De Saumarez, Admiral Lord   172, *212*
Devins and Bolton   183
Digby   113, 117
Dinan   14
Diocletian   69, 72, 73
Diodorus   65
*Directoire*   135
Donop, Baron   24, 25
Drogo de Barentin   88
Dumaresq, Philippe   125
Dupré, Guillaume   109
Dürer, Albrecht   163
Durotriges   20, 38, 59

Ecréhou   100
Edict of Nantes   106, 112
Edict of Pitres   81
Edward I   *91*
Edward II   91, 95
Edward III   90, *93*, 97
Edward VII   157, 173, *174*
Edward the Black Prince   97, 139
Edward 'the Confessor'   83
*Eidgenössische Technische Hochschule*   121
Electronic Money   188
Elizabeth I   104, *105*
Elizabeth II   170, *175*
Elizabeth Castle   127, 171, *257*, 302
Elizabeth College   179, *180*, 201
Elizabeth, the Queen Mother   *175*, 188, *343*
*Enseignes de pallyn*   103
*Epicerie française*   182
Epona   53
Evans collection   26, 31
Evreux   83
Exeter   113, 116, 118, 119, 120, 121, 122

Fairfax   113
Faldouet dolmen   *293*
Fall   23
Farquhar, Helen   117, 120
Faustina II   72
Feuillerat, Bertin   182
Flanders   78, 99, 100
Flavius Josephus   55
Fort Regent   5, 23, 72
Fountain Street   201
François I   102, 103
François II   104
Franks   75, 78
Frédéric Maurice of Sedan   109
*Freluques*   103, 109, 110

Galbraith, J.K.   187, 188
Galerius   73
Gallo-Belgic 'D'   38
Galpidus de Lucy   89
Gardiner, Sir Robert   107
Gascony   128
Gaston de Dombes   109
Gee, Henry   268
General Hospital   74
Geoffrey of Anjou   84
George III   128, *130*, 131, 136, 139, 159, *192, 193*
George IV   136
George V   169, 173, *175*
George VI   173, *175*
German Occupation   163 f., 207 f., 253 f.
Gibraltar   276, 277, 283
Giotto   55
Gironde   12
Gondebaud   76
Gorey Castle   *72*, 74, 91, 97, 98, 102, 103, 104, 125, 137, 172, *256, 258,* 294, *295*
Grainville   114
Grand Hotel   181
Greenland   187
Gregory of Tours   75, 77
Gregory (Pope)   79, 88
Gresham, Sir Thomas   187
Grosnez   *94*, 172, *297*
Grouville   100, 132
Grugyn   65
Guerdain   114, 115
Guernsey   6, 39, 72, 77, 85, 86, 88, 89, 90, 91, 92, 94, 95, 96, 102, 103, 105, 106, 109, 110, 111, 125, 128, 131, 132, 136, 137, 138, 139, 143, 155 f., 199 f., 305 f.
Guernsey coins   305 f.
Guernsey Commercial Banking Co.   *200*
Guernsey Electrical Exhibition   180
Guernsey Horticultural Society   180
Guernsey Lily   *325, 338, 339, 346*
Guernsey States Notes   202 f.
Guillaume de Vauville   85
Guillaume de Vernon   86
Guillaume d'Ouville   89
Gwrhyr   65

Hadrian   72
Halley's Comet   55, 56
Halliday, Thomas   191, 192, 194, 195, 196
Hamon & Co.   181
Harley   115
Hasculfus de Soligny   89
Heaton   157, 267, 310 f., 321 f., 327 f.
Helvetii   20, *30*
Hengistbury   38, 59, 70

361

Henri d'Albret  *102*
Henri de la Tour d'Auvergne  141
Henry I  84
Henry II  84, *85,* 89, 90
Henry III  *88,* 89
Henry V  *97,* 98
Henry VI  98
Henry VII  103
Henry VIII  101, 103
Henry I of France  89
Henry II of France  103
Henry III of France  *105,* 106, 120, 121
Henry IV of France  104
Henry IV of Navarre  *106, 108*
Heraclea  73
Heraclius  76
Hereford  117
Herm  77, 85, 96, *161*
Hermitage Chapel  76, *77,* 172, *290*
Hervé, Archbishop  *82*
*HMS Crescent*  172, 346
Holland  105, 111, 136
Hopton  113, 118, 119
Hoskyns  116, 120
Hougue Bie  6, *177*
Howard  127
Hugh the Great  *82,* 89
Hyde, Sir Edward  *113,* 117, 118, 119

Iberians  9
Ile Agois  72, 82
India  6, 57, 129
Ireland  6, 59 f., 86, 101, 117, 137
Isle of Man  187, 200, 276, 283

James I  107
James II  137
Jeanne d'Albret  104
Jerbourg Monument  201
Jermyn  119, 120
Jersey  5, 6, 7, 8, 9, 10, 11, 14, 15, 16, 17, 18, 19, 20, 23 f., 49, 54, *60,* 70 f., 76, 77, 81, 82, 86, 88, 89, 90, 91, 92, 94, 95, 96, 97, 98, 99, 101, 103, 104, 107, 111, 113 f., 125, 126 f., 131, 132, 137, 138, 139, 145 f., 215 f., 261 f.
Jersey Coins  261 f.
Jersey Eisteddford  180
Jersey Evening Post  34
Jersey Lily  *297*
Jersey Notes  215 f.
Jersey Trades & Industries Exhibition  180
Jersey Weekly Post  170, 171
Jethou  90
Jettons  *104*
Joan of Arc  98

John  86, 87, 88, 89, 90
John V of Brittany  97
John, Duke of Bourgogne  98
John 'le Bon'  *96*
Justin I  76
Justin II  79
Justinian I  76

Kernunnos  9, 53
Kings Arms  181
Krauwinckel, Hans  104
Kruger-Gray  160, 161, 271, 273, 274
Krugerrands  171

L. Cassius Longinus  71
L. Scribonius Libo  71
L. Titurius Sabinus  71
Labraid Loingsech  61
La Cotte  5, 6
La Cotte à la Chèvre  6
La Guerdainerie  114 f., *114*
La Marquanderie  16, 31, 32, 49, 57
Lanarkshire  59
L'Ancresse  6
Languedoc  30
La Rochelle  81, 128
La Tène  59, 65
La Vauroque  21
Law, John  125, 126, 129, 131
Le Catillon  16, 17, 18, 19, 20, 33 f., 45, 52, 56, 62, 63, 64, 66
Le Caudey  182
Lechfeld  82
Le Couperon  39
Le Couteur, François  125
Le Hocq Tower  172
Leinster  61
Lelong, Auguste  179
Le Mans  78, 79, 80, 85 f.
Lemprière, Jacques  125
Leo I  75
Le Quesne, Charles  126, 127
Leuci  *30, 54*
*Liards*  112
Liberation  175
Licinius I  73, 74
Lihou  90, 92, 96
Lisieux  83
Lockett, R.C.  16, 120, 122
Londinium  73
Longy Common  70, 74
Lorraine  9, 129
Lothaire I  81
Louis II  82
Louis VI  89

Louis VII 89
Louis VIII 89
Louis IX 89, *90*, 91
Louis X 91
Louis XI 100, 128
Louis XII 102
Louis XIII *108,* 109, 119
Louis XIV 111, *112,* 124, *129*
Louis XV 129, *130*
Louis XVI *130,* 135
Louis XVIII 135, *136*
Louis the Pious *81*
'Love-tokens' 183
Lowsley, Lieut. Col. B. 31
LSD 80 f., 85 f.
Lugaid 63
Lugdunum 73
Lukis Museum 39
Lydia 7
Lyons 76, 79
Lyre *47, 55*

M. Aemilius Scaurus 71
M. Sergius Silus 70
Mabinogion 65
Maccullock, Allaire, Bonamy *199*
Macedon 13, 14
Machin, Arnold 287, 342
Mack, R.P. 34 f.
Madame de Pompadour 129
Madame du Barry 129
Maiden Castle 59
*Maison de Paris* 182
Majorian 76
Malta 61
Manche 61
Marcus Antonius 31, 42, 71, 72
Marcus Aurelius 72
Maria Theresia 112
Marine Hotel 182
Marmoutier 85
Marseille 10, *20, 54,* 78
Marshall Fraser 145 f.
Mary Stewart 104
Masonic Penny 184
Mauger 23, 24, 70
Maurice Tiberius 76
Maxentius 73
Maximianus 73
Maximinius II 73
Maximus of Tyre 56
Mazarin 111
Medals 173 f.
Melesches 114
Melle 81

Mendips 60
Mérovée 75
Meroringians 70, 75 f.
Messervy, Jurat 159, 169
Messervy, Maximilian and François 111, 117
Minquiers 39
Mint in Jersey 113 f.
Mirabeau 131
*Moneyage* 92, 93
Mont St. Michel 85, 86, 94, 95, 96, 100
Morbihan 7, 61

Napoleon 41, 135
Narbonne 79
National Debt 186
Navarre 104, 105, 106
Néel II 85
Neel, Elias 139, 191
Neustria 77, 78, 81
Nevers 76
New Grange 59, 61
New Jersey *124*
Newton 178, *179*
Nicholas, Sir Edward 117
Nivillac 7
Noirmont 94, 95, 114
Norman Conquest *275, 286*
Normandy 78, 82, 83 f.
Northumberland 59
Nüremberg 104

Octavianus 71
Odo *82*
Old Bank 200
Olwen 65
Orléans 77
Osanne des Isles
Osismii 13, 15, *18, 19,* 26, *36,* 43, 59, *64, 65*
Ostia 73
Otho de Granson 94
Oxford 114
Oxford Hotel 182

P. Clodius *71*
P. Crepusius 22, *71*
P. Maenius Antiaticus 70
P. Plautius Hypsaeus 71
Paeonians 56
Paris 77
*Parisis* system 88 f.
Parity 185, 186
Partridge & Co. 309, 320, 326, 327
Paying Agents 251 f.
Peirson, Major 172, *257*
Pepin the Short 80, 81

*Peplum* 57
Pepys, Samuel 119
Perkins, Bacon Ltd 171
Philip II of Macedon 13, *14*
Philip I 'the Arabian' 72
Philippa of Hainault 139
Philippe I 89
Philippe Auguste 88, 89
Philippe II 84
Philippe III 'le Hardi' 91
Philippe IV 'le Bel' *91,* 92
Philippe V 'le Long' 91
Philippe VI de Valois 92
Philippe d'Albigny 89
Philippe d'Orléans 125
Phocas 76
Pictones 30
Pinnacle Rock 39, 70
Pippin I 81
Pippin II 81
Pistrucci 159
Pitt 141, 176
Plees 145
Pocahontas 123
Poland 105
Pontac 97
Popinjay 102
Portugal 105
Postumus 72
Pottier, John 119
Pretextatus 78
Prince of Orange 132
Prince of Wales 113 f., 139
Prince of Wales Hotel 182
*Proud Black Eagle* 118
Provence 78

Q. Cassius Longinus 71
*Queen of the Isles* 184
Queenston Heights *143, 211*
Quenvais 73, 74

Raoul of Hermesthorp 96
Ration Books *167*
Rauraci *54*
Reading 139
Redones 13, 15, *22, 18, 19, 36,* 56
Remi *30*
Rennes 79, 82
*Rentes* 92, *158*
Richard I 86
Richard I 'the Fearless' 83
Richard II 'the Good' 83
Richard III 83
Richards & Co. 199

Richelieu 108, 112
Robert I 83, 89
Robert, Duke of Normandy 84
Robert, Duke-Abbot 82
Roettiers 129
Rollo 82, 83
Roman coinage 12, 22, 23, 26, 31, *40,* 69 f., 157
Rome 10, 73
Rouen 78, 79, 80, 83, 85 f.
Royal Guernsey Militia 178
Royal Jersey Golf Club 180
Royal Jersey Militia 172, 178, *297,* 298
Royal Mint 137, 171, 261 f., 309
Royal Mint, Paris 103, 115, 125, 129
Royal Wedding *299, 343,* 344
Rozel 24, 25, 31, 72
Ruding 139, 156
Russian coins 132
Rullecourt, Baron 172
Rybot, Major N.V.L. 14, 32, 33, 51, 73, *165, 166, 177*

St. Aubin 131
St. Aubin's Fort 171, *256*
St. Brelade 100
St-Claire-sur-Epte 82
St. Clement 72, 94, 95, 96, 100
St. Helier 9, 76, *298*
St. Julien's Club 181
St. Lawrence 7, 132
St. Magloire 77
St. Malo 7, 59, 70, 117, 119, 127
St. Marculf 76
St. Martin 78, *80, 82, 87,* 89, 173
St. Marie du Voeu 86, 89
St. Mary 109
St. Ouen 7
St. Ouen's Manor 171, *255, 256*
St. Peter 95, 109
St. Peter Port 183
St. Sampson *72,* 76, 77
St.-Sauveur-le-Vicomte 86, 95
St. Saviour 102
St. Saviour's Bank *148*
Salt 9, 70
Santones 20, *29,* 30
Sark 20, 21, *22,* 42, 71, 72, 77, 85, 86, 96, 132, *161,* 170, 173, 201, 300, *337, 338*
Sarnian Club *182*
Saumarez, Captain James 172
Saumarez, Captain Philip 173, 176
*Schweiz. Landesmuseum* 39
Scilly Isles 114, 300
Scotland 61, 107
Seine 12

Sequani  20, *30, 54*
Seymour Tower  172, 292
*Shekel*  7
Shrewsbury  114, 116
Sigismond  76
Sillman, Norman  295
Simon, Thomas  119
Singleton Copley, J.  171
Siscia  73
Smith, Adam  170
Smith, John  123
Smyth, Col. William  113 f.
Smyth, Robert  113
Société Jersiaise  26, 31, 32, 33, 39, 43, 82, 97, 109, 131, 132, *177*
Society of Antiquaries  21
Soho Mint  139, 155, 191, 305, 317
Solothurn  30, 54
*Sols marqués*  128
*Sou*  70, 75 f.
South Sea Bubble  125
Spanish 'dollars'  136, 139
Stephen  84
Stephen de Oxford  89
Strabo  59
*Sus gallicus*  47, 53, *54,* 65
Syagrius  75
Sydenham  70
Syracuse  52

Tacitus  53, 59
*Talent*  7
Terry, John  *183*
Theodosius I  74
Thessalonika  73
Thierry  77
Thomas de Ferriers  96
Ticinum  73
Tin  9
Tinchebrai  84
Tokens  135 f., 191 f.
*Torques*  9, *30,* 61
Torteval  201
Tournai  75
*Tournois*  88 f., *105, 106,* 107
Tours  76, 78, 79, 80
Touzel, Edward  178
Tower Mint  103
Town Hospital  183
Toy, Henry  306, 318, 326
Trajan  42, 71, 72
Treasure Trove  111

*Tremisses*  75 f.
Trèves  79
Treviri  73
Truro  116, 118, 119, 120
Twrch Trwyth  65, 66
Tyery, Nicholas  *101*

Unelli  15, 26, 33, 36

Vale  77, 95, 96
Vannes  79
Vaughan  117, 119
Veliocasses  20, *54*
Vendée  61
Veneti  12, *13,* 14, 15, *37,* 41, 55, 59, *63*
Vespasian  72
Victoria  157, 173, *174*
Victoria College  172, 179, *180, 257*
Victory Inn  182
Vincze, Paul  316, 334
Violet, Thomas  115
Visigoths  22, 76
Volcae Arecomici  *38*
Vouillé  76
Vyvyan, Sir Richard  118, 119, 120, 122

Wace  83
Wales  61, 66
Walpole  176
Wargrave  5
Warin, Jean  109, 119
Waysum's Albion Hotel  182
Weimar  164
Wellenheim  159
Werdun  142
Wesley, John  *177,* 178
West of England Inn  *182*
Whitehouse  183
William I 'Long-Sword'  83
William II (William I of England)  *83,* 85, *335*
William Rufus  84
Wodehouse, P.G.  25
Woolfe, George  171
Wren, Sir Christopher  169
Wüthrich  *30*
Wyon, Leonard Charles  265
Wyon, Thomas  137, 191

York  114, 116
Yorkshire  59
Ysbaddaden  65, 66